READING ALOUD EFFECTIVELY

OTHER RINEHART BOOKS
IN ENGLISH COMMUNICATION

ANDERSCH AND STAATS: *Speech for Everyday Use*

HENNEKE AND DUMIT: *The Announcer's Handbook*

MOORE: *Effective Writing,* Second Edition

PARATORE: *English Dialogues for Foreign Students*

PARATORE: *English Exercises: English as a Foreign Language,* Forms A and B

PRATOR: *Manual of American English Pronunciation*

TAFT, MCDERMOTT, AND JENSEN: *The Technique of Composition*

WATT: *An American Rhetoric,* Revised Edition

The English Pamphlet Series

BOWDEN: *An Introduction to Prose Style*

CARR AND CLARK: *An ABC of Idiom and Diction*

JORDAN: *Elements of Good Writing*

MOORE: *Plan Before You Write*

OGGEL: *Thoughts into Themes*

By LIFE Photographer Alfred Eisenstaedt. Courtesy of TIME Inc.

The Professional Reads Aloud.

BEN GRAF HENNEKE

Professor of Speech, University of Tulsa

Reading Aloud
EFFECTIVELY

HOLT, RINEHART AND WINSTON

New York

January, 1961

Copyright, 1954, by Ben Graf Henneke
Printed in the United States of America
Library of Congress Catalog Card Number: 54–9559

23575-0214

DEDICATION

For my mother, who first introduced me to reading aloud and who early convinced me it should be done effectively.

Preface

❖꘎❖꘎❖꘎❖꘎❖꘎❖꘎❖꘎❖꘎❖꘎❖꘎❖꘎꘎❖꘎❖꘎❖꘎❖꘎❖꘎❖꘎❖꘎❖꘎❖

Reading Aloud Effectively is intended for two publics: college students of interpretation, and all others who need help to develop skill in reading aloud.

Today more and more people are reading from manuscript in their public utterances. These persons fall into well-defined professional categories: the businessman, the lawyer, the teacher, the preacher, the army officer, the radio and TV announcer and newscaster, and the parent. The average college student knows for which of these professions he is training and is convinced of the usefulness of a text that recognizes his preprofessional interests.

The needs of these two publics are the same. Both wish to learn how to communicate from the printed page. Both need information on the understanding and preparation of a manuscript. Both need training in effective reading skills.

This book is divided into three parts. The first includes information on preparing a manuscript for reading aloud; the second, information on presenting a manuscript by reading aloud; and the third, practice material which I have chosen with both publics in mind. The reader's professional interest has been my major criterion. There are selections for the parent, businessman, politician, minister, lawyer, teacher, and radioman, as well as selections of general interest.

The text and the practice selections have been tried out on both publics before their publication here. I have been a college teacher of interpretation for many years. At odd times over the years, I have coached businessmen, radio announcers, and college professors in the techniques of reading aloud. For the past four years I have been an active speech consultant for the Stanolind Oil and Gas Company. These experiences have convinced me that the problems of reading aloud effectively are the same for both publics. In the course of these experiences, I have pretested the text and practice material.

I am indebted to all the teachers and writers in the field of interpretation for my knowledge. I am indebted to men of radio and oil businesses for my experience.

I am further indebted to Mark Twain, Henry David Thoreau, Robert Benchley, and Edmund Burke. If these seem strange bedfellows, there is a blanket term that covers them. They are individualists. Since communication is an individual act, the writings of these men seemed most suitable for practice material.

Detailed acknowledgment to all the writers and publishers represented in this text is given elsewhere.

I cannot adequately acknowledge my debt to my wife, Ellen Eaves. She was a teacher of interpretation before I became interested in the subject. In the preparation of this book she contributed ideas, information, and virtually all the commas.

Others who added ideas and lesser-used punctuation marks were Dr. George Kernodle and Dr. Portia Kernodle of the University of Arkansas faculty, and Dr. Beaumont Bruestle and students of the Speech Department of the University of Tulsa. For assistance on the manuscript and the technical details of copyright clearance I am indebted to Miss Bette Davis, Miss Emma Jo McConnell, and Mrs. Francis Jones.

B. G. H.

Tulsa, Oklahoma
September, 1954

Contents

PART TWO

IN ACTION

PART THREE

PRACTICE MATERIAL

· 1 ·

Why Learn
to Read Aloud?

❖·❭❭·❭❭·❭❭·❭❭·❭❭·❭❭·❭❭·❭❭·❭❭·❭❮·❭❮·❮❖·❮❖·❮❖·❮❖·❮❖·❮❖·❮❖·❮❖

Why learn to read aloud?

Chances are you'll have to. These days, nearly everyone of us is called upon to read aloud at some time or other. And since reading aloud is not "doing what comes naturally," you'll need to acquire certain skills to read aloud effectively.

At the dedication of the new library at Oklahoma Agricultural and Mechanical College, one of the speakers remarked that he would imitate previous speakers and read his paper, not only because the proceedings were being broadcast, televised, reported, and printed, but also because he would be loath to trust his technical remarks to the whims of an erratic memory. After he had pulled out a rumpled manuscript and adjusted his reading glasses, he peered out at the audience and promised he would attempt to make contact with them by glancing up occasionally.

In his explanation for reading the paper, he gave several of the reasons why public speakers have become readers. In his promise to make contact, he gave at least one reason why all of us should learn how to become readers.

Reading aloud is an ever-growing business. Charles Laughton and other professionals have, as *Time* magazine said, "turned the old pastime of reading aloud into a booming big business."[1]

[1] "The Happy Ham," *Time*, Vol. LIX, No. 13 (March 31, 1952).

But reading aloud was the concern of millions before Laughton and other entertainers capitalized on its commercial possibilities.

Who are all these people who read aloud?

Of course, you've seen scientists reading papers and politicians reading speeches. You may remember that the minister leads a devotional reading. Given the time to think about it, you'll remember teachers who read from texts or notes, lawyers who read depositions, businessmen who read reports, commencement speakers who read their talks.

But the largest group of people reading aloud today are parents. You may never be called upon to read a speech or formal material, but, in the normal course of things, you will be badgered into reading a story before bedtime.

The chances are that you'll be called upon to read aloud on other occasions, as well.

You may think expertness is not necessary for reading to a child, but your greatest sense of inadequacy will come when the child says, "I don't want you to read to me; I want Mother, she doesn't mumble." True, Mother may not be much better than you at reading aloud. True, what you're reading is only "kid stuff." The material may not be important, but the act of reading aloud to children is.

Reading aloud is one of the ways children share affection with their parents. Flora Straus of the Child Study Association of America says,

> Reading aloud, and being read to, are among the most treasured links between parent and child, to be deeply remembered and woven into the pattern of quiet togetherness. There is a special preciousness in the boom of the father's voice, the comfort of mother's arm as the little one snuggles down to look as well as listen—to match the real pictures in the book with the "mind pictures" formed by the words.
>
> We would like to think that the deep-rooted values of such a family hour might continue as the children grow up. Even when boys and girls can read for themselves, reading aloud by parents adds immeasurably to the warmth of family living and growing through the years. Especially in an era such as ours, with radio and television bringing, even to our littlest ones, experiences all too unselected for their needs, this intimate and personal sharing of reading acquires a double value, to be carefully nurtured by parents.[2]

Reading aloud to children is one of the ways of teaching children about the life about them. It is one of the ways of teaching them speech

[2] Flora Straus, Preface to *Read Me Another Story*, compiled by the Child Study Association of America, and published by Thomas Y. Crowell Company, New York. Copyright, 1949.

By LIFE Photographer Carl Iwasaki. Courtesy of TIME Inc.

The parent reads aloud.

and acceptable behavior patterns. It is a means of establishing wholesome moral and ethical values. In short, it is one of the most valuable preschool teaching devices.

What is read to the child is not so unimportant as might be supposed.

While the fairy tales have no immediate purpose other than to amuse, they leave a substantial by-product which has a moral significance. In every reaction which the child has for distress or humor in the tale, he deposits another layer of vicarious experience which sets his character more firmly in the mould of right and wrong attitude. Every sympathy, every aversion helps to set the impulsive currents of his life and to give direction to his personality.[3]

Businessmen make up the next largest group of persons reading aloud. This has become so apparent in recent years that the Standard Oil Company (New Jersey) has had written, printed, and distributed a booklet on the subject. The booklet "contains hints on the preparation and reading of speeches . . ."

The most suitable method for delivering a speech is often indicated by circumstances. For example, it might be pretentious to read a prepared script before a small group or even before a large but relatively informal meeting. And when a speaker is an expert on the subject of his address and has all the facts at his mental finger-tips, he may speak more effectively from a few notes than from a full text.

On the other hand, when a businessman is giving a "policy" address, it is probably advisable that he read from a manuscript. Then his exact words are available for later reference. In the event of misquotation or misunderstanding, the text can be cited to set the record straight. It is for these reasons, of course, that the major addresses of responsible statement are prepared in advance and thoroughly reviewed before delivery.

There are other things that can be said for reading a speech. A complete text before you on a lectern is reassuring. You know that if you lose the thread of your thought—if your mind suddenly goes blank, as happens to all of us at times—you're not going to be left with your mouth open, eyes glazed and panic growing in your chest.

A speaker who reads a speech is less likely to ramble from the subject than one who speaks without text. He will not "er" and "ah" while he searches for a word or casts about in his mind for the next point. His talk will probably be better organized and free of tedious repetitions. Assuming that his text has been well written, he will not get involved in those sentences which start out all right, trip on a phrase, get tangled in a welter of clauses, and end in mid-air. A speech that is read can be clocked in advance, so the speaker can be sure not to exceed the time allotted him.[4]

[3] Laura F. Kready, *A Study of Fairy Tales* (Boston: Houghton Mifflin Company, 1916), p. xxii.

[4] *Mr. Chairman . . . Distinguished Guests . . .* (New York, 1953), pp. 2–3. Courtesy of the Standard Oil Company (New Jersey).

In nearly every department of business activity there is occasion for reading aloud. Research and technological workers read scientific papers and reports. Men engaged in sales promotion, public relations, and industrial relations are all readers. The sales-promotion man and his staff have become such expert readers they are almost actors. At a typical sales meeting they will make presentations of new products; they will read reports from science, industry, and government affecting possible sales; they will demonstrate selling techniques. If you want to see reading aloud done effectively, ask to attend a Coca-Cola or Pepsi-Cola sales meeting.

The public-relations and industrial-relations men are no less effective in their presentations. Because their functions so often overlap in business today, they will be considered together. New products, new lines, new models all come on the market today in presentations. New merchandise is given especially organized and staged public showings. New plants, new buildings, new techniques are given similar public showings. Industries in Youngstown, Ohio, and Houston, Texas—to name only two cities—hold public training programs for opinion leaders. Teachers, clergymen, doctors, and lawyers are taken on especially planned business tours where they witness one demonstration after another. New employees are informed of safety measures, company progress and plans, economic trends, and government actions in especially prepared programs. In every instance, skillful reading aloud animates the presentation.

The businessman whose work is management finds that one of his biggest jobs is communication. He has become a reader of papers on departmental structure and function; a reader of reports to stockholders, suppliers, merchandisers, and employees. Because of his position, he is also a public figure, called upon to read statements and papers to widely divergent groups on a variety of topics.

At any time, any of these businessmen may be asked to present opinions, advice, or testimony before government agencies. The businessman has become a speaker whether he wanted to be one or not. He has become a reader because of the need for compression and accuracy.

Politicians make up another large group of oral readers. Many were readers before the advent of mass communications, but nearly all of them are today. Since most campaign speeches are filmed, broadcast, and televised and the time is purchased by the candidate's party and backers, he prepares, times, and follows a manuscript.

Should the politician win office, he continues to be a reader. He now reads statements into the record; he reads testimony, depositions, bills, and speeches. He makes prepared statements on legislation and policy. No matter what the occasion, from campaigning to officeholding, the politician is a reader because of the contemporary demands for accuracy, timing, and talk.

> Today the pen is as potent as the sword in the making of a despot. Tyrants used to be great generals. Now they are strategists in communication, beguiling orators or propagandists. Their weapons are radio and the press . . . .[5]

The teacher has always been an oral reader. Stories, assignments, illustrative material, lectures, reports, and papers may all be read. The more formal the teaching situation the more likely the teacher is to read. The teacher has always been aware of the restrictions of accuracy and timing. All teachers are readers: the schoolmarm, the college lecturer, the Sunday-school teacher, the industrial-job teacher, and the armed-forces instructor.

Apropos of the armed-forces instructor, it should be noted that almost every officer today is a reader. He is a reader of notices and bulletins, either at parade or over a public-address system. He is a reader of citations and regulations. He is a reader of especially prepared material for indoctrination of the serviceman. He is a reader of explanatory talks, like the businessman; a reader of public comment, like the politician; a reader of lectures, like the teacher.

The lawyer, too, is an oral reader of long standing. In many courts the lawyer is expected to read depositions into the record, to read testimony or the court reporter's records. Many lawyers are public readers as well, appearing before school groups, civic clubs, and public gatherings.

Clergymen have always been readers. They read the daily lessons, announcements, the ritualistic services, the responses, the sacred books. Most clergymen read occasional services such as the wedding and funeral services. Many clergymen read their sermons. The mass-communications media have opened up new areas of persuasion for the clergy; and motion pictures, radio, and television are employing the reading talents of a host of ministers. The clergyman, like the lawyer, is a public reader.

The performers in the mass-communications media are readers, of course. Motion-picture and television performers may memorize, but they, like radio performers, read from a manuscript in the first stage of the communicative process. Actors, directors, commentators, analysts, dubbers; experts in cooking, fashion, hobbies, farming, sports, and war; newsmen, narrators, commercial announcers—all are readers.

A host of other persons are occasionally called upon to read aloud,

[5] Mortimer J. Adler, *How to Read a Book* (New York: Simon & Schuster, 1940), p. 367.

and their hearers wish they did it more effectively. The professional secretary reads dictation aloud, the interpreter reads translations, the club
member reads papers, the·theater performer reads for a role, the writer
reads from his own works.

There would be little need for this book if everyone did an adequate
job when reading from a prepared manuscript. Unfortunately, many
people who read aloud do it badly; relatively few do it effectively. We
have all heard the shy and mumbling scientist, the inarticulate teacher, the
strangled minister, the droning businessman, the "punchy" announcer,
and the bad actor.

An oil man of my acquaintance was called upon to do considerable
speechmaking because of his position. Being a busy part of top management, he left the writing of his speeches to the public-relations department. He never worried about his delivery of those addresses, claiming
he didn't have time to practice. He sounded just as you would expect—
uninterested, dry, and prosy.

Then some legislation regulating oil was proposed in Washington,
and a congressional committee was appointed to consider it. The proposed
law would affect the oil company's operation by millions of dollars in
extra taxes. My acquaintance was asked to testify on the forthcoming bill.
This was one occasion when he did want to say his piece. No one else
could write this speech for him. He wrote it himself. He wanted all the
time he could get for practice. He wanted all the help he could get on his
delivery. He wanted to tell that "so-and-so committee" what he thought
of their "so-and-so legislation." He was inspired, passionate, and demonstrative—all the things he had never been before. He worked on that
presentation as he had worked on few things in his life. His ability as a
reader improved a thousandfold.

I would like to say the oil man's speech swayed the committee—it
did. I would like to say the legislation failed—it didn't. But the oil man's
comment on his experience is the point of this story.

"I made a good speech for the oil industry," he said after he returned
from Washington. "If I had been making as good speeches all my life, that
legislation would never have been proposed, much less passed."

Reading aloud effectively can be learned. Reading aloud is just
another form of communication and, like all communication, it has as
its goal complete response by the listener to the speaker's words.

We talk because we want something. We may want an object, or
companionship, or guidance or help, or we may want to give instruction
or companionship. Since we are human beings, we make our wants known
through speech. Don Marquis put it this way.

All religion, all life, all art, all expression come down to this: to the effort of the human soul to break through its barrier of loneliness, of intolerable loneliness, and make some contact with another seeking soul, or with what all souls seek, which is (by any name) God.[6]

Good reading should sound like good speech. It should be direct, unaffected, conversational, vital, and clear. You don't need a book like this for your daily conversation. Your normal speech when you are interested usually shows the qualities essential to the reader. But something happens to you when you get up before a group with a manuscript in your hand. Yet your aim should be to sound as natural as your most effective everyday speech.

Your reading can sound like good communicative speech if you spend enough time in the right kind of preparation. One preparation you do at your desk. The other preparation you do in action. Neither can be slighted if you want to read aloud effectively.

Desk preparation is the work you do to understand the material you are reading, to choose appropriate material for the audience to whom it will be read, and to prepare for the reading act. It is the subject matter of Part I of this book.

The preparation you do in action is a continuing process to improve your communication skills. It is not enough for you to understand your material and to have prepared it for an audience; you must win the listener's response. To do this you will need to develop or improve certain skills, such as the communication of ideas and emotions, the projection of personality, the use of movement and voice. Like all other skills, they can be improved through practice. Defining such skills and outlining areas for practice is the subject matter of Part II of this book.

Then there are other values to be gained from learning to read aloud effectively. They are secondary values, to be sure, but real values for all that. (1) Learning to read aloud is a way to improve your ability in analysis and synthesis—your ability to interpret printed material. (2) Developing your communication skills is a means of developing your personality. (3) The subject matter of your reading aloud is literature of greater or less value; prolonged study of any selection you read aloud adds to your knowledge and appreciation of literature.

The oral reader is an interpreter per se. Government and business leaders today rank interpretative ability as one of the most necessary assets of management. Events and decisions of all sorts need interpreta-

[6] Don Marquis, *Chapters for the Orthodox* (New York: Doubleday & Co. Inc., 1934), p. 220. Copyright, 1934, by Don Marquis, reprinted by permission of Doubleday & Company, Inc.

tion to the people affected. The Economic Cooperation Administration (ECA) needs interpretation to the people of America as well as to the people of Europe. Old-age benefits need interpretation to the employer, the employee, and the beneficiary. The president of an oil company recently wrote,

> It seems apparent that one of the most important jobs industry faces today involves neither a technical nor a financial problem. The problem, is, instead, a social one. We must interpret business to the public.[7]

Like all other communication skills, reading aloud helps to develop personality. Psychologists are agreed that there are three major components of personality: thinking, feeling, and doing. Reading aloud contributes to the development of positive traits in each of the components. The reader uses analytical thinking to understand his material. He works to feel and project the emotional content of his material. He practices and performs.

Reading aloud also serves as a mental discipline. The analysis, research, and clear thinking required of even the most casual reader, as described in the next chapter, is excellent training in reasoning, organization, and understanding.

> I got through my head at an early age a few simple truths: that the proper reading of a good writer requires energy and application; that reading is not mere "diversion"; that it is impossible to admire writing you do not understand; that understanding it does not destroy but rather enhances its beauty; that unless a writer's mind is superior to, more complicated than, your own, it is a bore to read him.[8]

The Greeks believed the oral reader developed moral and ethical values because he was exposed to the best in writing. The literary experience cannot be undervalued today. The reader learns grammar, vocabulary, diction and, at the same time, spends repeated moments with some of the world's greatest thinkers. The intensive study and frequent rehearsal of a manuscript for oral presentation can heighten the reader's literary appreciation.

> One learns a great deal about literature in general from reading even one good book aloud slowly. Our forefathers, for whom such

[7] E. F. Bullard, "The Technical Man's Role as Interpreter," *Journal of Petroleum Technology,* II, No. 7 (July, 1950), 7.

[8] Reprinted from *Reading I've Liked,* by Clifton Fadiman (New York: Simon & Schuster, 1945), p. xxiv. Copyright, 1941, by Simon & Schuster, Inc.

reading was a usual thing, read fewer books than we do, but probably also had a finer feeling for literary values than we have.[9]

Reading aloud is not just a method of understanding literature, however; it is a part of the total learning process. The child learning to read starts by reading aloud. At that level of education the emphasis is not on the child's work as a communicator but on his work as a receptor. Elementary teachers use the technique of reading aloud to help the child to better understanding. In remedial-reading schools for more mature students, the emphasis is on reading aloud for comprehension. What may be too difficult to understand when read silently becomes clear when read aloud.

> The process of making monotonous black characters on the page vividly stir the latent sense-perceptions is, however, relatively slow and irksome. Few people have ever learned to do it consistently; and hence, it is fair to say, few have ever truly learned to read. The moral is read slowly. Take ample time. Pause where the punctuation bids one pause; note each and every comma; wait a moment between a period and the next capital letter. And pause when common sense bids you pause, that is, when you have not understood. As the line of sentences comes filing before the window of your soul, examine each individual expression with the animus, and more than the animus, you would maintain were you paying teller in a bank, saying to yourself continually, "Do I know this word?" and, "What is this phrase worth?"
>
> Read aloud; read slowly, read suspiciously. Re-read. What a busy man has time to read at all, he has time to read more than once. Was it not Emerson who held that he could not afford to own a book until it was ten years old—had at least to that extent proved its ability to survive? Jealous of his time, he let others sift the ashes. And was it not Schopenhauer who considered no book worth while that was not worth a third perusal? If we read a thing but once, that usually is but so much lost time. The most industrious student forgets a large part of what he tries to retain. The best-read man is the one who has oftenest read the best things.[10]

▶ *Conclusion.* Why learn to read aloud? Because so many people nowadays are being asked or forced to read aloud that you may have to, too. It can be an effective way to present material. Like all communication, reading aloud has only one end: the complete response of the listener.

[9] *Ibid.,* p. xxxi.
[10] Lane Cooper, *Two Views of Education* (New Haven: Yale University Press, 1922), p. 118.

To achieve this, you have to learn how to analyze your manuscript and to improve your communication skills. In learning analysis and communication skills, certain other educational values will accrue to you.

Why learn to read aloud?

Why not learn to read aloud?

EXERCISE

(*The following selection is all the proof you need that reading aloud should be done effectively. Read it to yourself; then try reading it aloud.*)

The Treasurer's Report [11]

(*The report is delivered by an Assistant Treasurer who has been called in to pinch-hit for the regular Treasurer who is ill. He is not a very good public speaker, this assistant, but after a few minutes of confusion is caught up by the spell of his own oratory and is hard to stop.*)

I shall take but a very few moments of your time this evening, for I realize that you would much rather be listening to this interesting entertainment than to a dry financial statement. . . . But I am reminded of a story—which you have probably all of you heard.

It seems that there were these two Irishmen walking down the street when they came to a—oh, I should have said in the first place that the parrot which was hanging out in front of the store—or rather belonging to one of these two fellows—the first Irishman, that is—was—well, *any-* way, this parrot . . .

(*After a slight cogitation, he realizes that, for all practical purposes, the story is as good as lost; so he abandons it entirely and, stepping forward, drops his facile, story-telling manner and assumes a quite spurious business-like air.*)

Now, in connection with reading this report, there are one or two points which Dr. Murnie wanted brought up in connection with it, and he has asked me to bring them up in connec—to bring them up.

In the first place, there is the question of the work which we are trying to do up there at our little place at Silver Lake, a work which we feel not only fills a very definite need in the community but also fills a very definite need—er—in the community. I don't think that many members of the Society realize just how big the work is that we are trying to

[11] Robert Benchley, *The Treasurer's Report* (New York: Harper & Brothers, 1930), pp. 298–306. Copyright, 1930, by Robert C. Benchley.

do up there. For instance, I don't think that it is generally known that most of our boys are between the age of fourteen. We feel that, by taking the boy at this age, we can get closer to his real nature—for a boy *has* a very real nature, you may be sure—and bring him into closer touch not only with the school, the parents, and with each other, but also with the town in which they live, the country to whose flag they pay allegiance, and to the—ah—(trailing off) town in which they live.

Now the fourth point which Dr. Murnie wanted brought up was that in connection with the installation of the new furnace last Fall. There seems to have been considerable talk going around about this not having been done quite as economically as it might have—been—done, when, as a matter of fact, the whole thing *was* done just as economically as possible—in fact, even more so. I have here a report of the Furnace Committee, showing just how the whole thing was handled from start to finish.

(*Reads from report, with considerable initial difficulty with the stiff covers.*)

Bids were submitted by the following firms of furnace contractors, with a clause stating that if we did not engage a firm to do the work for us we should pay them nothing for submitting the bids. This clause alone saved us a great deal of money.

The following firms, then, submitted bids:

Merkle, Wybigant Co., The Eureka Dust Bin and Shaker Co., The Elite Furnace Shop, and Harris, Birnbauer and Harris.

The bid of Merkle, Wybigant being the lowest, Harris, Birnbauer were selected to do the job.

(*Here a page is evidently missing from the report, and a hurried search is carried on through all the pages, without result.*)

Well, that pretty well clears up that end of the work.

Those of you who contributed so generously last year to the floating hospital have probably wondered what became of the money. I was speaking on this subject only last week at our up-town branch, and, after the meeting, a dear little old lady, dressed all in lavender, came up on the platform, and, laying her hand on my arm, said: "Mr. So-and-So (calling me by name), Mr. So-and-So, what the hell did you do with all the money we gave you last year?" Well, I just laughed and pushed her off the platform, but it has occurred to the committee that perhaps some of you, like that little old lady, would be interested in knowing the disposition of the funds.

Now, Mr. Rossiter, unfortunately our treasurer—or rather Mr. Rossiter our treasurer, unfortunately is confined at his home tonight with a bad head-cold and I have been asked

(*he hears someone whispering at him from the wings, but decides to ignore it*)

and I have been asked if I would

(*the whisperer will not be denied, so he goes over to the entrance and receives a brief message, returning beaming and laughing to himself.*)

Well, the joke seems to be on *me! Mr. Rossiter has pneumonia!*

Following then, is a summary of the Treasurer's Report:

(*Reads in a very business-like manner.*)

During the year 1929—and by that is meant 1928—the Choral Society received the following donations:

B.L.G.	$500
G.K.M.	500
Lottie and Nellie W.	500
In memory of a happy summer at Rye Beach	10
Proceeds of a sale of coats and hats left in the boat-house	14.55
And then the Junior League gave a performance of "Pinafore" for the benefit of the fund which, unfortunately, resulted in a deficit of	300
Then, from dues and charges	2,354.75
And, following the installation of the new furnace, a saving in coal amounting to $374.75—which made Dr. Murnie very happy, you may be sure.	
Making a total of receipts amounting to	$3,645.75

This is all, of course, reckoned as of June.

In the matter of expenditures, the Club has not been so fortunate.

There was the unsettled condition of business, and the late Spring, to contend with, resulting in the following—er—rather discouraging figures, I am afraid.

Expenditures	$23,574.85
Then there was a loss, owing to several things—of	3,326.70
Carfare	4,452.25
And then, Mrs. Rawlins' expense account when she went down to see the work they are doing in Baltimore came to $256.50, but I am sure that you will all agree that it was worth it to find out—er—what they are doing in Baltimore.	
And then, under the general head of Odds and Ends	2,537.50
Making a total disbursement of (hurriedly)	$416,546.75

or a net deficit of—ah—several thousand dollars.

Now, these figures bring us down only to October. In October, my sister was married, and the house was all torn up, and in the general confusion we lost track of the figures of May and August. All those wishing the *approximate* figures for May and August, however, may obtain them from me in the vestry after the dinner, where I will be with pledge cards for those of you who wish to subscribe over and above your annual dues, and I hope that each and everyone of you here tonight will look deep into his heart and (archly) into his pocketbook, and see if he cannot find it there to help us put this thing over with a bang

(*accompanied by a wholly ineffectual gesture representing a bang*)

and to help and make this just the biggest and best year the Armenians have ever had. . . . I thank you.

(*Exits, bumping into proscenium.*)

PART ONE

At Your Desk

❖‑)❯‑)❯‑)❯‑)❯‑)❯‑)❯‑)❯‑)❯‑)❯‑)❯‑❮‑❮‑❮‑❮‑❮‑❮‑❮‑❮‑❮‑❮‑❮‑❮‑❮‑❮‑❖

· 2 ·

Understanding Your Material

✦)) ✦)) ✦)) ✦)) ✦)) ✦)) ✦)) ✦)) ✦)) ✦✦ ((✦ ((✦ ((✦ ((✦ ((✦ ((✦ ((✦ ((✦ ((✦

The assistant treasurer in the Benchley sketch obviously didn't know what he was talking about. As a result, no one else knew what he was talking about, either. That's the humor of *The Treasurer's Report*. But would you have thought the report so funny if you had been a member of the club hearing that report? If you had been a member, wouldn't you have wanted a better accounting of the funds? Just how inefficient can a treasurer be? For that matter, just how ineffectual can a reader be?

If you want to make a better presentation than the assistant treasurer, you must know what you are talking about. You, the reader, must comprehend your material before your listener can. In other words, *you can't communicate what you don't understand.*

You will understand some material just by reading it through. Other material will require study and analysis before you can understand it. Your reading aloud will be most effective, however, if you give study time to each selection no matter how simple it may seem on first reading. Your study should be from the script and all the related materials at your disposal.

Briefly, here are some of the considerations that should motivate your study. You should understand the selection as a whole, what it means, what it implies, why it is. You should determine the author's purpose. You

17

should understand the form of the author's writing. You should recognize the structural pattern used by the author.

You will need to analyze the author's ideas. You must understand the over-all structure, the relation of each paragraph to the whole, and the relation of each sentence to the paragraph of which it is a part. You must understand the different types of sentences, the usages of grammar, the functions of punctuation. You must become aware of individual words, what they mean singly and together, what they denote and connote. You will need to understand the purpose and meaning of references, allusions, and imagery. In fact, you must try to know as much as the author about your material.

For purposes of example, let's take two well-known selections and analyze them as the reader must if he expects to achieve complete comprehension.

The Lord's Prayer

Our Father, Who art in heaven, Hallowed be thy Name. Thy kingdom come. Thy will be done, On earth as it is in heaven. Give us this day our daily bread. And forgive us our trespasses, As we forgive those who trespass against us. And lead us not into temptation, But deliver us from evil. For thine is the kingdom, and the power, and the glory, for ever and ever. Amen.

This is one of the widely used versions of this prayer. Let us try to understand it. It is a prayer, and, like all communication, it states a want. The supplicant wants bread, forgiveness, and deliverance. The purpose of the writing is to persuade. The form is rhythmic prose. The structure is simple and makes use of cumulative detail. Now let's examine the author's ideas.

Take the first sentence. It is an attention-getting salutation. Do you know what it means? Any unfamiliar words? Better look up *hallowed* just to be sure. *Webster's Collegiate Dictionary* says, "(hăl'ōd; *in the solemn or liturgical style often* hăl'ô·ĕd), *adj.* Blessed; consecrated." The first sentence now reads, "Our Father, Who art in heaven, blessed be thy name."

Since the dictionary has been helpful both on meaning and pronunciation, you may decide to look up *art*. The same dictionary says, "2nd person present indicative singular of the verb *be;*—now only in solemn or poetic style." You know now that *hallowed* should be pronounced with three syllables to be consistent with the solemn style.

As you continue to study that first sentence, you begin to see its real meaning. You're saying, "Our Father, blessed be thy name." "Who art in heaven" is a modifying clause telling you which father it is; it is not our earthly father but our heavenly Father.

But why would you bless a *name?* Is that what the sentence really means? Looking up *name* in Webster's dictionary, you find the noun form has seven meanings. The first meaning, "the title by which any person or thing is known or designated," is not much help. That definition changes the line to read, "Our Father, blessed be thy designation which is Father." But it might be some help, at that. Maybe the ancient Jews had a different concept of the importance and power of a father? Maybe *father* connotes more than we realize. Let's look at other meanings. "A descriptive or qualifying appellation; an epithet, often disparaging in nature: as, to call one *names.*" That is not applicable. "Reputed character; reputation; esp., illustrious fame; honorable reputation; as, he has made a *name* for himself as a writer." That is some help. Using *reputation* and *illustrious fame* in the sentence, we have, "Our Father, blessed be thy reputation, thy illustrious fame."

Does the sentence really mean that? We had better do some research outside the dictionary for further help. The first place to go when you are puzzled by a selection is back to the whole piece of writing of which it is a part. There read the selection in context.

Beginning at the fifth verse of the sixth chapter of the Gospel of St. Matthew, you will find Jesus' instructions to His followers with regard to prayer. This prayer is the Nazarene's answer to the question, "How shall we pray?" Read the verses from five to sixteen. You'll probably be using the King James Version since it is the one most frequently used. The first thing you'll discover is different wording in the prayer itself.

> Our Father, which art in heaven, Hallowed be thy name.
> Thy kingdom come. Thy will be done in earth, as it is in heaven.
> Give us day by day our daily bread.
> And forgive us our debts, as we forgive our debtors.
> And lead us not into temptation, but deliver us from evil: For thine is the kingdom, and the power, and the glory, for ever. Amen.

If your copy has the center column references, you'll find a reference to "Deut.32.6." Checking back to it, you'll find this verse:

> Do ye thus requite the Lord, O foolish people and unwise? is not he thy father that hath bought thee? hath he not made thee, and established thee?

This is just confirmation of what we already knew, that the father to whom we are addressing this prayer is the Lord.

There is a second reference, "Ch.23.9.," which is to the ninth verse of the twenty-third chapter of the Gospel of St. Matthew.

> And call no man your father upon the earth: for one is your Father, which is in heaven.

That could be some help to us. It may be that Matthew is telling us that the name *Father* is a sacred thing and should only be used when referring to our heavenly Father. Therefore, the name is consecrated.

The third reference is to the second verse of the eleventh chapter of the Gospel of St. Luke. This turns out to be another version of the same prayer, with several word differences.

> Our Father which art in heaven, Hallowed be thy name. Thy kingdom come. Thy will be done, as in heaven, so in earth.
> Give us this day our daily bread.
> And forgive us our sins; for we also forgive everyone that is indebted to us. And lead us not into temptation; but deliver us from evil.

That doesn't help us much, except to show us some synonym choices in the later sentences in the prayer.

The references to Romans and First Corinthians are not very helpful either, but the reference to the ninth verse of the twelfth chapter of Hebrews can give us a clue.

> Furthermore, we have had fathers of our flesh which corrected us, and we gave them reverence: shall we not much rather be in subjection unto the Father of spirits, and live?

Here is the suggestion that we reverence or give subjection to the Father. The first line could go something like this now: "Our Father (who art in heaven) we give reverence or subjection to thy name." Not a completely satisfactory meaning yet, but let's move on.

A quick check of this reading in a modern translation of the Bible, Goodspeed's, for example, shows our meaning to be essentially sound In Goodspeed's translation the prayer reads,

> Our Father in heaven,
> Your name be revered!
> Your kingdom come!
> Your will be done
> on earth as well as in heaven!

> Give us today bread for the day,
> And forgive us our debts, as we have
>   forgiven our debtors.
> And do not subject us to temptation,
> But save us from the evil one!

Revered makes more sense to us today than *blessed* and the dictionary of synonyms gives it as an analagous word with *hallowed*. Further perusal of the thesaurus shows that *revere* implies "a recognition of the exalted character of that which is so respected and honored"; that "one reveres not only persons who are entitled to respect and honor but also things which are associated with such persons; the word commonly connotes tenderness of feeling and deference."

This much research and we are still on the first line! You may have a new understanding of that first line. Let's continue our analysis for purposes of illustration, but let's continue with Goodspeed's translation, since the language is more nearly contemporary. "Your kingdom come" seems a simple enough concept. The next line amplifies that idea. "Your will be done on earth as well as in heaven." In other words, we are simply asking for the kingdom of God on earth, where the will of the Lord will be done in everything, just as it is now done in His kingdom of heaven. The word *kingdom* should give you no trouble because we are speaking of an autocracy, where one person's will is law. We don't need to quibble about whether it is "in earth" or "on earth"; the meaning is essentially the same. "Give us today bread for the day" may seem like an unnecessary troubling of the Lord. It is a more meaningful phrase in the barren hills of Israel than it is in the fruitful land of America, but, if we can imagine a society where famine is an ever-current threat, then we begin to understand the import of such a line. "And forgive us our debts, as we have forgiven our debtors" presents a problem. Does *as* mean *just as* or *like* or *in the same degree?* Let's go back to the context, to the sixth chapter of Matthew, fourteenth verse. In Goodspeed's translation it reads,

> For, if you forgive others when they offend you, your heavenly Father will forgive you too. But if you do not forgive others when they offend you, your heavenly Father will not forgive you for your offenses.

That clears that up. *As* in that sentence means *just as,* according to St. Matthew.

The last lines are clear in any of the versions. Our last request of the Lord is that He keep us from temptation, but if that is impossible that He deliver us from ultimate evil, because He is all-powerful.

By LIFE Photographer Howard Sochurek. Courtesy of TIME Inc.

The layman reads aloud.

There may be other work you will want to do. You may want to look up *debts, trespasses,* and *sins* in the dictionary to see just what emphasis is most meaningful to you. You may want to do other supplementary research on the purpose and the technique of prayer; you may want to discover what scholars have had to say about the Lord's Prayer. However much more you may want to do, you have moved one big step closer to listener comprehension. You have begun to comprehend.

Try analyzing another familiar selection, the Pledge of Allegiance.

I pledge allegiance to the flag of the United States of America and to the Republic for which it stands, one Nation, indivisible, with Liberty and Justice for all.

Here is a straightforward bit of writing. The purpose is to inform or persuade, depending upon the occasion; the form is prose; and the selection is only one sentence long. The meaning seems quite clear. We pledge allegiance to the flag. But is that really what it means? What's a flag? A symbol, isn't it? Do we pledge allegiance to a symbol? Yes, we do, as long as we remember the entity for which the symbol stands. We would pledge allegiance to the entity, if we could, but since we can't focus our attention on an object as great as the United States, we focus on a symbol—in this case, the flag. But the author has tried to help us by adding to the pledge to the flag a statement of the nature of the entity for which the flag is a symbol, "the Republic for which it stands."

Let's dissect this selection to be sure we comprehend it. Do you know what *pledge* means? Are you sure? Better look it up. You'll find it has several meanings and all of them have the connotation of a promise with a guarantee of "forfeiture for nonperformance." Do you know the meaning of *allegiance?* You'll find it has two meanings in *Webster's Collegiate Dictionary.*

1. The relation of a feudal vassal to his superior, or liege lord; the duty of fidelity to one's king, government, or sovereign state.

2. Devotion or loyalty to that which is entitled to obedience or service and respect.

At first glance we see that it is the second meaning that applies to our flag. The sentence now reads, "I promise, with forfeiture-of-something-for-nonperformance, devotion to this *flag* which is entitled to respect. It is the symbol of the United States of America, a republic." Do you know why we say *republic* instead of *democracy?* Why do we in this pledge make a point of "one nation, indivisible"? Was this pledge written before or after the War between the States? Why do we in this pledge stress "Liberty and Justice for all"? Why those precise words? Why not *freedom and law?* Why not *life, liberty, and the pursuit of happiness for all?* What is the difference between *liberty* and *freedom?* What is the difference between *justice* and *law?* Is it really for "all"?

We need to know the answers to all these questions before we completely comprehend this simple, much-recited selection.

At this point, you probably think you should have resisted that impulse to learn to read aloud; there is too much work to it. "When Judge Pusey asked Lon Moon, who murdered his wife, if he had anything t' say before being acquitted, he replied, 'I never would have shot her if I'd know'd I'd have t' go thru so much red tape.' "[1]

Yet all this analytical "red tape" is essential if you are to achieve effective communication with your audience. You are attempting to get from a group of listeners maximum comprehension of a selection you are

[1] Kin Hubbard, *Abe Martin* (Indianapolis: Bobbs-Merrill Company, Inc., 1926), p. 35.

reading aloud. Since the listener cannot comprehend what you do not understand, let's look systematically now at this business of understanding.

COMPLETE MEANING OF SELECTION

We start with the work from which the selection is taken. The first thing we seek is total meaning. In many writings the meaning is straightforward and obvious, but in others it may be diametrically opposed to what the words seem to say. A parable means more than the bare words describe. Fables mean more than the simple tale relates. George Orwell's book *Animal Farm* does not mean literally that the animals took the farm away from the farmer or that pigs are the smartest of the barnyard animals. It is a fable about communism. The pigs represent one segment of a Communist society. It is also a parable, meaning much more than it says. The reader must know what Orwell means before he can intelligently interpret the book.

When sarcasm and irony are used in humor, they frequently make use of the double meaning. The words say one thing and their sum total implies something else. A "something else" that is often at variance with the literal meaning. In countries where censorship is strict, humor may be the only means of saying something very serious.

After you have read a selection in its context and are certain of the total meaning of the work, ask yourself these questions: what is the author's purpose, what form does he use, what mood does he create? The answer to each of those questions will affect the way you finally read the selection to your listeners.

AUTHOR'S PURPOSE

What is the author's purpose; what is he trying to do? Is he trying to tell you something; that is, is he explaining something (called *exposition* in English textbooks), or is he recounting an experience (called *narration*)? If he is trying to explain or recount, his purpose is to inform. If he is trying to convince you of something, or inspire you, or swing you to his opinion, his purpose is to persuade. If he is trying to amuse you, or just spend some time enjoyably with you, his purpose is to entertain.

It is not always easy to be sure of an author's purpose after your first reading. While he is aiming to persuade you, he may inform you of much you did not know. While he is entertaining you, he may also cause you to change your opinion on some matter. Nevertheless, he will have an over-all purpose in the work you are reading. Make sure you know what it is.

STRUCTURE OF MATERIAL

Your first reading of a selection in its context should also reveal to you what structural form the writer used. If poetry, did he use the ballad, the ballade, the sonnet, the lyric, the epigram, the ode, and so forth; if prose, did he use the article, the fable, the story, the essay, the novel, and so forth?

Having discovered the writer's purpose and recognized the form in which the prose or poetry is cast, you are ready to analyze the structure of the selection on which you are working. A first reading will certainly not reveal all the details and interrelationships of this structure. But a careful analysis will.

The writer is a communicator just like you. He tries for the reader's complete comprehension by gaining his attention, his interest, his understanding, and frequently his belief. Artificial devices are often employed to gain attention: the headline or picture in the newspaper, the illustration and layout in a magazine, the cheesecake cover on a paper-bound book.

After our attention has been arrested, the writer has to interest us or the communication is incomplete. If the headline speaks to us of some subject in which we too have an interest, we will probably read further into the story. If the cheesecake cover attracts our eye, we may still not read the book if the kind of story fails to interest us; the book is a western and we only like mysteries.

Attention and interest alone are not enough to insure complete comprehension; what is written must be understood by the reader. The government has our attention and interest when it sends our income-tax forms, but it is far from winning our understanding. When we read the instructions, most of us feel as Robert Benchley felt.

A little farther on in the book I found, under Sec. 25 (a) "dividends received from domestic corporations, except corporations taxable under Section 251 of the law and corporations organized under the China Trade Act." Now I am frank to say that I do not know about the China Trade Act. I don't really suppose that it applies to me, but how am I to be sure? In Supplement K there is a paragraph (d) which is headed: "Definition of China" which says: "As used in this section the term 'China' shall have the same meaning as when used in the China Trade Act, 1922." This more or less brings us back to where we were in the beginning. If the Government thinks that it has cleared up anything at all in that "definition of China," it is crazy. I sometimes wonder if it isn't anyway.[2]

Let's say the writer has won our understanding. Comprehension is not complete until he has won our belief. Assume, for example, that the writer is telling us we should drive more carefully. He catches our attention by some arresting device. He gains our interest by talking about a subject in which we are interested. He points out the dangers of careless driving; he cites the number of highway accidents each year; he shows that nearly all were the result of carelessness. We understand everything he has to say. But he fails to make sufficient impression on us to affect our driving. We put down the article and continue to pass other cars on hills. He did not convince us. He did not make believers of us.

This last step, the belief step, does not occur in all writing. It is absent in much writing to inform, it seldom occurs in writing to divert. But it is always present in writing to persuade.

Let's see if these four steps involved in comprehension can be found in various forms of writing; for example, the public speech. Pick up any textbook on public speaking and you will find that the authors all name three parts of a speech: the introduction, the body, and the conclusion. If you'll study their remarks, you'll find they speak of the introduction as a means of getting attention. Then, they say, the introduction is followed by a statement of the speaker's aim. Some texts call this the speaker's purpose, his central idea, main thought, or thesis. That statement is the interest step. It is the reason for your continued attention to the subject being discussed. The body of the speech is given over to argument, proof, and explanation of the main idea. It strives for our understanding. If the argument of the body of the speech is sufficiently persuasive, we believe it. Then the conclusion is a restatement of the central idea of the speech, a summing up and tying together. It reminds us of the conviction we have reached, or the action we should take.

Let's glance at other forms of writing. The play, the novel, the newspaper article, the essay, the magazine article, the radio commercial, and the advertising layout all have a structural form that makes use of the steps for complete comprehension.

The play, according to Aristotle, has three parts: the beginning, the

[2] Robert Benchley, *Chips off the Old Benchley* (New York: Harper & Brothers, 1949), pp. 13–14

middle, and the end. The beginning reaches for our attention and states the problem to be solved, the middle is the involvement of the problem, and the end settles the problem. We are interested in the problem or we would not give it our continued attention, the middle gains our understanding and maybe our belief, the ending restates and ties together.

Critics of the novel claim for it the same structure.

The newspaper article is organized so that interest, attention, and understanding are all in the first paragraph, the rest of the space being devoted to restatement. In recent years, this style has been undergoing a change, but, since most reporters pack "who, when, what, where, why, and how" into the first sentence, the rest of the story becomes extended anticlimax.

The essayist usually begins with some attention-getting device, then states the particular bit of minutiae the essay will concern itself with (the interest step), then goes into a development of that basic idea (the understanding step), and eventually comes to a conclusion. Usually the essay is dedicated to too frail a subject for the author to burden it with a conviction or belief step. The magazine article most frequently follows the same pattern.

A radio commercial, if it is good, is so organized that all four comprehensive steps are present. The attention step is usually some type of casual sneak-up on the listener, or some raucous jingle or sound effect. The interest step is usually a statement of why you should be interested in a certain product. This step varies with each day's sales message. The understanding step is the sales message. The conviction step in radio is an action step. It usually begins with the word *so:* "So why not ask your grocer for a box today!"

"So" it's fairly safe to say that all communicative writing follows a formula—the introduction, central idea, body, and conclusion—and that formula uses the four steps necessary for gaining complete comprehension.

Thus far you have asked yourself questions about the author's purpose, and about the form and structure of his material. Now question yourself on the mood of the selection. How were you affected when you read it? If the author's purpose was informative, the material may have had no prevailing mood. But, if his purpose was to persuade or to entertain, there may have been a very definite mood, a pervasive emotion or state of mind which you will need to recreate for your audience. For the present, put a label, for your own purposes, on the mood he created, and remember the emotional impact of the selection. The relationship of mood to communicating emotion is dealt with in Chapter 7.

ANALYSIS OF MATERIAL

You are now ready to start an intensive analysis of the manuscript.

Writers do not convey information by an outline. They amplify that structure with material that—in their opinion—interests the reader and insures his understanding. Authors may use some or all of these amplifying devices to gain comprehension from a reader: restatement; definition; breakdown of an idea into its component parts; illustrations, such as anecdote, hypothetical situations, contrasts, and comparisons; evidence in the form of statistics, opinions, interpretations, beliefs, and authoritative statements.

Here is a curtain speech made on the opening night of a New York play by one of the authors. Read it through.

> This is a very remarkable play. I don't know as you noticed it as it went along; but it is. The construction of this play and the development of the story are the result of great research, and erudition and genius, and invention—and plagiarism. When the authors wrote it they thought they would put in a great lot of catastrophes and murders and such things, because they always enliven an evening so; but we wanted to have some disaster that wasn't hackneyed, and after a good deal of thought we hit upon the breaking down of a stage-coach. The worst of getting a good original idea like that is the temptation to overdo it; and in fact when the play was all done we found that we had got the stage-coach breaking down seven times in the first act. It was to come right along here every seven minutes or so, and spill all the passengers over on the musicians. Well, you see, that wouldn't do; it made it monotonous for the musicians: and it was too stagey; and we had to modify it; and there isn't anything left of the original plan now except one breakdown of the coach, and one carriage breakdown, and one pair of runaway horses. Maybe we might have spared even some of these; but you see we had the horses, and we didn't like to waste them.
>
> I wish to say also that this play is didactic rather than anything else. It is intended rather for instruction than amusement. The Chinaman is getting to be a pretty frequent figure in the United States, and is going to be a great political problem, and we thought it well for you to see him on the stage before you had to deal with that problem. Then for the instruction of the young we have introduced a game of poker. There are few things that are so unpardonably neglected in our country as poker. The upper class know very little about it. Now and then you find Ambassadors who have a sort of general

knowledge of the game, but the ignorance of the people at large is fearful. Why, I have known clergymen, good men, kindhearted, liberal, sincere and all that, who did not know the meaning of a 'flush'; it is enough to make one ashamed of one's species. When our play was finished, we found it was so long, and so broad, and so deep—in places—that it would have taken a week to play it. I thought that was all right; we could put 'To be continued' on the curtain, and run it straight along. But the manager said no; it would get us into trouble with the general public, and into trouble with the general government, because the Constitution forbids the infliction of cruel or unusual punishment; so he cut out, and cut out, and the more he cut out the better the play got. I never saw a play that was so much improved by being cut down; and I believe it would have been one of the very best plays in the world if his strength had held out so that he could cut out the whole of it.[3]

How soon did you realize that the speaker's purpose was to entertain you? Did you doubt that this was prose? What was the prevailing mood? How did you respond to it? Obviously, the total meaning of the speech is different from the meaning of any of the parts. The total meaning of the speech is that this play is a piece of theatrical fustian with little to differentiate it from other horse operas. Yet the individual sentences and paragraphs say just the opposite. Mark Twain claims it is a "remarkable" play and uses a number of illustrations to prove it. The whole speech is a tongue-in-the-cheek spoofing of the theater, theater writers, Twain and his collaborator, and the audience.

This selection is a good example of the necessity for understanding the meaning and purpose of an item as a whole before attempting to understand all of its parts. Understanding of the parts of this speech without the essential understanding of the whole might lead the unhumorous reader into a ridiculous predicament.

Assuming now a knowledge of the purpose and meaning of the whole, let's consider the speech as an example of the way a writer amplifies his outline. Take the following analysis of the speech, sentence by sentence.

1. This is a very remarkable play.

> *Sentence 1 is the statement of the central idea of the talk. There is no introduction; evidently Twain thought the occasion called for none. He starts immediately with the interest step.*

---

[3] Mark Twain's curtain speech at the opening of *Ah Sin,* a play written by Mark Twain and Bret Harte. Fifth Avenue Theatre, July 31, 1877. Quoted by Joseph Francis Daly in *The Life of Augustin Daly* (New York: The Macmillan Co., 1917), pp. 234–236.

2. I don't know as you noticed it as it went along; but it is.

> *This sentence—as dead-pan as the first—sets the facetious tone of the whole speech. The drawled, colloquial structure hints to the listener that a joke is in the making. Mark Twain is about to be funny.*

3. The construction of this play and the development of the story are the result of great research, and erudition and genius, and invention—and plagiarism.

> *Sentence 3 is the first sentence of the body of the speech, the proof or argument part. Twain begins to prove that the play is remarkable and with the "and plagiarism" makes his first outrageous or humorous remark. The mood has been established with this sentence. The speech will be droll but will follow a straight-faced pattern of exposition. Humour will be achieved through the ridiculousness of the incidents. Had the speech been lengthy, Twain would have elaborated on each of the five items in turn: (1) research, (2) erudition, (3) genius, (4) invention, and (5) plagiarism.*

4. When the authors wrote it they thought they would put in a great lot of catastrophes and murders and such things, because they always enliven an evening so; but we wanted to have some disaster that wasn't hackneyed, and after a good deal of thought we hit upon the breaking down of a stage-coach.

> *For the purposes of this speech he dwells on invention and plagiarism in sentence four.*

5. The worst of getting a good original idea like that is the temptation to over-do it; and in fact when the play was all done we found that we had got the stage-coach breaking down seven times in the first act.

> *Sentence 5 elaborates the idea of catastrophes.*

6. It was to come right along here every seven minutes or so, and spill all the passengers over on the musicians.

> *Sentence 6 uses specific example to make the point of 5.*

7. Well, you see, that wouldn't do; it made it monotonous for the musicians: and it was too stagey; and we had to modify it; and there isn't anything left of the original plan now except one breakdown of the coach, and one carriage breakdown, and one pair of runaway horses

> *Sentence 7 limits the elaboration of 5.*

8. Maybe we might have spared even some of these, but you see we had the horses, and we didn't like to waste them.

Sentence 8 is the final statement on "invention of catastrophes."

9. I wish to say also that this play is didactic rather than anything else.

Sentence 9 is a second reason why the play is remarkable.

10. It is intended rather for instruction than amusement.

Sentence 10 is a restatement of the idea of sentence 9.

11. The Chinaman is getting to be a pretty frequent figure in the United States and is going to be a great political problem, and we thought it well for you to see him on the stage before you had to deal with that problem.

Sentence 11 is an example of the type of instruction that makes the play remarkable.

12. Then for the instruction of the young we have introduced a game of poker.

Sentence 12 is an example of another type of instruction.

13. There are few things that are so unpardonably neglected in our country as poker.

14. The upper class know very little about it.

15. Now and then you find Ambassadors who have a sort of general knowledge of the game, but the ignorance of the people at large is fearful.

16. Why, I have known clergymen, good men, kindhearted, liberal, sincere and all that, who did not know the meaning of a 'flush'; it is enough to make one ashamed of one's species.

Sentences 13, 14, 15, and 16 give reasons for the need of instruction in poker.

17. When our play was finished, we found it was so long, and so broad, and so deep—in places—that it would have taken a week to play it.

Sentence 17 is a third reason why the play is remarkable.

Sentence 18 is implied. (How will an audience see a play that takes a week to perform?)

19. I thought that was all right; we could put 'To be continued' on the curtain, and run it straight along.

Sentence 19 gives one solution to the implied question.

20. But the manager said no; it would get us into trouble with the general public, and into trouble with the general government, because the Consti-

tution forbids the infliction of cruel or unusual punishment; so he cut out, and cut out, and the more he cut out the better the play got.

Sentence 20 gives another solution.

21. I never saw a play that was so much improved by being cut down; and I believe it would have been one of the very best plays in the world if his strength had held out so that he could cut out the whole of it.

> *Sentence 21 is the result of the solution in sentence 19 and gives a final reason for the play's remarkableness. It is the conclusion of the speech.*

You see, all writing is just a string of ideas. Some ideas are of major importance, while others of less importance are subordinate to the main ideas. The subordinate ideas amplify, prove, or comment on the main ideas. We think in idea groups. In order to convey those idea groups on paper, the writer uses certain tools: paragraphs, sentences, punctuation, and words. The paragraph is an idea group. In it are thought units that are subordinate to the principal idea but are complete in themselves. These units are called sentences. Sentences themselves may have dominant and subordinate clauses and phrases, and to show this interrelationship the writer uses punctuation. Phrases are made up of words that do not constitute a complete thought unit.

The reader, eager to comprehend what the writer is trying to communicate, must recognize the interrelationship of words, phrases, sentences, and paragraphs. Here we must indulge in a certain amount of study that may seem like busy work. We all know what sentences are. We all are familiar with the more common punctuation marks. And we can name the parts of speech.

SENTENCES

In most of our reading we may not need to worry about these simple matters. But occasionally we find a writer who states his ideas in such a complex way, or whose ideas are inherently so complex, that we must take time for sentence analysis. We will need to know just what is the subject of the sentence, what the verb, what the object. We will need to scan the punctuation for guideposts through the maze. We will need to know the parts of speech in order to find all the writer's meanings.

Below is a good example of why we need a brief review of the writer's tools.

> There isn't any reason
> Why a sentence, I suppose, once it begins,

Once it has risen to the lips at all
And finds itself happily wandering
Through shady vowels and over consonants
Where ink's been spilt like rivers or like blood
Flowing for the cause of some half-truth
Or a dogma now outmoded, shouldn't go
Endlessly moving in grave periphrasis
And phrase in linking phrase, with commas falling
As airly as lime flowers, intermittently,
Uninterrupting, scarcely troubling
The mild and fragile progress of the sense
Which trills trebling like a pebbled stream
Or lowers toward an oath-intoning ocean
Or with a careless and forgetful music
Looping and threading, turning and entwining,
Flings a babel of bells, a caroling
Of such various vowels the ear can almost feel
The soul of sound when it lay in chaos yearning
For the tongue to be created: such a hymn
If not as lovely, then as interminable,
As restless, and as heartless, as the hymn
Which in the tower of heaven the muted spheres
With every rippling harp and windy horn
Played for incidental harmony
Over the mouldering rafters of the world,
Rafters which seldom care to ring, preferring
The functional death-watch beetle, stark, staccato,
Economical as a knuckle-bone,
Strict, correct, but undelighting
Like a cleric jigging in the saturnalia,
The saturnalia we all must keep,
Green-growing and rash with life,
Our milchy, mortal, auroral, jovial,
Harsh, unedifying world
Where every circle of grass can show a dragon
And every pool's as populous as Penge,
Where birds, with taffeta flying, scarf the air
On autumn evenings, and a sentence once begun
Goes on and on, there being no reason
To draw to any conclusion as long as breath
Shall last, except that breath
Can't last much longer.[4]

If you have been convinced by this selection that you may need a

[4] From *Venus Observed,* by Christopher Fry. Copyright 1949 by Christopher Fry. Reprinted by permission of Oxford University Press, Inc.

brief review of the writer's tools for conveying meaning, let's begin with sentences.

Sentence, in grammar, means a set of words complete in itself, having either expressed or understood in it a subject and a predicate, and conveying a statement or question or command or exclamation.[5]

A sentence is a group of related words expressing a complete thought. . . . A sentence when completely expressed must contain at least one independent clause. Some sentences, however, do not have every part expressed. Occasionally, something—a subject, a verb, a clause—may be omitted when the meaning of the sentence would be perfectly clear with the omissions.[6]

PUNCTUATION

Within every written sentence there are symbols other than words that aid your understanding. These symbols are punctuation marks. Let us turn our attention to them. There are two kinds of punctuation: punctuation for the eye and punctuation for the ear. Since we are working from the printed page, we will discuss punctuation for the eye first.

The use in written or printed matter of the arbitrary set of symbols called *punctuation marks* is for one of the following purposes: *grammatical punctuation,* to show the varying degrees of relationship of ideas, as by division into sentences, clauses, and phrases, to aid in their quicker comprehension; *inflectional punctuation,* to show the varying degrees of emphasis, as by italics, underlining, quotation marks, and dashes; *rhetorical punctuation,* to indicate who is speaking, as by quotation marks, commas, and colons; *word punctuation,* to show variations in the formation, use, or omission of words or parts of words, as by the apostrophe and the ellipsis; *punctuation for reference,* to point the reader to other places on the page or in the books, as by footnotes, parentheses, and numbering.

When we are talking, of course, we don't use any punctuation marks. We use a system of pauses, varying in length, to join or separate our ideas, and we raise or lower our pitch to indicate varying degrees of emphasis. In other words, we make ourselves understood not only by words but also by pauses, stress, and pitch.

Punctuation gets pauses and stress (but no pitch) down on paper.

[5] H. W. Fowler, *A Dictionary of Modern English Usage* (Oxford: At the Clarendon Press), p. 523.

[6] George P. Wilson, *A Guide to Better English* (New York: Appleton-Century-Crofts, Inc., 1942), p. 102.

The system is simple to get the hang of:

	Between Words	Between Sentences
Normal pause	White space	Period
Shorter pause	Hyphen	Semicolon (or colon)
Longer pause	Dash	Paragraph
Normal stress		Normal type (or writing)
Unstressed		Parentheses (or two dashes)
Stressed		Italics (or underlining)

Let me explain this little table: As long as you use normal pauses and normal stress in talking, don't use anything but periods and commas in writing. When you run two or more words together with almost no pause between them (because you use them in that sentence as one word), hyphenate them. When you use a longer pause—Watch out for the next word—make a dash. Same with sentences: When you run two or more sentences together (because you use a string of sentences as one), use a semicolon or, if the first sentence introduces the second, a colon. When you use a longer pause—Now comes something else! —make a paragraph. And don't forget to use italics or parentheses for emphasis or casual mention.

When you put plain talk in writing, two punctuation marks are particularly important for you: hyphens and semicolons. The reason is this: The fewer empty words you use and the more you rely on word order, the more important it is for you to show which words belong closely together; this you do by using hyphens. On the other hand, in plain talk you often use two or more short sentences instead of one long one and show the connection by semicolons.[7]

Mr. Flesch omits two writing devices for stress that you should be familiar with: the quotation mark for stress; the comma for no stress. Here is an example.

I have often wondered that no philosopher has considered the strange affinity between crime and whiskers. The campaign so capably conducted some years ago by Mr. Frank Richardson against what he pleasantly terms "face fittings" did not, I think, invade this region of the hostile province. That most of the homicides of history have been hairy faced folk, sealed of the tribe of Esau—Cain was certainly unshaven—admits of no dispute, and invites to curious reflection, a subject upon which, luckily for the reader, I lack space to dwell. I shall content myself with reminding him that King James the Sixth and M. Landru were both, though unequally, bearded— James affording, in comparison with the fertile Frenchman, but poor

[7] Rudolf Flesch, *The Art of Plain Talk* (New York: Harper & Brothers, 1946), pp. 92–93.

soil; and that the moustaches of the Kaiser and of his subject Oscar Slater each influenced evilly the wearer's fortunes.[8]

Notice that the quotes around "face fittings" lead you to stress that phrase just as much as if it were underlined. Notice also how you drop the stress on "I think" in the same sentence. The commas there act as if they were parentheses. Notice the subordination of ideas in the next sentence. "Cain was certainly unshaven" is subordinated to "sealed of the tribe of Esau," which, in turn, is subordinated to the first phrase of the sentence.

We can do some generalizing now. "Ear punctuation" we use naturally in speech. To achieve the same naturalness in reading from the printed page we must become familiar with "eye punctuation." Visual punctuation is used in sentences to act as traffic markers along the straightaway of the main idea. A comma, a parenthesis, or a dash warns us of changes in direction. A semicolon or a colon are blinkers at intersections. A period is a stop sign.

WORDS

Finally, you are ready to investigate words. Words, grammatically, are parts of speech; semantically, they are abstractions of ideas.

▶ *Nouns.*   Nouns are the names of the subject of discourse, as persons, places, things, qualities, ideas, actions. Like most names, they are capsule histories of civilization. Nouns denote meanings while being strong in connotative values for the reader.

Talk about learning our *letters* and being *literate!* Why, the roots of *letters* are *things*. Natural objects and phenomena are the original symbols or types which express our thoughts and feelings, and yet American scholars, having little or no root in the soil, commonly strive with all their might to confine themselves to the imported symbols alone. All the true growth and experience, the living speech, they would fain reject as 'Americanisms.' It is the old error, which the church, the state, the school ever commit, choosing darkness rather than light, holding fast to the old and to tradition. A more intimate knowledge, a deeper experience, will surely originate a word. When I really know that our river pursues a serpentine course to the Merrimack, shall I continue to describe it by referring to some other river no older than itself which is like it, and call it a *meander?* It is no more meandering than the Meander is *musketaquidding.* As well

[8] William Roughead, "Poison in the Pantry," from *Malice Domestic*. (Edinburgh: W. Green & Son, 1928); reprinted in *The Murderer's Companion* (New York: The Press of the Reader's Club, 1941), pp. 60–61. By permission of the author's agent.

sing of the nightingale here as the Meander. What if there were a tariff on words, on language, for the encouragement of home manu-facturers? Have we not the genius to coin our own?[9]

▶ *Verbs.* Verbs express action, occurrence, or mode of being. It is the verb that gives life to any sentence; it makes the sentence go.

The boy in Saroyan's *Beautiful People* wrote only one-word books. As he said, he wasn't going to write a two-word book until he knew two words.

#1 I've got to find out about nouns before I move to verbs. You've got to be careful about verbs, otherwise you'll get things all mixed up—even worse than they are already. *Is. That's* a verb. I've got to be careful when I use a word like that.[10]

#2 The verbs you want to use are those that are in active business doing verb work; if you use a verb in the passive voice or make a participle or noun out of it, you have lost the most valuable part in the process: it's like cooking vegetables and throwing away the water with all the vitamins in it.[11]

#3 Generally use transitive verbs, that strike their object; and use them in the active voice; eschewing the stationary passive, with its little auxiliary *it's* and *was's,* and its participles getting into the light of your adjectives, which should be few. For, as a rough law, by his use of the straight verb and by his economy of adjectives you can tell a man's style, if it be masculine or neuter, writing or "composition."[12]

▶ *Adverbs.* Adverbs qualify a verb or another qualifier, whether adjective, adverb, verbal noun, or qualifying phrase or clause. The greater number of English adverbs are formed by adding the suffix *ly* to adjectives and participles.

One reader of the Times finds words being used too wastefully in the news of the day. Apparently he thinks that there is so much violence and waste operating in the world that one should practice moderation where it is still possible. Official statements in Washington flatly deny a dispatch from Europe; in the opinion of our reader it is enough to deny without the flatness. The report is characterized a second time as completely erroneous, when "completely" is super-fluous, just as absolutely is unnecessary in "absolutely incorrect."

[9] Henry David Thoreau, *Journal,* ed. Bradford Tarrey and Francis H. Allen (Boston: Houghton Mifflin Company, 1949), 14 vols., October 16, 1859.

[10] William Saroyan, *Three Plays* (New York: Harcourt, Brace and Co., Inc., 1941), p. 67.

[11] Flesch, *op. cit.,* p. 67.

[12] Arthur Quiller-Couch, *On the Art of Writing* (New York: G. P. Putnam's Sons, 1916), p. 166.

Mr. Churchill is called to account for offering not only a denial but a "strong" denial, and for saying that a German U-boat was "effectively sunk."

On the other hand, to insist on the highest verbal purity under circumstances like that attending Mr. Churchill's speech is going pretty far. And after all, there is often an undeniable force in the marshaling of unnecessary adjectives and adverbs. Like the gentleman who was caught with a lighted cigarette behind stage in disregard of a large sign saying "NO SMOKING": he argued that the sign did not say "Positively No Smoking."[13]

▶ *Adjectives.* Adjectives modify nouns. Some adjectives define the noun; some merely comment.

Voltaire once said: "the adjective is the enemy of the noun." This sentence is one of the most famous epigrams about language; many young journalists have been started off with it, and taught to hunt adjectives in their copy.

It's a good rule, but a little confusing. The fact is, grammarians still can't agree on what an adjective is. If you say, for instance, *A ravishing math teacher,* some of them will tell you that *ravishing* and *math* are adjectives; some will say that *ravishing* is a verb form; some others will insist that *math* is a noun (if they admit it is a word at all). The best thing for us is to leave grammatical labels behind and see what the words do in and to a sentence. Then, at once, we see that *math* defines *teacher,* and that *ravishing* is a comment on the math teacher. In other words, there are two kinds of so-called adjectives: commenting and defining. Now we can see what Voltaire meant: obviously he didn't mean that a defining adjective is the enemy of the noun, because it really belongs to the noun (*What is she teaching?—Math*); in fact it is a part of the noun and you could just as well write *math-teacher,* with a hyphen. On the other hand, the commenting adjective is hostile to and literally kills the following noun: what we remember is that she is ravishing, not that she teaches math.[14]

▶ *Other parts of speech.* Pronouns stand for nouns. Prepositions denote relationship. Conjunctions connect words, sentences, or parts of sentences. These "other parts of speech" are receiving scant attention because the experienced reader usually gives them little stress. (See Chapter 6.)

▶ *The meaning of words.* The words used by an author have several possible meanings, denotative and connotative. The words can be exact or approximate in meaning. It is up to the reader to determine by study

[13] New York *Times,* October 13, 1941.
[14] Flesch, *op. cit.,* p. 74.

whether the author has used words exactly or loosely, and whether the meaning he intends is denotative or connotative. After the reader makes the decision, he must decide further whether he will change the words, cut them from the text, or use them and try to give them their proper value in his reading. In Chapter 7 you will find selections in which the object of the reader is to extract all the connotative values. In Chapter 5 there are selections for drill in denotative meaning. As for exactness in word usage, listen to Mark Twain.

. . . I do not find that the repetition of an important word a few times—say, three or four times—in a paragraph troubles my ear if clearness of meaning is best secured thereby. But tautological repetition which has no justifying object, but merely exposes the fact that the writer's balance at the vocabulary bank has run short and that he is too lazy to replenish it from the thesaurus—that is another matter. It makes me feel like calling the writer to account. It makes me want to remind him that he is not treating himself and his calling with right respect, and, incidentally, that he is not treating me with proper reverence. At breakfast, this morning, a member of the family read aloud an interesting review of a new book about Mr. Gladstone in which the reviewer used the strong adjective "delightful" thirteen times. Thirteen times in a short review, not a long one. In five of the cases the word was distinctly the right one, the exact one, the best one our language can furnish, therefore it made no discord; but in the remaining cases it was out of tune. It sharped or flatted, one or the other, every time, and was as unpleasantly noticeable as is a false note in music. I looked in the thesaurus, and under a single head I found four words which would replace with true notes the false ones uttered by four of the misused "delightfuls"; and of course if I had hunted under related heads for an hour and made an exhaustive search I should have found right words, to a shade, wherewith to replace the remaining delinquents.

I suppose we all have our foibles. I like the exact word, and clarity of statement, and here and there a touch of good grammar for picturesqueness; but that reviewer cares for only the last mentioned of these things. His grammar is foolishly correct, offensively precise. It flaunts itself in the reader's face all along, and struts and smirks and shows off, and is in a dozen ways irritating and disagreeable. To be serious, I write good grammar myself, but not in that spirit, I am thankful to say. That is to say, my grammar is of a high order, though not at the top. Nobody's is. Perfect grammar—persistent, continuous, sustained—is the fourth dimension, so to speak; many have sought it, but none has found it. Even this reviewer, this purist, with all his godless airs, has made two or three slips. At least,

I think he has. I am almost sure, by witness of my ear, but cannot be positive, for I know grammar by ear only, not by note, not by the rules. A generation ago I knew the rules—knew them by heart, word for word, though not their meanings—and I still know one of them: the one which says—which says—but never mind, it will come back to me presently. This reviewer even seems to know (or seems even to know, or seems to know even) how to put the word "even" in the right place; and the word "only," too. I do not like that kind of person. I never knew one of them that came to any good.[15]

Many words are used as allusions, that is, as indirect references to something generally familiar. You cannot gain the comprehension of the listener unless you understand each allusion and all of its implications. To understand allusions you will have to refer to dictionaries, biographical dictionaries, classical mythologies, and encyclopedias. You are all familiar with such allusions as "persecuted as Job," "poor as a church mouse," and "Quisling," but do you understand the references in these selections?

1   WORDS
    shake out their wings, and soar and sing like birds
    of flashing, gleaming feathers—
    peacock-blues,
    Red Admiral scarlets,
    shimmering, silk-robe greens
    fit to adorn Jade Button Mandarins;
    and jewel-colours,
    turquoises, topazes,
    and milk-blanched moonstones, Nicholas,
    all the hues
    th' imprisoning rainbow holds—
    words, words, words, words
    O bright!
    Lovely to say and sing, and beautiful to write.

    There's Palimpsest—
    a grand word old and stately,
    to do with History, and Manor Lands,
    and great possessions men once valued greatly.
    There's Ortolan—which is itself a bird—
    and Chivalry, a noble-sounding word
    by which, one day, Nicholas, you will be spurred
    as knights were, when men's faith in words was strong.

[15] Samuel L. Clemens, *Mark Twain's Autobiography* (New York: Harper & Brothers, 1924), I, 172. Copyright, 1924, by Clara Gabrilowitsch. Copyright, 1952, by Clara Clemens Samossoud.

There's Parasang—
a word to shout to stars,
and when you understand its meaning, too
as thrilling as the note of a great bronze gong.

There's Burgundy
(a Duke, also a wine
and both magnificent),
there's Damascened—
a word that goes back, Nicholas, to the line
of the Crusaders; Crusaders, Nicholas,
a word as well-rubbed as an ancient brass
in a Cathedral (which is Norman, too,
like the Crusaders). Old words shine mint-new

as Basilisk does if you but learn to seek
whether they come—as that one does—from Greek
or Latin (like Regency), or were fetched away
with silks and ginger in a bygone day
from the far borders of remote Cathay,
or brought with looted Ingots from the Main,
exchanged for English words by way of Spain.

There's Roc
(a word that has a hard, fierce beak)
and Nightshade
(that's a dreamlike, deadly flower);
Nicholas, I could repeat words by the hour
as you do, when you fall in love with them:
oh, even the commonest of them is a gem,
like Dust, from which both you and I, Nick, spring.
One day, when you grow up, you'll understand
our lovely English words, and make them sing.[16]

#2   We had a Scrooge in our office a few minutes ago, a tall, parched man, beefing about Christmas and threatening to disembowel anyone who mentioned the word. He said his work had suffered and his life been made unbearable by the demands and conventions of the season. He said he hated wise men, whether from the East or from the West, hated red ribbon, angels, Scotch Tape, greeting cards depicting the Adoration, mincemeat, dripping candles, distant and near relatives, fir balsam, silent nights, boy sopranos, shopping lists with check marks against some of the items, and the whole yuletide stratagem, not to mention the low-lying cloud of unwritten thank-you

[16] "Words for Nicholas at Nine," *Punch,* Vol. CCXXI, No. 5787 (September 26, 1951). Reproduced by permission of the Proprietors of *Punch.*

letters hanging just above the horizon. He was in a savage state. Before he left the office, though, we saw him transfigured. The difference was that whereas Scrooge was softened by visions, our visitor was softened by the sight of a small book standing on our desk—a copy of Fowler's "Modern English Usage."

"Greatest collection of essays and opinions ever assembled between covers," he shouted, "including a truly masterful study of *that* and *which*."

He seized the book and began thumbing through it for favorite passages, slowly stuffing a couple of small gift-wrapped parcels into the pocket of his greatcoat.

"Listen to this," he said in a triumphant voice. " 'Avoidance of the obvious is very well, provided that it is not itself obvious; but, if it is, all is spoilt.' Isn't that beautiful?"

We agreed that it was a sound and valuable sentiment, perfectly expressed. He then began a sermon on *that* and *which,* taking as his text certain paragraphs from Fowler, and warming rapidly to his theme.

"Listen to this: 'If writers would agree to regard *that* as the defining relative pronoun, and *which* as the non-defining, there would be much gain both in lucidity and in ease. Some there are who follow this principle now; but it would be idle to pretend that it is the practice either of most or of the best writers.' "

"It was the practice of St. Matthew," we put in hastily. "Or at any rate he practiced it in one of the most moving sentences ever constructed: 'And, lo, the star, which they saw in the east, went before them till it came and stood over where the young child was.' You've got to admit that the *which* in that sentence is where it ought to be, as well as every other word. Did you ever read a more satisfactory sentence than that in your life?"

"It's good," said our friend, cheerfully. "It's good because there isn't a ten-dollar word in the whole thing. And Fowler has it pegged, too. Wait a minute. Here. 'What is to be deprecated is the notion that one can improve one's style by using stylish words.' See what I mean about Fowler? But let's get back to *that* and *which*. That's the business that really fascinates me. Fowler devotes eight pages to it. I got so excited once I had the pages photostated. Listen to this: 'We find in fact that the antecedent of *that* is often personal.' Now, that's very instructive."

"Very," we said. "And if you want an example, take Matthew 2:1 '. . . there came wise men from the east to Jerusalem, saying, 'Where is he that is born King of the Jews?' Imagine how that simple clause could get loused up if someone wanted to change *that* to *who!"*

"Exactly," he said. "That's what I mean about Fowler. What was the sentence again about the star? Say it again."

We repeated, "And, lo, the star, which they saw in the east, went before them, till it came and stood over where the young child was."

"You see?" he said, happily. "This is the greatest damn book ever written." And he left our office transfigured, a man in excellent spirits. Seeing him go off merry as a grig, we realized that Christmas is where the heart is. For some it is in a roll of red ribbon, for some in the eyes of a young child. For our visitor, we saw clearly, Christmas was in a relative pronoun. Wherever it is, it is quite a day.[17]

Since Fowler has been mentioned, it might be well here to quote what he has to say about words.

Any one who wishes to become a good writer should endeavour, before he allows himself to be tempted by the more showy qualities, to be direct, simple, brief, vigorous, and lucid. This general principle may be translated into practical rules in the domain of vocabulary as follows:—

Prefer the familiar word to the far-fetched.
Prefer the concrete word to the abstract.
Prefer the single word to the circumlocution.
Prefer the short word to the long.
Prefer the Saxon word to the Romance.

These rules are given roughly in order of merit; the last is also the least.[18]

PARAPHRASING

Words, punctuation, sentences—all that study just to understand what a writer is trying to say! But you are not finished. After you have made an analysis of the author's ideas, you may have to put the manuscript from you, and paraphrase and outline it. To be sure you understand what you're trying to read, put the material in your own words, maintaining the writer's sequence of ideas.

If you can't rephrase the author's ideas, it usually means they have not yet become your own. If you can't keep the material in the proper order, it means you have not understood the structure of the article. In some cases, of course, it may mean the author did not write well. But this is no place to quarrel with writing. Some writers claim they could

[17] *New Yorker*, XXIV, No. 44 (December 25, 1948), 11. Reprinted by permission. Copyright, 1948, by The New Yorker Magazine, Inc.
[18] H. W. Fowler and F. G. Fowler, *The King's English* (Oxford: At the Clarendon Press, 1925), p. 1.

and would write better if the persons who read their words aloud would do better. This is especially true in the fields of radio and speech writing. Continuity writers claim that there is no incentive for careful writing, because the announcer will butcher the script anyway. The announcer claims he can't do good work unless he is given something to work from. The speech writer claims that the reader emphasizes all the wrong points and throws away the writer's finest efforts. The reader denounces the writer, because, "I don't talk like that and I feel uncomfortable saying it."

Since our concern in this book is principally with the reader, we will take his part. But the reader can expect to get better writing only if he deserves it. You should strive to read so well that the writer is challenged to do better for you. You should read so well that you make the writer's every effort sound worth hearing.

But back to this matter of paraphrasing. If you really want to know what is in the manuscript you are reading, rewrite it in your own words. There is nothing like writing to impress ideas on your mind. Old-time stage managers dictated roles to the members of their acting companies and found that the actors learned the lines faster by writing them from dictation than by any other way devised. There is an unearned increment for you in paraphrasing, too. It is a way to perfect your own writing style. Ben Franklin used it.

> About this time I met with an odd volume of the *Spectator*. It was the third. I had never before seen any of them. I bought it, read it over and over, and was much delighted with it. I thought the writing excellent, and wished, if possible, to imitate it. With this view I took some of the papers, and, making short hints of the sentiment in each sentence, laid them by a few days, and then, without looking at the book, try'd to compleat the papers again, by expressing each hinted sentiment at length, and as fully as it had been expressed before, in any suitable words that should come to hand. Then I compared my *Spectator* with the original, discovered some of my faults, and corrected them. But I found I wanted a stock of words, or a readiness in recollecting and using them, which I thought I should have acquired before that time if I had gone on making verses; since the continual occasion for words of the same import, but of different length, to suit the measure, or of different sound for the rhyme, would have laid me under a constant necessity of searching for variety, and also have tended to fix that variety in my mind, and make me master of it. Therefore, I took some of the tales and turned them into verse; and, after a time, when I had pretty well forgotten the prose, turned them back again. I also sometimes jumbled my collections of hints into confusion, and after some weeks endeavored to reduce them

into the best order, before I began to form the full sentences and compleat the paper. This was to teach me method in the arrangement of thoughts. By comparing my work afterwards with the original, I discovered many faults and amended them, but I sometimes had the pleasure of fancying that, in certain particulars of small import, I had been lucky enough to improve the method of the language, and this encouraged me to think I might possibly in time come to be a tolerable English writer, of which I was extremely ambitious.[19]

RESEARCH

If you can do with your manuscript what Franklin taught himself to do with the *Spectator,* you need have no fears about understanding. In ninety-nine cases out of a hundred, the preparation you have now made is sufficient to comprehend any author's manuscript; analysis and paraphrase will ferret out the author's meaning. But there is always that hundredth case. Sometimes you will have to go to supplemental materials, finally, to track down the real meaning of your manuscript.

Research techniques may be needed for complete comprehension of your script. You may need to study the author's life to know why he wrote what he did, as he did. You may need to study critical comments on the author's works: contemporary criticism for present-day evaluation, historical works for the criticism of his contemporaries. You may need to study the history of the author's period to know the audience for whom he wrote and the situation that evoked his writing. Above all, you will need to know the context from which your selection is taken.

Study of an author's life may give you a clue to the workings of his mind. Perhaps he is a writer of parables, such as the Biblical writers, and when he speaks of a "lost sheep" is not speaking of a "sheep" at all, but of a sinner. Perhaps he is a humorist and, when he appears to speak in the sanest logic, is merrily pulling your leg.

If study of the author's life does not give you this information, perhaps the critics will. Here is an example of the help a critic can give. John Mason Brown deals with *The Cocktail Party,* by T. S. Eliot.

I have my other reasons for being shy about discussing Mr. Eliot's text in detail. He is a great one for playing solemn jokes upon his public—to the delight of his academic devotees. It amuses him

[19] Benjamin Franklin, *Autobiography* (New York: Garden City Books, 1916), pp. 25–27.

to interlard his own creations with lines borrowed here and there from the works of others, as a test of his readers' scholarship. Edmund Wilson, for example, pointed out that in "The Waste Land," a poem of only 433 lines (to which are added seven pages of notes), Mr. Eliot managed to include "Quotations from, allusions to, or imitations of, at least thirty-five different writers (some of them, such as Shakespeare and Dante, laid under contribution several times)—as well as several popular songs; and to introduce passages in six foreign languages, including Sanskrit."

I remember the late Theodore Spencer smiling happily when he told me that a speech which I had admired of one of the knights in "Murder in the Cathedral" had been snipped as a merry jest from A. Conan Doyle's "The White Company." Whether or not Mr. Eliot has been indulging in such playful appropriations in "The Cocktail Party," I do not know. I only remember Shaw's warning to critics when, for fun, he rewrote his novel "Cashel Byron's Profession" as a play in blank verse called "The Admirable Bashville." Shaw confessed he had purposely stolen or paraphrased lines from Marlowe and Shakespeare (not to mention Henry Carey) so that, if any man dared quote him derisively, he should do so in peril of inadvertently alighting on a purple passage from "Hamlet" or "Faustus."[20]

The principal help of this criticism is warning you away from such playful authors. But even such negative advice is valuable. Current critical opinion and historical opinion can be of further help in establishing the merit of the author's work for your audience. Everyone is familiar with the story of the reception Lincoln's Gettysburg Address was given in the daily papers of that time; everyone is equally familiar with the present opinion of it. Similar stories can be recounted of other works. Such information, if it is available, can be of value to the reader and his listener. A knowledge of the audience and the situation for which a piece was written can also help the reader. One audience may have had a special background for a subject, which made the writer's task simple. Our audience may not have such a background, and we will have to establish one for them or describe the audience for which the speech was first devised. The audience for which a piece was written may have met for some special reason; our audience will need to know that fact if it affects the meaning of the script. What seems vulgar to us, may not have been vulgar at all for its original audience.

You must study the material from which an excerpt is taken. Many times, a selection out of context is meaningless. Many times, the opposite

[20] John Mason Brown, "Seeing Things," *Saturday Review of Literature,* Vol. XXXIII, No. 4 (February 3, 1950).

of its meaning out of context may be its meaning within the entire work. You should know the entire work. Here is a selection from Stephen Vincent Benét's *America*. Notice the differences in meaning when passages are taken out of context. First let us read an excerpt.

> Who were the Pilgrims and why did they come to America? Were they adventurers, conquerors, gold seekers?
>
> No, they were not. A few of those on the *Mayflower* came on the chance of getting land and farms of their own.

Now read the same lines in context.

> Who were the Pilgrims and why did they come to America? Were they adventurers, conquerors, gold seekers?
>
> No, they were not. A few of those on the *Mayflower* came on the chance of getting land and farms of their own. But most came for another reason. They came because they wished to worship God in their own way—a simple and faithful way, but not the way of the Established Church of the England of their time.
>
> They were family men, for the most part. They brought their wives and their children with them on a 64-day voyage, in a small tossing ship. One child was born on the voyage, two others just after the landfall. The whole company numbered a little over a hundred human beings. It was backed by an English company whose investors put money into the venture. But the backbone of the venture was this group of quiet, family men, bringing their wives and children to a coast at the world's end.
>
> Why did they do such a crazy thing? Why on earth did they take such a chance? Nobody ordered them to do it, bribed them to do it. They went to great trouble and pain, uprooted their homes, left everything they had known behind, from the memories of childhood to the things in the house that one looks at and cannot take because there will be no room, and yet remembers.
>
> They wanted to worship God in their own way. They were resolved and determined to worship God in their own way . . . .[21]

▶ *Conclusion.* What has been said in this chapter? Above all, there can be no listener comprehension unless first there is reader comprehension. You cannot communicate what you do not understand. To understand your material you must first analyze it. You must search for

1. The total meaning.
2. The author's purpose. Does he write to inform, persuade or entertain?

---

[21] Stephen Vincent Benét, *America* (New York: Rinehart & Company, Inc., 1944), p. 11.

3. The script's form and structure. Does it follow a pattern of getting attention, interest, understanding and belief?
4. The script's mood.
5. The script's ideas. What are the main and subordinate ideas?

To understand your material you must recognize the writer's tools for conveying meaning. These are
1. Sentences.
2. Punctuation.
3. Words.

To be sure you understand your material, you should be able to restate the author's ideas. The techniques for restatement are
1. Paraphrasing.
2. Outlining.

To understand some material, you may need to do research. The sources of information are
1. The author's complete script.
2. The author's life.
3. The author's critics, both contemporary and historical.
4. The author's times.

· 3 ·

Preparing Your Material for an Audience

❖❖❖❖❖❖❖❖❖❖❖❖❖❖❖❖❖❖❖❖❖❖❖❖❖❖❖❖❖❖

The church in your home town on a Sunday morning is a familiar place. You know the Sunday-school rooms, the choir rooms, the offices, the church itself. You know the clergyman— in and out of his Sunday best. You know the folks in the congregation. The people who sit in front are neighbors. The folks over there live on the other side of town. Over there is a girl you went to school with. You may know nearly everyone in the church in one way or another. You all sit together on Sunday morning and listen to the clergyman speak.

But suppose you were to trade places with that clergyman. You go up into the pulpit and let him sit in your pew. Suddenly, all those people you know are different. They are no longer acquaintances and friends; they have become an audience. They are still the same individually, but your position before them has changed them into an "audience."

In this chapter, whenever an audience is mentioned, remember that it is just such a group of individuals as the one mentioned above. The audience is made up of people someone knows, people you could know if you had the time and opporutnity. If you will bear this in mind, preparing your material for an audience will be easier.

Whether you plan to read your own words or another's, you will need to know all you can about the audience who will hear you. In either case,

49

our alphabet of knowledge begins with *A* for audience. Up to now we have been concerned with you, the reader, or with him, the writer, with only a side glance given the listener. Let's think about the audience now.

> Talk about reading!—a good reader! It depends on how he is heard. There may be elocution and pronunciation (recitation, say) to satiety, but there can be no good reading unless there is good hearing also. It takes two at least for this game, as for love, and they must cooperate. The lecturer will read best those parts of his lecture which are best heard. I saw some men unloading molasses-hogsheads from a truck at a depot the other day, rolling them up an inclined plane. The truckman stood behind and shoved, after putting a couple of ropes one around each end of the hogshead, while two men standing in the depot steadily pulled at the ropes. The first man was the lecturer, the last was the audience. It is the duty of the lecturer to team his hogshead of sweets to the depot, or Lyceum, place the horse, arrange the ropes, and shove; and it is the duty of the audience to take hold of the ropes and pull with all their might. The lecturer who tries to read his essay without being abetted by a good hearing is in the predicament of a teamster who is engaged in the Sisyphean labor of rolling a molasses-hogshead up an inclined plane alone, while the freight-master and his men stand indifferent with their hands in their pockets.[1]

AUDIENCE INFORMATION

Who is the audience? Who is our listener? What is he like?

These questions must be answered before you can feel reasonably sure of your success in preparing your communication.

An audience is a group of people assembled under similar conditions to listen to a speaker. That definition is like a definition of humour: it will serve until you think of an example that won't fit it. A radio audience certainly doesn't fit it; and, with the exception of radio, all audiences, except the blind, assemble to look at as well as to listen to the speaker. Admitting some inadequacy in the definition, let's accept it for the present.

An audience has group characteristics that are different from the characteristics of the individuals who comprise it. An audience thinks more slowly than an individual, but laughs more quickly and more loudly. An audience is more restrained and polite when paying attention than is an individual, but more demonstrative when moved.

[1] Henry David Thoreau, *Journal,* ed. Bradford Tarrey and Francis H. Allen (Boston: Houghton Mifflin Company, 1949), 14 vols., March 3, 1859.

An audience thinks and acts with a group identity. The speaker, by his presence and his speaking, creates uniformity in the audience's thinking. An audience likes to feel it is smart, tolerant, discerning, and logical. It can be more easily flattered than could most of the individuals in it; it can react more vigorously when antagonized.

Who will be in your audience? Can you characterize those listeners to whom you will read? Why will they come to hear you? In order to help you prepare the material you will read, let's set up a guide for the analysis of your audience.

► *The size of an audience.* Find out in advance the probable size of the audience you will meet. The size of the audience will affect your preparation. If the audience is to be small, you can use an informal and conversational presentation. If the audience is to be very large, you will probably need a more formal presentation.

► *The occasion for the audience.* Again, find out in advance the reason for this gathering. Is the audience assembled for worship, information, amusement? If the audience has met for amusement and you are prepared to persuade them, or if they have met for worship and you are prepared to amuse them, you had better change your preparation or claim illness in the family,

► *The place of meeting.* You can find out in advance the meeting place of your audience. The manner of your delivery and often the content of your remarks will be affected by the place. Material and language suitable for an out-of-door gathering may seem sacrilegious in a church.

► *The audience's characteristics.* Find out in advance as much about your audience's probable characteristics as you can. If of one sex, it can be either a "stag" or a "hen" audience. Will the audience be of both sexes? A mixed audience varies in emotional reactions; informational backgrounds; interests; attitudes toward money, religion, war, and security; and taboos.

One of the most interesting chain reactions observable in audiences is the response of a mixed audience to a remark that may be thought to be taboo. You can see the audience understand the allusion, then you can see the men in the audience control themselves until they have looked at their wives. If the wives laugh, the men laugh. If the women look shocked, the men will look shocked—also a little strangled. The chain is longer and funnier in most high schools. The students do not laugh until they have looked at their teachers, who will restrain their laughter until they can find the principal and note his reaction. If he laughs, the teachers laugh, and finally the students.

Such a chain reaction is not confined to mixed audiences and schools. Will Rogers noted it in another situation.

> Now Pershing was in Mexico at the time, and there was a lot in the papers for and against the invasions. I said "I see where they have captured Villa. Yes, they got him in the morning Editions and in the Afternoon ones let him get away." Now everybody in the house before they would laugh looked at the President, to see how he was going to take it. Well, he started laughing and they all followed suit.[2]

What is the age range of this audience? Are they all adults, all children, or a mixture of both? What a high-school audience may get without elaboration may have to be amplified for little children or adults. Children and adults are easier to move emotionally than adolescents. Each group separately is easier to convince or to inform than all of them together. Don't do as I did—prepare a speech for a cattle breeders' association on the assumption of an adult audience, only to find that the association membership ranges in age from an octogenarian to a nine-year-old youngster, a boy with his first young heifer.

What is the intellectual level of this audience? Are the listeners likely to be college graduates, high-school graduates, illiterates, or a mixture of all? Are they persons of manual dexterity, number dexterity, or word sense? Are they capable of thinking in abstractions or in practical terms? You will be lucky to discover any of these facts for most of your listeners, but such information can help you.

What are the vocational interests of this audience? Is your audience made up of white-collar workers or manual laborers? Are the white-collar workers of managerial, technical, or clerical level? Are the laborers skilled, unskilled, agricultural, or industrial? Over and beyond their jobs, have they avocational interests that tie them together; for example, are they all members of the company choral society or company bowling league?

What are the political beliefs of this audience? Know this before you quote from Karl Marx, Franklin D. Roosevelt, or Herbert Hoover! Does this audience believe in big government or big business, in states' rights or centralized government? Is it left, middle-of-the-road, or right?

What are the religious backgrounds of this audience? Will the group be of mixed backgrounds, as in most public meetings? Will it be of like backgrounds, as in most churches and sectarian schools? Will it be Christian, Jewish, or agnostic?

---

[2] Reprinted from *Enjoyment of Laughter* by permission of Simon and Schuster, Publishers. Copyright, 1936, by Max Eastman.

What will be the probable attitude of this audience? Will it be an audience that gathered for the express purpose of hearing you? Will it be some type of captive audience: school assembly, church meeting, employee meeting? Will the audience be friendly toward you and your subject, or is it apt to be hostile? Will the audience know you and your qualifications for speaking?

If you can ascertain the size, reason for being, location, and characteristics of your audience, you can apply that knowledge now to the preparation of your material.

You will take three steps in preparing your presentation for an audience. The first step will be the choice of a selection or selections to read aloud to your particular audience. The second step will be the arrangement of this material. And the third step will be the preparation of a suitable introduction.

CHOOSING YOUR MATERIAL

Choose your material with your audience in mind. But, while never forgetting it, never forget yourself either. You should read something you like and enjoy. As Charles Laughton said, "Pick a book that you know and enjoy. Since it will be more fun for you, it will be more fun for your listeners."[3]

The beginning reader usually complains that he knows nothing an audience would be interested in hearing. In refutation, let me suggest that you get from a library any volume of familiar essays and check the subject matter. Here is a group of subjects discussed informally with an audience—your problem. The subjects range through waking, lying in bed, getting breakfast, old china, safety pins, going on a journey, starting a fire, highway markers, reading a book, clothes, personal habits and study habits, holidays, unusual jobs, and the most-remarkable-man-I-ever-met. The essayist is a silent reader aloud.

Another frequent complaint of the beginning reader is that he doesn't know where to turn for suitable material. No one can know all that has been printed. One easy source of material is the practice material in this book. The bibliography appended to this book names other sources. A source I have found helpful is Bartlett's *Familiar Quotations.* Try using it this way. Let's assume that you have been asked to read some selection for a special occasion, say Thanksgiving. Look up that topic in Bartlett

[3] "How to Read Aloud at Home," *Time,* Vol. LIX, No. 13 (March 31, 1952).

and, from the list of quotations on the subject, make a list of sources. From this list you will find several selections that are likely to be appropriate.

Three criteria will help in your choice of material: appropriateness to the audience, appropriateness to the occasion, and appropriateness to you.

Choosing material that is appropriate to your audience makes use of all your knowledge of audiences generally, this specific audience, and previous audiences you have met. If you knew in advance just what would please an audience, you could make a fortune in radio, the movies, television, or any mass media. All you can do is take the information available on the age range, intelligence, interests, and characteristics of your audience and judge your selected material accordingly.

If the audience is interested solely in football, *Casey at the Bat* may be inappropriate, but *Casey* may be more appropriate than a selection from a minor lyric poet. Better yet, try reading to such an audience James Thurber's story of the football player in the economics class.[4]

Probably, the way you will go about finding an appropriate selection for that audience is something like this. You will determine why the audience has met. Let's say it is the annual-awards banquet for the members of the team. The members of the team, their families, the coaches, the athletic council, and interested friends will be present. A moment's thought will convince you that the Thurber selection is inappropriate. Appropriate as it may be to you, it does not show the football player in the most heroic light. Someone in the audience might be offended by an implied comparison. At best, it might be thought to be in dubious taste. So you are left with no selection to read. Now you check the reasons why you were invited to be part of the program. Why were you asked to appear at this banquet? Were you chosen because they needed some entertainment and someone had heard you on a previous occasion and thought you were entertaining? Did the program chairman say, as so many do, "I'd like to have you say a few words. Kinda entertain the boys before the awards are made. You know, nothing heavy. Just kinda be funny for a little while, while they're clearing the tables."

If that's your assignment, start digging. Go to the index of periodical material and start looking for articles on football. Ask the librarian for help. She can be looking through the volumes of collected material while you explore the magazines. You know that most magazines feature football stories and articles during the fall months of the year, so you can pretty well skip the spring and summer issues. You know that the *Saturday Evening Post* runs comments by coaches and short stories about football

[4] See p. 308 in the practice material.

By LIFE Photographer Michael Rougier. Courtesy of TIME Inc.

The statesman reads aloud.

from August on, so you lose no time in flipping through the back copies of that magazine. The librarian, in the meantime, is going through Ring Lardner's works, John Lardner's essays, Bill Stern's book, and others like them.

By this time you have a number of possible selections. You have one article by a famous coach on why football is valuable training for later citizenship. You have another, in a humorous vein, on why a certain coach sucks his thumb during the nerve-straining moments of the big game. Another article is on how much first-aid equipment a team uses in the course of the football season. Another is about great and decisive plays. Another is an entertaining account of weird mistakes and plays. You have a stack of biographical stories on football greats.

Now you start applying all the other information you have about the audience to these selections. You may decide to reject the article on the thumb-sucking coach since most of your audience will be more interested in anecdotes about players than in coaching problems. You may reject the first-aid article because it is not appropriate to this particular team—or because this team had so many injuries during the season that it would be cruel to remind it of the painful past. You will probably reject the article on football as a trainer for citizenship because it is inspirational and you have been asked to be entertaining. You finally settle on the account of football mistakes.

Let's take another example. Around Thanksgiving time last year, my second-grader came home from school and told us of a wonderful poem about fall her teacher had read to the class. Since the poem was about fall, it was appropriate to the occasion. The teacher who read it aloud had a rural background, so the selection was appropriate to her. But mine is a city child and the selection was remarkably inappropriate to her. In fact, the communication act broke down completely. "When the frost is on the pumpkin and the fodder's in the shock," became, in the version we heard at our house, "When the frost is on the pun'kin and my father's in the shop." Conclusion: an inappropriate selection for the audience.

We can dispose of "appropriateness to the occasion" quickly. You are not apt to read the Thanksgiving Day proclamation at Easter time. With a little thought about the occasion, the average reader can make an appropriate selection.

"Appropriateness to you" deserves more consideration. This will require an honest evaluation of yourself as a person and as a reader, and of your goal as a reader. You may have to tell yourself some bitter truths. Most clowns aspire to play *Hamlet* and all stagehands know they can act.

However, most readers are too modest, rather than too presumptuous.

They are unwilling to try to read something they like because they don't think they can. Our purpose is to help you learn how to read; your job is to have material you want to read. If you have found a selection that you understand and like, one that gives you a lift when you reread it, then that selection is likely to be an appropriate one for you.

If, in your self-scrutiny, you discover that you understand, like, and get a lift from Edgar Guest when you reread his poetry, you may disparage your reading ability. You may have heard that Guest is not considered a first-rate poet. You may find that a reading of so-called first-rate poets leaves you cold. Your concern about your level of appreciation is a wholesome sign. If you want to sharpen your literary appreciation, you can begin a study of literature. You can try to find reasons for the critical estimates of Guest. Such a study program is not within the province of this book, except in this one respect: start "reading up." Rudolf Flesch, in his book *The Art of Plain Talk,* lists the understanding level for various types of magazines and books. From that list find what your present level is and then try reading one level above yourself.

> Well, the course my brother gave me, via that blessed trinity Cunliffe, Pyre, and Young, was calculated to make me understand that literature, beyond helping one to discover oneself, has a higher, more impersonal function. It is a challenge issued by a higher mind, the author's, to a lower mind, the reader's. Even if the challenge is not met, much pleasure may still result. But if it is met, or if a sincere attempt to meet it is made, a finer, rarer pleasure is experienced. If you read for pure diversion, well and good, but if you read for any other purpose, always read above yourself. One of the reasons for the general mental fuzziness of most "cultivated" people we know is that publishers have become too shrewd. They have learned, the cunning little fellows, just how to temper their books to the lamb-like mental innocence of their readers. The result is that every week we are deluged with books which, the publishers assure us, we can understand. It is quite true. We can understand them, all too easily. It would be much better for us if now and then we read a book just a few rungs beyond our mental capacities in their most relaxed state.[5]

You can't begin the study of anything where some teacher thinks you ought to be; you have to start from where you are and go as far as you can in the time allotted. Remember, in your preparation of material to be read aloud, you are starting from where you are now. Read for an audience's pleasure those selections that, after several readings, continue

[5] Reprinted from *Reading I've Liked* by Clifton Fadiman, p. xxv. Copyright, 1941, by Simon and Schuster, Inc.

to give you pleasure and stimulation. Read aloud for an audience what you already enjoy. Read silently what you wish to learn to enjoy.

If you desire the widest possible audience acceptance, then you should choose material that already receives the widest possible acceptance. That is the technique of selection used by most movie, television, and radio producers. "Find out what the public wants and then give it to them." There is here no ethical or moral or pedagogical criteria. You strike for the lowest common denominator.

If your reading goal is to inform or to persuade, then you have a higher responsibility. Right here you bump into the problem of standards. Who has standards, who sets them, and for whom? Deems Taylor has an urbane discussion of the problems of standards in his book *The Well-tempered Listener*. He says, in part,

> . . . you can't legislate against bad taste. The minute you start regulating people's likes and dislikes in music or books or what not, you're confronted by the question of who is to decide what is good and what is bad. And you soon discover that there's no Emily Post of the arts.
>
> In the second place, I'm not so sure that Bach himself would fall on the floor in a fit if he heard a swing version of his Toccata in D minor. If there's one thing I'm pretty sure of, it is that the so-called classic masters were not aware that they were classic masters. As Gilbert Seldes once wrote, "The Japanese are not Oriental to themselves." . . .
>
> Don't misunderstand me. I'm not saying that it's a laudable thing to play swing versions of the classics or that anyone ought to try not to be revolted by hearing a piece of familiar and beautiful music distorted. But the distortion itself, while it may be a nuisance, is hardly a crime.
>
> Besides, if you're going to be completely consistent about this question of altering a composer's original work, where are you going to stop? After all, a so-called "swing" version of a piece of music is merely a debased form of a set of variations. And if it's wrong for a jazz band arranger to write his particular variations on a theme by Bach, why is it right for Brahms to write his particular variations on a theme by Haydn? Now there's a very obvious answer to that, of course, which is that Brahms variations are great music and the jazz band's variations are trash. But while you and I may believe that, we can't prove it. We can only say, in the last analysis, "That's what I think." Most people would agree that we were right in an extreme case such as I have chosen. But cases are not always extreme. . . .
>
> Do you know, I'm afraid I think it's a good thing that we do hear so much cheap humor and bad sentiment and bad music on the radio. Mind you, I think it would be an even better thing if we

heard nothing but good stuff on the radio—*if* everybody wanted to hear it. But as long as there are people who want to hear bad stuff, they should be allowed to listen to it if it isn't obscene or criminal. Because if they're *not* allowed, they won't listen to anything else. . . . It's one thing to offer a listener something, and it's another thing to get him to listen. So long as his receiving set is working, no matter how low his tastes are, you always have the chance of luring him into hearing and learning to like something better than what he thought he liked; in other words, of elevating his taste. But you can't elevate a man's taste through a dead radio.[6]

Elevating the listener's taste is the work of the minister, the teacher, and the parent. It may be the interest of all other oral readers, but they should not make it a crusade if they wish to keep their audience's attention and interest. Just as you must remember that you start from where you are in this matter of learning, so the members of an audience can only start from where they are. You can't begin by reading Henry James aloud to a man reared on comic books, but, if you want to elevate his taste, you might start with *Treasure Island*.

My concern in elevating taste is not primarily with the audience. It is with you. If you can become a better oral reader, you will do something for the taste level of your audience. They will expect the next reader to be equally expert, and you have begun a progression of professional competence, which in itself is an alteration of taste. There are two attacks on this problem of standards: you can complain because of the low standards to which everyone else is subjected; you can try to do something about it by elevating your own.

This brings us back to our original point. What standard have we for selecting written material? If the selection is appropriate to you, your audience, and the occasion, if the selection is consonant with your personal aim as a reader—if your selection meets these tests and you still can't choose among two or three items, the final choice must be made on a basis of taste. And your taste may be as good for you as another's is for him. As Taylor said, ". . . there's no Emily Post of the arts."

ARRANGING YOUR MATERIAL

The material you have chosen to read aloud will need to be arranged for each particular reading situation. You must bring the selection within

---

[6] Deems Taylor, New York Philharmonic Symphony Orchestra intermission talk, later published in *The Well-tempered Listener* (New York: Simon & Schuster, 1940). Reprinted by permission of the author.

time limits; you must build an organizational pattern if you are reading more than one selection; you may have to edit the content of your selection.

The first axiom in arrangement is this: shape the selection as if it were your own. Another person's material is not sacrosanct; do with it what he would do if he were appearing before your audience.

You will be given a time limit for your reading. Whatever it is, adhere to is scrupulously. There is no greater sin than taking more time than is allotted you. And if you wish to remain friendly with the chairman, don't run short. The selection you have chosen will seldom be timed, in its original length, exactly to the needs of the program chairman. If it is long, cut. It is always better to cut in large segments than to prune a bit here and a bit there. Always remember, however, to keep the organizational pattern of your material clear. Do not leave just an introduction and a conclusion and omit the body. Do not have an introduction and body and no conclusion. Do no injury to the intent of your selection by your cutting. Don't, in other words, lift a selection out of essential context. Keep your audience constantly in mind as you cut. Leave in the material that you think will most please them, omit the material that will interest them least.

The best advice for cutting for time is this: choose a selection that very nearly fits into the time limits. The adjustments you make then will be minor. Don't choose a novel for a ten-minute selection and try to cut to time.

If the time you have been given is long enough for more than one selection, or if you think several selections will be more interesting than just one, choose selections that fit together and arrange them so that your program has a beginning, middle, and end. Order the selections to make the best use of contrast, variety, and interest. Prepare original material to bridge the selections. Organize your program so that your first selection catches attention and your last selection is conclusive. And build this organizational structure with your specific audience in mind. It is conceivable that you might read three separate selections in three different orders for three distinct audiences. For a Rotary Club luncheon on Lincoln's birthday you might have chosen three short selections: Lincoln's letter to Mrs. Bixby consoling her for the loss of her son, his Gettysburg Address, and the conclusion to his Second Inaugural Address. You might organize the program by beginning with the Second Inaugural Address, using the letter as the second selection for a simple contrast to the rolling oratory of the first selection and keeping the familiar Gettysburg Address for the conclusion. Now assume that in the evening of that day you are reading the same program to a group of Gold Star mothers. You might arrange the program so that you begin with the Gettysburg Address, continue with the Second Inaugural Address, and conclude with the letter, which, for such an audience, would have a greater emotional impact. The transitional material you prepare for each occasion should clarify the organizational pattern.

In arranging any selection for a specific audience, you may have to edit. An author writes for a particular audience, in a certain language, for a particular occasion. Audiences change, language changes, occasions differ. How absurd to read for an audience a part of a selection that no longer makes sense because of language shifts, or that no longer is appropriate because the occasion is different, just because we feel the author's words to be inviolate.

The author was seeking the complete comprehension of his audience; so are you. He chose his language and illustrations for a specific audience; you should do the same for your audience. If Shakespeare's bawdiness pleased his audience and offends yours, whom you want to please, then cut the bawdiness. If the table of "begats" in Genesis interested the tribes of Israel as a genealogical history but bores your Christian congregation, then cut the "begats." If the financial report of debenture bonds interests your board of directors and confuses your employees, then cut the debenture report for the employees.

If the Scriptures use words your listeners do not understand, change the words so the meaning is clear. If the terminology of the scientist obscures his meaning, then find simpler terms. Your task as a reader is to be comprehended; anything that detracts from comprehension should be avoided.

You may edit your manuscript for four reasons: (1) to meet the structural requirements of your presentation; (2) to meet the time limitations of your audience or occasion; (3) to contribute to comprehension; (4) for good taste

PREPARING A SUITABLE INTRODUCTION

You will write, or at least prepare, an introduction for your presentation. This is extremely important since your introduction will be your means of catching your audience's attention.

Here are a few suggestions that may be helpful.
1. Speak to your listeners. Use the word *you,* rather than the word *I.*
2. Be fresh and interesting in your selection of words, phrases, and

anecdotes. Avoid the categorical listing of all the persons on the platform. Avoid such bromides as "Unaccustomed as I am," "This reminds me," "As I look out."

3. Be funny if you want to and can be.

> . . . Their chief used to introduce me to the audience; but these introductions were so grossly flattering that they made me ashamed, and so I began my talk at a heavy disadvantage. It was a stupid custom. There was no occasion for the introduction; the introducer was almost always an ass, and his prepared speech a jumble of vulgar compliments and dreary effort to be funny; therefore after the first season I always introduced myself—using, of course, a burlesque of the time-worn introduction. This change was not popular with the committee chairmen. To stand up grandly before a great audience of his townsmen and make his little devilish speech was the joy of his life, and to have that joy taken from him was almost more than he could bear.[7]

4. If you are reading another's work, include in your introduction all the information the audience needs, such as the name of the author, the title of the selection, the date of composition, the occasion of composition, the reason for its present use.

5. If you are ad-libbing your introduction and reading your presentation, keep the speaking and reading styles harmonious. Don't be colloquial in one and formal in the other. Don't present one in front of the speaker's stand and the other behind it. Don't do one without your reading glasses and the other with them. Keep the presentation all of a piece.

6. Use all the vocal tricks for attention you can master. Speak loudly enough to be heard easily; err on the side of being too loud rather than too quiet. An actor on the road in a strange theater tests out his voice for distance in his opening lines; after he has the range of the back wall, he moderates his volume.

7. Remember, if you fail to get the audience's attention, you cannot hope for their interest, understanding, or belief.

▶ *Conclusion.* In preparing to read an author's selection for entertainment or edification, you will take three steps. You will analyze your audience. You will choose a selection suitable in length and appropriate to the audience, the occasion, and you. You will write your introduction to the author's selection in a style consonant with your whole presentation.

[7] Samuel L. Clemens, *Mark Twain's Autobiography* (New York: Harper & Brothers, 1924), I, 160. Copyright, 1924, by Clara Gabrilowitsch. Copyright, 1952, by Clara Clemens Samossoud.

· 4 ·

Preparing to Face Your Audience

A speaker friend of mine received the accolade after a presentation on "Private Enterprise." The chairman of the meeting grabbed him by the shoulders and said, "You convinced me. You either care a heckuva lot about private enterprise or you practiced a long time."

The truth is the speaker both cared and practiced.

You must practice, too, if you want complete comprehension from your audience. Practice does not mean just reading your manuscript over. It means preparing your presentation in every way so that you will leave nothing to chance. It means using visual aids, if they will help gain comprehension. It means preparing the manuscript so that it can be read easily. It means rehearsing the manuscript and dress rehearsing the presentation under performance conditions. It really means thorough preparation.

Although Simeon Ford's speeches had an air of spontaneity they were the result of a lot of hard work. Each speech represented weeks of preparation—writing, rewriting, and memorizing. For, after all, the best spontaneous speeches are carefully prepared. In the parlance of the theatre it's "rehearse your adlibs carefully before you pull 'em."

Simeon Ford gave a humorous inkling of the work involved in

preparing a funny speech when in one of his talks he said: "The idea generally obtains that all an after-dinner speaker has to do is to assume a dress suit and an engaging smile, rise up when called upon, and captivate his audience with wit and eloquence, born of the moment and inspired by the surroundings. This is largely the fault of the speakers themselves, who spend most of their allotted time jollying the listeners into the idea that the call is unexpected and the speech spontaneous.

"This is not only untrue, but robs the orator of the credit which is his due. How much more honest it would be if he would only admit that for two long sickening weeks his speech had been rankling in his vitals; that for two long weeks his innocent wife and children had been made wretched by having to listen to rehearsals thereof; that he had aroused suspicions as to his sanity by muttering in public places, and had been shadowed by the police as he patrolled lonely streets at night addressing imaginary after-dinner audiences."

To Simeon Ford, being funny was fun only to the audience.[1]

SCRIPT PREPARATION

Preparing a script may seem like busywork to the beginning reader. Why not read directly from the book containing the selection? There are several good and—to my mind—sufficient answers to that question. (1) Book type is usually too small and cramped for a reader to follow easily. (2) Book margins seldom are large enough for a reader's markings. (3) Book pagination is not set up with an oral reader's convenience in mind. I recommend that every reader use a specially prepared manuscript of his own—one that he can treat in any way he likes.

Preparing the typescript for your presentation takes some doing. It is not just a matter of making a clean copy of your selection. The typescript should be so prepared that you spend a minimum of time looking at it and a maximum of time in contact with your listeners.

Your copy of the script should be an original. It should be on good paper that does not rustle, wrinkle, or fold over when held up. The color of the typewriter ribbon should be determined by a check of the lighting where you will speak. (This is more important than most readers realize. Some readers can read blue type on white paper better than black type on white paper. Some radio stations where fluorescent lighting is used prefer purple type on a green paper because of the color characteristic of the

[1] Ed ("Senator") Ford, "Being Funny Isn't Much Fun," *New York Times Magazine* (June 25, 1944).

lighting.) The typewriter type size should be one you are familiar with. Pica type is the largest and easiest to read. The script should not be typed in all capital letters, unless you are accustomed to reading all caps; radio newsmen read copy that is little else and are confused by lower case.

Have carbons made and have them available. They may be wanted by reporters or persons in the audience. They may not be, but it is always better to be prepared.

The typing should be so arranged that each idea is complete on the page. Sentences and paragraphs should not spill over to the next page, unless there is a special reason for it, such as getting the page turned before both hands become busy with a demonstration.

The typing should be so arranged that business and action cues are clearly differentiated from the copy you read aloud. Such cues should be typed in a different color, or underlined, or bracketed. An example of a typescript is appended to this chapter.

The typescript should be arranged for your convenience and ease of reading. If you want only one phrase to a line, or if you want the lines triple-spaced, or if you want unorthodox punctuation, have it typed that way.

After a typescript is prepared and you begin practicing with it, start marking it.

> The definite indication of an amateur actor, to a director, is to see a script page which, after hours of rehearsal, is as free of notations as a blank check. Every possible marking should be used as a sign-post to a good performance. . . . A good memory is the leaning-post of the stage actor; a good pencil is the bulwark of the radio performer against the uncertainties of inspiration at the time of actual broadcast.[2]

Use any marking system that makes sense for you. Use the single virgule / for short pauses, the double // for longer. Use underlining, quotation marks, circling, carets in the margin—anything you like—if it helps you. If you want to emphasize *you* in a sentence and you sometimes run over the word in practice, you can have it typed in caps, or underlined on the typewriter, or you can underline it with a marking pencil, or set it off by quotes, or virgules, or use a combination of all these ways. Stressing *you* in that sentence is the important consideration, not the appearance of your manuscript.

You may want to substitute parentheses for commas to set off ideas. You may want to underline quotes. You may want to hyphenate run-on

[2] Arch Oboler, *This Freedom: Thirteen New Radio Plays* (New York: Random House, Inc., 1942), pp. xv–xvi.

words. You may want to put dashes in for breath marks. You may do any of these things you wish, if you bear in mind (1) that the audience is concerned solely with what is heard, (2) that you must understand what your own marks mean, (3) that the audience must comprehend the full statement.

Here, by way of illustration, is a marked script of Westbrook Van Voorhis, announcer for "The March of Time on the Air." It was used in an advertising campaign by *Time* magazine. The following letter was sent out by *Time* with the script, to explain its markings.

All of us have to make speeches sometime.

And so I thought you would like to see some speaking tricks that may come in handy the next time you have to give a talk or read a report to some group of your associates.

Attached is an actual example of how our famed "Time Marches On" announcer marks up a script before he steps up to the microphone.

Van Voorhis does this $\sim$ under a word to remind himself that although he might be tempted to inflect it with unusual emphasis he should give it only its natural weight in the sentence.

When he does this ____ under a word it means hit the word hard. This ____ means not quite so hard, but do not slur....

This / means a partial stop; this // means a complete stop; this /// means the end of the story.

The double underline means "slow down first and then give this word all you've <u>got</u>," and when Van puts quotes around a word it means he's probably had trouble with it in rehearsals, that it's an unusual word and he has to give it specially careful "orthoepic" handling.

VAN....

Endeavoring to keep up with <u>world</u> <u>affairs</u> is <u>never</u> an <u>easy</u> <u>job</u>./ Today, when there are so <u>many</u> tremendous events in the making, it is more <u>difficult</u> than <u>ever</u> <u>before</u>.// That is why Americans <u>now</u> have <u>greater</u> <u>need</u> than <u>ever</u>/ for <u>frank</u> and <u>forthright</u> reporting of the <u>news</u>/ - <u>realistic</u> <u>facts</u>.// As <u>many</u> an American believes today-//

MAN...

In those communiques we get from the front....they boil the news down to where you can hardly see it. And when you start reading those crystal gazers... why you just get more confused than ever.

```
                    VAN...
(quick cue)
Yes, as a result of cryptic communiques and hopeful
crystal gazers, there is a special need today for
TIME's kind of reporting.// Time Magazine's frank
and forthright reporting is relentless in its
presentation of the facts./ Pleasant or unpleasant,
the facts are reported to Time's readers in Time's
own analytical style, which helps them understand
what is happening/ and why.// Because of that,
realistic Americans in all parts of the nation....
(from the largest cities to the remotest crossroads)
....have come to rely on Time.// In Time/ they
know they can get the facts they need to make their
own plans./.. the facts they need to take part in
the public discussions through which the nation's
plans are made.// To provide those facts through
frank, forthright and realistic reporting/ is the
all-important wartime function of Time Magazine.///[3]
```

VISUAL AIDS

This section does not apply directly to the problems of the reader who is reading material other than his own. I say this with some hesitation, since I think the failure to use visual aids is one of the great mistakes of the beginning reader. However, if visual aids will not help you in presenting your current selection, you may skip the next pages.

When you were collecting the data for your presentation, you may have decided you needed visual aids to win complete comprehension from your listener. If you did, these aids will have to be prepared with the same care as your typescript.

A parent reading a book knows the child gets more from the reading if he can look at the pictures. Most parents point out the details in the pictures as they read along. To explain some ideas to a child, you need to demonstrate familiar objects or draw pictures or go on field trips. A book about airplanes may lead to trips to the airport and to the construction of models. That is good teaching and it certainly is winning comprehension from the listener.

If you are a teacher, you may use the blackboard, or a map, or a chart to clarify a statement. You are using visual aids. If you are a

---

[3] Reprinted by courtesy of Time, Incorporated.

clergyman and you use church fixtures for purposes of example, you are using visual aids. If you are a politician and you have the platform decorated with posters and flags, you are using visual aids. If you are a businessman or teacher and you use films and slides and Vu-Graphs and displays, you are using visual aids.

All of us use them at one time or another. They are valuable adjuncts to speech because they use sight as a medium for getting attention and holding interest, and sight impressions are received more quickly and retained more accurately than sound impressions. Of course, you should remember that every movement you make is a visual aid. Your posture, walk, gestures, and facial expression are visual aids that contribute to the effectiveness of your presentation.

Since visual aids must be built into the structure of your presentation and should be rehearsed with your manuscript, let's see how they can help your speech.

There are a number of visual devices now in general use by speakers and readers. There are films, filmstrips, slides, balopticans, and visual casts. There are handouts, charts, displays, mock-ups, flannel boards, and blackboards. Each has its advantages and disadvantages.

Films have many disadvantages. They must be shown in a darkened room, and the reader is merely a voice from the darkness. Too often he is in the dark himself, serving only the function of a sound track. The film focuses interest and places emphasis on the picture and not on the reader. Films are expensive and, in many cases, they must be made especially for your specific need. They require expensive projection equipment and, even with good equipment, they cannot be used in every auditorium. The high cost puts them beyond the reach of the average reader.

But no one can deny that films are an excellent device for holding attention and for teaching complicated skills. Almost all schools today use films as part of the audio-visual training. Sunday schools are beginning to use them. Industrial-relations men use them liberally in job training and in safety programs. The filmstrip has all the disadvantages of the motion picture, except that it is less costly. It also has like advantages.

If you are going to use a film, prepare your presentation with the film or filmstrip in mind. Will it precede your comments, follow them, or interrupt them? If the film precedes you, be sure your talk is related to it. If the film follows you, make its showing the climax of your remarks and give it a build-up. If the film interrupts you, be sure your remarks make the film an integrated part of the organization of your presentation. However you use it, tie it in with what you say so that the whole presentation has form and unity.

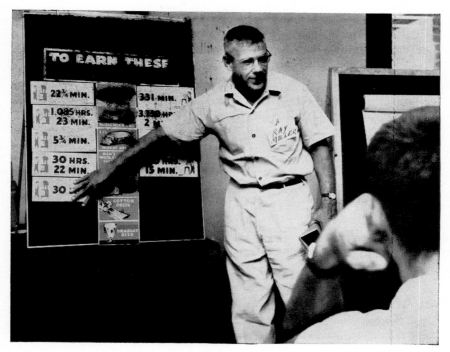

Courtesy Stanolind Oil and Gas Company.

Reading aloud from a visual aid.

In fact, whatever the type of presentation, build your part of the program into the program as a whole. When you are getting information about the audience, find out about the entire program. Will you be the only speaker? Will there be a meeting, or ritual, or program before you? What sort of introduction will you receive? What follows you? Will the audience want to ask questions? How long is the whole program or presentation?

Remember that when your presentation appears as part of a program, the whole program has an identity of which your communication is a part. Like your own speech, the program has a beginning, one or more high points leading to a climax, and an end. If you are to be the first speaker, you may conceive of your function as that of introducing the presentation as a whole. The second speaker may present the body of the whole program, and the third speaker, the conclusion. If you appear in some other part of the presentation, your function may shift accordingly. You know by now that, in any case, your presentation will be structurally complete and self-contained.

If you have any control over the program, you may want to have a break before you speak. You may want to defer all questions to the end of the meeting or have questions following each speaker. Whatever you do, do it as the result of your consideration of the total meeting.

The slide and baloptican projectors are common visual aids. They, too, must be operated in a darkened room. Also, they require an operator whose efforts must be coordinated with the reader's words. Another disadvantage is that they have become associated in the listeners' minds with "some fine pictures I took on my vacation," or with biology classes in junior high school. An advantage is the relatively low cost of the equipment and of preparing the illustrative material.

The Visualcast, Visualizer, Vu-Graph, and Keystone Overhead Projector will project words, diagrams, graphs, and all such material on a screen in back of the speaker, in a lighted room. The advantage is obvious: the listener can see the reader at the same time as he sees the illustrative material. Again, there is the problem of expense, but these devices are less costly than motion-picture equipment.

Handouts are the most frequently used visual aids. Special consideration should be given their use. As soon as printed matter is distributed, the audience ceases to listen and begins to read. Distribute supplementary material after you have concluded your presentation. But remember to mention that you are going to distribute it and explain why.

Amplifying materials must sometimes be distributed during a break in your presentation, so that everyone can follow the ensuing portion of the speech. Avoid this if you can; but if you can't, read the material aloud along with the group so that their attention stays with you and is not absorbed by the printed page.

Charts are one of the most common types of visual aids and, when figures are to be presented, they are invaluable. Carefully prepared, they can convey a world of information that would be just dull statistics if read aloud. Charts are usually displayed on easels and, when he uses a chart, the reader should be sure that it can be seen by the audience, that it is well lighted, and it is used throughout the talk. While using a chart, the reader should be careful to read from the chart itself, so that the terminology heard is the same as that which the audience sees. He should cover the chart when he is through with it, so that the audience does not continue to read it after he has passed on to another point. Charts, like slides, are relatively inexpensive.

Displays are used in teaching, sales meetings, and training programs of all types. The first requirement is that they be big enough to be seen by everyone in the audience. If they are not big enough, mock-ups should be used. If they are big enough, some stage management is necessary. They should be kept out of sight until they are needed. This requires curtains, or stage assistants, or both. If many displays are to be used, careful organization is required. Have you ever seen a style show where the reader was talking about "something interesting for the man about the house," meaning a woman's housecoat or workdress, and a model strolled on out of turn in black scanties?

Use mock-ups if the display is too small for everyone to see and appreciate. If you are showing a new line of fountain pens to an audience of a hundred, use a mock-up the size of a baseball bat. If you are demonstrating a lubricating oil's action on ball bearings, use bowling balls if the audience is very big, use baseballs if it is small. Again, you are confronted with the problem of what to do with the mock-ups when they are not needed. You have the additional problem of having only two hands. How to lubricate two bowling balls presents a nice problem. But don't do what an oil company I worked for did. Don't have a scantily clad pin-up girl apply the lubrication. No one to this day knows what kind of oil she used.

Flannel boards are a recently popular device that are really as old as Sunday school. They too are easels, but they are made of flannel. Topic sentences, main points, and illustrative material are lettered on cardboard backed with flannel. Then, as the reader makes each point in his presentation, he slaps the appropriate cardboard on the flannel-board easel and it sticks there. This technique has several advantages: (1) there is no fuss getting the exhibit to stay up—no Scotch tape, no thumb tacks; (2) the reader need never look away from his audience while placing the exhibit; (3) the exhibits can be removed easily to make way for other exhibits; (4) since the exhibits are used to point up the oral statement, they can be put in place in a manner that also accentuates the idea; in fact, one manufacturer calls them "slap boards."

The reader needs extensive rehearsal with a flannel board before he can use it effectively. The initial expense is slight, but preparing the cardboard exhibits takes time. Flannel boards can be as visually stimulating as any advertising layout. The ease with which changes can be rung on them contrasts with the static quality of prepared charts.

The blackboard is one of the oldest of the visual aids and still one of the best because the cost is negligible. The reader does not have to make extensive preparations to use it, but the reader does have to learn how to use it

Use of the blackboard should be planned in advance. Know when and how you are going to use it. Coordinate the work at the blackboard with the material of your speech. Since you will be writing on the blackboard while you are talking, remember to keep your head and shoulders out of the way so that the audience can see what has been written. Don't talk to the blackboard, but don't stop talking while you write. Write just a little at a time so that you can maintain contact with your audience. When you have finished writing for a time, turn around and use the other hand to point with. That is, if you wrote with your right hand, use your left hand for pointing at statements. Plan your material as if it were a layout; use different colored chalks for interest and emphasis. Some diagrams and drawings will have to be put up before your presentation begins. Try to have them covered until they are needed.

Erase material when you have finished with it so that the audience doesn't continue to look at it after it has served your purpose. Any writing, printing, or drawing you do should be neat, legible, and large enough to be seen.

Remember that the purpose of visual aids is to interest and convince your listener. They are valuable only when they help you communicate. They are worse than useless if they distract. When you have visual aids, make them structurally important in your talk and then practice with them so they will serve your purpose.

PRACTICING THE PRESENTATION

How do you practice? "Often and vigorously" is the simple answer. "With an objective" is a better answer. You should have a goal for each practice session. That goal should be attainable in the time allotted to the practice session. For example, after you finish preparing the typescript, your first practice session should be devoted to one thing—proofreading the script. Don't try to mark the script or to practice voice work, or movement, or reading aloud, or all four together at this time. Do just one thing, but do it thoroughly.

When you have proofread the script and are satisfied with it, you are ready for your second practice session. The goal of this session should be reading for intelligibility. This time you read aloud and you read the script to make sense of it. You check yourself and your script for clearness of ideas.

At some later practice session, your goal will be projection. At another, your goal will be mastering the visual aids. At another, your goal will be timing your presentation. At another your goal may be to record your talk on tape. Whatever the particular goal may be, you should have one, and only one, goal for each practice session.

When you practice, do nothing else. Don't practice where you can be interrupted. Don't try to practice while you have other chores pending. Allocate a few free moments to practice and then use them.

Approach each practice session with the proper attitude. "Today I am going to improve over yesterday," is a helpful attitude once your practice sessions are devoted to the whole presentation. If you don't try to do better at each session, you will find you are just spinning your wheels—using a lot of effort, but getting nowhere. Try to be rested when you practice. This can be a matter of attitude. You don't have to be completely rested physically to be mentally alert. Practicing a speech is different enough from your daily routine to be refreshing. Most of us don't need rest as much as we need diversion. Think of your practice session as a "turning-aside" and you'll get more from it.

Remember, you learn what you learn. If you practice your speech lying down, that may be the only position from which you can present it effectively. If you twirl your key chain while you practice, you will want to twirl it in performance.

If you must stop during practice sessions, stop, each time, at a different place in the script. When you resume practice, start a paragraph or two before your stopping point. Better yet, summarize in a few sentences what went before, then begin. The reason for this suggestion is implied in the previous paragraph; we learn what we learn. Good musicians can tell you where the singer turned each page of music while learning a song. Directors can tell where actors have had trouble learning lines. They can hear the frequent stops and false starts in the learning process.

Since you learn what you learn, you frequently learn incorrectly. That is why you should not try to study your presentation at the first practice session. If you begin practice as soon as you have a typescript, you may practice phrases that won't be part of your final presentation, you may practice pronunciations that are incorrect, you may learn ideas that should not be there. After you have your typescript in proper form, then begin practicing and, after you begin practicing, make few changes, because it is very difficult to unlearn something you have already learned.

If you are going to memorize your presentation, don't do it by rote, do it by ideas. Let the memorization grow out of your knowledge of what you are saying. Strive to get the ideas right first, even if the words are all wrong. The words will come later. And don't start each memorization session with the beginning of the speech. If you do, you may be glib on the first part and faltering on the last. Give every part of the speech equal attention at some time in your practice. But practice and practice until you have it thoroughly learned.

> . . . As time went on he increased his repertoire and learnt all the scenes by heart, so that he was independent of the book. He rehearsed himself continually, and after one trial reading to a few friends, including Browning, Fechter, Collins and Forster, he said: "There! If I have gone through that already to myself once, I have gone through it *two-hundred times!*" He strove for perfection; corrected his utterance of certain words by repeating them constantly to himself; went through each scene in his study again and again with as much pains as he gave to the public rendering; and was not satisfied until he had made himself master of every episode and had exhausted every means of reproducing the humour and pathos and oddity of his characters.[4]

After you are familiar with the manuscript—when you think you know what to do, and when and how to say what is written—start practice with a speaker's desk and your visual aids. Don't be upset if you forget everything you thought you'd learned up to this time. Learning is a long, involved, and painful process, and we are likely to forget one thing while trying to master another. As soon as you have mastered coordination with the visual aids, your previous mastery of the spoken words will return.

"In speakin' from manuscript allus toss th' pages aside when read so th' audience kin git some idee o' how much longer it'll have t'be bored." Kin Hubbard's advice is pertinent at this point in rehearsal. What do you do with the pages you have read? If you are using a free manuscript, one not in a notebook or binder, slide the page you are reading to the left, face up. By this method you can see the material on that page and the material on the page to follow, and you can make an effortless transition from one to the other. Don't turn pages if you can avoid it. Don't slide the one you have finished under the rest of the manuscript. Don't toss them on the floor. If you are using a bound manuscript and you want to get away as much as possible from turning pages, you can place page one on the left side of the binder and page two on the right, staple page three to the back of page two, and so on through. That will cut down half the page turning.

Hubbard is right in one respect about the reaction of an audience to a manuscript; a bulky manuscript disheartens an audience. If you can have your manuscript on the speaker's stand before the audience arrives,

---

[4] Hesketh Pearson, *Dickens: His Character, Comedy, and Career* (New York: Harper & Brothers, 1949), p. 272.

it is a good plan to do so. If you can't, have it in a folder or binder. Don't pull a wad of folded papers out of an inner pocket as you walk to the speaker's stand. That gesture, followed by putting on your reading glasses, is guaranteed to discourage the most interested audience.

About this time in your practice sessions, you may feel the need for constructive criticism. A teacher can give it to you, or, if a teacher is unavailable, you may get help from a friend whom you ask to listen. Accept what he has to say when he comments that you weren't talking to him, or that you didn't look at him often enough, or that he couldn't hear, or couldn't understand. But look out when he says you are too slow, or too fast, or not forceful enough, unless he is a qualified critic. His technical comments may be valid and then again they may not be.

George Bernard Shaw is talking about theater rehearsal here, but his comments can also warn the reader about his lay critics.

> Only geniuses can tell you exactly what is wrong with a scene, though plenty of people can tell you that there is something wrong with it. So make a note of their dissatisfaction; but be very careful how you adopt their cure if they prescribe one. For instance, if they say a scene is too slow (meaning that it bores them), the remedy in nine cases out of ten is for the actors to go slower and bring out the meaning better by contrasts of tone and speed.[5]

After one or two "dress rehearsals" of your whole presentation—on your feet, in action, with someone listening—you should be ready. But don't perform until you have had a chance to check all the last-minute details.

LAST-MINUTE PREPARATION

If it is at all possible, before the audience arrives go to the room where you will perform and check it. Test its acoustics: find out if you can be heard at the back of the room, or under the balcony; find out just how much projection you will need in order to be heard. Charles Dickens "made a point of testing the acoustics of every hall before reading in it, and correcting echoes by means of carpets and curtains."[6]

Check the lighting in the hall with equal thoroughness. Will you be able to see your manuscript easily? Will the audience be able to see you? Will there be a glare or distraction? If you are using electrical visual aids,

[5] George Bernard Shaw, *The Art of Rehearsal* (New York: Samuel French, Inc., 1928), p. 10.
[6] Pearson, *op. cit.,* p. 274.

check the wiring for them. Is there a connection for your projector and is there an extension cord? Do you know where the fuse box is located and are there spare fuses?

> He took his own staff and equipment wherever he went, but he always superintended the fitting of the screen and the erection of the gas battens, and he personally supervised the copper gas tubes to make sure that they were safe. The sides of the stage or platform on which he read were curtained off. At his back was a screen of maroon-coloured cloth. In front of him was a table covered with velvet of a lighter shade than the screen. On the table was a reading desk, and to the left and right of the table were projecting ledges, one for a water bottle and glass, the other for his gloves and pocket handkerchief. About twelve feet above the platform, in advance of the table, was a row of gas jets with a tin reflector; sidelights and footlights, also with reflectors, made his face and figure absolutely distinct to the audience, the light being equally strong from every angle.[7]

Check your probable position on the speaker's platform. Be sure that there is a speaker's stand and that it is the right height and size and strong enough for your needs. Find out where you will sit and practice getting from there to the speaker's stand. Some program committees apparently like the speaker to thread a maze before he reaches his position. Decide how you will steer your course among the chairs, palms, baskets of flowers, and laps of dignitaries who will share the stage with you.

If you are going to use visual aids, superintend their placement. Be sure the screen is hung where it can be best seen by everyone. Place the projector in proper relationship to the screen and try to get it out of the way of the audience. Place the speaker's stand where it can command maximum interest when the film is not in use, but where it is out of the way and where no light will spill when the film is being shown. Place the easels for charts or flannel boards. Prepare your blackboard exhibits. See that all arrangements are the best that can be made. Then mark the locations of the paraphernalia on the floor with crayon or masking tape. This is a safeguard in the event that your equipment should be moved before you appear. Be sure the marks can't be scuffed off.

All this exactness may seem superfluous, but notice a good speaker in action and you will see that he leaves no detail to the last minute or to chance. Part of his proficiency and most of his calm are the result of his careful preparation.

Just before performance, when you are off stage getting ready to

[7] *Ibid.*, p. 275.

go on, check these last details. Do you have your manuscript? Is it in the right order, page two following page one and so on? (Don't laugh at this; at some time in his career every performer has been caught with pages out of order.) If there is a staple in the corner of the manuscript, take it out. Is your equipment still where you planned to have it? If you are using the blackboard, do you have a spare piece of chalk? (One in the pocket is safest.) Do you have a handkerchief? Is your fly zipped?

Okay? Go on! They're waiting for you!

ON STAGE

Getting from the wings to your seat on the stage may seem like walking "the last mile." Those people out there may appear to be two-headed monsters, or they may appear all eyes and no other features, but they are human beings who can be interested in your script and you. There may be times when you will agree with Mark Twain, "All that I care to know is that a man is a human-being—that is enough for me; he can't be any worse."

While you are sitting on the platform waiting to be introduced, look at that audience and re-examine your presentation in terms of the particular audience you are now facing.

If the hall is big and the audience is smaller than you expected, you may need to be more informal than you had originally planned. If the hall is big and the audience scattered, you will need to be more forceful and vital. If the hall is small and the audience big, you may need to curtail your remarks because of the listener's discomfort. If the hall is big and the acoustics bad, you may need to use the public-address system or an orotund type of delivery. If the hall is big and the sight lines bad, you may need to omit all visual aids. If the hall is not a hall at all, but a vestibule with people wandering in and out, you may need to repeat your main ideas, cut amplifying details, and reorganize your whole presentation. These decisions are made while you look out at the audience before you begin to speak.

That's your name the chairman is announcing. Listen carefully to him now. Just because he has mentioned your name, it does not follow that you are to speak immediately. Too many chairmen don't know how to make introductions, so be sure he has finished his remarks before you stand up. When he has finished, you should move directly from your seat to the speaker's stand, going in front of the chairman. He is supposed to relinquish the rostrum to you. Watch out, though; the chairman may not know this and the two of you can look as if he has just said, "Shall we dance?"

If, at this point, you are nervous, that's all right. Stage fright is just the recognition of responsibility in the midst of strange surroundings. (For a further discussion of stage fright see Chapter 8.) Begin your speech only when you are in position before the speaker's stand and have acknowledged the audience's applause by a smile.

Now, communicate.

Keep your attention on the audience throughout your presentation. Watch the audience to be sure they comprehend. On another level of consciousness, keep a record of your audience's reaction, if you can possibly do it. Such awareness can be a part of your learning process. From it you can discover what ideas the audience grasped readily, what concepts were funny, what concepts failed to be funny, what unforeseen reactions you received, what distractions marred your effect. Of course, "nobuddy kicks on be'in interrupted if it's by applause."[8]

IT IS ALL OVER

After the program is over and other listeners compliment you on your presentation, remember these don'ts.

1. Don't be shy. One of the pleasures a listener takes is speaking to the performer after the meeting; don't deprive him of that pleasure.

2. Don't apologize for the job you did. Don't say, "I could have done better"; don't say, "You are very kind, but"; don't belittle your own efforts.

3. Don't disclaim credit for the presentation. If you didn't write it, but it is assumed you did, don't disillusion the listener; the ghost writer is a little-understood medium of communication whose spirit can't be crushed. If you didn't write it all, don't try to acknowledge all the people who gave you help. No quarterback after a touchdown names all the players who blocked for him.

4. Don't accept their congratulations as if they were your due. Turn a compliment back if you can. If they say you were fine, say that they were an inspiring audience or that it was a pleasure to talk to them.

And when it is all over, don't be misled by the comments. Did you really make a good presentation? Evaluate yourself and your presentation.

[8] Kin Hubbard, *Abe Martin* (Indianapolis: Bobbs-Merrill Company, Inc., 1926), p. 126.

Only from an honest appraisal of the event can you learn your strengths and weaknesses; only from a scrupulous evaluation can you build a better presentation for the next time.

EXERCISE

(The following speech by R. D. Karns is an example of a typed script that shows the use of visual aids. The speaker stood at a reading desk between two visual-aid props: an easel display on his right, and a slap board on his left. The easel had a cover and a prearranged set of pages attached at the top. When the speaker came to the cue word flip *in his manuscript, he turned over one of the pages, revealing the next picture page. When he finished with the easel chart he covered both chart and pages by flipping back the turned pages until he reached the blank cover. The slap board was blank when the speech began. The individual flannel boards were stacked in piles behind the slap board. That is, flannel boards one to nine were in one stack, ten to seventeen in another, and so on. When he saw the cue* reach, *the reader picked up the appropriate stack and then slapped the cards on individually as each cue was reached. In effect, he made a visual outline of his talk on the slap board. The script was so typed that he did not at any time have to turn a page while he was using the visual aids.)*

FIRST PORTION OF A SPEECH BY R. D. KARNS[8]

Thank you, Mr._____.

.....public relations for Stanolind is easy. As you all know, our business and industrial relations' record is a fine one. I was reminded the other day just how good our record was when I was interviewing a man for public relations work.

I showed him the O.R.C. presentation you have just seen. He was impressed by the public's economic ignorance. But before he was willing to work, he wanted to know about Stanolind's business record.

He asked if he was being employed to do a whitewash job. So I reviewed for him our record in industrial relations, our employment practices, and our various employee plans; I not only convinced him Stanolind has a good business record, but I reassured myself that Stanolind was a company that could profit from a vital public relations program.

We all know that Stanolind has never done much in the past to cultivate the public.

[8] Reprinted by permission of the author.

Stanolind is doing better now. Most of you have received the statement of public relations policy issued by Mr. Bullard last April.

REACH

That statement is the proof if you need it, that Stanolind is doing something in public relations and that the program stems right from the top of the organization.

FLANNEL BOARD #1

STANOLIND PUBLIC RELATIONS

As further proof of Stanolind's interest in good public relations.

FLANNEL BOARD #2

PRESENT ACTIVITIES

Let me review some of the activities in this field.

FLANNEL BOARD #3

OPEN HOUSES

Many of you have helped us in our program of open houses. You know how effective they have been.

FLIP (Easel montage of open house brochure covers)

Ten thousand people have had the opportunity to see how our plants operate; how well they are kept; what a tremendous investment they represent; and what benefits the community derives from the plant's being there.

FLANNEL BOARD #4

PUBLICATIONS

We have printed and distributed 125,000 copies of booklets and other printed materials that tell the Stanolind and free enterprise story.
FLIP (Easel montage of printed material covers)
Through these booklets we have emphasized the fact that Stanolind is a good place to work. We have shown that Stanolind is willing to tell the public the facts about its operation.
FLANNEL BOARD #5

SPEECHES

Speaking tours inside and outside the company areas have been arranged.
FLIP (Easel picture of executive making speech)
Our executives and technical personnel have made 311 speeches throughout Stanolind's operating areas. Those speeches were designed to tell the Stanolind story.
FLANNEL BOARD #6

OIIC

We have worked with the Oil Industry Information Committee providing speakers, materials, presentations and funds. All this to tell the story of the place of Stanolind and the Oil Industry in the free enterprise system.
FLANNEL BOARD #7

RADIO

Many of Stanolind's recent activities have been broadcast over local and regional networks.
FLIP (Easel montage of microphones and radio station call letters)
Radio stations have been eager to give us time on the air. For they recognize that the oil industry is important to the community and operates in the public interest.

FLANNEL BOARD #8

MOVIES

Company and industrial films have been made and distributed throughout the country. There have been more than 600 separate showings. These films have told the story of Stanolind, the Industry, and free enterprise.

FLANNEL BOARD #9

THE PRESS

I am sure all of you have been aware of the increased activity in our public relations with newspapers and trade journals.

FLIP (Easel montage of newspaper and journal clippings).......

There's a concrete example of the results that can be obtained from a good public relations program.

COVER FLIP

Now, it may seem to you that this activity does not quite measure up to the goal of public relations —"getting all the public to know us and think well of us."

REMOVE FLANNELS 2,3,4,5,6,7,8,9.

I report it to show you Stanolind is aware of the need for public relations, and is beginning to take steps to fight the public's economic ignorance.

REACH

But now what are we going to do in the future?

FLANNEL BOARD #10

FUTURE PLANS

First: We will continue the present company PR program

FLANNEL BOARD #11

COMPANY PR PROGRAM

that is, to set up and organize company open houses;
print and distribute booklets; arrange speaking tours
for our personnel; handle newspaper and magazine
stories and pictures; use radio and movies.

We will continue to tell the Stanolind story.

But we can use your help.

. . . .

PART TWO

In Action

✦)〉✦〉〉✦〉〉✦〉〉✦〉〉✦〉〉✦〉〉✦〉〉✦〉✦〉✦〉✦〉✦〉〈✦〈✦〈✦〈✦〈✦〈✦〈✦〈✦〈✦

· 5 ·

Communicating Ideas—Phrasing, Inflection, and Pauses

❖⫸⫸⫸⫸⫸⫸⫸⫸⫸⫸❖⫷⫷⫷⫷⫷⫷⫷⫷⫷❖

One school of thought in this country believes it is easy to communicate ideas. Just make the idea simple enough, repeat it often enough, and eventually your audience will get it. Many teachers, preachers, and advertising men subscribe to this theory. Just say "two-plus-two-equals-four" often enough, and the second-grader will remember it and be ready for the third grade. Just say "God is Love" often enough, and the churchgoer will believe. Just say "Lucky Strike means fine tobacco" often enough, and the listener will buy a pack.

This theory has drawbacks, however; all ideas cannot be reduced to that lowest of all denominators—it is not uncommon for the listener to rebel at the din. The second-grader may rebel inwardly at the two-plus-two reiteration and become a third-grader just to get away from the noise, never really knowing why two plus two equals four. The churchgoer may not have understood the concept "God is Love" and lose his faith in a moment of trial when mere repetition won't help. The radio listener may turn off his radio, or his hearing, or may react violently in the opposite direction and buy anything but the cigarette so advertised.

Since some of the ideas you will be dealing with may be complex, and since you cannot afford to offend your listener, we will approach the problem of communication of ideas from a different viewpoint. There are three prime requisites for the successful communication of ideas: (1) your comprehension of the ideas, (2) your desire for the listener to comprehend, and (3) your skill in interpreting the ideas for the listener.

Methods of understanding the ideas in your script have been discussed in Chapter 2. As for desire and skill—actually, if your desire to e comprehended is great enough, you have the necessary communication kills. A hungry man can get food; a shot-down pilot can find friends; a zealot can make converts. When the need is great enough, any of us can become effective communicators. When we communicate, our needs are not usually as elementary as hunger, food, and shelter, and we must make up in skill what we lack in emotional drive. The skills discussed here and in the following chapter are basic to the interpretation of ideas for a listener. They are phrasing, inflection, pauses, stress, and variety. These skills can be acquired by practice and drill. They are the vocal techniques necessary for winning the listener's complete comprehension.

PHRASING

To communicate an idea, we do not begin with words. Words have meaning, it is true, but most words have too many meanings. Take the word *nice* as an example.

ME., foolish; OFr. *nice, niche, nisce,* stupid, foolish <L. *nescius,* ignorant, not knowing. <*nescire,* to be ignorant; *ne-,* not *scire,* to know.   1. difficult to please; very careful, fastidious; refined.   2. delicate; precise; minute; discriminative; subtle: as, a nice distinction.   3. calling for delicacy, accuracy, or precision in handling, discrimination or adjustment; calling for great care, tact, etc., as a nice problem.   4. (a) able to make fine or delicate distinction; delicately skillful; finely discriminating.   (b) minutely accurate, as an instrument.   5. having high standards of conduct; scrupulous.   6. (a) agreeable; pleasant; delightful.   (b) attractive; pretty.   (c) kind; thoughtful, considerate.   (d) modest; well-mannered; reserved.   (e) in good taste.   (f) good; excellent. A generalized term of approval, having very wide application.   7. (Obs.) (a) ignorant; foolish.   (b) wanton.   (c) tender; delicate.   (d) coy; shy.[1]

It is only when the word *nice* is used with other words that we understand the import of the idea and the value to be given the word.

[1] *Webster's New World Dictionary of The American Language* (Cleveland: The World Pub. Co., 1951).

The word group, and not the separate word, is the unit of thought. We speak in word groups. Sometimes those groups are sentences; always they are phrases. A phrase consists of either a whole or those parts of an idea that logically belong together.

In conversation, phrase length is determined by two factors: breathing and comprehension. We voice our idea the way we want to say it, and then pause for breath. This breathing is unconscious. Most people are as unaware of breathing as they are of the beating of their hearts. That natural breath pause gives the listener a chance to comprehend what has been said.

Here is an example of natural phrasing. Each phrase is indicated by //.

> No one can tell you // just how many publicity men // the federal government employs. // Even the Hoover commission // couldn't count them all. // But here are a few // figures // the commission did bring to light. // For the fiscal year // 1949 // the Executive Branch of the government // spent: // salaries // 12 million, // 65 thousand dollars.[2]

If you try to read that, following the phrase marks, you will notice that some pauses seem to need to be shorter than others. If you try to breathe at each of those marks, you will find yourself panting like a lizard. The original speaker was not aware of breathing at those spots, because he was concerned with communicating. Each time he paused, air rushed naturally into his lungs. He did pause at all the points marked, as a tape recording of his speech testifies.

A foreigner listening to this talk might have thought that all the words between pause marks were single words. Hearing "no one can tell you," the foreigner might have attempted to write it "nowunkentlyu."

Phrasing is dictated principally by the reader's desire to be understood. Usually, the simpler the material, the longer the phrases; the more complex the material, the shorter the phrases. Phrases shorten with the reader's desire to make each word count with the listener. Sometimes a phrase is only one word long.

Phrasing is often indicated by punctuation, but the infinite variety of shadings possible to the human voice is beyond the scope of printed symbols. Punctuation frequently is a stumbling block.

"Oh, no, Joe, you're not going to try that, too?"

There is an example of acceptable punctuation. Used as a guide to phrasing, the punctuation is confusing to the reader. If you tried to read

[2] Speech by R. D. Karns. Reprinted by permission of the author.

the punctuation, you would sound like a second-grader. Speaking the sentence, you might phrase it in one of several ways: "Oh no Joe // you're not going to try that too"; "Oh // no Joe // you're not going to try that // too"; "Oh no // Joe you're not going to try that too."

"Phrasing is dictated by the reader's desire to be understood."

There's another example of acceptable punctuation that does not indicate the possibilities for phrasing. You could read that sentence as if it were, "Phrasing // is dictated by the reader's desire to be understood"; or "Phrasing is dictated // by the reader's desire // to be // understood."

Punctuation is our first guide to vocal phrasing. Here is where all the work you did on understanding your script begins to pay off. If you followed the instructions given in Chapter 2, the work now will be easier. Let's phrase a few examples.

> She said it like a trained broadcaster, breaking it up so it would sound natural but arranging the inflections so that listeners of any mental age whatever would get it.[3]

She did what we are now going to try to do. The comma shows us one phrasing break: "She said it like a trained broadcaster" is one phrase, the rest of the sentence can be another or several more. Punctuation does not help us on the rest of the sentence. "Breaking it up so it would sound natural" at first blush seems to be a phrase. "But arranging the inflections so that listeners of any mental age whatever would get it" seems to be another. Look at that last phrase again. The idea is complete if we just read "so that listeners would get it." Therefore, "any mental age whatever" is another phrase.

You might read it like this now: "She said it like a trained broadcaster // breaking it up so it would sound natural // but arranging the inflections so that listeners (of-any-mental-age-whatever) would get it."

You can do more with the sentence than that. While you're talking about breaking it up, you can break it up into even shorter phrases. If you phrase after "breaking it up," you might read, "Breaking-it-up // so-it-would / sound / natural // but // arranging / the-inflections / so-that / listeners // of-any-mental-age-whatever // would get it."

Let's leave that and take another example.

> When, as you say, I made an utter fool of myself, believe me, I made a poetic fool of myself.

Here, commas set off phrases that are obviously subordinate. The

[3] Rex Stout, *And Be a Villain* (New York: The Viking Press, Inc., 1948), p. 10.

sentence can be read, "When I made an utter fool of myself, I made a poetic fool of myself." The remaining comma is also helpful, setting off an adverbial clause. The spine of the sentence remains: "I made a poetic fool of myself." The phrases "as you say" and "believe me" are so subordinated to the main line of the sentence that they are really parenthetical. "When (as you say) I made an utter fool of myself, (believe me) I made a poetic fool of myself." Finding and tagging the phrases in this sentence should make it easier to read aloud. Because you know that the spine of the sentence is the last phrase, you will read it with more stress than the preceding phrases. You will subordinate—throw away—the drop-in phrases.

Here is a more complicated problem in phrasing.

> But how you can imagine, after that, that I can suspect you of the smallest feeling for me except the inevitable feeling of early youth for late age, or imagine that I have any feeling for you except one of shrinking humiliation, I can't understand.

The first duty here is to find the subject of the sentence. It is "I." The sentence could read, "I can't understand how you can imagine . . . ." "After that" is easy. It is subordinate; the commas show it. We can ignore it for a while. Worrying the rest of the sentence, you find the verb *imagine* used before two parallel phrases. "How you can imagine that I can suspect you of the smallest feeling for me . . . or imagine that I have any feeling for you . . . ." In other words, the sentence spine—what you're trying to get across—could be simply, "I can't understand how you can imagine these things." But since we are trying to phrase this author's words, let's try it like this: "But how you can imagine (after that) that I can suspect you of the smallest feeling for me (except the inevitable feeling of early youth for late age) or imagine // that I have any feeling for you (except one of shrinking humiliation) I can't understand."

INFLECTION

Your voice has been making observable glides and shifts while you have been phrasing main and subordinate ideas. It is time to recognize those vocal movements and identify them. They are pitch inflections and pitch shifts. They—with pauses—are the principal vocal means of showing the interrelation and separation of ideas. A Victor Borge with his oral punctuation marks is an amusing oddity. We, as readers, will use sound

Courtesy Stanolind Oil and Gas Company.

Reading aloud from an easel chart.

and no-sound to indicate word groups; we will use variation in the sound pattern for further differentiation among phrases.

Pitch is the characteristic of the voice that relates vocal tone to the musical scale. A pitch inflection is an upward or downward movement of tone without cessation of sound. A pitch shift is a similar movement during the cessation of sound. A pause is a cessation of sound.

Try reading this aloud.

> That public virtue, (which among the ancients was denominated patriotism), is derived from a strong sense of our own interest in the preservation and prosperity of the free government of which we are members.[4]

In order to read that sentence so that it made sense for the listener, you used a number of pitch inflections and two pitch shifts. The pitch shifts were used to indicate the parenthesis. The shift is the principal vocal technique for indicating the parenthesis to a listener. It is also a helpful technique for indicating subordinate ideas.

To indicate a parenthesis vocally, you should consider the main phrase as one pitch group and the enclosed phrase as another. The parenthesis may be spoken in a higher pitch or in a lower pitch, but there should be a marked difference between the main pitch and the subordi-

[4] Edward Gibbon, *The History of the Decline and Fall of the Roman Empire* (New York: Heritage Press, 1946), I, 7.

nate pitch. In the example above, the pitch used on the word "virtue" is identical with that used on the word "is." If the sentence were scored for singing, you could conceive of the main phrase being sung on *E,* for example, while the subordinate clause was sung on *C* below or *G* above.

Pitch shifts are also used to denote new ideas. After completing one thought, the effective reader begins the next on another pitch to indicate to the listener that he has reached a new idea in the selection. Notice how naturally you will make such shifts in the following selection.

It is a friendly thing to read from great books to large numbers of people. I have always been a nervous actor and scared of appearing before audiences. I have never yet been scared when I have had a bundle of books under my arm.

I have been asked which of the great authors people seem to like best. I have read to audiences varying in size from several hundred to six thousand or so, and the main impression that I have taken away is that people have just liked hearing things out of real books. Sometimes they have said, "I liked Dickens best"(it may have been snowing outside—it was in Detroit); sometimes James Thurber (they wanted to laugh together); sometimes a Psalm (they wanted to be solemn together); and sometimes Shakespeare's magic wood from *A Midsummer Night's Dream* (they were indulging in magic together). There has been no preference . . . .[5]

A further comment on parenthesis can be made. Reading the parenthesis in the Laughton selection, your pitch probably dropped and you spoke just a shade more rapidly; in the Gibbon parenthesis, however, your pitch probably rose and you spoke more measuredly. A conclusion can be drawn from these instances. When the parenthetical idea is subordinate to the main idea, the voice drops and the rate increases—you throw the phrase away, in order words. When the parenthetical idea is important, the voice rises and the rate decreases.

Needless to say, the voice does not remain monotonously on the *E* pitch until it shifts to the *C* or *G* pitch. In speaking, the voice continually slides from one pitch to another, expressing various shades of relationship and degrees of meaning.

A single spoken word may vary in pitch by gliding through several notes of the musical scale. On "You did?" the "did" may begin on middle *C* and slide up a full octave. A sung word may slide the same octave, but it will pause momentarily on some or all of the pitch frequencies. Here is the principal difference between the melody of speech and the melody of

[5] Charles Laughton, "Storytelling," *Atlantic Monthly,* Vol. CLXXXV, No. 6 (June, 1950).

song: spoken syllables are held on constant pitch for a shorter length of time than are sung syllables.

In the English language, pitch glides coming at the conclusion of each phrase indicate by their movement whether the phrase is complete in itself or connected to what follows. That is why you make a preliminary analysis to find main and subordinate ideas. After you know the relationship of ideas, you can give them proper interpretation by the use of inflections.

A downward glide in pitch usually expresses (1) completion of the phrase, (2) authority, (3) decision, (4) emphasis, and (5) finality. Here are some downward glides. "She's lovely. She's engaged. She uses Ponds!"

An upward glide in pitch usually expresses (1) the thought is incomplete, (2) indecision, (3) disbelief, (4) a question, (5) courtesy, and (6) gayety.

Notice the variety of pitch inflections possible in the following selection.

As I remember my school requirements (I am both a public and a private school boy myself, having always changed schools just as the class in English in the new school was taking up Silas Marner, with the result that it was the only book in the English language that I knew until I was eighteen—but, boy, did I know Silas Marner!), I would substitute a list something like the following in place of that sent out by the clothing store:

One sheet of note paper (with envelope to match) for letter home. This should do for the school year. Requests for money can be made by telegraph, collect.

Five hundred pairs of socks, one to be thrown away each day.

One very old T-shirt.

Three dozen neckties, for use of roommates.

One set of name tags, to be sewn on clothing to insure roommates getting them in return for clothing marked with roommates name.

There is no sense in trying to provide handkerchiefs.[6]

Did you notice that your voice did not fall on every period? A period is not necessarily a full stop, with the voice sliding downward, pause, breath, new subject. A period may be as unimportant to the reader as a comma. That is another concept about phrasing that you need to acquire.

But if you don't stop for periods, where do you stop? You stop on

[6] Robert Benchley, *Chips off the Old Benchley* (New York: Harper & Brothers, 1949), p. 32.

pauses. But before we discuss pauses, there is another technique of phrasing through inflection that you should become acquainted with.

> Even now I can smell London—its acrid fragrance of sea-coal smoke pressed to earth by the soft and heavy London air. I can hear it, too—hear the unending grinding and thumping of coach wheels and cart wheels on the round boulders of the streets; the bellowing of chariot drivers, chair boys, draymen, street hawkers, with which the roads are filled; the clacking of women's pattens on the sidewalks; the screaking of the heavy signs that overhang every street.
>
> I can see it, hear it, smell it; but I can't describe it satisfactorily for nowhere in the world is there such a city of opposites. In no other hive of humanity are there so many kind and generous people, or so many thieves and rascals; so many beautiful homes and so many hovels; so many wise statesmen and so many political dolts; so much honesty and so much knavery; so much education and so much pitiable ignorance; so much cleanliness and so much filth; so much patriotism and so much treachery; so much sobriety and so much drunkenness; so much virtue and so much vice; so many frigid natures and so many warm hearts.[7]

In that selection you will find a new type of inflectional problem—contrast. In order to communicate the sense to a listener, you will use pitch variations to show the contrasts in mood. The average reader will take the pitch upward on the good quality and downward on the bad, as in "so much virtue and so much vice." He will also balance one pitch with another; the "goods" with the "goods," and the "bads" with the "bads." Contrast is a good writing device for conveying impressions. Mastery of it technically by the reader is a means of achieving variety in pitch and inflections; but, watch out, it can become a monotonous pattern.

Now, pause.

PAUSES

The pause is where you breathe and the audience thinks. A better way to phrase it would be to say that a pause is where you think and the listener comprehends.

The pause is potentially one of the most useful instruments of vocal expression. Only long experience with audience reaction can enable you to understand all the possibilities in a pause.

[7] Kenneth Roberts, *Northwest Passage* (New York: Doubleday & Co., Inc., 1946), p. 345.

You pause because you have come to the end of one idea group; because you breathe; because the listener needs time to comprehend; and because you are assembling vocal symbols to communicate the next idea.

What do pauses mean? Suspense, omission of words, lapse of time, change of scene, reflection—those are some of the things a pause may indicate.

▶ *Suspense.* The suspense pause is best exemplified in the act of an aerialist in a circus. He pauses for effect, swaying on the slack wire high up in the tent. He pauses there while you hold your breath. When he tries his trick, whatever it may be, you aren't built up sufficiently for the trick, so he misses. The second time he attempts the trick, he pauses just a little longer, getting set. The third time he tries—he'll make it this time—the suspense is excruciating and the pause is long drawn out. That pause is filled with suspense—the performer's calculation and our imaginative projection of the danger.

The suspense pause is your best story-telling device. Suppose, for a moment, you are telling a story instead of reading one. You are a good story teller. You have a group of listeners seated around you. They are interested in the story; they are hanging on your every word. You are trying to get the most out of every story turn and every surprise.

"And although Bluebeard had told her not to open the door, she went up to it and tried the key in the lock. (Pause) It didn't work. (Pause) She jiggled the key, a-n-d the door began to s-w-i-n-g o-p-e-n. Finally, she could look into the room. And what do you think she saw there? (Big pause)."

As you can see, it is the same technique used by the circus performer. You can use it in almost every reading situation. To know where to put such a pause, ask yourself at the end of each phrase if you could insert the question, "What do you think happened next?"

You're a ham if you use the suspense pause, but good ham. You should learn to use it. And you can hold the suspense pause in direct ratio to the amount of surprise that follows; in the Bluebeard story, for example, you can't hold the key pause too long. After all, the key is or isn't going to work and you can't protract the agony, for your audience is running ahead of you. But when the door is open and the wife looks in, then you can really pause, because what she sees is a big surprise. If what she saw was fifty pairs of shoes, a big pause would be foolish. If what she saw was canned goods and we had been built up to a big surprise by a long pause, we would feel as if we had been cheated; there would be an anticlimax. But since she saw the corpses of the other wives—believe me, quite a sight and quite a surprise for the listener—the pause, if it is big enough and long enough, adds to the satisfaction of the listener.

Get an audience of children for the acid test of the suspense pause. They are better for your present purpose, because they are not afraid to respond to the reader. Read them a story like the Bluebeard story and pause frequently for "What do you think happened next?" questions. If you're doing your job, they'll fill the pauses for you with possible answers. When you say, "What do you think she saw there?" you'll get answers that will make your blood run cold. "Dynamite," says one. "Russian spies," says another. If you get such answers, you are getting complete audience response; you are truly communicating. And the value of the exercise is in what you can learn from the experience. You can begin to see how big a pause can be, how effective a pause can be, and how frequently you can use the pause.

They knew that the time a man could cling to a slippery rock in the face of that driving current was a matter of minutes, and they ran as fast as they could up the bank to a point far above where Thornton was hanging on. They attached the line with which they had been snubbing the boat to Buck's neck and shoulders, being careful that it should neither strangle him nor impede his swimming, and launched him into the stream. He struck out boldly, but not straight enough into the stream. He discovered the mistake too late, when Thornton was abreast of him and a bare half-dozen strokes away while he was being carried helplessly past.

Hans promptly snubbed with the rope, as though Buck were a boat. The rope thus tightening on him in the sweep of the current, he was jerked under the surface, and under the surface he remained till his body struck against the bank and he was hauled out. He was half drowned, and Hans and Pete threw themselves upon him, pounding the breath into him and the water out of him. He staggered to his feet and fell down. The faint sound of Thornton's voice came to them, and though they could not make out the words of it, they knew that he was in his extremity. His master's voice acted on Buck like an electric shock. He sprang to his feet and ran up the bank ahead of the men to the point of his previous departure.

Again the rope was attached and he was launched, and again he struck out, but this time straight into the stream. He had miscalculated once, but he would not be guilty of it a second time. Hans paid out the rope, permitting no slack, while Pete kept it clear of coils. Buck held on till he was on a line straight above Thornton; then he turned, and with the speed of an express train headed down upon him. Thornton saw him coming, and, as Buck struck him like a battering ram, with the whole force of the current behind him, he reached up and closed with both arms around the shaggy neck. Hans snubbed the rope around the tree, and Buck and Thornton were jerked under the water. Strangling, suffocating, sometimes one uppermost and sometimes the other, dragging over the jagged bottom, smashing against rocks and snags, they veered in to the bank.

Thornton came to, belly downward and being violently propelled back and forth across a drift log by Hans and Pete. His first glance was for Buck, over whose limp and apparently lifeless body Nig was setting up a howl, while Skeet was licking the wet face and closed eyes. Thornton was himself bruised and battered, and he went carefully over Buck's body, when he had been brought around, finding three broken ribs.[8]

The suspense pause is also used to build up an anticlimax. When an event is seemingly over, there is a pause following it. If there is to be an anticlimax, it should come soon enough after the event for the spectator to know it is related to what preceded, but there must also be the element of surprise at something being added. In retrospect we recognize the pause to have been one of suspense, building us up for the surprise of the anticlimax. Rudy Vallee had such a pause for anticlimax in an act with his band. He told the fairy story "The Frog-Prince" against the background music of the orchestra. He told the story straight and very well. He ended the story,

And when the Princess opened the door, the frog came in and slept upon her pillow as before, till the morning broke. And the third night he did the same. But when the Princess awoke on the following morning she was astonished to see, instead of the frog, a handsome Prince, gazing on her with the most beautiful eyes she had ever seen and standing at the head of her bed.

He told her that he had been enchanted by a spiteful fairy who had changed him into a frog; and that he had been fated so to abide till some princess should take him out of the spring and let him eat from her plate and sleep upon her bed for three nights. "You," said the Prince, "have broken this cruel charm, and now I have nothing to wish for but that you should go with me into my father's kingdom, where I will marry you and love you as long as you live."

Saying that, Vallee turned to the orchestra, and the act appeared to be over. After a well-calculated pause, he turned back to the audience and said, "Her mother didn't believe the story, either."

[8] Jack London, *The Call of the Wild* (New York: The Macmillan Co., 1903), pp. 177–179. Reprinted by permission of The Macmillan Co.

▶ *Omission of words.*   Here are two selections with ellipses.

#1   I would have to tell them they had to learn to tell stories or poems to another person and that if they wanted to learn to read aloud well they must learn to seek the response in somebody else's eyes as they read; and so I would get them reading to each other . . . . I find myself objecting every time I either say or hear the phrase "reading aloud." Stories were told and retold for hundreds of years before they were set down and these are the best stories . . . .[9]

#2   Among the three or four million cradles now rocking in the land are some which this nation would preserve for ages as sacred things, if we could know which ones they are. In one of these cradles the unconscious Farragut of the future is at this moment teething— think of it!— . . . . In another the future renowned astronomer is blinking at the shining Milky Way with but a languid interest—poor little chap!—and wondering what has become of the other one they call the wet nurse. In another the future great historian is lying—and doubtless will continue to lie until his earthly mission is ended.[10]

In those selections you paused at the ellipsis marks, which indicated that words were missing. In the second selection, you paused to indicate that two different kinds of words were missing: those deleted from the text and those expected by the listener. In the pause following "lying," the speaker omitted no words, nor did the listener. But the words the listener supplied during the pause were not the ones the speaker used when he resumed speaking. The switch of ideas makes the selection funny. The pause is the speaking device that permits this mental switching of ideas.

In the next example there is an exaggerated use of the omission-of-words pause. It is a powerful example of the possibilities of a pause. To fully appreciate Artemus Ward's success with this pause, imagine the results had he failed.

The opening night of the show Hingston introduced him in a neat little speech, and claimed the indulgence of those present for any nervousness the entertainer might display on this his first public appearance in London. He said it was a critical moment for Ward, and his fate trembled in the balance. Then Ward rose, came down to the footlights, and stood silent, casting his deep-set, brilliant eyes over the vast audience, and twiddling his thumbs in the most unconcerned way. A minute or two passed; under such circumstances it

[9] Laughton, *op. cit.*
[10] Albert Bigelow Paine, ed., *Mark Twain's Speeches* (New York: Harper & Brothers, 1923), p. 61.

seemed much longer. The audience became fidgety. I heard one gentleman sitting near me exclaim to a lady at his side: "What a fool! Why doesn't he say something?" Once more a silence fell upon the assembly, but the imperturbable man stood twiddling his thumbs. A murmur of disapproval swept like a wave over the audience, then a little more clapping, a little more stamping, followed by a silence during which a pin might almost have been heard to fall. At last, in his inimitable drawl, Ward spoke:

"Ladies—and—gentlemen. When—you—have finished this—unseemly interruption, I guess I'll begin my discourse."

It was as if an electric shock had passed through the people. They saw the humor of the situation. They rose to it. And seldom had a showman received such an ovation. The audience almost raised the roof with their cheers and applause, and it was fully five minutes before he could proceed. From that moment he became the idol of London.[11]

▶ *Lapse of time.* The reader uses pauses to indicate to the listener the actual passing of time. The simplest use of this pause is found in radio. "In just ten seconds, when you hear the musical note, it will be nine o'clock," says the announcer. Then he pauses ten seconds, strikes the musical note, and begins a new program.

The reader uses a lapse-of-time pause with such expressions as "after a pause," "there was a long period of silence," "several moments later," "that afternoon," "next week." The speaker may pause either before or after the line describing the lapse of time, whichever is more effective in a given selection.

Here is an example of such a lapse-of-time pause.

If you've ever heard Abbott and Costello go
through that "Who's on First" routine   you'll
understand what sort of a mess Seaman Herbert Duty
found himself in.
Herb was drowsing through his watch in Atlantic
Fleet Headquarters when the phone rang.   A deep
firm voice asked, "Who's the duty driver?"
Herbert said, "Duty, sir."
The deep voice took on a trace of irritation.
"Yes, that's it," he said, "who has the duty?"
Seaman Duty gulped and said, "Duty, sir."
There was a pause, then the voice came back with,
"Listen, son, this is the skipper speaking.   Knock
off this funny business and tell me who the duty
driver is."
Herbert pulled himself together and tried once

---

[11] Quoted by Don C. Seitz, *Artemus Ward* (New York: Harper & Brothers, 1919), pp. 207–208.

more. "Like I told you, sir, Seaman Herbert Duty has the duty, sir."

There was one more long silence. Then the skipper's voice said, "That's all right, son, I'll call a taxi."[12]

A third use of the lapse-of-time pause is for allowing time between ideas. Without any verbal indication from the reader, the audience recognizes that such a pause means the passing of time. The first of the following selections is a clear example. In the Wodehouse selection following it, you may pause to show the lapse of time after "soul," after "door," after "fit for," and after "thank you, Jeeves."

#1   He had brought tumblers from the automobile, so that we could drink in comfort, and indeed it was delicious beyond the nature of water.

When I had finished drinking, I looked around with satisfaction. This was a fat little estate . . . .[13]

#2   "Oh? Well, let me tell you that the man who has not music in his soul . . . ." I stepped to the door. "Jeeves," I called down the passage, "what was it Shakespear said the man who hadn't music in his soul was fit for?"

"Treasons, stratagems, and spoils, sir."

"Thank you, Jeeves. Is fit for treasons, stratagems and spoils," I said, returning.[14]

The greatest literary example of the lapse-of-time pause is in Marlowe's *Doctor Faustus*. In the last scene Faustus indicates the passing of an hour in fifty lines of poetry! The pause is the only device to make this passing of time credible. And the spectator witnessing a good performance does believe that an hour has passed.

► *Change of scene.*   One of the obvious uses of the pause is to indicate a change of scene. In narrative and descriptive material we have located our listener with us somewhere. Then we change locale. The change is indicated by the words of the script. The changing is indicated by the pause.

At last evening began to fall, and they drove the cow home together, and Sylvia smiled with pleasure when they came to the place where she heard the whistle and was afraid only the night before.

[12] FK247A8/24, United Press Radio, August 24, 1950.

[13] Rebecca West, *Black Lamb and Grey Falcon* (New York: The Viking Press, Inc., 1941), p. 964.

[14] P. G. Wodehouse, *Thank You, Jeeves* (Boston: Little, Brown & Co., 1934), p. 10.

> Half a mile from home, at the farther edge of the woods, where the land was highest, a great pine-tree stood, the last of its generation.[15]

Think of this change of scene as if it were being done in the movies. A motion-picture director might use a slow dissolve on Sylvia as she smiles with pleasure thinking of the whistle she had heard. The scene fades away, there is a moment of darkness, and then there is a new scene. All that takes time. You should take the same time in your pausing.

Or think of this change as it might be done in the theater. Should the playwright want to make a real break here, he might have the curtain come down slowly with a dimming of the lights, then the curtain would rise again on the new scene—a time-consuming operation. Your pause could take a comparable amount of time. If the playwright does not want so complete a break, he could have simply a dimming of the lights, but again it would take time.

This change of scene in radio would be done by a fade-out of the noises of the cattle, a moment of evening sound effects, silence, and then a fade-in of the sounds of the new locale—a device similar to your pausing.

As a reader, you are the movie director, the playwright, the radio sound man. You create the same effects for your audience; your most telling device for gaining effects is the pause.

▶ *Reflection.* You use a reflective pause when you are thinking of your own thoughts, marshaling the words for a new statement. A frequent example is, "Let's see, that happened about . . . two years ago." If you wish to give the impression of searching for words, you use a reflective pause.

> . . . the thought precedes the word. Of course there are passages in which thought and language are borne along by the streams of emotion and completely intermingled. But more often it will be found that the most natural, and most seemingly accidental, effects are obtained *when the working of the mind is evident* before or as the tongue gives it words.[16]

You often use the reflective pause to give the audience time to think with you. If you are showing a list of figures and then you give their total, you normally pause to allow the audience time to add with you.

---

[15] Sarah Orne Jewett, *A White Heron, and Other Stories* (Boston: Houghton Mifflin Company, 1887).

[16] Henry Irving, *The Drama* (Boston: Joseph Knight Company, 1892), pp. 83–84.

"Twenty dollars for insurance and eighty dollars for rent, and thirty-five dollars for utilities comes to . . . one hundred and thirty-five dollars a month."

If you ask a simple question of your listener, give him a chance to answer. "Were you one of the people who failed to vote in the last election?"

If you ask a more complex question of a listener, give him a chance to review the question before you supply the answer. In other words, let him reflect on his answer. "What are we going to do about this rise in taxes?"

Give the listener time to remember, if you ask him to. "Remember the good old days in high school . . . ."

If you say "think of" in your speech, give the listener time to think. "Think of the number of times you've mispronounced e-r-r."

The reflective pause is the most frequently used pause. It is the natural pause that comes at the conclusion of each idea, the pause you make meaningful by your active thinking of the next idea, the pause the audience utilizes for thinking.

The answer to the question, "What do I do while I pause?" is supplied in the preceding paragraph; you think. In all the situations for pauses listed in the foregoing pages, there was the need for active thought by the speaker.

You don't hesitate during a pause; you forget about the rule you may have once learned—pause one count for commas, two counts for semicolons, three counts for colons, and four counts for periods; you fill the pause with thinking. If the pause is for omission of words, you think of what has been omitted. If the pause is for lapse of time, you fill in the pause by a review of how that time was spent. In the Wodehouse selection, you walk to the door in your imagination. If the pause is for change of scene, you summon up the image of the new locale. If the pause is reflective, you think the ideas. Pauses are not just devices, they are moments of cerebral activity.

Then, how long do you pause? A time comparable to the amount of mental activity going on. If it takes time to add the three figures on household expense given as an example above, you take the time necessary to add those figures. If it takes some time to get to the passage door in the Wodehouse selection, take that time.

Because there is so much disagreement over the proper length for a pause, some writers of material for the oral reader do not use conventional punctuation. They use dashes and ellipses to separate phrases and leave the decision of how long each pause should be up to the reader. Maurice

Maeterlinck in his play *The Bluebird* uses this device. Radio writers—script, continuity, and news—use the same device. Here is a random sample.

```
    Washington - - Nineteen-fifty may be known on the
weatherman's book as the year in which summer gave
up the ghost a month ahead of time.
    The weather has been acting very strangely indeed
--upsetting the best-laid plans of farmers and
countryfolk.  With the season only two months along,
rural residents report that fall seems to be bursting
out all over.  The signs are indisputable - first
frost... birds flying south... leaves turning red.¹⁷
```

Don't worry about your pauses being too long. If the pause is filled with meaningful thought, the listener continues to be interested. The greatest problem in pausing is taking *enough* time. Don't be afraid of "white space," "dead air," or whatever you may call it. If thinking the thoughts of your manuscript does not cause you to pause long enough for reflection, if awareness of the listener who is trying to comprehend does not halt the flow of your words, maybe the knowledge that the pause is the greatest contributor to an easy conversational style may give you pause.

The surest sign of the novice reader is his failure to pause. The greatest observable difference between the speaker who reads his manuscript and the one who ad-libs his ideas is the difference in the use of pauses. If you want an easy, conversational reading style—learn to pause.

Throughout this book, there are many opportunities for practice in the use of pauses. As a suggestion about pauses before you try any drill material, remember—a pause after a word makes what has preceded important; a pause before a word or phrase makes what is to come important, for it arouses interest and builds suspense.

▶ *Conclusion.* In this chapter, we have discussed phrasing, inflection, and pauses. We have talked about them as if they were three distinct and separate entities. Actually they are mutually dependent. You indicate phrases by pauses and inflection. You achieve variety in inflection by the use of pauses. You take short pauses when the phrases are closely linked together and the ideas are interrelated; you take longer pauses when the phrase ideas can be separated. The longer the pause, the greater the shift in pitch when you begin to speak again. If you have time to concentrate on only one of the communication skills, concentrate on pauses. They will make phrasing obvious and inflectional variety easy.

¹⁷ HXR146, United Press Radio, August 23, 1950.

EXERCISE

(After reading the introductory statement by Samuel Clemens [Mark Twain], try out your ability with pauses on "The Golden Arm," following Twain's suggestions; they are good ones.[18])

The pause is an exceedingly important feature in any kind of story, and a frequently recurring feature, too. It is a dainty thing, and delicate, and also uncertain and treacherous; for it must be exactly the right length —no more and no less—or it fails of its purpose and makes trouble. If the pause is too short the impressive point is passed, and the audience have had time to divine that a surprise is intended—and then you can't surprise them, of course.

On the platform I used to tell a negro ghost story that had a pause in front of the snapper on the end, and that pause was the most important thing in the whole story. If I got it the right length precisely, I could spring the finishing ejaculation with effect enough to make some impressible girl deliver a startled little yelp and jump out of her seat—and that was what I was after. This story was called "The Golden Arm," and was told in this fashion. You can practise with it yourself—and mind you look out for the pause and get it right.

The Golden Arm

Once 'pon a time dey wuz a monsus mean man, en he live 'way out in de prairie all 'lone by hisself, 'cep'n he had a wife. En bimeby she died, en he tuck en toted her away out dah in de prairie en buried her. Well, she had a golden arm—all solid gold, fum de shoulder down. He wuz pow'ful mean—pow'ful; en dat night he couldn't sleep, caze he want dat golden arm so bad.

When it come midnight he couldn't stan' it no mo'; so he git up, he did, en tuck his lantern en shoved out thoo de storm en dug her up en got de golden arm; en he bent his head down 'gin de wind, en plowed en plowed en plowed thoo de snow. Den all on a sudden he stop (make a considerable pause here, and look startled, and take a listening attitude) en say: "My *lan'*, what's dat!"

En he listen—en listen—en de win' say (set your teeth together and imitate the wailing and wheezing singsong of the wind), "Bzzz-z-zzz"—

[18] Samuel L. Clemens, *How to Tell a Story* (New York: Harper & Brothers, 1897), pp. 12–15.

en den, way back yonder whah de grave is, he heard *a voice!*—he hear a voice all mix' up in de win'—can't hardly tell 'em 'part—"Bzzz-zz—W-h-o—g-o-t—m-y—g-o-l-d-e-n *arm?*—zzz—zzz—W-h-o g-o-t m-y g-o-l-d-e-n *arm?*" (You must begin to shiver violently now.)

En he begin to shiver en shake, en say, "Oh my! *Oh,* my lan'!" en de win' blow de lantern out, en de snow en sleet blow in his face en mos' choke him, en he start a-plowin' knee-deep towards home mos' dead, he so sk'yerd—en pooty soon he hear de voice agin, en (pause) it 'us comin' *after* him! "Bzzz—zzz—zzz—W-h-o—g-o-t-m-y—g-o-l-d-e-n *arm?*"

When he git to de pasture he hear it agin—closter now, en a-*comin'!*—a-comin' back dah in de dark en de storm—(repeat the wind and the voice). When he git to de house he rush up-stairs en jump in de bed en kiver up, head and years, en lay dah shiverin' en shakin'—en den way out dah he hear it *agin!*—en a-*comin'!* En bimeby he hear (pause—awed, listening attitude)—pat—pat—pat—*hit's a-comin'* up-stairs! Den he hear de latch, en he *know* it's in de room!

Den pooty soon he know it's a-*stannin'* by *de bed!* (Pause.) Den—he know it's a-*bendin down over him*—en he can't skasely git his breath! Den—den—he seem to feel someth'n *c-o-l-d,* right down 'most agin his head! (Pause.)

Den de voice say, *right at his year*—"W-h-o g-o-t—m-y—g-o-l-d-e-n *arm?*" (You must wail it out very plaintively and accusingly; then you stare steadily and impressively into the face of the farthest-gone auditor—a girl, preferably—and let that awe-inspiring pause begin to build itself in the deep hush. When it has reached exactly the right length, jump suddenly at that girl and yell, *"You've* got it!")

If you've got the *PAUSE* right, she'll fetch a dear little yelp and spring right out of her shoes. But you *must* get the pause right; and you will find it the most troublesome and aggravating and uncertain thing you ever undertook.

· 6 ·

Communicating Ideas —
Stress and Variety

❧

So far, we have discussed the vocal techniques of phrasing, inflection, and pauses. We need an understanding of the skills of stress and variety, before we will have discussed all the skills basic to the interpretation of ideas for a listener.

Stress is used in a generic sense to refer to the relative prominence given to a sound, syllable or word by any vocal means and for any purpose whatever. *Emphasis* is logical stress for the purpose of expressing meaning and pertains primarily to words. *Accent* is syllabic stress, referring thus to the prominence of syllables. The adjectives *unstressed, unemphasized* and *unaccented* pertain to conditions of relative lack of prominence.[1]

Variety is the all-inclusive term we shall use for diversity in the techniques of spoken communication. Variety is all the skills of the writer to create continued interest, all the vocal tricks of the reader to capture attention, all of the physical movements of the speaker to drive home comprehension. Stress is just one means of achieving variety.

[1] Grant Fairbanks, *Voice and Articulation Drillbook* (New York: Harper & Brothers, 1940), p. 218.

108 · IN ACTION

STRESS

In all the selections you have read so far, certain key words have carried the burden of the thought. They were more important than the other words. They received the greater stress; the types of stress you used, your pauses, and your phrasing lent variety to the reading.

Stress can be given a word or an idea by any of the four controllable properties of the voice: loudness, time, quality, and pitch. Loudness is the easiest of these techniques to acquire. To give importance to an idea, we instinctively increase the loudness of our voice. The reader must guard against too much loudness for stress, rather than against too little. In your desire to stress key words, you are apt to punch too hard, and your phrases and sentences are apt to sound like a transoceanic broadcast—alternately loud and soft for no apparent reason.

#1 Emphasis is regarded by many readers as the all important thing; but it is really the least important. Any untrained voice can emphasize. The difficult thing to do well is the opposite of emphasis— the slighting of certain subordinate parts of discourse. Whatever is sufficiently implied, or should be taken for granted or has been anticipated, and, in short, all the outstanding relations of the main movement of thought and feeling, require to be slighted in expression, in order that they may not unduly reduce the prominence and distinction of the main movement. Only the well-trained voice can manage properly the background of what is presented; and if the background is properly managed, the foreground will generally have the requisite distinctness. When a reader endeavors to make everything tell, he makes nothing tell. Ambitious reading often defeats its own end.[2]

#2 A common, unexplainable fault in emphasis, even among experienced radio actors, is the prominence constantly given the personal pronoun. The letter "I," perhaps because it is a capital letter, or perhaps for some egocentric reason, is too frequently stressed, with a consequent distortion of the meaning intended. The word "you" is also too often pounded by radio actors. The truth is that the pronouns are sometimes more important and sometimes less important than other words in a sentence . . . .[3]

Loudness is the principal stress device used in the "interpretation

[2] Hiram Corson, *The Aims of Literary Study* (New York: The Macmillan Co., 1894), p. 123.
[3] Edwin Duerr, *Radio and Television Acting* (New York: Rinehart & Company, Inc., 1950), p. 139.

game." Shifting the stress to different words in the same sentence is a good game, and it can quickly show you how meaning can be altered by stress.

I thought you were dead.   (But no one else did.)
I *thought* you were dead.   (But I wasn't sure.)
I thought *you* were dead.   (You've been away such a long time.)
I thought you *were* dead.   (You looked as if you were.)
I thought you were *dead*.   (But you were just asleep.)

The "interpretation game" is provocative because in ordinary speech we tend to stress nouns and verbs and play down the other parts of speech.

Studies made of superior speakers show that the amount of stress given the different parts of speech prove that our tendencies are correct. Stress follows a set scheme, although thought content or type of material may affect the order occasionally.

Here is a tabulation of the parts of speech arranged in a descending scale of degrees of emphasis: nouns,[4] verbs, adverbs, adjectives, pronouns, prepositions, conjunctions, and articles.[5]

Remember that nouns, the names of things, receive the greatest stress in the speech of superior speakers, and verbs receive the next greatest. If you will bear in mind this tabulation of stress, you should have little difficulty with some of the common reader faults, faults that make the reader sound more "readery." Have you heard the poor reader who said, "He saw A fox," or "He came to THE car." Articles receive the least stress in the speech of good readers.

Conjunction hitting is a second common, unexplainable emphasis fault. Nine of ten inexperienced microphone performers insist on hitting the frequent "ands" and "buts" in their speeches. Not that these two words are never important; often they are. Not that these two words are not constantly given a wrong importance in actual, everyday conversations; often they are. Conjunction hitting is a bad, useless habit of speech.[6]

Stress by voice quality is a seldom-used device for understanding. It falls within the category of "vocal gimmicks." All readers use it occasionally; the parent and radio announcer use it often. Try reading "The Three Billy-Goats Gruff" or a "whispering power" commercial without using vocal quality for stress. All animal, mechanical, and fanciful sounds

---

[4] Studies of radio announcements show that verbs receive the greatest stress with nouns next. The rest of the list remains the same.
[5] Fairbanks, *op. cit.,* p. 219.
[6] Duerr, *op. cit.,* p. 141.

are stressed by means of vocal quality. The sensory attributes of words are indicated by vocal quality, but that is not so much a technique of stress as it is a technique of variety.

Stress by pitch is another "vocal gimmick." The circumflex stress of sarcasm and irony, the arbitrary use of low or high pitch for shock are common uses of pitch for stress. The radio announcer talking of Lifebuoy soap, and the parent reading of the little pig who cried all the way home are making use of pitch for stress.

Time stress is achieved principally by the prolongation of sounds. Impressiveness is given a sound by prolongation. It is used for effects of dignity and grandeur—but watch out—it is also used for effects of pathos and girlish enthusiasm. Dorothy Parker used it acidly in her monologues about "sweet" young things.

> I'll just get this chair and put it over—oops, I'm sorry I joggled the bed—put it over here, where you can see me. There. But first I want to fix your pillows before I get settled. Well, they certainly are *not* all right, Mona. After the way you've been twisting them and pulling them, these last few minutes. Now look, honey, I'll help you raise yourself ve-ry, ve-ry slo-o-ow-ly. Oh. Of course you can sit up by yourself, dear. Of course you can. Nobody ever said you couldn't. Nobody ever thought of such a thing. There now, your pillows are all smooth and lovely, and you lie right down again, before you hurt yourself. Now, isn't that better? Well, I should think it was![7]

While loudness, time quality, and pitch may be used separately for stress, most good, easy-to-listen-to readers use them in some combination to achieve a desired result. "This little pig's 'wee-wee-wee-wee-wee-wee' " is apt to be faster in time and higher in pitch than the story about the rest of the pigs. The dread troll of "The Three Billy-Goats Gruff" may have a voice that is slow, loud, and low-pitched, as well as hoarse or guttural.

VARIETY

Variety is essential in communicating ideas interestingly. Using variety may not affect your communication of the sense of an idea, but it does affect the interest with which the audience listens. You can communicate sense just by the proper use of phrasing, pauses, and emphasis; but the listener may not comprehend because he has lost interest in your unvaried

---

[7] From "Lady with a Lamp" in *The Portable Dorothy Parker,* reprinted by permission of The Viking Press, Inc., New York.

delivery. A monotonous delivery will deaden the listener's perceptions, permit his attention to wander, fail to convince him, and may lull him to sleep. In order to keep his attention, you must constantly restimulate him to listen. Variety is the sum of the vocal techniques you use.

A writer attempts to restimulate interest by illustration, anecdote, contrast, evidence, and all the other devices mentioned in Chapter 2. A speaker can restimulate interest by vocal variety and movement. Variety is possible through loudness, pitch, quality, and time. Using loudness to stress a word is the simplest and most common technique for achieving variety through loudness. The whisper, *sotto voce,* and shout are other means. Speakers today do not use a wide range of loudness, as they did twenty-five years ago. The movie sound track, the radio amplifier, and the public-address system have curtailed the use of loudness. Should a reader whisper for an effect, the constant loudness level at which the electronic device is set would boost his whisper up to the volume of his normal speech. You can recognize the reader's whisper only by the aspirate quality of his voice. Should the reader shout, the volume level would remain the same. You can recognize a shout only by the coincidental changes in the reader's voice quality. But the whisper and the shout are important means of giving variety to the reader's communication. When he is performing without the questionable aid of amplification, he should attempt the varied use of the wide scale of loudness, ranging from the whisper through the barely audible sound, the *sotto voce,* and normal speech to intoning, calling, and shouting.

Any reader can see the need for variations in loudness in these speeches of Bottom in *A Midsummer Night's Dream.*

> Let me play the lion too: I will roar, that I will do any man's heart good to hear me; I will roar, that I will make the duke say, 'Let him roar again, let him roar again.'
>
> . . .
>
> . . . but I will aggravate my voice so, that I will roar you as gently as any sucking dove; I will roar you an 'twere any nightingale.

There is occasion for like "aggravation" of the voice in much of the material the reader will encounter.

▶ *Variety in pitch.*   The reader usually errs in not making his inflectional variations sufficiently extensive. The voice has a possible speaking range as wide as the singing range, and both are capable of being extended. No singer would think of singing a selection that encompassed only one or two tones. He would expect the audience to be uninterested in such limited melodic variation. But many a speaker is willing to appear before an audience with a comparably circumscribed speaking range and is surprised when the listener does not react favorably. Pitch variety can be achieved through voice training.

Whitestone Photo.

The radio man reads aloud.

▶ *Variety in quality.* Variation of the quality of the voice is a much needed, if often neglected, technique in reading. All sensory perceptions are recreated by vocal quality. The softness of the dove and the fierceness of the lion in Bottom's speech can be indicated by the vocal quality used on the words "dove" and "lion." The "harshness" of a cigarette or the "smooth, melt-in-your-mouth quality" of some food can be conveyed to a listener through vocal quality. The Biblical statement,

> Though I speak with the tongues of men and of angels, and have not charity, I am become as sounding brass, or a tinkling cymbal,

depends on vocal quality for much of its inherent variety.

What are some of the qualities possible to the voice?

1. The aspirate quality. It is distinguished by the absence of tone

and by breathiness and is most commonly used in the whisper. It is also used to characterize gentle, ineffectual people.

2. Guttural quality. It is distinguished by a low pitch. It is used for depicting unsavory and loathsome sensations. It is also used to characterize unsavory and loathsome persons. The giants and wolves and bad men in children's literature usually are characterized as having deep, growly voices. The same quality, exaggerated, is used for comic effects. In fact, any vocal quality is comic when exaggerated.

3. Raspy quality. It is distinguished by harshness and a sense of strain. It is used for depicting harsh, tense sensory images, such as the *bitter, biting words*. It is also used to characterize persons under mental or emotional strain, or persons of innate meanness.

4. Strident quality. It is distinguished by a higher pitch than that used for the raspy quality, but the sound is equally harsh and strained. It is used for depicting the sensation of insistence. We speak of a strident voice as being "nerve-racking." It is used to characterize dominating, insistent persons who are under strain because of their ambitions or their warped desires.

5. Hoarse quality. It is distinguished by a rough, uncomfortable sound. It is a sound that makes the listener want to clear the speaker's throat. It is used for depicting sensations of weakness, illness, and dissipation. It is used to characterize the ill or dissipated person. It is often used to express extreme passion, when the emotion is of almost pathological intensity.

6. Metallic quality. It is distinguished by a brassy sound, as if the voice were being reflected by a tin pan. It is used to depict sense images of hardness, and metal-like characteristics; for example, the *clanging* of a fire bell. It is used to characterize brash, overly forward persons.

7. Orotund quality. It is distinguished by a too round, too firm, too fully packed sound. It is used to depict sense images of overripeness and fulsomeness. It is used also to characterize the pompous, officious, self-satisfied person.

8. Muffled quality. It is distinguished by a low pitch and a hot-potato-in-the-mouth sound. It is used to depict sense images of softness and mushiness. It is also used to characterize persons of indecisive manner —the Casper Milquetoast.

9. Whiny quality. It is distinguished by a thin, nasal, reedy tone. It is used to depict small, unpleasant, unmasculine sensations. It is used to characterize the unpleasant, insignificant, immature person.

10. Pleasant quality. This quality is observable when none of the other qualities are present. It is distinguished by clarity of tone, full

resonance, and discriminating modulation. It is used to depict sensations of beauty, affection, and charm. It is used to characterize heroes, heroines, and whatever other pleasant people there are.

All these vocal qualities should be at the command of the reader who wishes to convey the connotative implications of his words as well as the denotative ideas. The use of them can add infinite variety to the reader's presentation. For further discussion of communicating connotations see Chapter 7, Communicating Emotions, because many of the attributes of vocal quality are emotional in nature.

▶ *Variety in time.* There are three ways of varying time: (1) the use of pauses of varying length, (2) the use of sounds of varying length, (3) the use of variations in rhythm.

That pauses of varying lengths would add variety to reading seems most obvious, yet it is frequently ignored by the reader. Think of pauses as the musician thinks of rests: this measure has an eighth-note rest, another has a half-note rest, and this measure is nothing but rest. Shaw recognized the relationship of reading and music in this comment.

> In playing Shakespear, play *to* the lines, *through* the lines, on the lines, but never between the lines. There simply isn't time for it. You would not stick five bars rest into a Beethoven symphony to pick up your drumsticks; and similarly you must not stop the Shakespear orchestra for business. Nothing short of a procession or a fight should make anything so extraordinary as a silence during a Shakespearean performance.[8]

Sounds of varying length are supplied us by the writer, by the persons who invented words, and by our desire to be understood. Short, chopped sounds—staccato—and long, smooth sounds—legato—add variety to speaking because of the variations in the time of sound formation.

Each of us has a distinctive speech rhythm that is the outgrowth of our total physical, social, emotional, and educational experience. Writing has its distinctive rhythms, too.

> Rhythm is one of the principal translators between dream and reality. Rhythm might be described as to the world of sound, what light is to the world of sight. It shapes and gives new meaning. Rhythm was described by Schopenhauer as melody deprived of its pitch.[9]

[8] Christopher St. John, ed., *Ellen Terry and Bernard Shaw* (New York: G. P. Putnam's Sons, 1931), p. 59. Reprinted by permission of The Public Trustee and The Society of Authors, London, and Reinhardt & Evans, London.

[9] Edith Sitwell, "Some Notes on My Poetry," *The Canticle of the Rose* (New York: Vanguard Press, Inc., 1949), p. xi.

Your job as a communicator is to adjust your rhythms to the rhythms of your selection—no small task. Your job, also, is to make positive use of rhythm for interest. An acceleration in rate can quicken the listener's interest. A slowing down in rate makes the ideas more momentous. A change of pace is important for variety and interest.

Here are three examples varying in rhythm: first, a selection with a slow rate; second a selection with an accelerating rate and an abrupt change of pace in the last line; and third, a poem with a moderate rate in the first four lines and a quick change of pace in the fifth.

#1   A man's life should be a stately march to a sweet but unheard music, and when to his fellows it shall seem irregular and inharmonious, he will only be stepping to a livelier measure, or his nicer ear hurry him into a thousand symphonies and concordant variations. There will be no halt ever, but at most a marching on his post, or such a pause as is richer than any sound, when the melody runs into such depth and wildness as to be no longer heard, but simplicity consented to with the whole life and being. He will take a false step never, even in the most arduous times, for then the music will not fail to swell into greater sweetness and volume, and itself rule the movement it inspired.[10]

#2   How can a man sit down and quietly pare his nails, while the earth goes gyrating ahead amid such a din of sphere music, whirling him along about her axis some twenty-four thousand miles between sun and sun, but mainly in a circle some two millions of miles actual progress? And then such a hurly-burly on the surface—wind always blowing—now a zephyr, now a hurricane—tides never idle, ever fluctuating—no rest for Niagara, but perpetual ran-tan on those limestone rocks—and then that summer simmering which our ears are used to, which would otherwise be christened confusion worse confounded, but is now ironically called 'silence audible,' and above all the incessant tinkering named 'hum of industry', the hurrying to and fro and confused jabbering of men. Can man do less than get up and shake himself?[11]

#3   If all be true that I do think,
          There are five reasons we should drink:
          Good wine—a friend—or being dry
            Or lest we should be by and by—
            Or any other reason why.[12]

[10] Henry David Thoreau, *Journal,* ed. Bradford Tarrey and Francis H. Allen (Boston: Houghton Mifflin Company, 1949), 14 vols., June 30, 1840.

[11] *Ibid.,* March 6, 1838.

[12] Henry Aldrich translation of *Causae Bibendi,* by John Sirmond.

Below is an example to test your variety in pitch, volume, and time. To get this right you must watch several things: (1) don't start too loud or you'll blow your top; (2) the pauses must be in rhythm with the rest of the piece and they must vary in length; (3) there is a gradual acceleration of rate, along with a rise in pitch and an increase in volume; (4) there must be a marked rhythm; imagine the emcee in the wings swaying to the beat, waiting for your build-up to explode him onto the stage; don't trip him, don't stagger him; don't deflate him; you're the springboard on which he is bouncing higher and higher and higher and off!

```
(INTRODUCE COMEDY SHOW AND M.C.)
     The following program will be heard in Canada
through the facilities of the Canadian Broadcasting
Corporation.
(PAUSE)
From Coast to Coast -- it's Club Matinee!
(PAUSE)
With Fran Allison and Johnny Johnston!
(PAUSE)
Frankie Rullo and the Vagabonds!
(PAUSE)
Rex Maupin's Music -- and yours truly_____.
(PAUSE)
And now, friends, here he comes --- your Tuesday
master of ceremonies; Baltimore's gift to network
radio -- and SHAME on Baltimore.  It's that little
man with the close-cropped hair -- that hair that
almost isn't there, Gus Glutz.[13]
```

If you did that right, Gus came on to thunderous applause. He was the climax of your introduction. To achieve a climax you may have used all the ingredients of emphasis and variety: pitch, volume, time, and quality. Did you rasp out "Gus Glutz" in a Betty Hutton coal-car-unloading sound? That is the way you could have achieved stress through quality. Climax requires the total use of all your skills to drive home your point, arouse to action, or demand belief.

Your reading, for the most part, is a preamble to the climax, and that climax is the consummate statement of the reader's intention. If your reading follows the pattern of structure discussed on page 25, the climax is the end of the progression of ideas, unless there is a specifically conceived anticlimax. The Clifton Fadiman excerpt that concludes this chapter has an anticlimax.

[13] Announcer's audition, National Broadcasting Company.

Anti-climax is allowable only when the implications of the actual climax are too far-reaching to be fully absorbed at that moment.[14]

Usually, as you approach a climax the rate increases, the pitch mounts, and the volume increases. When it is reached, there is a pause, and then the reader works for a finale rhythm: a pitch, volume, and time beat that bring the reading to a close. In the theater this finale rhythm must be so sufficiently accentuated that the closing or dropping of the curtain seems the logical final beat to the preceding sound pattern. You have heard the finale rhythms of classical music. The speaker needs some similar rhythmic pattern to conclude his presentation. Without such a finale, the listener feels uncomfortable—left up in the air. In the theater an ending without a finale rhythm calls for a "curtain hook," a symbolic tool needed to get the curtain down.

Work for a finale rhythm on the first example below, the conclusion to Lincoln's famous Second Inaugural Address; and for climax and finale rhythm on the second example, a contemporary speech on business trends. The third selection has a climax, and an absolutely necessary anti-climax. Try and get all the variety you can in reading each of these.

#1   With malice toward none; with charity for all; with firmness in the right, as God gives us to see the right, let us strive on to finish the work we are in; to bind up the nation's wounds; to care for him who shall have borne the battle, and for his widow, and his orphan— to do all which may achieve and cherish a just and lasting peace among ourselves, and with all nations.

#2   American management has a wonderful story to tell, but it seems obvious that it has far to go in getting that story out to the people. Continuity and repetition are valuable aides in getting the major points across. Spasmodic and scattered efforts are of course far less effective.

If we are to preserve our American system and the democracy on which it rests, we must maintain our huge productive capacity with its high level of employment. The productive machine is at once the envy and the hope of all the people of the world.

If our society is to realize in fullest measure the great potentials of this machine, management must help men to understand that the "Security" they all want is not the static kind that comes through closed shops, seniority, feather-bedding, and government guarantees. These things will, in fact, guarantee only insecurity.

[14] Worthington Miner, "Directing a Play: The Complete Procedure," in John Gassner, *Producing the Play* with the *New Scene Technician's Handbook*, by Philip Barber (New York: The Dryden Press, Inc., 1941), p. 223.

Rather, we must continuously demonstrate to people that the things that really make for true "Security" are:

Productivity and low unit cost
Research
Aggressive advertising and selling
Fair profits and
Team play.

The key fact is that the United States with less than 7 per cent of the world's people now produces almost half of the world's manufactured goods and uses nearly all it makes. The qualities which have enabled Americans to perform this miracle still live in them. And, as Herbert Hoover stated in a recent address, "It is not yet too late to summon these qualities in our people."

This is an enormous challenge and yet not beyond the power of the communications instruments at management's disposal. It is a matter of deciding the job is worth doing, and then appropriating the time and money and manpower to do it.[15]

#3 Mr. Jones was, as I have indicated, a Shakespeare addict, but of a highly specialized sort. He was really familiar, in an unintelligent way, with all of Shakespeare, but his particular interest lay in those passages of an inflammatory, lickerish, and erotic nature. He had, for example, memorized the whole of Venus and Adonis, a rather long poem. It was my duty, book in hand, to listen to him recite. It was mildly fantastic: the locked door with its furniture barricade, Mr. Jones hopping about, Martini in hand, quoting, in a voice that mingled a shriek, a snarl, and a whine, some torrid passage, and myself, crowded into a corner, doing my best to handle the old gentleman tactfully. Naturally, he would stumble from time to time, but woe to me if I prompted him! His emendations of Shakespeare were extraordinary but I soon found it expedient to let them stand.

On Saturdays we would repair to the golf links. I had two duties there. One was to keep shouting, as he addressed the ball, "Keep your head down!" The other was to listen to him recite his favorite passages of Shakespeare between strokes. The caddy, had he possessed any Elizabethan vocabulary, would surely have been shocked.

My association with Mr. Jones must have been satisfactory to him, or else his love of the bard gradually deepened, for one day he proposed to me an additional duty; that I accompany him downtown in his car every morning, attended by good old Shakespeare. As I got five dollars an hour for these services (ten on Saturday, for

---

[15] Hugh Rusch, *Guides for Management from Current Opinion Trends* (Princeton: Opinion Research Corporation, 1950), pp. 56–58. From "The Public Opinion Index for Industry" of the Opinion Research Corporation.

some reason) and as I was receiving a free education in a great classic, I made no objection.

Now part of the story is somewhat indelicate. I must warn you that Mr. Jones, like many elderly people, was troubled with an inconvenient weakness of the bladder. In the morning we would start out in the car, Shakespeare going full blast. The drive took about forty minutes. But forty minutes just about represented the limit of Mr. Jones' endurance. The last five minutes of the drive may have sounded something like this:

"Now quick desire—O God!—hath caught the yielding prey—how much longer is it?—and glutton-like she feeds, yet never filleth—God Almighty, you're driving like a damn turtle—where was I?—Her lips—her lips are conquerors, his lips obey—Lord, how everybody makes me suffer!—his lips obey—OW!—Paying what ransom the insulter willeth—hurry, you confounded slow-coach!—O Lord!"

Shakespeare was never intoned in stranger circumstances. Sometimes art won and sometimes nature.[16]

► *Conclusion.* It takes skill to communicate your ideas. You will need techniques of phrasing, inflection, pause, stress, and variety to completely communicate those ideas. They are all techniques that can be acquired.

[16] Reprinted from *Reading I've Liked,* by Clifton Fadiman, p. xxxiii. Copyright, 1941, by Simon and Schuster, Inc.

· 7 ·

Communicating Emotions

❖⟩⟩❖⟩⟩❖⟩⟩❖⟩⟩❖⟩⟩❖⟩⟩❖⟩⟩❖⟩⟩❖⟩⟩❖◇◀⟨◇⟨◇⟨◇⟨◇⟨◇⟨◇⟨◇⟨◇⟨◇❖

1. Emotion is a quality shared equally by both sexes; as many men as women marry.

2. Booing the umpire, cheering the touchdown, and grousing about taxes result from emotions just as surely as love scenes, death-bed repentances, and tears.

3. Unbridled emotions are shown on the caucus-room floors of Congress as well as on the cutting-room floors of Hollywood.

4. Honest emotion is as easy to convey as honest thought; it is more convincing than feigned emotion.

These comments on emotion seem necessary because so many beginning readers revolt when the word *emotion* is mentioned. Unfortunately, here in America, the word *emotion* all too frequently connotes flamboyance and lack of restraint. The average reader thinks he must chew scenery to show emotion. Nothing is further from the truth; nothing embarrasses an audience more.

The scientist at his laboratory sink is just as emotional as the Hollywood starlet in her Labrador mink. He feels more than he shows; she shows more than she feels. She and her kind have given emotion a bad name. They have forced the average person back into further corners of his puritanical repressions. Emotions have come to be associated with sprees, with breaking the rules, with shore leaves and liberties.

In this chapter we will try to understand genuine emotions and we will investigate techniques of communicating them so that the listener is moved to supply our wants.

120

In order to accomplish adequately the aims of this chapter it will not be necessary for the reader to point a wavering finger at "My Last Duchess," nor to rub away the cuticle trying for Lady Macbeth's last "damned spot." He will not have to carry "A Message to Garcia" nor chirrup "Little Boy Blue."

You may be asked, however, to let yourself go as completely as *Lutie*. (See practice material.)

Each of us has experienced every emotion there is. We have known fear, terror, hysteria; we have known ecstasy, exaltation, love; we have known anger, hate, frenzy; lust, loathing, cupidity.

> If you are a sensitive and normal human being, all life is open and familiar to you. After all, poets and playwrights are human, too. If they find experience in their lives to use, why shouldn't you? But you will have to use your imagination; you can never tell where you will find the thing you are after.
>
> THE CREATURE: All right, suppose I have to play murder. I have never murdered anybody. How shall I find it?
>
> I: Oh, why do actors always ask me about murder? The younger they are the more murders they want to act. All right, you have never murdered anybody. Have you ever camped?
>
> THE CREATURE: Yes.
>
> I: Were there any mosquitoes around?
>
> THE CREATURE: It was in New Jersey.
>
> I: Did they annoy you? Did you follow one among them with your eyes and ears and hate until the beast landed on your forearm? And did you slap your forearm cruelly without even thinking of the hurt to yourself—with only the wish to . . . .
>
> THE CREATURE: To kill the beast.
>
> I: There you are. A good sensitive artist doesn't need any more than that to play Othello and Desdemona's final scene. The rest is the work of magnification, imagination and belief.[1]

The author, like us, has experienced all emotional states. He attempts to capture those emotions in his writing, and if he can make the reader feel as he has felt, his job of communication is complete. The reader's job, then, is to take the author's script and reinfuse the emotion, so that the listener can feel the experience as the author revealed it and as the reader himself felt it.

The writer uses words, images, and the total effect of those words and images—mood—to convey his emotions. His medium is type, a set

[1] From *Acting: The First Six Lessons,* by Richard Boleslavsky (New York: Theatre Arts Books, 1933), pp. 43–44. Quoted with the permission of the publishers.

of inanimate symbols. We have an easier task than he, for we will use the living mechanism to recreate emotion

CONNOTATION

Words and phrases have connotative as well as denotative meanings. Your scripts are filled with action verbs and color words that imply more than their usual dictionary definitions. These implications are associative and emotional in nature.

Take the word *grog* for example. Denotatively, it means an unsweetened mixture of liquor and water. Connotatively, it may mean barefoot seamen on the blood-splattered decks of a sailing vessel; or pirates bound for Treasure Island—"Drink and the devil had done for the rest"; or it may mean the story from which the drink got its name. The English admiral Edward Vernon issued an order to dilute the sailors' rum. He was nicknamed "Old Grog" by his men because of the grogram cloak he always wore, so the drink he ordered was "Old Grog's drink," and eventually just grog.

Take the word *excruciating*. Denotatively, it means torturing that is agonizingly painful. Connotatively, it may mean to you a session in the dentist's chair, or an earache, or stomach cramps, or any extreme suffering you have known; or it may mean Christ's agony on the cross: *ex*—out + *cruciare,* to crucify.

From these two examples you can see that a word has several meanings. A story can be told by a word alone. In fact, words are stories; "fossilized poetry," someone has called them. The more you know of words, their derivations, their literal meanings and their associative meanings, the more emotional values you can reinfuse into your reading.

Words can have a beauty in themselves. Part of that beauty is in their sound; part of that beauty is in their evocative melody; part of that beauty is in their memories. Thomas Wolfe, who loved sounds and words as few other twentieth-century Americans have, wrote part of this chapter for me in his book *Of Time and the River*. Speaking of the homesickness of the American in foreign lands, he wrote that the expatriate hungered

> First for the thunder of imperial names, the names of men and battles, the names of places and great rivers, the mighty names of the States. The name of The Wilderness; and the names of Antietam, Chancellorsville, Shiloh, Bull Run, Fredericksburg, Cold Harbor, the Wheat Fields, Ball's Bluff, and the Devil's Den; the names of Cowpens, Brandywine and Saratoga; of Death Valley, Chickamauga,

and the Cumberland Gap. The names of the Nantahalahs, the Bad Lands, the Painted Desert, the Yosemite, and the Little Big Horn; the names of Yancey and Cabarrus counties; and the terrible name of Hatteras.

Then, for the continental thunder of the States: the names of Montana, Texas, Arizona, Colorado, Michigan, Maryland, Virginia, and the two Dakotas; the names of Oregon and Indiana, of Kansas and the rich Ohio; the powerful name of Pennsylvania, and the name of Old Kentucky, the undulance of Alabama, the names of Florida and North Carolina.

In the red-oak thickets, at the break of day, long hunters lay for bear—the rattle of arrows in laurel leaves, the war-cries round the painted buttes, and the majestic names of the Indian Nations: the Pawnees, the Algonquins, the Iroquois, the Comanches, the Blackfeet, the Seminoles, the Cherokees, the Sioux, the Hurons, the Mohawks, the Navajos, the Utes, the Omahas, the Onondagas, the Chippewas, the Crees, the Chickasaws, the Arapahoes, the Catawbas, the Dakotas, the Apaches, the Croatans, and the Tuscaroras; the names of Powhattan and Sitting Bull; and the name of the Great Chief, Rain-In-The-Face.

. . . the names of the mighty rails that bind the nation, the wheeled thunder of the names that net the continent: the Pennsylvania, the Union Pacific, the Santa Fe, the Baltimore and Ohio, the Chicago and Northwestern, the Southern, the Louisiana and Northern, the Seaboard Air Line, the Chicago, Milwaukee and Saint Paul, the Lackawanna, the New York, New Haven and Hartford, the Florida East Coast, the Rock Island, and the Denver and Rio Grande.

. . .

Finally, the names of the great rivers that are flowing in the darkness (Sweet Thames flow gently till I end my song).

By the waters of life, by time, by time: the names of the great mouths, the mighty maws, the vast, wet, coiling, never-glutted and unending snakes that drink the continent. Where, sons of men, and in what other land, will you find others like them, and where can you match the mighty music of their names? The Monongahela, the Colorado, the Rio Grande, the Columbia, the Tennessee, the Hudson (Sweet Thames!); the Kennebec, the Rappahannock, the Delaware, the Penobscot, Wabash, the Chesapeake, the Swannanoa, the Indian River, the Niagara (Sweet Afton!); the Saint Lawrence, the Susquehanna. The Tombigbee, the Nantahala, the French Broad, the Chattahoochee, the Arizona, and the Potomac (Father Tiber!)—these are a few of their princely names, these are a few of their great, proud, glittering names, fit for the immense and lonely land they inhabit.[2]

[2] Thomas Wolfe, *Of Time and the River* (New York: Charles Scribner's Sons, 1935), pp. 866–868.

IMAGES

Word groups form images. They are created by metaphors, similes, personifications, or any of the other figures of speech. Still confused about metaphors and similes? "A simile is a comparison proclaimed as such, whereas a metaphor is a tacit comparison made by the substitution of the compared notion for the one to be illustrated."[3] Here is an example of each by Don Marquis.[4]

"Poetry is what Milton saw when he went blind." That's a metaphor.

"Publishing a volume of verse is like dropping a rose-petal down the Grand Canyon and waiting for the echo." That's a simile. The word *like* in the comparison makes it unmistakable.

In the practice material you will find a group of selections filled with images that should have associative values for you. Do the authors catch moments out of your own experience? Is there a sensation of yours brought sharply into your memory by the author's words? If there is, can you recreate it for the listener?

You should recreate through your imagination the sensations suggested by the words and phrases you read. You should see in your mind's eye the picture the author sees. You should hear the sounds and smell the odors, feel the tactile and kinesthetic sensations embodied in the script. You must recognize the image and translate it into your own experience. Just as you must understand an idea before the listener can, so you must *sense* before the listener can.

Al Siegel, one of the most successful singing coaches employed by the motion-picture industry, makes some suggestions to singers that are valuable to the reader, too. Here is his advice on handling images and emotional material.

> "Now listen, Alice," he said; "I'll play it over. You talk the first verse. Then sing the chorus. It's a sad song about a boy and a girl in the lamplight. You stand over there by the window and watch the sun setting into the Hudson. That will get you in the right mood."
>
> . . .
>
> "You got to tell the story," he said. "You got to paint a picture. You got to feel as if you were right there in the lamplight with your fiancé, or someone . . . .
>
> "Keep delivering the story of the song, and keep your singing sec-

---

[3] H. W. Fowler, *A Dictionary of Modern English Usage* (Oxford: At the Clarendon Press, 1949), p. 536.
[4] Don Marquis, "The Sun Dial," New York *Sun*.

Photograph by Fred Plaut.

The poet reads aloud.

ondary to the story. Now here, where it says, 'a boy, a girl, a lamplight,' you got your punch line. Sing 'boy' strong. Don't ever senti-
mentalize men too much. They don't like it. Then sing 'girl' soft,
because girls are always soft and sort of clinging. In songs, I mean.
And sing 'lamplight' very soft. It's lamplight, not electric light. Soft,
see?

. . . "explode the word 'bump' when you come to 'they bumped
into each other' . . . they didn't slip or slide, did they?"

. . .

"The audience which listens to popular songs wants to be moved—
and you can do this best by delivering the words effectively."

"Most people remember tunes by words, anyhow. Many musically
cultured people can't hum over an operatic aria unless they know
the words to start them off, and Sigmund Spaeth, the tune detective,
suggests making up words for symphonic themes as an aid to remembering them. That should give you an idea of how important lyrics
are to songs."

. . .

"So, I figured that if a singer wants to entertain an audience, she's
got to sing in English, and she's got to sing so everyone can under-

stand her. I think of a song as a one-act play, with the singer as director, producer, backer, and all the actors rolled up together. She should tell the story of her song just as effectively as she can, with all the tricks of the stage—timing, emotion, drama, suspense and climax . . . ."[5]

MOOD

The total effect of an author's words and images is the mood he creates. It is part of the reader's job in the communication of emotion to establish that mood for the listener. The mood may be one of light playfulness or one of solemnity. It may be nostalgic, exalted, satiric, rapturous, vengeful, condemnatory, whimsical, hopeless.

An author conveys mood by his choice of images, his choice of the sounds forming the words that impart those images, and his use of rhythms. Since images connote as well as denote, the skillful author selects images that connote similar emotional states. If he is trying to create a mood of solemnity, he does not include images that might connote gaiety and vivacity.

Suddenly the notes of the deep-laboring organ burst upon the ear, falling with doubled and redoubled intensity, and rolling, as it were, huge billows of sound. How well do their volume and grandeur accord with this mighty building! With what pomp do they swell through its vast vaults, and breathe their awful harmony through these caves of death, and make the silent sepulcher vocal!—and now they rise in triumphant acclamation, heaving higher and higher their accordant notes and piling sound on sound.—And now they pause, and the soft voices of the choir break out into sweet gushes of melody; they soar aloft and warble along the roof, and seem to play about these lofty vaults like the pure airs of heaven. Again the pealing organ heaves its thrilling thunders, compressing air into music, and rolling it forth upon the soul. What long-drawn cadences! What solemn sweeping concords! It grows more and more dense and powerful—it fills the vast pile, and seems to jar the very walls—the ear is stunned—the senses are overwhelmed. And now it is winding up in full jubilee—it is rising from the earth to heaven—the very soul seems rapt away, and floated upwards on this swelling tide of harmony![6]

[5] William A. H. Birnie, "How's Your Umph?" *American Magazine,* CXXVII (February, 1939), 28–29.

[6] Washington Irving, "Essay on Westminster Abbey," *The Sketch Book* (Chicago: Scott, Foresman & Company, 1906), p. 190.

The Irving selection is also an example of the author's choice of sounds as an aid in creating mood. He has chosen words comprising sounds that reinforce the imagery and the mood. For this description of the sound of an organ he chose words with long vowel sounds: laboring, burst, doubled, intensity, rolling, billows, volume, grandeur, accord, mighty, building. He might have chosen words with like meanings but with shorter sounds that would have shattered the mood, not reinforced it: working, erupted, increased, loudness, pushing, wavelets, and so forth.

The Irving selection also makes use of rhythm to further amplify the mood. The cadence of the long vowels is not interrupted by sharp, unrhythmic sounds; the cadence of the sentences is as measured, as swelling, as uninterrupted as the sound. In combining these three elements—images, sounds, and rhythm—the author has created a mood that the reader must recreate. The technique of so doing is implied in the analysis of the author's technique: search out the connotations of the imagery, listen for the sounds, and feel for the rhythm.

"EMOTING"

Most of our discussion so far has been *about* emotions: recall, imagery, mood. The emotions we have dealt with have all been reflective in character; you have been asked to do very little "emoting" yourself. There are several reasons for this. In the first place, you don't swim the English Channel before you learn to dog-paddle; in other words, you learn simple skills before you attempt the complex. Secondly, the act of reading with its convention of the manuscript places you in the position of recreating emotion rather than creating it. Thirdly, the intensity of the American emotional climate is low—we shy away from displays of emotion. And finally, the emotion inherent in the manuscript is sufficient for most listeners.

▶ *From the simple to the complex.* The principal advantage in this approach is that the learner feels secure when he attempts no more than he can do. He knows what he is striving for and can concentrate on it. The steps from dog-paddling to the Australian crawl in the communication of emotion are these.

1. Understand the material. This you can do.

2. Recognize the author's techniques for communication of emotion. This you can do.

3. Recreate the author's emotional intent. This you can do.

4. Move an audience emotionally.

Here is one way to approach the fourth step. What happened to you when you read the author's writing is what you wish to have happen to the audience. You stand in the place of the author; you recreate for the audience as the author recreated for you. When you read the selection and were moved by it, the author's words and images created freshly in you the experience he had captured and set on paper. Now, when you read to an audience, you recreate with your voice (and to a lesser extent with your face and body) the author's experience so that it may come into fresh being in the mind and spirit of the listener.

► *Recreation of emotions.* When you are mad and you "chew somebody out," you do it ad libitum and there is nothing to constrain the free flow of your emotions save the thickness of your office walls, the size of the person who inflames your anger, and certain social conventions. When you are mad and you are using a manuscript, you don't have to worry about office walls or the size of your annoyer, but the social conventions create an even greater barrier. The first barrier is the immediacy of the emotion. Your audience knows you are angry, but they know the anger did not well up just at that moment. It first flared at the original stimulus; you recalled it when writing your speech (anger once removed); you voiced it when reading the manuscript (anger twice removed). If, while you are reading, you should voice your anger with the vigor and abandon you felt at the original stimulus, your audience would be embarrassed for you; you would be out of character as a reader.

The reader's communication of emotion is different from the actor's, although both use many of the same tools. The actor is trying to create the impression of the "first time." He is not Jimmy Stewart, but Mr. Somebody Else. Mr. Somebody Else gets mad at Mrs. Else and tells her off. The actor tries to achieve the effect that his anger is inspired just at that moment and that what he is saying is springing unrehearsed to his lips. We, in our "willing suspension of disbelief," accept this convention of the theater. The reader, however, is not Mr. Somebody Else. He remains himself and his words are not unrehearsed. The actor's attention is on the immediate situation; the reader's attention is on his prepared material and the audience.

The listener accepts the convention of the manuscript and the reader's part in that convention. The listener's reactions are colored by two other conventions. First, he knows that the speaker's material is shaped into some sort of order. Second, he knows that the material serves some purpose. Because of these conventions, the listener is at least once removed from the reader's emotion. You do not want to make the listener angry at yourself, you want to direct his anger to the cause of your emotion, you want him to understand why you are angry. He is a listener, not a participant in your emotion.

> But in our reaction to a work of art there is something more— there is the consciousness of purpose, the consciousness of a peculiar relation of sympathy with the man who made this thing in order to arouse precisely the sensations we experience.[7]

▶ *The American emotional climate.* The American tendency is to shy away from emotional displays. Sales-promotion men have learned that playing upon emotions is dangerous; the client can be "oversold." One of the first rules a new prosecuting attorney must learn is not to "overprosecute"; a jury will begin to react in favor of the defendant. We feel deeply, as deeply as the people of any other nation, but we don't like to "slop over." We prefer our expressed emotions leavened with irony and belittlement. No matter how serious the moment, we seek the light touch, the wry, self-mocking deflation. We accept as our standard of heroic speech the apocryphal "Nuts!" of the Bastogne commander, rather than McArthur's rhetoric.

▶ *Emotion inherent in the manuscript.* We Americans like to make our own decisions on the emotional merits of a situation. We don't want someone else to force us to be sad or grave or jubilant or ecstatic. We like to feel that the emotion is inherent in the situation and that the reader does not need to do anything extra to bring out the values. Most ministers have learned that their congregations want the marriage ceremony read effectively, but nothing more. The listeners will supply the emotion. The service for the dead must be solemn, but restrained; the mourners will supply the emotion. The radio newsman (Winchell excepted) is to read the news and comment on it, if he must, but the listener will supply the emotional values. Our humorists for the most part are the dead-pan variety. They tell the story; you laugh at it.

The one near-emotion we do allow ourselves is exaggeration. That fits in with our national character. The tall tale is humorous, it is self-conscious, and it allows the listener to be belittling.

▶ *Conclusion.* Part of your job as a reader is to recreate for the listener the emotional content of your selection. Your communication is incomplete if you bring out only the meanings of a selection; you must evoke also the emotional quality. This you can do by sensing and recreating the connotative quality of the words, the imagery of the language,

---

[7] Roger Fry, *Vision and Design* (London: Chatto & Windus, 1929), p. 30. Reprinted with the permission of the author's executors and Chatto & Windus.

and the moods of the selection. You must feel in order that the listener may be moved.

EXERCISE

(*This is a tall tale; a bravura piece. Caution: don't let sound and fury take the place of true emotion.*)

Roadside[8]

TEXAS: I wasn't borned in the ordinary way.
(*Waggishly.*) I'd a-thought you'd knowed that by lookin' at me.
(*Lyrically.*) No, sir! I'm gonna tell you jist the way it was—Way out on the Texas prairie jist this side the tall mountains set a small cabin made outa oak. And in that cabin, set a man and womern with a growed gal as purty as purty could be! Name was Liza. Mornin' came, she'd hop on her pony to ride the range, her old pap and mammy a-runnin' after to stop her. "Come on back, Liza," they'd say—"the plains is full of coyotes. Them big old growly mountain b'ars has started to sharpen up their spring teeth." And seein' she didn't answer, they'd say, "Don't go fur, then, and come back soon." And away she'd go! Greased lightnin'! Dynamite on wings! Her pony stretched hisself out like a tentpole headed West! When she was seven mile and half away, she'd stop and look around. Now a funny thing! She had rid into a valley whur a river used to flow in the year one. The tall grasses stood up like trees. A quair kind of a roarin' like lions come from some'eres along the tall grass. She'd git off her horse, look around, suspicious like, and go into that valley on foot. She'd stay all day. Who did she see thar? Whut did she do thar? Fer it soon was evident's the nose on yer face, she was gonna produce a infant. Who was its pappy? Whut kind of a roarin', hell-shootin', brawny big mountain of a man was she a-consortin' with? Somebody! With a whole valley fer his house, and a sky fer a roof over him! A nameless wonder of a giant with all out of doors to call his front room. A secret man that roared when he talked and shuck the ground like a earthquake rumblin'. Fin'lly one night—Liza lay in her pappy's cabin. Wild hosses came a-nickerin' and trompin' around. Great big b'ars as high as hills begin to growl sump'n fierce. All of a sudden, there was a crash and a bang and a clatter! Thunder and hail and lightnin', hell f'ar and brimstone. The cabin whur Liza lay cracked itself wide open from stem to stern, beam-end to beam-end, hind-end to gullet! And when the smoke cleared away, out I stepped, full-size, dressed to kill, in a ten-gallon hat, boots and chaps, a gun in ary hand, and both guns a-poppin'! And that's how I got started.

[8] Lynn Riggs, *Roadside* (New York: Samuel French, Inc., 1930), p. 46.

· 8 ·

Projecting Personality

If you will look up the word *personality* in the dictionary, you will find that it stems from the Latin *persona,* which means literally "player's mask." The word has come a long way in meaning since it was coined. In fact, today, a desirable personality for a reader is the antithesis of the idea of a masked actor. Today, personality means the quality of being a person, being individual.

Personality traits are both positive and negative. The reader who would be successful in his task of communication must have as many of the positive personality traits as possible. It is easier to gain attention if your personality is arresting; it is easier to win understanding if you are friendly and sincere; it is easier to win belief if you are vital.

Your success as a communicator is affected by your personality; your personality can be affected by your study of communication. The study and practice of good speech can help you acquire desirable personality traits.

When you appear before an audience, your personality is judged as a whole. Audiences form likes and dislikes, and they find it hard to state their reasons why. They form an impression based upon your total effect, the sum of all your personality traits. If that impression is unfavorable, you should do something about yourself. If that impression is favorable, your task of communication is much easier.

Let's analyze the factors that operate in an audience's reaction to you.

131

APPEARANCE

The audience makes its first decisions about you from your appearance. What do you look like? How are you dressed? How do you stand? How do you move? What is your manner? What sort of personality do you project when someone looks at you?

What do you look like? Thank heavens you no longer have to be pretty to satisfy an audience. All an audience expects of you now is that you be clean, well groomed, and not overly made up. You can't be too clean, but you can look as if you had just come from the barber's chair which may affect your audience adversely. You can be too well groomed; you can be judged to be vain and finicky if you are overcareful about the part in your hair and the line of your eyebrows. Too much make-up (this goes for both men and women now that television is here) makes you look actorish or worse; remember, the audience is there to hear what you have to say, not to be distracted by too much awareness of you.

How are you dressed? Your clothing should be appropriate to the occasion and should be worn as if it were your own. Let's start at the top and work down. If you are a woman and the occasion calls for it, you will wear a hat. Not a creation, please, just a hat. Don't Daché your listener's expectations for an informative or entertaining afternoon with a hat they can't keep their eyes off. Next, jewelry; wear very little, and none of it ostentatiously. This goes for men as well as women. Most audiences feel that fraternity and lodge keys and emblems are in bad taste; they are a form of visual bragging. Jewelry reflects light, and some poor spectator may be blinded by a swinging Masonic tie clasp or jeweled pendant. Clothing also catches light; so women, don't wear sequins, and men, don't wear hard-surface suits.

Don't wear clothing or ornamentation that draws attention to your hands. Your hands will be busy with your manuscript and other paraphernalia of your presentation; don't make them distracting by wearing identification bracelets, frilly cuffs, or heavy rings.

The style of the clothes you wear should be determined by the situation. If the occasion calls for formal wear, dress accordingly; but don't wear your formal suit as if you rented it, even if you did. Get used to the collar you will wear, men. Get used to the hem and neckline you will wear, women. If the occasion calls for street wear, dress simply. Don't wear extreme styles either in color or cut. Let the Duke and Duchess of Windsor set new style trends; you stay back in the advanced conservative ranks. If the occasion might call for some other type of apparel, check on it. Don't think that because it is a 4-H Club meeting you are to wear blue jeans, unless you have been so informed. Don't wear cowboy regalia, even if it is Dress Western Week, unless the program committee demands it. And if you do wear some sort of costume, wear it as if it were something you were accustomed to. Don't look like a foreign dignitary in an Indian bonnet posing for the newsreels. The only way to gain familiarity with a costume is to practice in it; practice sitting, moving, eating, as well as reading, in it.

Finally, the legs and feet. Women, please check the hang of your hem, the length of your slip, and the seams of your stockings. Don't stand like a draggletail before your audience, and, please, wear shoes you can stand in! Men, wear shoes you are comfortable in and that show reasonable signs of care. Also, adjust the fall of your trousers at home. Beware of the too carefully pressed trousers. Check on your socks; no holes, no ladders, and some invisible means of support.

MANNER

How you stand and how you move are rightfully subjects for consideration in the next chapter, but, since your stage presence is part of your personality, let's look at you. You should stand and move as though you were poised and confident. You should not show signs of nervousness, hesitance, diffidence, fatigue, or lack of interest. Nor should you show signs of cockiness, pomposity, or pride. You should stand and move as if you were a guest who was sure of his welcome, a friend who was sure of others' friendliness. You should be alert and vigorous.

What is your manner? Are you nervous, troubled by shortness of breath, a dry mouth, dizziness, clammy hands, damp forehead? Are you self-conscious? Do your hands look like strangers? Is your collar too tight?

Do you wonder what you're doing reading before an audience? Will they be interested? Will they like you? Are you apologetic for being there, and aware you might have made a better preparation? Are you interested in your subject? Are you interested in that audience out there? Do you want to tell them about your subject, make them understand and believe?

The attitude you take toward the reading situation and toward your material will determine your manner. An audience can sense your attitude. If you are suffering from stage fright, it will affect your manner, but something can be done about it. You must be interested in your subject and your audience before you will have a satisfactory public manner.

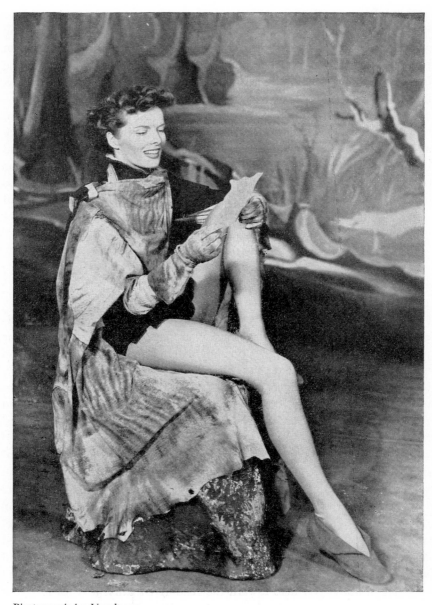

Photograph by Vandamm.

The actor reads aloud.

VOICE

Another factor in determining an audience's reaction to you is your voice. Your speech reflects your personality, and an audience will quickly judge you by what you say and how you say it. So far, we have been concerned to some degree with what you will say, and in succeeding chapters we will concern ourselves with how you will say it. Now let's examine the sort of personality you project when you talk.

A loud voice suggests dominance; a weak voice suggests diffidence; a hoarse voice, dissipation; a shrill voice, shrewishness; a too-loud voice, the bully and the show-off; a too-soft voice, effeminacy and weakness; an orotund voice, pomposity; a whiny voice, servility.

Speaking too fast shows nervousness and lack of consideration. Speaking too slowly suggests laziness and indifference. Abrupt speech suggests incoherent thought. If your speech is slovenly and mumbled, you indicate lack of interest and lack of training. If your speech is dialectal, you reveal educational limitations and insularity. If your speech is unsuited to the occasion, you disclose want of taste. Speaking in a monotone is a sign of lack of vitality. Speaking in an infantile tone signifies a lack of maturity. Speaking in a pattern shows lack of interest in your listener and your subject.

This list could be extended to almost any length, but these illustrations will suffice to show how your speech reflects your personality. As Don Marquis said, "An idea isn't responsible for the people who believe in it." We might add—"or voice it."

By your appearance and your speech you are judged, and the judgment results in an evaluation of your projection of personality. Now, what sort of personality traits should you project? Here are the principal ones: naturalness, vitality, and friendliness.

NATURALNESS

The personality trait most frequently looked for in readers is naturalness. The suggestion most often made to a beginning reader is, "Be yourself, be natural." Each of us is an individual with a different heredity, environment, and physical equipment. It is this individualness that makes us interesting. If we were all alike, no one would give anyone a second thought. Since you are individual, you are potentially interesting to others, but your individuality is apparent only when you are being yourself, being natural.

STAGE FRIGHT

You can't be yourself when plagued with stage fright, so let's analyze that bugaboo.

1. Nearly every person who has appeared before an audience has felt stage fright. People feel it in varying degrees; some are "pepped up" by it; others are moved to more careful preparation because of it; some are emotionally inhibited by it.

2. You may never get over it, but you can learn to control it. Performers with the experience of Helen Hayes and Charles Laughton still suffer from it.

3. Stage fright is not as observable to the listener as it is to the performer. The other people on the program, who look so calm and happy, may be suffering the same qualms as you and wondering at your calm exterior.

4. The use of stimulants, alcohol, or sedatives does little good at the moment and much harm in the long run, so don't depend on them. If your stage fright results in real physical disability, get proper medical advice. Remember that sound health—through proper eating, exercise, and regular habits of work, rest, and recreation—is the best way to combat nervousness.

5. Try to understand what causes stage fright. We tend to fear what we don't understand.

6. Talk about the problem with others. Such talk is the solace of the confessional and the comfort of psychiatry.

7. Assume a vital, positive, and assured manner and you are apt to be vital, positive, and assured.

8. Learn to relax. Try to yawn. Breathe deeply. Flex and then relax muscles individually. We don't know how relaxation affects emotional tension, but we do know that it helps many people.

9. Take it easy the days you must appear before an audience. Speaking is hard work for most people; it burns up energy. You can do your best only when you are rested and in good health.

10. When you are an after-dinner speaker, don't try to eat the dinner served, if you are at all concerned over your digestion or your presentation. Accept the food and look interested, but defer dinner until after your speech.

11. Be thoroughly prepared. If you know there is no justifiable cause

for embarrassment, you can forget about worry and concentrate on your presentation. If you have tried to foresee all the problems that might arise, you will have fewer last-minute fears.

12. Know so well what you are going to do that you are doing it before you have an opportunity to worry about it. Have the first line of your introduction well in mind. Know where your manuscript is. Know when you appear on the program and what sort of introduction you will receive, then listen to it.

If you will try to follow these precepts, you can overcome the worst aspects of stage fright and be on the way to naturalness in the performing situation.

Many unskilled readers complain that there is no naturalness in the performing situation, that it is unnatural. There is little real naturalness in any social situation. Social conventions dictate behavior that is at variance with the natural behavior of an untrained child. We learn to be natural within the framework of those conventions.

In all social intercourse we aim for a manner so unobtrusive that no one notices we are behaving. So it is on the platform. When you sit before an audience waiting to be introduced, you sit so that no one notices how you are doing it; you neither sprawl nor pose. When the situation is informal, you react so that no one remarks on your condescension or your abandon.

When something out of the ordinary happens during your reading, you react in such a way that the audience is not distracted by your reaction. If you should drop a page of your manuscript, you pick it up. The audience knows you are using a manuscript and will worry if they can see part of it on the floor. If you are using a visual aid and it fails to work properly, the audience knows something is wrong and you can't ignore their knowledge. If a baby cries so loudly it is a disturbance, you don't embarrass the family by commenting on the noise but, when the wailing has subsided, you do repeat what you were saying. In short, you are thought to be natural when you respond to your situation with tact, ease, and spontaneity within the conventional pattern of the social situation.

VITALITY

Another personality trait looked for in readers is vitality. To be vital connotes healthy interest in and enthusiasm for the opportunity to communicate with the listener. You should be interested in your subject, your audience, and the task before you. You should desire to stimulate your audience, to make them understand, to gain their credence. You should be energetic; you should speak with enthusiasm. You should be emphatic and convincing. To be interested, enthusiastic, stimulating, energetic, emphatic, and convincing requires vitality.

To be heard in a hall, your voice must be alive and strong; vital, in other words. To be understood amid the normal confusions of an audience situation, your speech must be athletic and vigorous; vital, again. To arouse an audience's attention and stimulate their interest, you must draw upon the resources of vitality within yourself. Vocal power and punch are not enough; there must be real enthusiasm in you.

You will need vitality to make your meaning clear to the audience. It takes verve to stimulate the imagination of an audience toward a full comprehension of the thoughts and emotions of your script. An audience, however sympathetic, tends to key downward because of mass inertia. Only your vitality can combat this downward drag.

If you want your audience to get into the spirit of the occasion and of your material, you must elicit that response through your vitality. You have seen performers who could make a situation electric by their enthusiasm. It was not just their enthusiasm for what they were doing, it was an excitement engendered by the audience. There is a flow from you to the listener and back again that you can start by vitally caring for the listener's interest.

Care about your listener. Before you start to read you should look at him: see him, realize who he is, respect him for what he is and like him; after all, he is *your* listener. Talk to him. See that he understands. Don't let your gaze flit and wander all over the hall. Look at one listener until at least one idea is completed. Then look for another listener whom you want to convince, and talk to him. See that he understands. Look at him until you see he is returning some of your enthusiasm. Then repeat the process. To make such audience contact requires vitality.

But all the vitality in the world is of no value if the listener thinks you are putting on an act. Your enthusiasm must rise from a real interest in your job; in other words, it should be a genuine personality trait— honest and sincere.

FRIENDLINESS

The third personality trait looked for in readers is friendliness. Friendliness is a predisposition to be favorably impressed. It must be rooted in honesty and sincerity. You should realize that all overtures of friendliness must be made by the reader. Like the individual members of your audience. Only then can they like you. We like those who like us, as a rule, and dislike those who don't. George Santayana says,

> Friendship is almost always the union of a part of one mind with part of another; . . . . Sometimes it hangs on passing pleasures and amusements, or on special pursuits; sometimes on mere convenience and comparative lack of friction in living together. One's friends are that part of the human race with which one can be human.[1]

Our friends are those with whom we can be human, with whom we can behave naturally. We cannot jeopardize this relationship by insincerity or dishonesty and still hope to hold the listener's friendly respect and esteem. Our sincerity must be observable in our attitudes, our thinking, and our emotions. Not for a moment can you let your audience question your sincerity. If they should, they might think of you as Samuel Hoffenstein feels about "little boys destined for big business!"

> Loyal be to loyal friends;
> Make them pay you dividends;
> Work, like the industrous bee,
> Your friends and foes impartially.[2]

Actually, the best advice that can be given a reader who is concerned with the positive aspects of his personality was stated centuries ago. It is just another application of the Golden Rule. Treat your audience as you would like to be treated if you were out there. Treat each individual listener as you would like to be treated.

Responding to a complimentary introduction, Mark Twain once said, "I am as fond of compliments as another, and as hard to satisfy as the average; but these satisfied me. I was as pleased as you would have been if they had been paid to you." What better example of the projection of personality do we need?

[1] George Santayana, "Friendships," *Soliloquies in England and Later Soliloquies* (New York: Charles Scribner's Sons, 1923), p. 55.

[2] From *Treasury of Humorous Verse,* by Samuel Hoffenstein. Published by Liveright Publishing Corporation, New York. Copyright, 1947.

· 9 ·

Movement

❖❖❖❖❖❖❖❖❖❖❖❖❖❖❖❖❖❖❖❖❖❖❖❖❖❖

Your total physical response to the reading situation, your movement, in other words, is an important part of your effectiveness as a communicator. Your posture, your gestures, all your movements—both good and bad—can affect the audience's response to your reading.

> When the layman walks, his only object is to get to Charing Cross; when he makes a gesture, it is to attract the attention of a cab driver or a bus-conductor; when he speaks it is to convey or demand information, to tell a lie, or otherwise further his prosaic ends; when he moves his hands it is to put up his umbrella or take out his handkerchief. On the stage (or before the cameras) these merely utilitarian purposes are only simulated; the real purpose is to produce an effect on the sense and imagination of the spectator.[1]

Bodily activity is inherent in the speech act. Just watch a small child for a few moments and you will see a total physical reaction to any speech stimulus. He wriggles with excitement, he jumps up and down, he uses his face, his arms, his hands, his torso, and his legs to voice a simple idea. But he is soon trained out of that! Parents and teachers spend much of their time "calming down" the expert communicator. "You don't have to whoop through the house like an Indian just because Aunt Drusilla remembered your birthday" is the sort of comment every child

[1] George Bernard Shaw, *Dramatic Opinions and Essays,* ed. James Huneker (New York: Brentano's, Inc., 1906), I, 206.

140

hears. And training is effective; the child soon learns to curb his physical expression. A mumbled "thank you" from a cigar-store Indian is all Aunt Drusilla gets in a few years. Then the child hears, "Well, aren't you pleased with the nice birthday present Aunt Drusilla brought? You don't act it!"

By the time he is an adult, that child has been so schooled in controlling himself that he must learn movement all over again when he becomes interested in vital communication. Now he is dead-pan, controlled to near rigidity, and giving the lie physically to anything he may say vocally.

Happily for him, however, all the physical responses are still there, though he may have learned to suppress them. The existence of these concealed responses can be proved in the laboratory by various instruments. The lie detector of the police courts is such an instrument, and its validity is based on the assumption that physical responses continue even though they are no longer expressed outwardly.

Although we are interested in what happened to you as a child, there is little that can be done about it now. Our concern now must be with what can be done to free movement and use it to aid in the projection of your personality and communication. You can't unlearn all the instructions of your childhood, nor can you shatter all the inhibitions you acquired during adolescence. Don't expect to. You can develop positive attitudes toward movement, you can learn to control distracting mannerisms, and you can acquire freedom of movement.

POSTURE

Since your body functions as a unit, the movement of any of the parts is freer if you have good posture. Good posture is simply that stance that produces a minimum of tension while allowing the normal functions of the muscles and organs. There is no best posture for all persons.

Posture is not standing erect. Say to someone, "Stand up straight," and they automatically go into a "brace," like a West Point cadet. There is more tension in that pose than in your normally erect position. Your posture should be comfortable and natural. It should make you appear to your best advantage. Get someone to criticize your posture. If they are adversely critical of you, you can do something about it.

Try this. Don't think about posture at all. Think about your feet. Try to feel the floor with your feet. Most of us never feel the texture of the surfaces we walk on. Modern shoes are so well built that we soon forget we have sensory organs in our feet. When you try this suggestion, you will discover you can't feel with your feet if they are too close together or too far apart. You will find you get no sensation from your heels. You will find you lost the sensations of the floor surface if you lock your knees. You can feel with your feet only when you are poised on the balls you feel through your feet, but not looking at them, you will discover you feel more athletic, more confident, more like a conqueror. That's natural. You are in the posture of the good athlete. You can move easily in any direction, forward, backward, to the side. You are not heel trapped. If you will stand like that for a few minutes, concentrating on the sensations you feel through your feet, but not looking at them, you will discover you are standing in a free, natural posture. You won't have to worry about getting your chest high or keeping your chin up. Those things will happen because your bodily center of gravity will be where it should be. There may have been truth in the Greek myth about Antaeus who took his strength from the earth, and who lost it when he was lifted from the earth

If you want some do's and don'ts about posture, here are a few.

1. Keep your chin slightly raised.

2. Keep your chest high. This is the ballet dancer's trick and makes possible the free, easy use of your arms.

3. Keep your buttocks well tucked in.

4. If your posture is right, your hands will fall naturally just back of the seam line of your trousers or skirt.

5. Make a strong base for your body by using your feet as if they were hands.

6. Don't duck your head.

7. Don't slump at the waist. You won't be able to breathe properly and you'll look uninterested and unsure.

8. Don't look like a figure S in profile. Remember, the bustle is no longer stylish.

9. Don't lock your knees. If someone should brush against you, you might fall over.

10. Don't sit back on your heels.

11. Don't stand with your feet together or spread too far apart.

12. Don't lean forward from the hips only. You can fall into the orchestra pit doing this.

13. Don't shift your weight from one leg to the other.

14. Don't teeter back and forth, rocking from your toes to your heels.

15. Don't just stand. Move around.

Yes, move around. But, in discussing movement, we will have to break up the subject into segments, and you may get the impression, as a result, that you move segmentally. Only a few burlesque queens and Hindoo dancers move that way. Your physical activity should be total and grow out of your desire to communicate. For clarity in exposition, let's split up movement into expression, gesturing, and other movements.

THE EYE

All movement is led by the eye, so let's start there. The audience looks where you look except when you are looking at them; then they look back at you. If you find this difficult to believe, just watch a television commercial for a few minutes. If the announcer is looking at you, all is serene. If he looks away, you want to know what he's looking at, and smart producers have used that desire to lead your attention to the automatic dishwasher, new car, or electric refrigerator being sold.

The eye has always been an important factor in communication. The salesman is told to make eye contact with the client. The speaker is warned not to look down at the floor, or up at the ceiling, or out of the window, but to look at his listeners. The television performer is told to look at the object he is talking about. All those admonitions are simple, good sense. In a normal situation you do look at the person to whom you're talking, unless you both are looking at some object.

The reader has a special eye problem. He must look at his manuscript and still maintain eye contact with his audience. His best answer is a compromise. His eyes should follow the manuscript until he is certain of what it is he is going to say. Then he may look at his audience until he has completed saying that phrase or group of phrases. As for keeping his place, there were some suggestions given on that in Chapter 4.

Television has created some new hazards for the reader. The listener is now able to watch him in a close-up. The eye work is much more noticeable. The appearance of the eye has become important.

If you wish to appear natural, you must look at what you are talking about. Most opera singers look stiff and unnatural because they are looking at the conductor's baton, watching the beat, while pointing at the evening star or the toreador or the girl of their dreams. Since they are not looking at the object of their affection, their gestures are wooden and badly timed. If you are before an audience and you are using visual aids, look at the displays as you talk about them. If you are on TV and you are talking about some object, look at it as you talk about it.

Attempting to use your eyes expressively may make you an eyebrow performer. TV has revealed how many people there are who think raising the eyebrows and corrugating the forehead adds emphasis to an idea. Wrinkling the forehead is distracting to an audience in a hall and maddening to a TV viewer. Happily, it is a habit that can be broken. The movie people used to use this recipe to make performers aware they were using their foreheads like Venetian blinds: smear the white of an egg on your forehead; it dries so that it is unnoticeable to the viewer but is just stiff enough to make you aware of each time you wrinkle your forehead. It is a cheap facial, as well.

THE MOUTH

Unfortunately, no such easy treatment is available for the reader who does gymnastics with his mouth. We need the mouth to talk with and to smile and laugh with. But too many speakers also use the mouth for contortions. Avoid such oral mannerisms as biting the lips, pursing the lips, wetting the lips, darting the tongue upward toward the nose, pushing the lower lip outward with the tongue. Break yourself of oral habits such as speaking out of the corner of your mouth, twisting your mouth downward, keeping a stiff upper lip. Such habits and mannerisms add nothing to your communication and they detract much—on TV they are disgusting.

Necessary movements of the mouth should be made like all other movements. They should be fully developed and they should end. If you are going to smile, smile. Don't half smile, like a baby with a gas pain. When the occasion for the smile is past, let the face return to its normal contours. Don't let the smile remain like that of the Cheshire cat, the only thing that can be seen, and that for no reason.

GESTURES

Beginning a gesture, carrying it through to its ultimate development, and then concluding it is the accepted progression for all movements. In a normal situation your movements follow this normal pattern. When you shake hands, you raise your hand from your side, extend it, clasp the other's hand, let go, and let your hand come back to rest.

No movement nor any part of a movement means anything in itself. Putting your hand on someone's shoulder, for instance, means nothing in itself. It could mean you are holding the person back from action that might be dangerous. It could mean you are going to turn the person

By LIFE Photographer Martha Holmes. Courtesy of TIME Inc.

The officer reads aloud.

around. It could mean you are indicating sympathy. It could mean you are being affectionate. The action is meaningful only (1) in relation to the actions that have preceded it and will follow, (2) in relation to the ideas being expressed by the speaker at the time of the gesture, (3) in relation to the emotions inherent in the situation.

Gesture is the physical extension of an idea or emotion. Gesture is not a separate entity divorced from other aspects of the communicative act. To say that a gesture starts from rest and returns to rest is misstatement. The speaker while communicating is never at rest. His arms are not at rest, even though they may be hanging at his sides. When you find the word *rest* used in descriptions of gesture and movement, do not conceive of it as a vegetative absence of motion. Think of it, rather, as a transitional stage of motion and you will be at a starting place in your understanding of movement.

Being alive means you aren't ever completely "at rest." Thinking an idea is being more alive; hence you are more active. Thinking a complicated idea is an active progression of cerebral movements that is evident to the listener through your physical response to this mental activity. Voicing an idea is one physical manifestation of thought. While you are speaking the conclusion of one idea, your mind is leaping ahead preparing the next. As a result, your body, which reflects the activity of your mind, is constantly displaying the development of one idea, while shifting and preparing itself for the display of the new idea. This being true, the body can never be said to be at rest during speech. Therefore, prescribed, set gestures are an abomination. They neither reinforce the activity of the speaker's mind as it is displayed in speech nor do they reflect the activity of the mind, which runs ahead of the voice. Set gestures are merely physical-training exercises.

If you can so observe someone talking to you that he is unaware that you are watching the natural flow of physical movement reflecting his mental activity, you will note that his movement follows a sequential pattern. All natural movement follows the same pattern.

The mind first creates an idea. Slightly behind the movement of the mind is the movement of the speech mechanism. But concurrent with the movement of mind is the movement of the eye. If you are thinking and talking about a chair, your eye travels to the chair as you think of it. Your head follows the eye movement; that is, the eye reaches the chair before the head is turned squarely toward it. The shoulder closer to the chair moves a fraction of time more slowly than the head.

If you are pointing to the chair, the chest goes into action. It raises as your torso follows the shoulder swing. The rising chest pulls up the whole arm, freeing it from the body. Notice how, in natural movement, the wrist seems to lead the arm movement in toward the chest and then out toward the chair. The pointing finger does not become apparent until the wrist snaps the arm into position, leveled at the chair. While all this activity is going on with one arm, the hips are swinging the feet into a position facing the chair, and the other arm is making a balancing movement to counterpoise the shifting body.

There you have a description of a simple natural movement. Reading the description took more than eighteen times as long as the movement itself. If you tried the action while you read, you are probably more wound up in arms, legs, and verbiage than the Laocoön statue. Keep trying it, however. If you are unsure of movement before an audience, you can retrain yourself to gesture.

Effective gestures help you communicate. Modern speech does not require them, though it profits from them. The speaker no longer has to point upward when saying, "The flag on high," nor sweep his hand downward when speaking of the devil. He does not have to clench his fist when angry, nor look like a recruiting poster when he says "you." He may, however, want to do all these things, and should if he feels strongly enough.

Your audience will appreciate it if you do use movement. An audience needs action to keep its attention focused. Actually, there is no such thing as continued attention. Our concentration span is measured in seconds. We are being constantly restimulated to give attention. The first movement that restimulates us is the movement of the speaker's mind. Secondly, his voice is an attention stimulant. That is why the speaker's voice must be capable of variety in pitch, time, loudness, and quality. Thirdly, the speaker's movements are stimulants to attention. The turning of a page, the shifting of weight, the play of facial expression, the gesture, all recapture our attention.

An audience appreciates movement because it enables listeners to respond empathically. *Empathy* is the label given your action at a football game. The home team is on the one-yard line and it is fourth down. The fullback tries to plunge over for the touchdown. You are high in the stands, yet, driving for that needed yard, you push the man next to you off the bench. Your legs drive with the fullback's. Your shoulders push forward. The man next to you would be annoyed, if he weren't doing the same thing himself. That is empathy. At a movie short on underwater play—you know the sort: girls doing ballet movements or pretending they're mermaids—you will find yourself gasping for air if the girls stay under water any length of time. That is empathy. It is the imaginative projection of one's consciousness into another's being.

An audience responds to your movement with empathy. If you are vital, they are vital. If you shake your head over the state of the world, they will shake theirs when they are completely with you; they will have a tightening of the neck muscles when they are only slightly with you. They enjoy moving with you. Give them the opportunity.

Other than gesturing, there are only a few types of movement you will be called upon to use as a speaker. You will need to practice sitting, rising, and walking. At this point, I can hear you say you're not interested in acting; you just want to read aloud so the listener can understand. You are not an actor? Sir Cedric Hardwicke, an actor, several years ago in a lecture at Cambridge said,

> The actor's voice has dropped from the declamatory to the almost confiding coo of the crooner, and his gestures are restricted to lighting a cigarette or putting an offending corner of a handker-

chief discreetly into its correct place in his jacket pocket. So that now the strain of comprehending a play is thrown entirely on the ear which, because of the absence of adequate gesture, is put to an increasingly severe test. Acting has given way to behavior and tends to become inarticulate . . . . I should say that there is more acting nowadays in a motor-car showroom when a potential customer enters and certainly more at the average business interview, than there is in the modern theatre. Perhaps we have arrived at a time when only the worst actors aspire to the stage.[2]

SITTING

Sitting down before an audience is not just crumpling from the waist and sighing, "Thank the good Lord that's over." It goes something like this. Locate the chair with a glance. Cross to it without further attention. Walk slightly past the chair and then turn toward the audience. Acknowledge their applause from a position in front of your chair. While responding to the audience, feel for the edge of the chair with the calf of the leg nearer the speaker's stand. This usually requires a backward step and is natural while you are bowing or nodding acknowledgment. After you have found the chair edge with one leg, keep the other leg slightly advanced, bend your knees slowly, and tilt your trunk forward as your leg muscles lower your body into the chair. Keep your feet where they are after you are in the chair. If you do you will be sitting on your buttocks and not on the base of your spine.

If you should have to rise to further acknowledge the applause, your feet are properly placed for getting up. The center of gravity of the body is in the center of the chest. In order to rise from a chair we must, therefore, start by bringing the chest over the foot that is to bear the weight. Many people do this by bending the head and body forward. This is awkward and involves a loss of presence. A better method is to sway forward from the hips until the weight is over the drawn-back foot, then push the body up with that leg. The forward foot will then take the weight, and your back foot is free for the first step forward.

When you are rising and sitting, your hands may be full of manuscript, so that they are no problem. If they are empty when you rise, place them on the arms of the chair, but don't push with them; let your legs do the pushing. If your hands are empty while you are sitting, let them fall

[2] Quoted by George Jean Nathan, "First Nights and Passing Judgments," *Esquire,* Vol. X, No. 5 (November, 1938).

on your knees as you settle back into the chair. But don't twiddle with your trousers.

WALKING

Walking should be thought of as a progression from one spot to another. You don't have any trouble walking from the front room to the dinner table. You shouldn't have any trouble on stage, if you will think of where you are going rather than of your means of getting there.

Walking is a falling forward and a recovery. That is the way a baby walks. That is the way a good athlete walks. Stand up and lean forward until you start to topple over. Your foot will move forward and catch you. The foot will go down first on the heel. Nijinsky, the great dancer, said, "Women have the tendency to put the tip of the toe to the ground first, to give the impression of grace and lightness, instead of first putting the heel down, which gives firmness and natural rhythm to the body. This is the way one should walk."

Your best walk as a reader is the walk that gets you to where you want to go. If you will think of your objective, you will not be thinking of your walk; if you aren't uncomfortably conscious of it, your audience won't be.

Here are some suggestions about movement to bear in mind.

1. All gestures and movement should be foreshadowed. Don't stand like an automaton and then suddenly burst into a frenzy of signal-flag waving. From the moment you take the platform, the audience should be given enough warning of the possibility of movement that they will not be surprised when large movement is used.

2. Gestures and movement should grow in size, frequency, and intensity as the communication grows in intensity toward its climax. That is, begin with few gestures and little movement—just enough to foreshadow your eventual use—and build them as the reading builds.

3. Movement before a key word makes the word important. Movement after a key word makes the movement important.

4. All movement and gestures should grow naturally out of your instinctive, physical response to the communication. They should be motivated.

5. The amount of action needed will vary with the audience. A big audience requires bigger movement than does a small audience. A tired, apathetic audience requires more movement than a small, alert audience.

A formal audience requires more formality in the speaker's movement.

6. You should avoid all movement that does not contribute to your effectiveness as a communicator. Avoid all physical mannerisms, such as buttoning and unbuttoning your coat, moving hands in and out of your pockets, jingling change and keys in your pockets. Don't play with buttons, handkerchiefs, ties, pendants, or necklaces. Don't play with a pencil, note-cards, or your manuscript. Don't clutch the speaker's stand. Don't torture your fingers, knuckles, or wrists. Don't fold and unfold your arms. Don't fidget with your clothing. Don't kick or scuff the speaker's stand. Don't pace about. Don't dodge back and forth around the speaker's stand as if you were a base runner on third.

7. Movement is good, so use it. If you can't gesture with any feeling of ease, then use visual aids with your presentation. They will create a reason for movement that has natural compulsion.

► *Conclusion.* If you care about your listener, if you want to keep him interested and attentive, move. If you care about what you have to say, if you believe in the importance of your communication, move. Movement is your total physical response to the meanings and emotions of your selection. Movement is the energizing of your material and your audience so that comprehension becomes a vital, active thing. You can move. Do so.

EXERCISE

(*Just for practice purposes, try making all the gestures described here while reading the selection aloud.*)

On Gesture, Action, and Delivery; Neglect of Them by Public Speakers in England[3]

Most foreign writers who have given any character of the English nation, whatever vices they ascribe to it, allow in general that the people are naturally modest. It proceeds perhaps from this our national virtue, that our orators are observed to make use of less gesture or action than those of other countries. Our preachers stand stock still in the pulpit, and will not so much as move a finger to set off the best sermons in the world. We meet with the same speaking statues at our bars, and in all public places of debate. Our words flow from us in a smooth continued stream without those strainings of the voice, motions of the body, and majesty

---

[3] Joseph Addison, Papers contributed to *The Spectator,* No. 407.

of the hand, which are so much celebrated in the orators of Greece and Rome. We can talk of life and death in cold blood, and keep our temper in a discourse which turns upon everything that is dear to us. Though our zeal breaks out in the finest tropes and figures, it is not able to stir a limb about us. I have heard it observed more than once by those who have seen Italy, that an untravelled Englishman cannot relish all the beauties of Italian pictures, because the postures which are expressed in them are often such as are peculiar to that country. One who has not seen an Italian in the pulpit, will not know what to make of that noble gesture in Raphael's picture of St. Paul preaching at Athens, where the apostle is represented as lifting up both his arms, and pouring out the thunder of his rhetoric amidst an audience of Pagan philosophers.

It is certain that proper gestures and vehement exertions of the voice cannot be too much studied by a public orator. They are a kind of comment to what he utters, and enforce everything he says with weak hearers better than the strongest argument he can make use of. They keep the audience awake, and fix their attention to what is delivered to them, at the same time that they shew the speaker is in earnest, and affected himself with what he so passionately recommends to others. Violent gesture and vociferation naturally shake the hearts of the ignorant, and fill them with a kind of religious horror. . . .

If nonsense, when accompanied with such an emotion of voice and body, has such an influence on men's minds, what might we not expect from many of those admirable discourses which are printed in our tongue, were they delivered with a becoming fervour, and with the most agreeable graces of voice and gesture?

We are told that the great Latin orator very much impaired his health by his *laterum contenito,* this vehemence of action, with which he used to deliver himself. The Greek orator was likewise so very famous for this particular in rhetoric, that one of his antagonists, whom he had banished from Athens, reading over the oration which had procured his banishment, and seeing his friends admire it, could not forbear asking them, if they were so much affected by the bare reading of it, how much more would they have been alarmed, had they heard him actually throwing out such a storm of eloquence?

How cold and dead a figure in comparison of these two great men, does an orator often make at the British bar, holding up his head with the most insipid serenity, and stroking the sides of a long wig that reaches down to his middle. The truth of it is, there is often nothing more ridiculous than the gestures of an English speaker. You see some of them running their hands into their pockets as far as ever they can thrust them, and others looking with great attention on a piece of paper that has nothing written in it; you may see many a smart rhetorician turning his hat in his hands, moulding it into several different cocks, examining sometimes the lining of it, and sometimes the button, during the whole course of his harangue. A deaf man would think he was cheapening a beaver, when perhaps he is talking of the fate of the British nation. I remember when I was a young man, and used to frequent Westminster-hall, there was a counsellor who never pleaded without a piece of pack-thread in his hand, which he used to twist about a thumb or a finger all the while he was speaking; the wag of those days used to call it the thread of his discourse, for he was not able to utter a word without it. One of his clients, who was more merry than wise, stole it from him one day in the midst of his pleading; but he had better have let it alone, for he lost his cause by his jest.

I have all along acknowledged myself to be a dumb man, and therefore may be thought a very improper person to give rules for oratory; but I believe everyone will agree with me in this, that we ought either to lay aside all kinds of gesture, (which seems to be very suitable to the genius of our nation), or at least to make use of such only as are graceful and expressive.

· 10 ·

The Voice

Almost as much has been written on the subject of voice as has been written on the subject of Shakespeare. The bibliography lists a number of books containing helpful information about the voice and how to improve it. Many of the books have been written by experts in the field. The following discussion is indebted to the researches of those experts; there is nothing original here. It will be limited to those aspects of voice affecting most oral readers. "Let us not be too particular," Mark Twain said. "It is better to have old second-hand diamonds than none at all."

The beginning public reader is too concerned with his voice. His first question after a performance usually is, "Did I sound all right?" Throughout this book the reader has been urged to ask, "Did you understand me?" If you are concerned with comprehension, you need not be much concerned with voice. If you are concerned with the listener instead of yourself, you will communicate more clearly.

Nevertheless, it is difficult for the reader not to be overconcerned with his voice. Listeners judge us by our voice. Our voice is our most effective instrument of expression. Any person who attempts to read aloud needs a better than an across-the-desk sort of voice. It may help you, though, to remember that most voice specialists agree that the reader who has no organic disorder of his vocal mechanism can exercise enough control over his vocal equipment to achieve effective communication. The voice can be trained; the superior voice most often is the result of conscious efforts at improvement.

Don't have the listener say of your voice what Bill Nye said of Wagner's music, "I've been told Wagner's music is better than it sounds."

What are the vocal attributes an effective public reader needs?

First, the public reader needs audibility, of course. For complete comprehension from the listener, you need to be sure you are heard before you worry about any of the other problems of interest, understanding, and belief. You need to be heard easily and without strain. Contrariwise, you should not be so loud that your volume hurts the listener's sensibilities.

Second, the public reader should have a pleasant voice. Listeners comment unfavorably on harsh voices, whiny voices, and strident voices. Listeners comment favorably on pleasant voices. "He has such a nice voice," or, "I could have listened all night," are frequent comments. Analyzing those comments, the reader discovers that his audience defines a pleasant voice as one that is clearly heard, of good and resonant quality, that is neither too fast nor too slow, that has elements of melody, and that is of medium or low pitch.

Third, the public reader should have fluency. He should be able to speak so that his ideas flow from word group to word group. If his manner is explosive or chaotic, if his speech is too fast or too slow, if his ideas are halted by *uhs, ahs,* and *ers,* the listener complains of his lack of fluency. Fluency is governed by your desire to be understood; each particular idea of your speech should be voiced as rapidly as the audience can follow it.

Fourth, the public reader should have vocal flexibility. The audience values flexibility in voice more than the other vocal qualities because it is the speaker's means of restimulating the listener's attention. You should strive for variety in pitch, loudness, rate, and quality, but you should beware of arbitrary variety—variety for its own sake, variety for show. A vital interest in your material will make you aware of potentials of vocal variety. Practice and training will increase your powers of flexibility.

Those, briefly, are the four vocal attributes needed for effective reading aloud. They are closely associated with the physical characteristics of sound. Audibility is related to loudness, of course. Pleasantness is primarily a characteristic of quality. Fluency is most closely akin to rate. And flexibility, although it can be applied to loudness, quality, and rate, is most closely related to the characteristic of pitch.

The physiological processes involved in the production of your speaking voice are breathing, phonation, resonation, and articulation. Articulation is the subject of the next chapter. Breathing, phonation, and resonance are the subject of this.

BREATHING

A good voice depends, first of all, on correct and efficient breathing, everyone tells me. Breathing, to me, continues to be something you do without thinking as long as you are alive. Some of my happiest school days were spent lying on the floor of a speech classroom, practicing breathing. I acquired many good habits from that experience. Since the class was held right after lunch, I grew accustomed to practicing after the noon meal. I still like to practice every afternoon. I do it now with a handkerchief thrown over my face—to prove I'm practicing. I have found that this is one of the speech exercises most businessmen are willing to practice, too. With a little experience, they become quite expert. I am, however, an authority on only this one exercise. Dr. Grant Fairbanks is a better teacher of the other aspects of respiration.

> In good speech this process of lung ventilation affords no problem because pauses are frequent, and each pause gives an opportunity to breathe. In general, if a speaker pauses as often as he should, and if he utilizes these pauses to ventilate his lungs, he will never "run out of breath," nor will he need to create a special pause for breathing alone. Furthermore, it is easier to take a shallow breath than a deep one. And since inspirations may be frequent in average speech, they also may be shallow.[1]

We lay on the floor in speech class to develop diaphragmatic breathing. Some of the students, who were not as expert as I, had to balance dictionaries on their bellies to acquire this skill needed to further develop their diaphragms. When we were erect in class, the teacher came around and poked us with his clenched fist in what Mrs. Jim Jeffries used to call "the kitchen." This was painful and served no good purpose, as far as I could see, so I remained prone—practicing. Fairbanks bears me out; speaking of the three breathing skills the speaker should develop, he says,

> 1. *Expansion and contraction in the proper regions of the torso.* The predominant region of expansion determines what is known as the "breathing type," and is a point of much controversy. It is mentioned here as an essential because, while there probably is no one "right way" to breathe, there is one "wrong way" which should be avoided. This "wrong way" is clavicular or high-chest breathing, in which the structures of the extreme upper chest, and sometimes

[1] Grant Fairbanks, *Voice and Articulation Drillbook* (New York: Harper & Brothers, 1940), p. 133.

even the shoulders, are elevated. There are three chief reasons why this is an inefficient way to breathe for speech; (a) It is fatiguing, (b) it increases throat and laryngeal tension and (c) you have poor control over expiration. Apart from this type, use the method that is easiest and most comfortable for you. This means that your expansions and contractions will be in the general region of the lower chest and abdomen.

"Use the method that is easiest and most comfortable for you." I know people who were in that speech class with me who, if they read that line, would take Fairbanks's book and poke our teacher with it—right in the diaphragm. And that's pretty hard to do, I discovered later, since the diaphragm does not run as a sheath over your belly, but cuts laterally across your torso just above the hip line.

Fairbanks continues with breathing skills two and three.

2. *Controlled expiration.* Use progressive contraction of abdominal and chest muscles accompanied by coordinated tension of all the breathing muscles. There is evidence to show that this contraction is steady in good voice usage, jerky in poor.

3. *Inspiration during the natural pauses of your speech.* Learn to coordinate inspiration with phrasing so that you need not make special breathing pauses.

Fairbanks's last comment makes excellent sense for the reader who is worried about breathing properly during his communication. "Learn to coordinate inspiration with phrasing so that you need not make special breathing pauses." When reading, if you will pause at the end of each phrase for the inspiration of the next idea, the respiration will take care of itself.

PHONATION

The vibration of the vocal cords by a column of air which produces vocal tone is called *phonation*. The pitch of your voice is created by the rate of vibration of the cords. The raising and lowering of pitch is controlled by the frequency of the vibrations.

RESONANCE

The lack or presence of resonance is responsible for the color and beauty of the voice. Qualities of voice that suggest personality traits and emotional conditions are often determined by the ways in which tones are resonated. The vowel sounds of speech are differentiated by characteristic resonance. The resonators are the amplifying system of the voice. The main vocal resonators are the throat, the mouth, and the nasal cavities.

Breathing, phonation, and resonance are the processes of voice production. Like the controllable properties of voice, they cannot be singled out in nature; we can only do that in textbooks. You can't have a pitch without loudness and quality at the same time. You can't have rate without pitch, loudness, and quality. While you practice using one controllable property of the voice, you are of necessity practicing the others. Your concentration can be on them one at a time, but the others will continue to coexist even if you try to ignore them. In fact, while you practice one aspect other aspects frequently improve.

LOUDNESS

Loudness is the property of the voice that determines whether we are heard or not. You achieve varying degrees of loudness by (1) greater breath pressure on the tenser vocal cords, and (2) amplification of the tone by the resonators.

If your voice is too weak, there may be many problems and the solutions are not easy. Your voice may be weak because you are speaking at too low a pitch level. Your habitual pitch may be wrong for you. (See section on pitch.) If your pitch is natural for you, you can achieve a louder tone by raising the pitch.

Your voice may appear weak because you are not taking sufficient time to voice the speech sounds. Try prolonging vowel sounds and see if your voice sounds louder. Calling pigs or trains or calling strikes and balls at a baseball game are good exercises for sound prolongation.

Your voice may appear weak because you are breathing improperly. Check your loudness problem while you are going through some of the breathing drills in the practice material.

If your voice is too loud, the solution is easy: speak more quietly.

Loudness is a common fault. Many readers begin each sentence at the same level of loudness and then become progressively weaker as the sentence continues. This fault has nothing to do with breathing or breath control. It is a matter of interest. When you are in conversation, your voice never sounds like a phonograph running down, because you are thinking your thoughts through to the end of the sentence. When you are reading, you run down simply because your mind leaps ahead to the next sentence and leaves your voice running. If you will think the thought of each sentence as you voice it, you will conquer this loudness problem immediately.

Another common loudness fault is monotony of volume. We strike a level of loudness sufficient to be heard and then never break away from that level. If you are guilty of this fault, the simple way to break it is to use short sentences or ask questions with one word answers. "Are we going to sit back and let people say our loudness level is monotonous? No."

PITCH

The pitch of the voice is its highness or lowness as measured on the musical scale. The frequency of the vocal-cord vibrations determines the fundamental sound wave and the pitch of the voice. The greater the frequency of vibration the higher the pitch, and contrariwise.

Every person has a habitual pitch and a pitch range. The habitual pitch is that tone around which the voice shifts in inflections either upward or downward, but which is constantly returned to. Such a habitual pitch is readily heard in its grosser aspects: we hear a man speaking and we know it is a man; we say he is a tenor or a bass because his habitual pitch is in the corresponding register. The pitch range is the extent of the highness and lowness of pitches possible to a person when speaking or singing. If a soprano can sing from middle C to C above high C, she is said to have a two-octave singing range. If her inflectional range is from C to E flat, she is said to have a two-and-one-half-tone speaking range. The wider the range, the greater the variety of effects possible to the speaker and the more subtle the shading of emotions and thoughts that may be conveyed.

According to research reported by Fairbanks, the habitual pitch of superior adult male speakers is located very close to C below middle C, while that of superior women speakers is near $G\sharp$ below middle C. Not every speaker's pitch will approximate these levels; they are merely what is thought to be the best pitch levels for men and women. If your habitual pitch varies markedly from these levels, put yourself into the hands of a skilled speech teacher for help.

Your habitual pitch is tied up with your pitch range, and your speaking range is related to the extent of your singing range. Fairbanks advocates a habitual pitch that lies somewhere one-fourth of the way up the scale of your singing range. That is, if you can sing sixteen tones, your habitual pitch should be four tones up that range. Many a reader's pitch is too low for him. It is not his best speaking pitch; it is merely his habitual pitch.

Good speakers use a range of just less than two octaves in reading factual material. Many poor readers use only one or two tones. You can build up your speaking range by singing. But maybe you feel you don't want to build up your speaking range because you may sound affected fluting about up in the air and then swooping down. To see just how much meaning you can pack into a sentence by the use of an extensive pitch range, try this. Say with great contempt, in your best top-sergeant manner, "Who do you think you are?" Now pitch the "Who" as high as you can in your natural range and say the sentence on a descending scale and let the last word hit the bottom of your range and settle there. More effective, isn't it?

Build up your speaking-singing range by daily practice. You may claim you are tone deaf and can't sing the scale. You may be. But few people are, although Abraham Lincoln claimed he couldn't tell one note from another. He said he knew only two pieces of music: "Hail Columbia," at which everyone stood up, and that other piece at which everyone sat down. If you are as badly off as he, you are in good company at least, but it is hard to say just what can be done about your speaking voice. If you have any ability to make a singing note at all, sing one and then sing down the scale until you have gone as far as possible. Repeat the same process several times daily. Try to raise your top pitch by reversing the process. Do it daily. You will be able to increase your singing range in a few days. Remember, don't strain your voice, and work with a piano if you can.

Variations in pitch are refreshing and can be used to restimulate the attention of the listener. These variations are of two types: pitch shifts and inflections. The pitch shift is the variation in pitch occurring when we end a word or a phrase or a sentence on one pitch and begin a new word or phrase or sentence on a different pitch. The pitch shift was discussed in Chapter 5, when we were considering the vocal techniques of communicating parentheses and new ideas.

An inflection is a pitch change that takes place without cessation of sound. These glides are what give relationship to ideas, emotional meaning to what we say, and melody to our speech. In voicing many of our ideas, we use inflection and tone to convey our true meaning while the words say something else. Such voicing is the technique for sarcasm and irony. Read this excerpt from Robert Benchley's essay on filling out his income tax. Read it silently until you know what it is about, and then notice what your voice does when you read it aloud.

It's their own fault that I am late. They print blanks for you to fill out, then pass a bill making the blanks no good, then send the blanks out anyway, with a little red slip telling you to disregard the blanks. If I had done a thing like that to *them,* what a howl they would have set up! I would have been just an old slipshod bungler, an impractical writer-man. But the Government can go out of its way to confuse and rattle *me,* and that's all right. Well, the Government makes me sick, that's what the Government does. And it always has, too.

In the first place, the little red slip got lost just as soon as I had taken it out of the envelope, so I never saw what it said. I can't sit right down the minute my blank comes and fill it out. I have certain other things which have to be attended to, although the Government may not think so. And a little red slip is very easily mislaid or lost these days. I don't suppose the Government ever loses anything, oh no! They're *perfect!*[2]

If you did that at all well you should have been able to hear the petulant melody. Mark Twain was aware that speech had a melody. One morning while shaving he cut himself and promptly let go with a hair-lifting round of profanity. His wife, who had overheard him, repeated the profanity to show him how vulgar it sounded. Twain listened critically and commented, "You have the words, my dear, but not the tune."

You have been aware, I'm sure, of the melody in the speech of many ministers and politicians. It is not a conscious attempt for melody; it is a conscious attempt to be heard. As was mentioned in the section on loudness, you can increase your volume by raising your pitch. You can also speak with good volume for longer periods of time if you will intone. This is the trick of the tobacco auctioneer and the square-dance caller. You can sing all day without tiring your voice, but you can't talk loudly for very long at a time without growing hoarse. The minister and politician have learned this and have developed a melodic speech that can be heard, but does not tire the speaker. Franklin D. Roosevelt's phrase, "My Friends," was an example of such intoned speech.

It could be heard by the great crowds that gathered to hear him in person. The need for such delivery is growing less today with public-address systems in wide use, but it is a good technique to add to your repertoire for the occasion when the PA breaks down.

Your normal speech utilizes all the pitch potentials. You use inflection naturally, you use pitch shifts naturally, you use range naturally. For reading aloud you need to develop those potentials until they are a real part of your skill in winning comprehension from an audience. The greater pitch and inflectional range you have, the wider the range of

2 Robert Benchley, *Chips off the Old Benchley* (New York: Harper & Brothers, 1949), p. 10.

meanings you can convey to an audience. Subtleties, nuances, and shades of meaning can be comprehended by listeners only if the speaker is capable of indicating them with his voice.

There are several common reader faults in the use of pitch that you should avoid. Retrain yourself if you are already guilty of them.

1. There is nothing so maddening as the reiteration of one pitch. The "beep-beep" of the automatic range finder and the automatic pilot are considered occupational hazards. The whirr of machinery and the chirr of the locust are all insistent sounds that may drive the listener to drink. To put a baby to sleep, you use a song with a monotonous melody. If you are a reader, don't treat your listeners as if they were babies by using too limited a range—commonly referred to as a monotone.

2. Too high a pitch level gives the impression of hysteria, of irritation, or of petulance. All are undesirable personality traits which we may indicate to our listeners. Ambrose Bierce said being positive was "being mistaken at the top of one's voice." The shrewish female uses a habitual pitch level that is too high.

3. Too low a pitch level may leave the impression that you are a stuffed shirt. It is undesirable because you have curtailed your inflectional range; you cannot inflect downward and you have cut down on the potential loudness of your speech. Your voice may be difficult to listen to because your audience is empathically wanting to clear its throat.

4. Habitual pitch patterns are recurrent melodic patterns in your reading. They usually result from not thinking the thoughts of your reading; they are the result of a short circuit between the eyes and the voice that by-passes the brain. If, after rethinking your material, your voice still goes down at the end of each phrase, try singing a sentence or two and arranging the melodic line to do just the opposite of what your voice does in speaking.

TIME

Time is the characteristic of the voice that refers to the duration of sounds and pauses. Rates of speaking vary according to the personality of the speaker and the nature of his material. Your rate should be slow enough to render your speech intelligible and should suit the material and the occasion. Rate should be determined by the speed of your thinking and the speed of the listener's comprehension. Your thinking is controlled by your material, of course. The audience's comprehension is determined by their characteristics, by the type of material you are reading, and by your manner of delivery.

Reading rates vary. Fairbanks believes that a rate is too rapid if it exceeds 185 words per minute and too slow if it is less than 145 words per minute.[3] Goldstein believes that a rate faster than 140 words per minute is too rapid for effective communication.[4] Franklin D. Roosevelt spoke between 110 and 135 words a minute. Radio announcers are expected to read at about 145 words a minute. In fact, radio stations sell 100 words as a one-minute announcement. But the script can be a few words longer and to those words the announcer adds the station break. Radio newsmen have gone as high as 225 words a minute.

So, how fast is too fast? If the listener complains you are speaking too fast or too slowly, you may be, no matter what your rate. Practice what George Bernard Shaw says about rate (page 75) and then, if listeners continue to complain, maybe you should do something about your own rate.

What the listener is complaining of, however, may not be your rate but your manner of voicing the individual words. Fred Waring has discovered that a group of singers can sing as rapidly as they can enunciate and not be singing too fast for comprehension. His technique is one the average reader would do well to study. Waring believes that any singer can be understood if he voices vowels as they sound in speech, has immaculate articulation of the consonants, and knows the ideas of what he is singing.

You may sound too fast because you are not giving vowels their full value and you are slighting consonants. By this time you should not be guilty of not knowing the ideas of your communication.

Giving vowels their correct value is a problem in prolonging sounds, the duration of tones.

> Vocal sounds may be grouped into three general classes on the basis of their durations. First of all there is normal duration of tones. Unemotional conversation provides a typical example. Secondly we have staccato speech, in which the tones are of very short duration. Such tones frequently are heard in expressions of anger and fear. In the third place we find tones which are prolonged, and such prolongation of vocal tones is common in the expression of the more pleasant emotions. Experimental studies of speech inform us that effective speakers tend to have a longer average duration of words than do poor speakers.[5]

In most regions of the United States, the greatest fault is too staccato

---

[3] Fairbanks, *op. cit.,* p. 142.

[4] Harry Goldstein, *Reading and Listening Comprehension at Various Controlled Rates, Contributions to Education,* No. 821, Columbia University Teachers College.

[5] Fairbanks, *op. cit.,* pp. 149–150.

an utterance. In the Southwest, the problem is just the opposite; too long a prolongation, or the drawl. I can get from the front door to the garage and have the car started before my second-grader gets out, "Let me give you a good-bye kiss." And while she is saying it she has mutilated the purity of every vowel. Kiss becomes "kih—ee—yuh—us." If your problem is staccato sounds, try imitating the drawl. If your problem is the drawl, try imitating Winchell. If your problem is too slow a rate of speech plus a drawl, try reading material that is sprightly and staccato. The Gilbert and Sullivan musical comedies are filled with good drill material for the slow speaker.

A common time problem for the beginning reader is jerkiness. If you read in fits and starts, if you sound as if you were using too heavy a grade of oil in winter weather, you can do something about it. Try reading rhythmic prose of some complexity in a smooth style. Edward Gibbon, or any of the eighteenth-century writers, is good for this exercise.

> . . . without some species of writing no people has ever preserved the faithful annals of their history, ever made any considerable progress in the abstract sciences, or ever possessed, in any tolerable degree of perfection, the useful and agreeable arts of life.[6]

Try reading that selection without a full stop until you reach the period. Read it with one of your arms outstretched, moving slowly and evenly back and forth on a level with your shoulder. Unless you are a person who can do a thing vocally in one rhythm while your body does things physically in another rhythm, moving your arm will help you overcome jerkiness. Most of us move our bodies spasmodically while reading in choppy spurts, move our bodies smoothly when speaking with a flow.

Two common time faults, phrasing poorly and neglecting pauses, are discussed in Chapter 5. Two other common time faults, monotony and time patterns, need consideration here. Monotony usually means you are overrhythmic. You are reading in a singsong style. This happens most often in the reading of poetry, but it can happen in the reading of some prose. If you will concern yourself with the ideas of your material and try for comprehension, you should have no trouble with a time pattern. If you become aware of rhythmic reading, do this: arbitrarily break the rhythm by pauses, insert words that will break the rhythm, rephrase the material or rewrite it.

[6] Edward Gibbon, *The History of the Decline and Fall of the Roman Empire* (New York: Heritage Press, 1946), I, 171.

QUALITY

Quality is the characteristic of the voice that differentiates one voice from another and one sound from another even when pitch, loudness, and time are the same. It is determined by the composition of the sound wave; that is, by the amplification of the original tone by the complete speech mechanism.

It is impossible to alter completely the characteristic quality of our voices. Yet much can be done to improve your vocal quality. More can be done to improve your use of quality in reading aloud. Like the other attributes of voice, quality depends upon your desire to communicate. If you are vibrant and alive, your voice is vibrant and alive. The quality of your voice is most affected by your state of health.

Here a word should be inserted on caring for the voice. Your voice is a delicate instrument. It can be wrecked by misuse. It is a part of your total physical make-up and as such responds to your physical condition. If you are tired, your voice is tired; if you are sick, your voice is sick. Another thing to remember is that the total speech act is an acquired skill. None of the physical equipment used in speech was intended primarily for that function. The lungs, the resonators, the lips, the tongue, and the vocal cords themselves have other primary physiological functions. As a result, it is impossible to speak when they are otherwise engaged. It is difficult and sometimes impossible to speak when you are laboring for breath, or are frightened, or angry. Unless you are a ventriloquist, it is impossible to speak while you are drinking a glass of water. It is difficult to speak when the resonators are clogged with a cold. The reader needs to know these truths about his vocal equipment so that he will treat it with proper regard.

We all know the importance of vocal quality. Listeners are favorably affected by a good voice. A good voice is an attention-compelling, interest-holding attribute. We enjoy listening to a good voice just because it is a good voice.

If you want to improve your voice, the place to start is by listening to it. Most of us have trouble hearing our "outside" voice—the voice that others hear. When we speak, the sound rumbles around inside our skull and resonating chambers, so that we hear a confusing mixture of vibrations, echoes, tone emission, and tone formation all at the same time. It may be a real shock for you to hear what you actually sound like to others.

In order to hear yourself, make a recording. Have someone with you who can guarantee that the recording sounds as you sound. After you get over the first shock, listen critically. Notice whether your voice sounds nasal, breathy, harsh or hoarse. Notice the vowel sounds. Are they clear and carefully voiced? Keep the record as a memento, but forget about it now and begin working.

Don't try to hear yourself, except on recordings. Don't do as so many singers and announcers do, listen to yourself while you are talking. Announcers have a trick of putting the tips of the fingers just back of the ear with the palm facing close to the cheek. They can hear themselves then. Too many announcers become so enamored of listening to themselves that you feel intrusive if you listen too. To paraphrase Dorothy Parker, the affair between the radio announcer and his voice will live as one of the prettiest love stories in the history of speech. Talk to the listener—don't talk to yourself.

What can you do about the quality of your voice? First of all, try whispering. Whisper violently—without hurting your throat—for a few seconds before you start to read. Your voice will show a marked improvement in quality immediately. I don't know why; I just know it works. Such whispering daily will progressively improve the quality of your voice. It's a good trick to practice while shaving.

As for bathroom vocal exercising, it is too bad more oral readers are not bathtub singers. A good operatic aria in the bathtub will do wonders for your voice and vocal quality. It is a safe place to practice; the acoustics make you sound at your best; and you are using otherwise wasted time, according to the father in *Cheaper by the Dozen*. I seriously advocate it.

A good voice demands that there be no tensions in the speaking mechanism. If you are poorly prepared, tired, nervous, self-conscious, or trying too hard, you have a tendency to tighten your jaw, your neck, or your shoulder; as a result, your tone production suffers. You must learn to relax the muscles affecting voice production.

A speaker tied up in knots might as well put a gag in his mouth. Many of his listeners might like to do it for him. Let your muscles go, not by sheer willpower but by thinking about what you want to say and how you are going to say it. Waggle your jaw a few times. Yawn frequently to relax the throat muscles. Grin and pucker your lips to release your face muscles. Roll your head around, stretching your neck. These exercises are taken before going on stage—need it be said?

▶ *Nasal quality.* Nasality can be the result of organic difficulties; if it is, see a physician. Nasality can be the result of improper vocal habits; you can do something about that yourself.

First of all, learn to hear nasality.

Second, check whether or not you are opening your mouth widely enough. That's your *mouth,* not just your lips; pry your teeth apart. You should be able to get three fingers, one on top of the other, between your teeth on an *ah s*ound. Opening the mouth sufficiently for the formation of the vowel sounds will improve nearly every case of nasality.

Third, place your fingers over the bridge of your nose and say *morning.* You should feel vibrations on the nasal consonants. Now try saying words that do not have nasals in them and see if you can feel vibrations. If you feel none, you shouldn't have any serious problem of nasality. If you can, try this. Say a word like *Dan,* with your fingers still over the bridge of your nose. Do you feel a vibration before you come to the final consonant? In other words, are you nasalizing the vowel too? If you are, that is the cause of your nasal quality. You are supposed to nasalize *m, n,* and *ng.* You are not supposed to nasalize vowels. To rid yourself of vowel nasalization before a nasal consonant, repeat *dad* rapidly, and at each fifth repetition slip in a *Dan* or *dam,* as the case might be. By this method you can train yourself to put the nasal consonant where it belongs, following the vowel, just where other consonants come. This exercise can be practiced with any word you are nasalizing just by the substitution of *b* or *d* or *g,* the letters listeners think we substitute when we have a cold. A cold is an extreme case of de-nasality. If you have nasal speech, talk as if you had a code in your dose, but bady tibes worse thad ady real code. Speaking so will help you remove your nasality.

▶ *Breathiness.* Breathiness is a characteristic of voice quality that is just what the name implies. If you sound as if you were out of breath, or your voice has a whispery quality, you are guilty of breathiness. You can test your voice for this quality by sounding words beginning with *h, t,* and *p.* Listen to your voice as you sound these words with varying time and loudness to see whether the breath used on the consonants continues into the vowel sounds that follow.

One of the ways to overcome this fault is by whispering violently and then speaking. Try a sentence whispered and then try it voiced; try to make as much difference as possible between the ways of speaking.

Another way to overcome this fault is to forcibly expel all the air in your lungs, take a shallow breath and then intone *ah* for as long a time as you can. Concentrate on getting as much sound as possible from each exhalation of breath.

Fairbanks suggests you sing an octave up the scale on *ah* as loudly and as long as you can, striving for a nonbreathy quality.

When you get to the upper *do* reverse immediately and sing back down to your natural pitch, still making each tone loud, long and non-breathy. The chances are good that elimination of breathiness will be easier as you ascend the scale and that you can retain the non-breathy quality to a certain extent as you descend.[7]

If you have a breathy quality and the simple exercises in this chapter fail to help you, check with a skilled teacher or with a doctor. The cause of your difficulty may be organic.

▶ *Harshness.* Harshness is the vocal quality all radio announcers use when speaking of another manufacturer's soap. It is characterized by rasping, unmusical tones. When your pitch is low and your quality is harsh, you sound like a truck unloading gravel. When your pitch is high and your quality harsh, you sound like Homer calling Henry Aldrich.

The two most common causes of harsh quality are pathological conditions of the vocal mechanism and excessive tension. A word of caution: don't let anyone do anything about a pathological voice ailment unless he is a highly skilled specialist in vocal disorders. Excessive tension you can do something about. First of all, try relaxing. Then try preceding all vowel sounds with an *h*. This will help you ease into the vowel. If when you say *ah* it sounds as if you had stepped on the cat, try easing into the same vowel by saying *hah*.

A less technical way, but an equally effective one, is trying to voice contrasting words. Get the mental image first and then practice the contrasting sentences aloud. Try to sound harsh in the first sentence of the pairs and not harsh in the second.

It was hard as iron.	It was soft as silk.
It's a big rock.	It's a tiny baby.
It's murder.	It's love.
He's beating her.	He's caressing her.

You can make up countless pairs for your own practice. Harshness is more the result of mental attitude than anything else. Quit driving the peasants with a whip; cajole them a little.

> . . . each of us has many qualities of voice, one of which we habitually over-use. The shrill yip yapping of the flapper, the growl of the paterfamilias, the dry incisiveness of the mathematician, each of these is not the one and only voice of its possessor. If the girl falls in love the whole timbre and range of her voice are transformed. If the father holds his infant in his arms there is an unaccustomed clearness and sweetness in his voice. If the scientist celebrates a victory there is a ring and sparkle in his words rarely heard in the classroom. Even a pessimistic college or dramatic school student in a

[7] Fairbanks, *op. cit.*, pp. 211–212.

required course in voice training can be happily moved from her conviction that "her voice", poor thing though it may be, is irrevocably and unchangeably hers, if you remind her that her family can always detect the "man at the other end of the line" by the change in the quality of her voice, however guarded her remarks.[8]

▶ *Hoarseness.* This is the vocal quality of the prize-fight announcer. It is also the vocal quality of the person who has chronic nose and throat infections or irritations. Medical examination and treatment are called for, not speech drill. Complete rest for the voice is always the best first aid, however.

▶ *Conclusion.* For most of us, the voice we have is satisfactory for casual reading aloud. For effective reading aloud we may wish we had a better voice. The first requisite for developing a better voice is a greater desire to be comprehended by our listener. The second requisite is an understanding of our own vocal shortcomings. Listen to your voice for purposes of criticism and diagnosis of faults then go to work on those faults. They may be faults of breathing, phonation, or resonance. They may be faults in the use of loudness, pitch, time, or quality. Most undesirable vocal qualities can be obviated if your formation of the English vowel sounds is correct. You can do something about any of your vocal inadequacies if you are willing to admit them and drill to correct them. Such drill is a continuing process over a period of time. It should continue until the desired skills have been mastered and put to work in your everyday speech.

[8] Henrietta Prentiss, "The Master Key to Understanding," *Theater Arts Monthly,* XX, No. 9 (September, 1926), 588.

· 11 ·

Pronunciation

◆)◆)◆)◆)◆)◆)◆)◆)◆)◆)◆ ◆(◆(◆(◆(◆(◆(◆(◆(◆(◆(◆

No one willingly and knowingly mis-
pronounces a word, except in jest. Each of us tries to say words so that
they will be understood by our listeners. Since this is true, pronunciation
should be the reader skill easiest to master.

Pronunciation is simply articulating all the speech sounds in a word
correctly and then accenting them properly.

This would be the simplest, least-controversial task you have been
set, if there were an Emily Post of pronunciation. But in the field of pronunciation there is no final arbiter of correctness. Actually, the word
correct should not be used in connection with pronunciation at all. *Correct*
implies that anything different from it is incorrect. In the case of many
pronunciations, there are only preferred and less-preferred classifications.
Look up the word *narrator* in more than one dictionary and notice the
different pronunciations given as preferred.

You cannot go as far as to say that one pronunciation is more acceptable than another. Acceptable to whom? The word *syrup* is pronounced
surp in the Ozarks. That pronunciation is acceptable there. Is *sih-rehp* not
acceptable? Who says so? Are you willing to accept that opinion? Dare
you set your own opinion against it? How do you arrive at a defensible
opinion?

There is no substitute for a good dictionary.
Get one.
Learn to use it.
Use it.

No one should cavil at your pronunciation, if you have used a standard dictionary as your source of information. Your speech also will be in keeping with the everyday speech of contemporary America if you use *A Pronouncing Dictionary of American English,* by Kenyon and Nott.

Using either of these sources, you may still tend to speak in a manner that differs from the majority of Americans. That is, you may speak in one of the regional dialects of America. Many speech teachers claim that this is bad, and many students defend their right to speak so the home folks will recognize them. For acceptance outside your region, the speech teacher is right. The more standard your speech is, the wider your acceptance. The other point of view is expressed by Charles Laughton.

> I have been asked about the techniques of reading aloud. I had better tell you something of my experiences in the hospital when the men came to me and asked me to teach them to read love poems to their wives or Mother Goose stories to their children. They would first of all start by imitating my English accent. I had to get them back to speaking in the accents of the place they came from. People always speak most beautifully in the accents of their home towns—I, by the way, do not think that standard speech is the most alive speech. . . .
>
> I know that some people could be angry about the remark about standard speech. I know someone who is a friend of mine who may be disappointed that I have made it. Her name is Margaret Pendergast McClean. She is a speech teacher and she has taught our Shakespeare class about the control of our voices. I know that standard speech is necessary in professional acting; otherwise in great centers such as New York and Chicago no plays could be put together if all the actors were speaking in the several accents of their home towns, but still I would like to hear *Julius Caesar* in Iowa in the speech of the Middle West, which is strong. And *Julius Caesar* in Oregon in the speech of the Far West, and *Julius Caesar* in New Orleans in the soft and lovely speech of the South. This would not work if your point of view is that *Julius Caesar* is chiefly about Ancient Rome, but I think *Julius Caesar* is more about man as a political animal in the town in which it is being played in that year and at that moment.[1]

By the relative space given the two points of view, it would seem that I agree with Mr. Laughton's viewpoint. I don't. His example of *Julius Caesar* can be reduced to its inevitable absurdity. I know a college where they produce Shakespearean plays in Pennsylvania Dutch. I have

[1] Charles Laughton, "Storytelling," *Atlantic Monthly,* Vol. CLXXXV, No. 6 (June, 1950).

never noticed that a man speaking standard English is thought to be an oddity in an area where others are speaking the local dialect. He might be thought an outlander, but he has no difficulty in being understood, whereas a person with a regional dialect outside his own region is an outlander who frequently may be misunderstood. The motion pictures and the radio networks have disseminated standard speech throughout this nation as *standard*. I would recommend standard speech as a desirable goal. But I would never recommend it if it would impair the effectiveness of your communication.

Articulate all the speech sounds in a word correctly.

Let's begin with the vowels and diphthongs since there are fewer of them. Needless to say these are the spoken vowels, not the *a, e, i, o, u,* and sometimes *w* and *y* of the printed alphabet. The vowels carry the tone of your speech. Their proper formation affects the quality of your speech.

Many mistakes are made in the sounding of vowels in English because a single letter often represents many different sounds. The letter *a* for example is used in writing to represent six different sounds, as in the words *take, zany, hat, about, arm, dawn.* You can't count on spelling to help you with this matter of proper pronunciation.

> As long as English spelling tolerates such words as knickknack—the same letter silent four times—why not spell the sawdust arena *psoloquoise?* Falk Johnson, instructor in English at Northwestern University in Illinois, went on to explain last week the *psoloquoise* is just another way of spelling "circus"—"ps" as in psychology for the initial "c"; "olo" as pronounced "ir" in colonel; the "qu" as in bouquet for the second "c"; and "oise" as in tortoise for the final "us." Reforms are held up, says Johnson, because the English-speaking world clings too closely to spelling customs: "The linguists just don't tolerate the *od* and the nu-fangld."[2]

VOWELS

▶ *The vowel* ee. The vowel *ee* is spelled in words of English speech as in b*e*, b*ee*t, b*ea*t, bel*ie*ve, dec*ei*ve, k*e*y, p*eo*ple, debr*i*s, C*ae*sar, Ph*oe*nix, qu*ay*, pr*i*ma.

Make the *ee* sound, as in *bee,* for all the capitalized letters in this list of words, no matter what the spelling.

[2] From *Newsweek,* XXXII, No. 12 (September 20, 1948), 92.

a-lum'nAE	E'ra	prI'ma-don'na
a-mE'na-ble	gab-ar-dIne'	quar'an-tIne
aus'pi-cEs	hE'don-is'm	rE-cre-ate'
ba'sEs	in-gE'nious	sac-ri-lE'gious
crE'dence	in-hEr'ent	scEn'ic
crE'ma-to-ry	mE'ter	skI
cri'sEs	pE'nal-ize	slEEk
debrIs'	pe-tIte'	tE'pEE
di-a-bE'tEs	prE-di-lec'tion	trEat
E'dict	prE-mo-ni'tion	vE'nal

▶ *The vowel* ih.   The vowel *ih* is spelled in words of English speech as in b*i*t, b*ui*lt, b*u*siness, b*ee*n, w*o*men, pr*e*tty, s*ie*ve, and, believe it or not, as in unaccented final syllables such as Tuesd*ay*, a*n*y, coff*ee*, coll*ie*, knowl-edg*e*, marri*age*. It occurs before *r* in such spellings as *i*rritate, st*ee*r, b*ee*r, b*ie*r, b*ea*rd, w*ei*rd.

Make the *ih* sound, as in *bit,* for all the capitalized letters in this list, no matter what the spelling.

ab'bEY	frag'Ile	rep'tIle
a-bYss'	gen'u-Ine	res'pIte
ag'Ile	grIm'ly	sa-tIr'I-cal
an'tI-dote	hos'tIle	sem'I
ar-Is'to-crat	Im'mI-nent	ser'vIle
com-pI-la'tion	In'fI-nIte	shrIv'el
con-spIr'a-cy	lIve'long	sIm'I-lar-lY
dI-ges'tion	mo'bIle	vIr'u-lent
dI-lap'I-date	mor'tIse	wInd (air)
dI-plo'ma	neu-rIt'Ic	wOm'en
fI-nan'cial	prEt'tY	

▶ *The vowel* eh.   The vowel *eh* is spelled in words of English speech as in l*e*d, l*ea*d (the metal), fri*e*nd, s*ay*s, s*ai*d, h*ei*fer, h*ei*r, G*eo*ffrey, b*u*ry, g*ue*st. It occurs before *r* in such spellings as *e*rror, f*a*re, f*ai*r, th*e*re, th*ei*r, b*ea*r, pr*ay*er.

Make the *eh* sound, as in *bed,* for all the capitalized letters in this list, no matter what the spelling.

a-gAIn'	as-cEt'ic	En'sign
al-lEge'	car'bu-rEt-er	En'ter-prise
a-mEnd'	Ed'i-ble	Es-sEn'tial
An'y	Ef-fEct'	eu-gEn'ics

fEt'id	mEt'ric	saId
hEr'o-ine	ob-scEn'i-ty	tEp'id
lEg	plEth'o-ra	trEm'or
lEg'ate	prEd'a-to-ry	zEAl'ot
lEp'er	quEr'u-lous	
lEv'i-ty	rEc'i-pe	

▶ *The vowel* a.   The vowel *a* is spelled in words of English speech as in hat, laugh, plaid.

Make the *a* sound, as in *hat,* for all the capitalized letters in this list of words, no matter what the spelling.

a-bAft'	cAst	mAsk
Ad'age	chAff	mAs-quer-ade'
ad-vAnce'	cAs'ket	mAs'ter
ad-vAn'tage	dAnce	mo-dAl'i-ty
Af-fect'	de-prAv'i-ty	nAs'ty
Af-ter-noon'	drAft	out'cAst
Al-low'	en-hAnce'	pAr'i-ty
Am'i-ca-ble	fAst	pAs'sa-ble
An'gle	flAsk	pAst
An-noy'	gAr'ru-lous	pAs'tor-al
An'swer	gAsp'ing	plAs'ter-ing
Ar'id	gi-rAffe'	rAft
Ar-rest'	glAnce	rAsp'ing
Ask	glAss	rAth'er
As-sume'	grAn'a-ry	shAft
Aunt	grAsp	slAnt
bAs'ket	guAr-an-tee'	tAp'es-try
bAth	hAlf	tAsk
blAst	hAlve	tAs'sel
brAnch	in-flAm'ma-ble	thAtch
brAss	ir-rA'tion-al	vAl'iant
ca-dAv'er-ous	lAnc'er	vAst
cAn't	lAr'nx	wAft
cAr'a-mel	lAst	wrAth
cAv'il	lAth	
clAsp	lAugh	

▶ *The vowel* uh.   The vowel *uh,* called the neutral or schwa sound, is heard most often as an unaccented glide sound. It is heard frequently, although incorrectly, in every vowel sound in *America.* It is spelled in words of English speech as in *ago, up, oven, young, blood, does, praises, possible, purpose, porpoise.*

Make the *uh* sound, as in *but,* for all the capitalized letters in this list, no matter what the spelling.

A-bout'	dOne	quo'tA
A-live'	gUn	rel'A-tive
an'Als	jUst	tOngue
A-nOth'Er	lOve	Ugly
A-re'nA	mOth'Er	Ul-tI-ma'tUm
bA-lloon'	Oth'Er	Ul'trA
bA-nan'A	Ov'en	Unc'tIOn
break'fAst	pa'pA	Ut'tEr
bUt	pEr-sua'sIOn	yOUng
cIr'cUs	pol'kA	yOUng'stEr

► *The vowel ah.* The vowel *ah* is spelled in words of English speech as in f*a*ther, b*o*ther, b*ah*, s*er*geant, h*ear*th, g*ua*rd, *ho*nest.

Make the *ah* sound, as in *father,* for all the capitalized letters in this list, no matter what the spelling.

Arch	En-sEm'ble	prOd'i-gy
A'ri-a	fa-cAde'	psAlm
bAr	gAr-nish-ee'	shOck
bOmb	hOm'age	sOl'ace
cAlm	hOs'tage	spA
can-tA'ta	knOck	stac-cA'to
cat-a-strO'phic	mel'an-chOl-y	stAr
cOl'umn-ist	nOd	ta-mA'le
de-bAr'	Om'i-nous	tAr'get
di-o-rA'ma	pa-jA'mas	ver-bOs'i-ty
dOm'i-cile	pAr'tridge	vi'vA
dOn	pOl'len	yOn
En-core'	pOs'se	

► *The vowel aw.* The vowel *aw* is spelled in words of English speech as in c*a*ll, c*aw*, c*au*se, f*ou*ght, *o*ft, br*oa*d.

Make the *aw* sound, as in *saw* for all the capitalized letters in this list, no matter what the spelling.

All	AU'thor	AWk'ward
Al'most	AU'to	AWn'ing
AU'burn	AW'ful	cAll

cAUght	fOUght	sOUght
cOre	gnAWed	tAUght
dAWn	lOrd	wAll
dOg	nAUght	wArm
flAW	pAWed	wrOUght
fOr	sAUce	

► *The vowel* ooh. The vowel *ooh* is spelled in words of English speech as in b*oo*k, f*u*ll, w*ou*ld, w*o*man, w*o*rsted. It occurs before *r* in such spellings as s*u*re and p*oo*r.

Make the *ooh* sound, as in *book,* for all the capitalized letters in this list of words, no matter what the spelling.

am'bUsh	hOOd	tOOk
bOUr'bon	nOOk	wOm'an
bUl'let	pUl'ley	wOOd
cOOk	pUl'pit	wOUld
cOUld	pUt	
crOOk	stOOd	

► *The vowel* oo. The vowel *oo* is spelled in words of English speech as in b*oo*th, bl*ue*, bl*ew*, b*ou*quet, d*o,* thr*ough*, fr*ui*t, sh*oe*, man*eu*ver, rendev*ous*.

Make the *oo* sound, as in *booth,* for all the capitalized letters in this list of words, no matter what the spelling.

a-lOOf'	de-tOUr'	rUse
bal-lOOn'	glU'ten	rUth'less
blUE	hOOf	slEUth
bOOth	pOOr	sOOth'say-er
bO'som	re-cOUp'	trU'ant
bOU-quet'	rOOf	trUths
brOOm	rOOt	tUlle
COU pe'	rOUte	up-rOOt'
cOU'pon	rU'di-ments	
cuck'OO	rU'mor	

So much for vowels, as such. Remember to make all the vowels with a loose jaw and a relaxed vocal mechanism. Open your mouth properly for each one. Here are the preferred mouth positions.

ee   Mouth almost closed. Lips slightly widened and extended in the smile position.

ih   Mouth open enough for the admission of your little finger.

eh   Mouth half open.

a   Mouth three-quarters open.

uh   Mouth open enough for the admission of your thumb.

ah   Mouth well open; get in three fingers.

aw   Mouth well open and rounded; get in two fingers.

ooh   Mouth open enough for the admission of your thumb. Lips partially slacked.

oo   Mouth almost closed. Lips rounded on your little finger.

Practice these, first forming the sound correctly with the mouth and lips, then voicing the sounds.

DIPHTHONGS

Diphthongs are two vowels voiced so that there is no interruption of sound. The mouth opening is always smaller for the second vowel than for the first, with the first vowel receiving the major stress. Watch out in sounding diphthongs that you do not substitute improper vowel sounds and that you do not prolong the sounds until you have more than two.

▶ *The diphthong* oh-ooh.   The diphthong *oh-ooh* is spelled in words of English speech as in g*o*, g*o*al, gr*o*wn, t*o*e, b*ou*lder, *o*h, *o*we, th*o*ugh, s*ew*, b*eau*, chauff*eu*r, y*eo*man, br*oo*ch, apropo*s*. You may want to think of this sound as a vowel, but say *go* and notice how your voice sounds an *ooh* as it closes off the *oh* sound.

Make the *oh-ooh* sound, as in *go* for all the capitalized letters in this list of words, no matter what the spelling.

AU re-voir'	hOm'ing	mOw (verb)
bOw (weapon)	jOlt	O'men
ca-jOle'	lOw'er	O'nus
com-mO'di-ous	mAUve	O'ral
dO'tard	mel-an-chO'li-a	O'ri-ent
drOll'e-ry	mis'an-thrOpe	swOl'len
fO'rum	mO'ron	trOw

▶ *The diphthong* ah-ooh.   The diphthong *ah-ooh* is spelled in words of English speech as in h*our*, c*ow*er, s*au*erkr*au*t.

Make the *ah-ooh* sound, as in *sound,* for all the capitalized letters in this list of words, no matter what the spelling.

a-bOUt'	flOUt	nOW
al-lOW'	flOW'er	OUnce
a-rOUnd'	fOUnd	OUr
a-rOUse'	gOUt	OUst
bOUgh	gOWn	OUt
brOW	hOUnd	plOW
brOWn	HOUr	some'hOW
cOWl	hOUse	sOUth
dOUbt	lOUd	thOU
dOUse	mOUse	tOWn
en-dOW'	mOUth	vOW
eye'brOW	nOUn	

▶ *The diphthong* ay-ih.   The diphthong *ay-ih* is spelled in words of English speech as in s*ay*, s*a*le, s*ai*l, gr*ea*t, gr*ey*, v*ei*l, n*eigh*bor, fianc*é*, fianc*ée*, croch*et*, g*au*ge, g*ao*l.

Make the *ay-ih* sound, as in *say,* for all the capitalized letters in this list of words, no matter what the spelling.

a-bEY'ance	frA'cas	plA'cAte
Ace	gA'la	plAgue
AId	grA'tis	pu-rEE'
AIm	hA'lo	re-gA'li-a
Al'ien-Ate	hEI'nus	rou-E'
A'pex	ig-no-rA'mus	sA'li-ent
ap-pa-rA'tus	im-plA'ca-ble	sA'line
Ate	lack-a-dAI'si-cal	sA'pience
au-dA'cious	lA'tent	sA'vo-ry
A-vi-A'tion	lAthe	slAke
bAI'li-wick	mAEl'strom	slAv'ish
bAIze	man-dA'mus	slEIgh
bA'nal	mat-i-nEE'	tor-nA'do
bla-sE'	mE-lEE'	ul-ti-mA'tum
blA'tant	mE'sa	vEIl
dA'ta	nApe	ver-bA'tum
e-mA'ci-ate	pas-sE'	whEY
flA'grant	pA'thos	yEA

▶ *The diphthong* ah-ih.   The diphthong *ah-ih* is spelled in the words of English speech as in *I*, *eye*, b*y*, p*ie*, *aye*, r*ye*, g*uy*, g*ui*de, th*igh*, *ais*le, h*eigh*t.

Make the *ah-ih* sound, as in *eye,* for all the capitalized letters in this list of words, no matter what the spelling.

ad in-fin-I'tum	hom'i-cI-dal	sI'ne-cure
AISle	ho-rI'zon	stEIn
al-bI'no	I'con	stI'pend
al-rIGHt'	I-tin'er-ant	su-pIne'
a-lum'nI	lIthe	tI'ny
an-nI'hi-late	long'-lIved	trI-bu'nal
bIde	mal-lIgn'	trI-sect'
bI-og'ra-phy	pI'e-ty	vI'and
bIte	rec'on-dIte	vI'ol-ist
er'u-dIte	sac'ri-fIce	vI'rus
fe'lIne	Sem'Ite	whIn'ing
fI'at	short'lIved'	wI'ly
fI'nIte		

▶ *The diphthong* aw-ih. The diphthong *aw-ih* is spelled in words of English speech as in b*oy,* b*oi*l.

Make the *aw-ih* sound, as in *boy,* for all the capitalized letters in this list of words, no matter what the spelling.

al'ka-lOId	de-spOIl'	pOInt
al-lOY'	de-strOY'	pOIse
bOIl	em'plOY-ee'	pOI'son
bOYs	en'vOY	rOY
clOY	fOIl	sa-vOY
cOIl	lOIn	sOIl
cOIn	jOIst	tOY
con-vOY'	jOY	vOIce
cor'du-rOY	nOIse	vOId
de-cOY'	pOIn-set'ti-a	vOIle

▶ *The diphthong* you. I know *you* is considered to be a consonantal vowel by some phoneticians. Fred Waring in his system of tone syllables calls it *ee-oo,* and for singing purposes that pronunciation seems to work. The *NBC Handbook of Pronunciation* refuses to recognize the existence of the sound, except in a few instances. But whatever it may be called we do make a different sound for *you* than we do for *oo,* and there are a number of words in our speech that are pronounced that way from prefer-ence. This diphthong is spelled in words of English speech as in c*ue,* c*u*te, l*ie*u, n*ew,* n*eu*ter, *you,* *ewe,* rev*iew,* bea*u*ty

Make the *you* sound for all the capitalized letters in this list of words, no matter what the spelling.

ab'so-lUte	en-thU'si-asm	ob-tUse'
al-lUr'ing	fU'ry	op-por-tU'ni-ty
al-lU'sion	grat'i-tUde	pU'ber-ty
as-tUte'	il-lU'mi-nate	pU'ri-tan
at'ti-tUde	im-mUne'	re-dUce'
bi-tU'men	in'sti-tUte	re'fUt-a-ble
bU'reau	in-tU'i-tive	res'i-dUE
cap'sUle	KU klux Klan	res-ti-tU'tion
con-sUme'	lIEU	ret'i-nUe
cos'tUme	lon'gi-tUde	sa-lUte'
cU'li-na-ry	lU-gU'bri-ous	se-cUre'
cU'ri-ous	lUre	spU'ri-ous
CUte	lU'rid	stEW
de-lUde'	ma-tUre'	stU'dent
de-lU'sive	mU'ci-lage	stU'pid
dEUce	mul'ti-tUde	sU'et
dEW	mU'tate	sUIt'or
di-lUte'	mUte	tUbe
dU'bi-ous	nEU'ter	tU'lip
dU'el	nEU'tral	tU'mor
dUEs	nEW	tU'mult
dUke	nEWs'pa-per	tU'nic
dUr'ing	nU'cle-us	tU'tor
dU'ty	nUde	un-U'su-al
e-lUde'	nUI'sance	U'su-ry
en-dUre'	nU'mer-ous	ZEUs

And those are the diphthongs. Again, take care to open your mouth sufficiently to voice them.

oh-ooh   Mouth open. Lips rounded on your thumb.

ah-ooh   Mouth open for *ah*, then rounding and closing for *ooh*.

ay-ih   Mouth half open, sufficient for a little more than one finger.

ah-ih   Mouth full open for *ah*, then closing and lips widening for *ih*.

aw-ih   Mouth nearly full open for *aw*, then closing and lips widening for *ih*.

you   Mouth set for *ee;* the tongue flaps downward and the lips purse for *oo*.

CONSONANTS

So much for the vowels and diphthongs. You should practice them until you can project them with the greatest clearness of tone you can manage. But your speech is just music if vowels are all you have. You need consonants to give it force and distinction. Consonants make the word.

> The theater in which we were going to speak was a large one. I glanced at it despairingly. "I shall never be heard, never!" I said. The chairman was about to murmur some encouraging fatuity when Augustus Thomas cut him short: "Look after your consonants," he said authoritatively; "and your vowels will look after themselves."
> How simple are the great truths of life. Since that day long past I have been ever mindful of my consonants, and I have been heard.[3]

Most speakers do not "look after" their consonants, because their articulators tend to be lazy. We do not use the lips, tongue, and teeth hard enough or fast enough.

The inadequacies in our articulation of consonants are these:

1. Substitution of one consonant for another: *w* for *wh; r* for *l;* the voiced *th* for the voiceless *th,* or *t* for both of these; *b* for *v* or *f; s* for *f; d* for *t.*

2. Distortion: a lisped *s;* a lateral *s* sounding like *sh.*

3. Omission: no *ng* on final *ings;* no *ts* in *sts* combination; no *n* in "government," and few finals on any word.

> The only difficulty about Prossy will be the usual difficulty—want of muscle in the enunciation of the words. When people intend to play the piano in public, they play scales for several hours a day for years. A pupil of Leschititsky (Paderewski's master) comes before the public with steel fingers, which give a quite peculiar quality and penetration even to pianissimo notes. *An actress should practice her alphabet in just the same way, and come before the public able to drive a nail up to the head with one touch of a consonant. For want of this athleticism, people get driven to slow intonings, and woolly execution.* Now for Prossy I want extreme snap in the execution; every consonant should have a ten pound gun hammer spring in it, also great rapidity and certainty of articulation. Of course Edy has

---

[3] Agnes Repplier, *Eight Decades* (Boston: Houghton Mifflin Company, 1937), p. 11.

not got all that yet; but I shall get more of it out of her than she dreams of troubling herself for at present.[4]

If we were to follow Shaw's advice and "drive a nail" with every consonant we spoke, we would have no difficulty in being understood. If you want to exercise your articulation of consonants, play with the tongue-twisters you learned as a child. Also try, as you practice pronunciation, to enunciate each consonant overprecisely. Drills and tongue-twisters are included in the practice material.

Work on your articulation while you consider the problems of pronunciation. It was said earlier that pronouncing was simply articulating correctly all the speech sounds in a word, and then accenting them properly.

ACCENTING

There are several common faults in accenting. One is accenting the wrong syllable; another is omitting a syllable; and the third is adding a syllable. Then, of course, there is the danger of being overprecise.

Here are some words on which you can practice your knowledge of accenting. They are arranged tabularly under headings that indicate the type of accent fault most commonly made on that particular word. When in doubt, consult your dictionary.

Misplaced Accent	Omitting a Syllable	Adding a Syllable
abyss	adenoid	accompanist
address	believe	athlete
adult	beneficiary	attacked
allies	burial	burglar
bizarre	champion	detective
campaign	celery	drowned
cement	considerable	elm
Detroit	cruel	film
finance	dandelion	grievous
kowtow	electric	hungry
insurance	eleven	yes
recourse	family	electoral
research	federal	hindrance

[4] Christopher St. John, ed., *Ellen Terry and Bernard Shaw* (New York: G. P. Putnam's Sons, 1931), p. 171. Reprinted by permission of The Public Trustee and The Society of Authors, London, and Reinhardt & Evans, London.

Misplaced Accent	Omitting a Syllable	Adding a Syllable
romance	guardian	mayoralty
technique	geography	preventive
robust	history	stupendous
debutante	laboratory	Westminster
excise	lavatory	Worcester

But why do we make these mistakes, if we care about proper speech? There are several answers. English spelling is a poor guide to pronunciation. It is a guide, but we all know that there are unnecessary letters in many words; that there are many ways of spelling the same sound; and that there is little consistency in the formation of comparatives, gerunds, gerundives, participles, and adverbial forms.

Another reason for mispronunciation is judging that words that look alike will be pronounced alike. This habit is an outgrowth of that early reading habit, learning new words by observing their similarity to other words we already know. The beginning reader learns to pronounce and read *Ted* and *Ned* because he knows how to read *red*. We carry this habit into adult life and many times it betrays us.

Parents, teachers, and other adults also betray us. Their speech affects ours and, unless theirs is unfailingly acceptable, we learn inaccurate pronunciations. My second-grader came home exclaiming about the catfish a neighbor had caught on a *trout* line. After awhile I discovered she was talking of a *trot* line. I explained the difference between *trout* and *trot* and she must have reported the lesson to the neighbor, for he brought it up in conversation that evening, saying he had always wondered why they were called *trout* lines since a trout was never interested in them.

The unpredictable, changing habits of words is another reason for our mistakes. Since ours is a growing language—and since ours is a people's language—what was incorrect the day before yesterday, and acceptable yesterday, may be preferred today and archaic tomorrow. Kin Hubbard said, "Ever'thing that used t'be referred to as 'unmentionables' are now called by their real names." That's an example of the point I am trying to make. The very style of Kin Hubbard is an example. We no longer find misspelling funny. It is torture now to try to read the writings of Josh Billings, even though what he has to say may still be funny. As for the names of the "unmentionables," they have changed frequently in the last thirty years. *Drawers* became *bloomers* which became *underpants* which became *panties* which became *step-ins* which became *scanties* which —where are we? Although pronunciation changes are a little less startling, there are changes: *poliomyelitis* has become *polio* and the two *os* have changed from *aw* sound to an *oh* sound; everyone today knows *penicillin,* although it was unknown ten years ago and the pronunciation today is not that used by its discoverer.

Another reason for frequent mispronunciation is our tendency to try out a word without first checking it. On the whole it is a good trait. But a word used incorrectly once is on the way to becoming a habit with a second misuse. None of us spends enough time with the dictionary. If you intend to read aloud, you will have to spend more time with it than you have in the past. Listeners are critical of mistakes. Always, in any audience, there is someone who knows the correct pronunciation of a word and who will be distressed by its mispronunciation.

There is one other consideration of pronunciation that must be touched on: foreignisms. When in your script you come across a foreign word, speak it using the sounds of English while attempting to approximate its foreign pronunciation. Fowler is speaking of French words here but what he says can be applied to words from any language.

> To say a French word in the middle of an English sentence exactly as it would be said by a Frenchman in a French sentence is a feat demanding an acrobatic mouth; the muscles have to be suddenly adjusted to a performance of a different nature, and after it as suddenly recalled to the normal state; it is a feat that should not be attempted; the greater its success as a *tour de force,* the greater its failure as a step in the conversational progress; for your collocutor, aware that he could not have done it himself, has his attention distracted whether he admires or is humiliated. All that is necessary is a polite acknowledgment of indebtedness to the French language indicated by some approach in some part of the word to the foreign sound, and even this only when the difference between the foreign and the corresponding natural English sound, is too marked to escape a dull ear. For instance, in *tête-à-tête* no attempt need or should be made to distinguish French ê from English ā, but the calling it tā′tahtā′ t instead of the natural English tātatā′ t rightly stamps it as foreign; again, *tour de force* is better with no unEnglish sound at all; neither r need be trilled, and *tour* and *force* should both be exactly like the English words so spelt. On the other hand, there are some French sounds so obviously alien to the English mouth that words containing them (except such as are, like *coupon,* in daily use by all sorts and conditions of men) should either be eschewed by English speakers or have these sounds adumbrated; they are especially the nasalized vowels (*an, en, in, on, un, am,* etc.), the diphthong *eu,* the unaccented *e,* and *u;* to say *bong* for *bon* is as insulting to the French language as to pronounce *bulletin* in correct French is insult-

ing to the man in the English street, and kooldesă'k for *cul-de-sac* is nearly as bad.[5]

▶ *Conclusion.* It is well to remember that pronunciation is the most mechanical of the reading skills. You can acquire effective pronunciation just by being careful. By using a dictionary you can learn the speech sounds and the accents in any word. Then all you need do is voice those sounds and only those sounds, giving them their proper accent.

[5] H. W. Fowler, *A Dictionary of Modern English Usage* (Oxford: At the Clarendon Press, 1949), p. 194.

· 12 ·

Special Reading Problems

>)>)>)>)>)>)>)>)>) ⊰(⊰(⊰(⊰(⊰(⊰(⊰(⊰(⊰(⊰(

The danger in heading a chapter "Special Reading Problems" is that you may get a wrong impression. You may think reading poetry or humorous or sacred material is different from reading other material. You may think reading for radio or television is a mysterious operation different from reading for an audience. Don't. Effective reading aloud is effective no matter what the material and no matter what the medium.

A good reader can read any type of material anywhere effectively. A good performer can switch from one medium to another without perceptible loss of stature. Ezio Pinza can move from opera to musical comedy, radio, motion pictures, and television without noticeable difficulty. Charles Laughton can read from the Bible, Shakespeare, and Charles Dickens without discernible change in his approach.

If you have mastered the requirements of analysis and preparation of materials, and if you have mastered the necessary skills for communicating ideas and emotions, you need have no concern, whether you are reading humor or poetry before an audience or before a camera.

The purpose of this chapter is to help you adapt your reading skills and techniques to different materials and media, to show you some of the minor differences in approach.

None of the sections in this chapter is intended for the professional person. The section on poetry is not intended for the professional reader of poetry; the section on humor is not intended for the professional humorist; the section on sacred material is not intended for the professional clergyman. These sections are intended for the person who plans to use poetic, humorous, or sacred material either as a quotation in a speech or as a reading experience to be shared with an audience for its edification or diversion.

Professor Churchill held the chair of Homiletics in the Seminary and also gave instruction in elocution in the Academy. He was an excellent preacher and writer, and one of the editors of the *Andover Review,* but his popular reputation throughout New England was due to his "readings." He had a singularly rich voice and features that expressed every color of emotion. His reading desk, lighted with lamps fitted with reflectors, was modelled after that of Charles Dickens. He invariably closed his programs with a humorous selection—"to send them home happy," as he told me—and his interpretations of Dickens, Mark Twain, and Bret Harte were masterly. Privately, I think he preferred to read *Hamlet* or *The Ancient Mariner* or Rossetti's *Sister Helen.* He never read in public from the Bible except when he was preaching, and I remember his saying to me that "a clergyman should always read the Bible as if he were himself listening to its message as well as conveying it to the congregation"; a counsel of perfection which is violated every Sunday.[1]

POETRY

It is assumed here that you will occasionally read poetry aloud when you want it for a quotation or when you think that poetry can express your idea better than prose. Poetry, when used for these purposes, is an extension of your communication, and you read for sense and variety and emotional impact.

The artist's reading aloud of poetry is a satisfying experience for himself and the audience. The average person's reading aloud of poetry can be equally satisfying if it is not pretentious. When you like a poem and read it out of your desire to have others share your delight, you will be forgiven many technical inadequacies. "He tried to recite two considerable batches of poetry—good poetry—but he lost confidence and turned it into bad poetry by bad recitation."[2]

Scholars, critics, and poets agree that poetry was intended to be read

[1] Bliss Perry, *And Gladly Teach* (Boston: Houghton Mifflin Company, 1935), p. 76.
[2] Samuel L. Clemens, *Mark Twain's Autobiography* (New York: Harper & Brothers, 1924), I, 280. Copyright, 1924, by Clara Gabrilowitsch. Copyright, 1952, by Clara Clemens Samossoud.

aloud. Reading poetry differs from reading prose because of the marked rhythm of poetry; poetic conventions, such as rhyme, assonance, dissonance, and alliteration; and the heightened perception of emotion in the contents of poetry.

To attack the problem of reading poetry aloud, the reader begins where he begins with all other material—with analysis. You try to understand the author's purpose, form, structure, mood, and ideas. You try to understand the poet's punctuation and words. Difficulties may arise there immediately.

"A poem compresses much in a small space and adds music, thus heightening its meaning," says E. B. White.[3] The meaning is heightened; but, at the same time, many of the traditional guideposts to meaning—word order, punctuation, and inclusion of all necessary parts of speech—are either changed or omitted.

▶ *Word order.* Emily Dickinson writes,

> Inebriate of air am I,
> And debauchee of dew,
> Reeling, through endless summer days,
> From inns of molten blue.[4]

Obviously, if this were prose it would be written, "I am an inebriate of air and a debauchee of dew, for I reel through endless summer days out of the inns of molten blue." It still has rhythm and rhyme, but it has lost much of its succinctness. If we were striving to write the exact idea we might rephrase it "In summer, I am inebriated by the air and debauched by the dew." Or, "Summer makes me drunk." However, the verb forms are much too strong for so simple and delicately stated an idea. As White said, the use of poetry has heightened the meaning, although certain poetic conventions may have made the whole meaning less perceptible.

▶ *Omission of necessary parts of speech.* Since the poet many times changes the word order of his speech to heighten meaning, he may of necessity omit words and some parts of speech necessary to structural completeness. Such omissions occur in prose. Emily Dickinson omitted the definite articles in the selection above. Robert Frost omits other words in this excerpt.

> Something there is that doesn't love a wall,
> That sends the frozen-ground-swell under it,

---

[3] *Here Is New York* (New York: Harper & Brothers, 1949), p. 121. Copyright, 1949, by The Curtis Publishing Company.

[4] Martha Dickinson Bianchi and Alfred Leete Hampson, eds., *Poems by Emily Dickinson* (Boston: Little, Brown & Co., 1947), p. 12.

> And spills the upper boulders in the sun;
> And makes gaps even two can pass abreast.[5]

Rearranged into prose, the excerpt might read, "There is something that doesn't love a wall, that sends the frozen-ground-swell under it and spills the upper boulders out into the sunlight; and that makes gaps big enough for two to pass through abreast." The added words in the prose version contribute little to our understanding of the poet's idea, but they do make it easier to follow the turn of the images. Without those added words, our task of vocal interpretation is greater.

▶ *Punctuation.* Because of changes in word order and the omission of words, the problem of punctuating poetry becomes more difficult for the poet and interpreting the punctuation becomes more complex for the reader. The commas become for the poet and the reader the warning of convolutions in construction, the interrelationship of clauses, and the listing of a series. True, the comma is used in all these ways in prose; but the increased frequency of such structures in the "small space" of which E. B. White speaks makes the comma look more omnipresent in poetry than it ever does in prose. The poet frequently makes use of the colon to indicate subordination of ideas.

> Gather ye rosebuds while ye may,
> Old Time is still a-flying:
> And this same flower that smiles today
> Tomorrow will be dying.

You may be tempted at this point to ask, why write poetry differently from prose? An answer might be, why sing what can be spoken? Poetry, like prose, is a means of conveying ideas and emotions; but because of its extreme compression and more strictly ordered form, it, like the other arts, speaks to us more deeply and subtly, if somewhat less obviously and directly.

> Good poetry seems so simple and natural a thing that when we meet it we wonder that all men are not always poets. Poetry is nothing but healthy speech . . . . The best lines, perhaps, only suggest to me that man simply saw or heard or felt what seems the commonest fact in my experience.[6]

If good poetry is simple and natural, why is it couched in verse? That question must be answered before it is possible to go further with

[5] Robert Frost, "Mending Wall," *Complete Poems of Robert Frost* (New York: Henry Holt & Company, 1949).

[6] Henry David Thoreau, *Journal,* ed. Bradford Tarrey and Francis H. Allen (Boston: Houghton Mifflin Company, 1949), 14 vols., November 30, 1841.

our analysis of poetic structure; the answer must be understood before we can begin using the techniques of the communicative skills to voice the poetry.

A great poet uses arresting language to clothe his ideas. He gains our attention by his phraseology, in other words. The poetic conventions of ordered rhythm and word harmony are interesting in themselves and enable the poet to constantly restimulate our interest. We remember a poem far more easily than a prose communication. The poet by his heightened perceptions can make truths understandable to us, not by the application of logic, but by insight and revelation.

> The creator, the artist, the extraordinary man, is merely the ordinary man intensified; a person whose life is sometimes lifted to a high pitch of feeling and who has the gift of making others share his excitement. The ordinary man lives by the creative spirit. He thinks in images and dreams in fantasy; he lives by poetry. Yet he seems to distrust it.[7]

As Untermeyer says, all of us think in images; much of our common understanding is gained by definition of likenesses. "Steering a Cesna Aircoupe is like driving an automobile," is an image that creates understanding. The poet deals principally in images, and oftentimes by his insight makes clear to us that which was obscure—he contributes to our understanding, in other words.

Since poetry contributes to our understanding, compels our attention, and is more memorable than prose, you will use it frequently when reading aloud. Few of us are fortunate enough to have such a broad knowledge of poetry that we can readily pull from our store the exact poem for every idea, occasion, and situation. However, the characteristics of your audience will help determine the type of poetry you will choose.

Having chosen a poem that says what you want to say, you meet the problems of communication of ideas by means of phrasing, inflection, pauses, stress, and variety, just as you did with prose.

The phrasing of poetry presents one immediate difference from prose: the run-on line.

> Some say the world will end in fire,
> Some say in ice.
> From what I've tasted of desire
> I hold with those who favor fire.
> But if it had to perish twice,

---

[7] Louis Untermeyer, "An Introduction," *The Pocket Book of Robert Frost's Poems* (New York: Pocket Books, Inc., 1946), p. 1.

> I think I know enough of hate
> To say that for destruction ice
> Is also great
> And would suffice.[8]

In the last five lines you have three run-on lines. If the problem were simply one of continuing the thought over the run-on, poetry would be little different from prose. But there is a metric cadence to the lines that must be observed even when the sense runs on. Using / for cadence breaks and // for phrasing, let's examine the last five lines.

"But if it had to perish twice, / I think I know enough of hate / to say // that for destruction ice / is also great / and would suffice. // " Obviously all this could be read as one phrase, although it might be too long for one breath. The phrasing of the lines "that for destruction ice is also great and would suffice" has to be kept together for sense, hence there can be no inflectional glide at "ice." The reader needs a pause there for cadence and rhyme, so he leaves the pitch up and prolongs the vowel, and then continues, on the same pitch with "is."

The run-on line is a fairly simple problem in most poetry; the reader needs only to analyse his material sufficiently to know where his phrases do end and where there is the possibility of a breath. The caesura, a rhythmic break within poetic lines, presents such a complex problem of phrasing that the study of it belongs to specialists in poetry.

The knowledge of how to voice contrasts through the use of inflections is essential to the reading of poetry. The poet achieves many of his sensory impressions through contrasting word against word or phrase against phrase. Shakespeare was especially enamored of this pairing of key words.[9] Sometimes he pairs six or more words against each other.

> Some grief shows much of love,
> But much of grief shows still some want of wit.

There *some* pairs with *much, much* with *want, grief* with *love,* and *grief* with *wit.*

Subordination in poetry is the same as in prose, except that it is elaborated. The poet subordinates two or three ideas to the main thought. To handle such multiples of subordination the reader must use all the tricks of rate, tone, and quality to convey the sense and use all his knowledge of sentence structure and paraphrase to be sure his listeners comprehend.

---

[8] From *New Hampshire,* by Robert Frost. Copyright, 1923, by Henry Holt & Co., Inc. Copyright, 1951, by Robert Frost. Used by permission of the publishers.

[9] See George R. Kernodle, "Basic Problems in Reading Shakespeare," *Quarterly Journal of Speech,* Vol. XXXV, No. 1 (February, 1949).

The new problem the reader meets with pauses in poetry is the blending of the pause into the metrical cadence of the poem. Shakespeare and many other poets drop beats in their poetry where they want the pause to take up the time. Tennyson's

> Break, break, break,
> On thy cold gray stones, O Sea!

is an example of the pause filling in the dropped syllables in the first line.

One new problem in stress faces the reader. That is the echo, the repetition of a word or an idea. Such a problem is found in the lines above. The rule for prose is this. A word is repeated for emphasis; therefore the second time it is voiced it differs from the first time either in volume, pitch, quality, or duration. In poetry, however, where phrases are often repeated, the repetition may be an echo rather than an emphatic reiteration. In

> The leaves they were crisped and sere,
> The leaves they were withering and sere,

the second line echoes the first and the stress would be on the new word; not on the repeated word. At this point is might be well to mention that all pronouns are echoes and should not be pounded. The noun and the verb receive the stress; the pronoun should be relegated to the background.

The reader needs no warning about variety in the reading of poetry; he needs to be warned away from too much variety. The up-hill and down-dale pattern of the reader who is enjoying the rhythmic gallop of the words and letting the sense limp slowly behind is only too familiar.

The emotional content of poetry is much more apparent than that of prose. The reader deals with more carefully chosen words, more meaningful and vivid images, and with definite mood. The techniques of conveying these emotions are the same as those studied in Chapter 7.

HUMOROUS MATERIAL

Need we assume here that you are only an occasional wit? If you have aspirations to be a professional humorist, there is nowhere you can be referred to for sure-fire training in how-to-be funny. If you want to spice your presentation with humor, or if you want to read a humorous selection because you like it, this section can be of some help.

You need to know what you are doing before you attempt it. Here is the most helpful discrimination of types of humor I know.

HUMOUR, WIT, SATIRE, SARCASM, INVECTIVE, IRONY, CYNICISM, THE
SARDONIC. So much has been written upon the nature of some of these
words, and upon the distinctions between pairs or trios among them
(wit and humour, sarcasm and irony and satire), that it would be both
presumptuous and unnecessary to attempt a further disquisition. But
a sort of tabular statement may be of service against some popular
misconceptions. No definition of the words is offered, but for each its
motive or aim, its province, its method or means, and its proper audience, are specified. The constant confusion between sarcasm, satire,
and irony, as well as that now less common between wit and humour,
seems to justify this mechanical device of parallel classification; but
it will be of use only to those who wish for help in determining which
is the word that they really want.[10]

	Motive or Aim	Province	Method or Means	Audience
Humour	Discovery	Human nature	Observation	The sympathetic
Wit	Throwing light	Words & ideas	Surprise	The intelligent
Satire	Amendment	Morals & manners	Accentuation	The self-satisfied
Sarcasm	Inflicting pain	Faults & foibles	Inversion	Victim & bystander
Invective	Discredit	Misconduct	Direct statement	The public
Irony	Exclusiveness	Statement of facts	Mystification	An inner circle
Cynicism	Self-justifica-tion	Morals	Exposure of nakedness	The respectable
the Sardonic	Self-relief	Adversity	Pessimism	Self

Being humorous with material already prepared requires skill above
everything else. Your analysis will be no different from that for any other
material. Your communication of ideas will make heavy demands on your
techniques for phrasing, inflection, pauses, emphasis, and variety. It will
make similar demands on your projection of personality.

The first suggestion all experienced funnymen make to the novice is
to take it easy. Humor should appear easy, effortless, and natural. The
second suggestion is that when you are being humorous you make it clear
that you are jesting. Unless you are in a playful mood, the audience cannot
be expected to understand that what you say is funny. Stephen Leacock
says,

> I always try to appear as happy as possible while I am lectur-
> ing. I take this to be part of the trade of anybody labeled a humorist

[10] Text and table from H. W. Fowler, *A Dictionary of Modern English Usage*
(Oxford: At the Clarendon Press, 1949), pp. 240–241.

By LIFE Photographer Al Fenn. Courtesy of TIME Inc.

Using the Teleprompter to read aloud.

and paid as such. I have no sympathy whatever with the idea that a humorist ought to be a lugubrious person with a face stamped with melancholy. This is a cheap and elementary effect belonging to the level of a circus clown. The image of "laughter shaking both his sides" is a truer picture of comedy. Therefore, I say, I always try to appear cheerful at my lectures and even to laugh at my own jokes.[11]

Other humorists of as great a stature as Leacock disagree with him heartily, believing that the speaker should remain deadpan and let the audience supply the laughter. All agree, however, that you must be known to be in jest before what you say can be taken as funny.

Max Eastman says there are ten commandments of the Comic Arts. (1) Be interesting. (2) Be unimpassioned. (3) Be effortless. (4) Remember the difference between cracking jokes and conveying ludicrous impressions. (5) Be plausible. (6) Be sudden. (7) Be neat. (8) Be right with your timing. (9) Give good measure of serious satisfaction. (10) Redeem all serious disappointments.

[11] Reprinted from *Enjoyment of Laughter*, by permission of Simon and Schuster, Publishers. Copyright, 1936, by Max Eastman.

1. Be interesting. Since you are not reading aloud your own humorous material, but that of another, this precept means for you—choose interesting material. Choose material that interests you and that you believe will interest your audience.

2. Be unimpassioned. Humor lies so close to deeper emotions that you must not arouse feelings that might get out of hand. If you should become impassioned, you might cease to be playful and, if you or the audience should get out of the play mood, you automatically cease to be funny.

W. C. Fields used to say that it was not funny to break things. People worried about the expense of broken objects and thus ceased to be playful. His recipe for humor—and he made a success from ringing changes on this idea—was this: if it bends it's funny; if it breaks it's tragic.[12]

3. Be effortless. This does not mean that you should not rehearse or work at the technical aspects of your humor. To prepare a half-hour radio program, Fred Allen used to work from one Sunday-night show to the next with only one evening off for relaxation. It means that you should sound as if your humor was easy and unlabored. If the humor must be dragged in, or if you have to work all around an idea to make the quoted joke applicable, you are working too hard to be in play; you are not playing, you are working, and hence you will not be funny to an audience. "Humor," as Josh Billings said, "must fall out of a man's mouth like music out of a bobolink."

4. Remember the difference between cracking jokes and conveying ludicrous impressions. A joke is a brief story with a "kicker" at the end. It depends upon plausibility, neatness, and timing for its effects. It has within it always the element of surprise. Bob Hope is a jokeman. The ludicrous impression is the rambling, humorous piling up of absurdities; it is the creating of ludicrous mental images in the mind of the listener. Many times it has no end. Fibber McGee and Molly are examples of this type of humor. Much of Fred Allen's fun is of this type. At a rehearsal of a skit for one of his radio programs, he argued to keep a line in the script that no one else in the cast thought funny; he believed it was ludicrous. He had Napoleon call Josephine his "big, beefy Oiseau." The laughter it provoked proved him more a comedian than the company he kept. According to Mark Twain, the humorous story can be spun out to great length. It can wander around as much as it pleases and arrive nowhere in particular. But the comic or witty story has to be brief and end with a point. "The humorous story bubbles gently along," Twain said, "the others burst."

[12] Alva Johnston, "Who Knows What Is Funny?" *Saturday Evening Post,* Vol. CCXI, No. 6 (August 6, 1948).

5. Be plausible. The joke you are telling must begin as sanely and as plausibly as the narration of any serious event. The effect of the "kicker" is in direct proportion to the credibility of the introduction to the story. Stories should be led into by the narration of logically related facts.

6. Be sudden. Most of the reasoning behind this commandment is included in Bennett Cerf's baker's dozen of don'ts for storytellers.[13] (1) Don't make a story too long. (2) Don't forget your point in the middle of the story. (3) Don't laugh too much yourself. "A hearty laugh at the end of the story, constituting yourself a sort of cheer leader, is not only permissible but, if not carried to excess, sound strategy. While the story is in progress, however, let your audience do the laughing . . . ." (4) Don't lay hands on your audience. (5) Don't tell your story more than once to the same audience. (6) Don't give the point of the story before you begin. (7) Don't insist on telling a story after your victim informs you he has heard it. (8) Don't oversell your story in advance. "The man who prefaces a recital with 'This is the funniest story you ever heard in your life' is apt to find the burden of proof sitting too heavily on his shoulders." (9) Don't tell your stories at the wrong place. Let it be appropriate to the audience, in other words. (10) Don't tell your stories at the wrong time. Let them be appropriate to the occasion, in other words. (11) Don't always know another version of someone else's story. (12) Don't tell stories that depend for their humor on events or personalities never heard of by your audience. (13) Avoid dialect stories if possible.

7. Be neat. This has nothing to do with grooming. It merely means that, allied to suddenness in storytelling, there should be an economy of motion and words to get to the point. The joke structure should be clear and orderly; neat, in other words.

8. Be right with your timing. This you learn with practice. It is the combination of change of pace, pausing, and rhythm generally. The "kicker" of a joke is usually held back for a split second. You use the pause for suspense. The comic effect is heightened by changing the pace of the surprise ending from that used in the body of the story. It cannot be explained on paper, nor can it be done the first time you try it. It is learned by frequent efforts to tell stories.

9. Give good measure of serious satisfaction. The best stories are relevant to serious concerns. Although they should be funny first, they should have one quality in common with poetry; they should give us fresh insight into a serious or perplexing problem.

10. Redeem all serious disappointments. One of the definitions of humor is that it is a disappointment. Your mind reaches for one idea and

[13] Bennett Cerf, "How Not to Tell a Story," *Saturday Evening Post,* Vol. CCXX, No. 17 (March 6, 1948).

is disappointed by not coming to the logical conclusion it sought. That is the fun of the anticlimax and the pun. Better humor is found in those stories where your mind reaches for one logical conclusion, does not find it, but finds a substitute idea. This is, again, the humor of the good pun, the surprise joke, and the carefully worked out anticlimax. It results in satisfaction of an unexpected kind. This commandment for humor means that the greater the disappointment at the failure to reach a predetermined end, the greater the brilliance of the substituted end must be. That is, let your surprises be real surprises, your puns be fresh ones, and your anticlimax as great as the legitimate climax might have been.

If you feel that humor is frivolous and has no place in public communication, if you feel that fun has no place in society today and is unbecoming in a public performer, if you feel that there should be a justification for the inclusion of humor in any presentation you make—if you feel any of these questions beginning to form in your mind, don't try to use humor in your presentation. To reform you, I would suggest that you sit with your audience while you make a humorless presentation, but, as Mark Twain said, the constitution prohibits the infliction of cruel or unusual punishments. If you must have rational justification for humor, give up the idea of being humorous; it is not for you.

> Laughs won't live on the knowledge about a thing; they live in the perception of it. You can learn to love—at least they say so—but you laugh at first or not at all.[14]

SACRED MATERIAL

A special section on reading sacred material is needed in any book that purports to discuss reading aloud effectively, for nearly every reader changes personality when he reads sacred material. For some inexplicable reason, as soon as the average reader addresses God, he assumes a lugubrious tone and harangues Him.

You should read sacred material aloud just as you would read any other material. You analyze the material, you prepare it for reading, and you use communication skills in exactly the same way you use them for all other material. There should be no difference in your style of delivery.

You should not assume a "ministerial" tone when reading sacred material. You need not intone nor chant your material. If the concept of God that you hold admits His omnipresence, you need no special volume level to reach Him. The assumption of an orotund quality of voice simply

---

[14] Eastman, *op. cit.,* p. 217.

removes your reading from the realm of ordinary communication for sense and lessens the possibility of the listener's complete comprehension.

> And ye shall seek me, and find me, when ye shall search for me with all your heart.
>
> —Jeremiah 29:13
>
> The Lord is nigh unto all them that call upon him, to all that call upon him in truth.
>
> —Psalm 145:18
>
> When you pray do not make your prayer mere routine, but a plea before God for mercy and grace.
>
> —Abot 2:13
>
> It is proper for you to know, my brother, that the aim of our devotion in prayer consists in naught save the soul's longing for God, humbling itself before Him and extolling the Creator with praise and gratitude unto His name, and casting all burdens upon Him.
>
> —Bahya ibn-Paquda, *Duties of the Heart,* 3

Why do we so often assume an unnatural manner of speaking when using sacred material? First, I believe, because of the difference in the language used. We are smitten with the words of the traditional versions of our holy books. They are magnificent words, granted; but the language is frequently incomprehensible to our audience. If similar language were used in some other communication you were reading, you would change or interpret the language to insure comprehension from your listener. For some reason we shy away from making similar changes in the seventeenth-century translations of the Bible. We no longer use the *thee, thou, thy, thine,* and *ye* forms for the second person; but the most colloquial speaker in America today, when called upon to pray, will invariably use and misuse them. As soon as we have established a language barrier between us and natural, sincere communication, as soon as we have assumed a florid language style, we tend to assume an equally unnatural and florid style of delivery, which has a dangerous potential for insincerity. How can we avoid these hazards? Whenever possible, your reading of sacred material should be from a good modern translation. Charles Laughton, in his argument that the reader should use the speech most natural to him, does not follow that through to its logical conclusion, for he reads from the King James Version of the Bible. But he is reading from the Bible as literature, not primarily as a sacred book.[15]

A second reason for the differences generally assumed in reading sacred and profane material is the feeling of the reader that the sacred material is sacred. You seldom approach the Bible with the attitude that

[15] See p. 170.

it is a book with something to say which you must understand clearly before you can read it aloud; you approach it rather with an attitude that the words are sacred per se. This is a mistaken attitude. When God spoke to man in the whirlwind or in revelations, He spoke in a language and accents that could be understood by His listeners; when we report His words today, we should speak in understandable language and accents. Few clergymen attempt to read the words of Holy Scripture to their congregations in the original Hebrew. Why then should they read them in archaic English or Latin?[16] If the language style were changed, the reader might lose the feeling that the "sacredness" of the communication absolves him from the necessity of active listening and full comprehension. Robert Louis Stevenson said,

> I believe it would startle and move anyone if they could make a certain effort of imagination and read it freshly like a Book, not droningly and chillily like a portion of the Bible.[17]

Many a beginning reader stands in similar awe of Shakespeare. He thinks he should not read Shakespeare as if the Bard had anything to say, but should treat him as if he were a "classic." This too is a mistaken attitude. Anything chosen to be read aloud should have ideas or emotions that are communicable. It is the reader's job to see that they are communicated.

You may on occasion be asked to read sacred material embodied in a ritual. In this case, you have no choice of language or style. Since you must accept the textual material exactly as it stands, approach the problem as if you were reading poetry. Get from your reading all the meaning you can; accept the traditional language as you accept the conventions of poetry. Realize that such ritual has strength and beauty and integrity of its own. Like poetry, it is a carefully worded, consciously ordered, rhythmic use of language deliberately aiming toward a heightened effect. Under no circumstances should you alter your usual speaking manner so that you will sound insincere, indirect, self-conscious—phony, in other words.

A third reason for the special reading style reserved for sacred material is in the emotion associated with the act. In a prayer, the reader implores or supplicates the Lord. The person praying knows this, and in order to indicate humility he frequently assumes a tone that is lugubrious,

---

[16] George Bernard Shaw points out in his play *Saint Joan* that although the Bishop of Beauvais thought Joan a heretic because she heard the voices of her Saints speak in French (when they should have spoken Latin), the English believed her a limb of the devil because the saints did not speak to her in English.

[17] Quoted in *The Bible Designed to Be Read as Living Literature* (New York: Simon & Schuster, 1936), p. 1,268.

but hardly humble. In reading from the scriptures, that tone carries over. Also, since most modern religious services and other religious functions are based upon emotional response, the reader of any material related to religion feels that he must use a tone fraught with emotion—hence the orotund voice, the hoarse quality. Here, as in all other reading, you must read as best you can to achieve your objectives; you must not read in your best imitation of someone else's interpretation.

The hushed "solemcholy" manner of reading sacred material is just as inappropriate in the occasional reader as is the too-emotional manner. One of the concepts of praise that is most forgotten by the average reader is the injunction to "make a glad noise unto the Lord." Joy is not out of keeping with solemnity; the word *solemn* means "observed with all the ceremony established by liturgy or tradition," as well as "highly serious; brave; deeply earnest." The Christian feasts of Christmas and Easter, the Jewish feasts of Hannukkah and Purim are first-hand evidence of the place of joy with solemnity in two major religions. The word *feast* itself stems from the Latin *festus* meaning joyful.

An elderly devil in hell writes to his nephew on earth—a junior tempter working on his first patient—on this subject in the eleventh of *The Screwtape Letters*. Remember that when the writer speaks of "we" or "us" he means the devils in hell.

> I divide the causes of human laughter into Joy, Fun, the Joke Proper, and Flippancy. You will see the first among friends and lovers reunited on the eve of a holiday. Among adults some pretext in the way of Jokes is usually provided, but the facility with which the smallest witticisms produce laughter at such a time shows that they are not the real cause. What the real cause is we do not know. Something like it is expressed in much of that detestable art which the humans call Music, and something like it occurs in Heaven—a meaningless acceleration in the rhythm of celestial experience, quite opaque to us. Laughter of this kind does us no good and should always be discouraged. Besides, the phenomenon is of itself disgusting and a direct insult to the realism, dignity and austerity of Hell.[18]

In conclusion, let me urge the reader of sacred material to attempt a direct communication with the listener. Strive for simplicity, naturalness, and sincerity. Strive for complete comprehension. It seems to me that we can better achieve the purpose of prayer, better achieve the stimulation toward a purposeful life, which contact with sacred materials can give us,

---

[18] C. S. Lewis, *The Screwtape Letters* (New York: The Macmillan Co., 1948), pp. 57–58.

if we have been meaningful, intelligible, and direct when reading sacred material aloud.

READING FOR RADIO

Let us assume that you have been asked to appear on the radio and you are going to use a manuscript. You are the occasional radio reader. If you want to be a professional reader on the radio, this section is not for you; you need a more intensive study of the special problems of radio.

The first consideration of the occasional radio reader is his audience. The radio and television audience isn't an audience at all. It is one or two people multiplied by a number of receiving sets. Although the radio industry has spent more money on audience analysis than has any other group in the history of communications, seemingly they have done little to apply logically the information they have obtained. We know that radio listeners are individuals in their homes or shops or cars. We know they listen as individuals. We know they are not moved by the same stimuli nor to the same degree as an assembled audience. The psychological motivations that characterize groups do not characterize individuals. Yet, knowing all this, most radio programs and most radio speakers aim their communications to a group. The average radio announcer is told to "punch" his copy, to use a volume level that "sells." "Huckstering" is an accepted technique. Contrariwise, many radio and television performers work for great intimacy. Ransome Sherman, Dave Garroway, Ben Grauer, and George Hicks are of the intimate school. You are alone listening to your radio and they talk directly to you, quietly and intimately. Such a style is more in keeping with the media of radio and television, in my opinion.

Unless the management of the radio station where you broadcast tells you differently, you should conceive of your audience as individual listeners to whom you are talking; you should not consider them an assembled audience to whom you are making a presentation.

Since the individuals to whom you will read are unseen, you should either recreate the individual listener in your mind or take along someone to whom you can direct your reading. Don't try to read to the announcer or the engineer; he will be busy with other duties. Have someone whom you can address. Gain his attention, hold his interest, secure his understanding, and it is likely you will win the belief of your unseen radio listener.

The second consideration for the occasional radio reader is preparing his material. You should prepare your communication with the same care as you would for any other oral presentation. Your copy of the manuscript should be on paper that makes no noise when it is handled, for the microphone is hypersensitive. You should have additional copies of your manuscript with you, since the radio station is supposed to file a copy of all material that is voiced on the air. In fact, many stations will require a copy in advance. All of the suggestions for preparing a typescript made in Chapter 4 are applicable to radio.

You will make the same kind of analysis of your material as you would make for any reading situation. You will make use of the communication skills in like fashion. The only problems you may have that will be different are (1) rehearsing, (2) posture, (3) loudness, (4) speech sounds, and (5) timing.

If you can possibly arrange it, have an on-mike rehearsal before you go on the air. Approach the problem of reading for radio with a desire to do as well as you can, and understand that it is mechanically different from other methods of reading aloud. Ask the announcer and engineer for advice on how best to make your presentation. Let them show you how to stand or sit and how to use the mike. Let them listen to you and give advice concerning your loudness level and any of your speech sounds that may adversely affect your delivery. That is part of their job. They are proud of their radio station and don't want to carry any more "dog" shows than they can help. They will appreciate your interest and concern. But don't approach them with an "I-know-it-all" attitude. An engineer can make even the best performer sound third-rate. An announcer can put you on the air in such a way that you can never recover from his introduction.

A former theater director of my acquaintance looked upon radio as a necessary evil. He was asked to make an appearance on a local station and he spent his first few minutes in that station exclaiming on the inadequacies of the equipment. Surely no one expected him to work with such inferior equipment; he was used to better things, he said. When it came time for him to go on the air, the announcer on duty, without changing a word of the prepared script, gave the director a Gus Glutz build-up (see page 116). All the director needed was the ability to live up to the newsreel-musical fanfare that the announcer gave him for a send-off. He could not maintain the rate, the volume, or the emotional intensity of his introduction; but he tried. He knew that if he did not rise to it, he would sound like an anticlimax; but that would have been better than trying to match the announcer's intensity, because the speaker fumbled, fluffed, repeated, and generally botched his presentation. This is an extreme example; but remember this—on the radio you sound only as good as the engineer and the announcer let you sound

The announcer may suggest that you sit down to read your presentation. This is far more comfortable than standing, but it is also a less vital position. Be sure that your delivery does not become too relaxed if you sit.

The engineer will tell you about your volume level. Since you are speaking to only an individual listener, you will not need to project to the back wall. A vigorous, conversational style of speaking is usually best. The engineer will caution you about getting too loud or too soft, because he must maintain a constant volume level for transmission purposes. He will warn you to lean away from the mike when you become loud and to lean in when you speak softly. Remember his injunctions; nothing infuriates an engineer more or is harder on his equipment than the sudden blasting of the mike by an inexperienced reader speaking too loudly. The engineer will also tell you of any of your speech sounds that may affect the mike adversely. Maybe you have a whistling *s;* the engineer can cut down the obviousness of that characteristic by using a different type of mike or by changing your position at the mike. After he has placed you and the mike, leave it alone. Don't touch radio equipment.

The announcer will probably go through your presentation with you for timing. When the arrangements for your reading are first made with the radio station, you may be told that you are to have fifteen minutes. At that time, you should check with the radio personnel about the exact time you will have in the clear. Most radio stations mean fourteen minutes and thirty seconds when they say fifteen minutes; also, they expect to have some kind of an opening and closing announcement added to your presentation. The time you have left is your time in the clear. Prepare your presentation to fit the time allotted. Don't take too much time; radio stations run by the clock and their time is sold. Don't take too little time; the radio announcer may not be able to fill the time adequately.

When you practice the presentation, watch your timing. Read for over-all timing at first. Then, after you have made the adjustments in your script necessary for meeting the time requirements, begin timing by the page. At the bottom of each page mark the time it takes to read that page. On the last two pages, mark the time by paragraphs. Arrange for possible cuts and mark the time they take. It may happen that your program will start late, or the radio station may sell adjacent time and you will have less time in the clear than you expected; be prepared to cut. If you know the time of your broadcast and if you get a rehearsal with the announcer, make your time markings the same as those that the clock will show when you broadcast. In other words, don't put down 1:30 at the bottom of your first page if you are broadcasting at a different time of the day. If you do that you will have to do mental arithmetic all the way through your broadcast. Let us say your presentation is at 6:15 and the announcer takes thirty seconds; if your first page is timed one minute and thirty seconds, put 6:17 on the bottom of the first page. Then, when you look at the clock, you will know whether you are reading on time.

After you have completed your broadcast, thank the announcer and the engineer for having been helpful. Thank the radio station for the opportunity to broadcast.

READING FOR TELEVISION

Let us assume that you are the occasional performer on TV. Again, your first consideration is your audience, and, like a radio audience, it is made up of many small groups; it is not an assembled audience. You will prepare your material in the same way as you do for all other reading performances.

Your typescript may be prepared differently. Most television copy is arranged in two columns: one column for action and business cues for the cameramen, one column for voice. Probably you will not read from a television manuscript. You are likely to read from an ordinary type-script, but the station should have your copy far enough in advance for them to prepare a TV script for their technicians.

You will make the same kind of analysis of your material as you would make for any reading situation. You will make use of communication skills in like fashion. The only differences in reading for TV and reading in other situations are (1) preparing the visual aids, (2) rehearsing, (3) eye contact, (4) working the microphone, and (5) appearance.

You have the possibility of visual aids to your presentation in TV. If you plan to use them, let the station personnel know so that they can arrange the proper studio setup and the proper shooting script. They will have many valuable suggestions on the use of visual aids; ask for them and follow them. Should you be using films or filmstrips, they may want to handle them in the control room where they have better facilities than you. Should you be using the slide projector or the baloptican, again they may want to divorce you from the equipment, or they may want to use different equipment. Should you be using charts, maps, displays, mock-ups, flannel boards, or the blackboard, let them see the illustrative material. They may want the charts remade in different colors for better photographic reproduction. The maps may need changing or enlarging. The displays may need to be redesigned and the color changed. In the hands of TV personnel, the flannel boards may become gray cardboard with white lettering, the blackboard may become a dark-green board with yellow chalk. The TV personnel will welcome your desire to use visual aids, and they can give you much helpful advice on their effective use.

The station producer may want to rehearse your presentation with you. You will probably get a dry run-through. You are lucky if you get a camera rehearsal. At the time of the run-through the producer will tell you about cameras, mike booms, floormen and stage managers. He will warn you of possible eventualities.

Unless he tells you differently, you will be expected to conduct yourself something like this. When it is time for you to begin your presentation, the floor manager will signal you. Don't whisper "now," or point to yourself, or react in any other way; just begin. You should begin your presentation by looking at your audience—remember that it is a couple of people at home before a receiving set, or a number of couples, each with little interrelationship with others present. Address your first remarks to them, then glance at your manuscript. Since you are reading a manuscript, don't try to act as if you were doing something else. Don't peck at the manuscript with your eyes; read from it. Glance at your listener as often as you can, but don't be ashamed of the script before you. No one expects you to ad-lib or to memorize, if you have told the station personnel in advance that you are going to read.

Unless you have been told otherwise, you will look at the lens of one camera—that is your listener. The station may use more than one camera on you, but that will be for effects. You look at the camera the producer designates as your audience.

The TV station will use a microphone to pick up your speech. You don't have to work it any special way, as you do in radio, but you might ask if there are any special suggestions the producer would like to make concerning your speech sounds or your volume level.

Ask for special guidance on clothing. Since, at the moment, the TV camera works only in black and white, the producer may have special suggestions on color of suit, color of shirt, pattern of tie, and the use of jewelry. He may have suggestions on the texture of your clothing. He probably will make no suggestions on clothing unless you ask for them, since he will be afraid to embarrass you about the state of your wardrobe.

He will see to it that you are made up properly for the cameras. Don't feel skittish about wearing make-up; the president of the United States wears it when he appears on TV—why shouldn't you? If you are a man, be freshly shaven before reporting for make-up.

The TV producer will also tell you about eye contact. He will tell you at what distance you should focus your eyes for proper contact with that listener who views you. He will tell you about smiling, facial mannerisms, and bodily mannerisms, if you will ask for his advice. He, like the radio producer, wants you to look and sound your best and he will welcome the opportunity to help you with your presentation.

No matter what happens, once you have gone on the air, give your principal attention to your presentation. Give the floor manager just enough attention so that you are aware when he signals you. He has many other duties and his movements and the movements of the cameras and mike-booms are not your concern. He may want to signal you about volume, or looking up, or keeping your chin up, or some other aspect of your presentation. If he does signal you, don't look directly at him and off camera; be aware of him and his signals while continuing your presentation. It's the presentation that is of paramount importance.

All that has been said so far about your manner before the TV cameras will hold true if you use the teleprompter. It, of course, is a device invented to make reading seem easy.

Through the use of Teleprompter service, established by the RCA Service Company and now available to public speakers in all parts of the United States, persons addressing business meetings, conventions and public gatherings no longer need worry about forgetting their lines. . . . Already, one hotel, the Statler in New York, has arranged to make the Teleprompter available for banquets, sales gatherings and other groups using its public rooms.

. . .

The Teleprompter service begins with the receipt by the Service Company of a typewritten copy of the speech. The text is then copied on a continuous roll of specially designed, glare-proof paper by an electric typewriter called the "Videotyper." This typewriter prints in large-size, clear, black letters which may normally be read from a distance of 25 feet. A half-hour speech can be prepared on the Videotyper in less than two hours.

After the typed speech has been carefully checked by experienced proofreaders, the paper roll is inserted into the Teleprompter script machine. An operator sits at a master control unit out of sight of the audience, and, with a duplicate script before him, can easily regulate the speed of the speaker's machine to conform with his speed of delivery. If the speaker adds comments not in the text or is interrupted by applause, the operator merely halts the movement of the script. When the lecturer returns to the printed speech, the paper begins again to move.

Use of more than one Teleprompter is sometimes required when it is desirable for the speaker to move about while demonstrating products and using charts or other visual aids as may be used at sales meetings, training courses or conventions. In such cases, the RCA Service Company is equipped to install as many as four units to keep the individual within reading range of his script. All machines are electronically synchronized so that each brings into view the same portion of the script at the same time.

The RCA Service Company also has available a Teleprompter concealed within a speaker's rostrum. This unit includes warning lights which flash when the speaker is ten, five, three minutes and one minute from the end of his address. Two clocks mounted on the rostrum indicate the time of day and the minutes of speaking time which have elapsed. With these aids, a speaker is able accurately to judge the speed of his delivery.

The RCA Service Plan for public speakers is highly flexible and can be tailor-made for different requirements. The Teleprompter permits a person to relax and to devote all his attention toward getting the subject across to an audience. It eliminates the tedious chore of memorizing speeches, avoids omitting important points and reduces rehearsal time to a minimum. The Teleprompter can make anyone a better speaker.[19]

► *Conclusion.* Reading poetry, humor, or sacred material aloud presents some special problems, but you need no additional special training to read them aloud effectively. Reading for radio or television is in some mechanical respects different from reading for an assembled audience, but your preparation should be no less thorough or extensive. Effective reading aloud is effective anywhere.

[19] E. C. Buurma, "Teleprompter Aids the Orator," *Radio Age,* Vol. XII, No. 2 (April, 1953).

PART THREE

Practice Material

❖⟩⟩❖⟩⟩❖⟩⟩❖⟩⟩❖⟩⟩❖⟩⟩❖⟩⟩❖⟩⟩❖ ❖⟨⟨❖⟨⟨❖⟨⟨❖⟨⟨❖⟨⟨❖⟨⟨❖⟨⟨❖⟨⟨❖

· 13 ·

How to Use
the Practice Material

※»)※»)※»)※»)※»)※»)※»)※»)※»(※(※(※(※(※(※(※(※(※(

Any selection in this book may be
used as practice material to acquire any single technique or skill. Any
writing you may read aloud may be used as practice material. The quotations in the text should be read aloud; the textual material itself might
be read aloud for practice purposes. There is no special magic in practice
material as such. The person who wishes to read aloud effectively can
pick up anything and read it for practice.

The selections included in Practice Material were chosen because
they met these criteria: (1) interest, both in intrinsic quality and in
attractiveness to preprofessional tastes; (2) variety, both in content and
in appeal for persons of varied interests; (3) application, both in usefulness as drill for a specific technique and in usefulness as supplementary
drill for other techniques; (4) familiarity, either in wide familiarity, so
that they cannot be excluded, or in unfamiliarity, so that they enlarge the
scope of the reader's interests; (5) general suitability to the reading-aloud
situation.

Let us take several exercises to see how they meet these criteria.
Lutie has already been mentioned. It is a selection to be read to children.
It is an exercise in the communication of emotion. It can also be used to
study organization, structure, sentences, punctuation, and language. It

can be used for vocal improvement—for practicing volume, prolongation, rate, and pitch—and for building toward climaxes. The story is high in amusement interest in itself.

"How Congress Makes a Law" is interesting as information. It can be used by the student interested in law, politics, teaching, and radio. It can be used for analytical study in purpose, organization, structure, sentences, punctuation, and words. It can be used for drill in the communication of ideas.

There are two selections on roots. John G. Coulter's prose selection is the sort of material the science teacher might use. Lloyd Frankenberg's poem might also be used by the science teacher. Both may be used for practice in communication of ideas. They are interesting in themselves, in their application, and in their differences.

All the practice material in this section was chosen for its usefulness in more than one category. The student is free to use all selections as he wishes. In the following List of Practice Selections, certain selections are noted as especially helpful for practice of a specific skill. The student may substitute other selections if he finds material that he feels is more interesting and useful.

All the practice material given for the study of organization, or structure, or purpose, and so forth, is intended for practice in reading aloud. All the material for reading aloud can be used for practice in the study of organization. The practice selections are arranged for the benefit of the student who is working without the assistance of a critic-teacher.

The items in the List of Practice Selections are arranged as follows: the name of the selection or excerpt; the name of the author; the specific technique or skill for which the material is suited; the preprofessional interest catered to in the content. The selections are arranged to coincide with the chapters of Part One and Part Two. No material has been included for chapters where practice material is not needed, or for chapters where practice material is available in other sources; for instance, no practice material is listed for pronunciation or voice, because excellent books on that subject are readily at hand in all colleges and libraries.

No selection of practice material can be complete or exhaustive. A list of supplemental books with excellent material in them is appended here. It is suggested that the student refer to them for additional selections. It is suggested, also, that the teacher have these, or other similar books, at hand in classes in reading aloud, so that a stimulating variety of material may be readily available for practice purposes.

BIBLIOGRAPHY FOR SACRED MATERIAL

The Holy Bible, Douay Version.

The Holy Bible. King James Version.

The Bible Designed to Be Read as Living Literature, ed. Ernest Suther-land Bates. New York: Simon & Schuster, 1936, 1,268 pp.

The Complete Bible: an American Translation. Translated by Edgar J. Goodspeed and J. M. Powis Smith. Chicago: The University of Chicago Press, 1948.

The Book of Common Prayer. New York: The Church Pension Fund, 1945, 611 pp.

The Union Prayerbook for Jewish Worship. Cincinnati: The Central Con-ference of American Rabbis, 1940, 395 pp.

The Broadman Hymnal. Edited by B. B. McKinney. Nashville, Tenn.: The Broadman Press, 1940.

Triumphant Service Songs. Compiled by Homer A. Rodeheaver, Yumpert P. Rodeheaver, Joseph N. Rodeheaver, and George W. Sanville. Winona Lake, Ind.: Rodeheaver-Hall-Mack Co., 1934, 288 pp.

BIBLIOGRAPHY FOR CHILDREN

Hollowell, Lillian, ed., *A Book of Children's Literature.* New York: Rine-hart & Company, Inc., 1949, 809 pp. (This book contains an inten-sive bibliography of children's books arranged by interest and by age levels.)

BIBLIOGRAPHY FOR LAW AND POLITICS

Brandeis, Louis Dembitz, *Other People's Money.* Philadelphia: J. B. Lippincott Company, 1914, 233 pp.

Chubb, Percival, ed., *Selections from the Addresses, Inaugurals, and Letters of Abraham Lincoln.* New York: The Macmillan Co., 1909, 208 pp.

Churchill, Winston, *Blood, Sweat, and Tears.* New York: G. P. Putnam's Sons, 1941, 462 pp.

Churchill, Winston, *The Dawn of Liberation*. Boston: Little, Brown & Co., 1945, 417 pp.

———, *Victory*. Boston: Little, Brown & Co., 1946, 307 pp.

———, *Winston Churchill's Secret Session Speeches*. Compiled by Charles Eade. New York: Simon & Schuster, 1946, 114 pp.

Clemens, Samuel, *Mark Twain's Speeches,* ed. Albert Bigelow Paine. New York: Harper & Brothers, 1923, 396 pp.

Vital Speeches of the Day. Published semimonthly. New York: City News Publishing Co.

BIBLIOGRAPHY FOR BUSINESS

Vital Speeches of the Day. Published semimonthly. New York: City News Publishing Co.

RADIO BIBLIOGRAPHY

Barnouw, Erik, ed., *Radio Drama in Action: Twenty-five Plays of a Changing World*. New York: Rinehart & Company, Inc., 1945, 397 pp.

Benét, Stephen Vincent, *We Stand United, and Other Radio Scripts*. New York: Rinehart & Company, Inc., 1945, 210 pp.

Burr, Jane, *Fourteen Radio Plays*. Hollywood, Calif.: Highland Press, 1945, 283 pp.

Cairns, Huntington, *Invitation to Learning*. New York: Random House, Inc., 1941, 431 pp.

Calhoun, Harold G., and Dorothy Calhoun, *Let Freedom Ring! Thirteen Scripts*. Washington, D. C.: U. S. Office of Education, 1937, 379 pp.

Corwin, Norman, *More by Corwin: Sixteen Radio Dramas*. New York: Henry Holt & Co., Inc., 1944, 412 pp.

———, *Thirteen by Corwin*. New York: Henry Holt & Co., Inc., 1942, 338 pp.

———, *Untitled and Other Radio Dramas*. New York: Henry Holt & Co., Inc., 1947, 558 pp.

Coulter, Douglas, ed., *Columbia Workshop Plays: Fourteen Radio Dramas*. New York: McGraw-Hill Book Co., Inc., 1939, 378 pp.

Duerr, Edwin, *Radio and Television Acting*. New York: Rinehart & Company, Inc., 1950, 417 pp.

Fitelson, H. William, ed., *Theatre Guild on the Air*. New York: Rinehart & Company, Inc., 1947, 430 pp.

Fox, Dixon Ryan, and Arthur M. Schlesinger, eds., *The Cavalcade of America*. Springfield, Mass.: Milton Bradley Company, 1937, 300 pp.

Henneke, Ben G., *The Radio Announcer's Handbook*. New York: Rinehart & Company, Inc., 1948, 308 pp.

Kozlenko, William, comp., *One Hundred Non-Royalty One-Act Plays*. New York: Greenberg, Publisher, 1940, 802 pp.

————, *One Hundred Non-Royalty Radio Plays*. New York: Greenberg, Publisher, 1941, 683 pp.

MacLeish, Archibald, *The American Story: Ten Broadcasts*. New York: Duell, Sloan & Pearce, Inc., 1944, 231 pp.

Oboler, Arch, *Fourteen Radio Plays*. New York: Random House, Inc., 1940, 257 pp.

————, *Ivory Tower and Other Radio Plays*. Chicago: William Targ, 1940, 79 pp.

————, *Oboler Omnibus: Radio Plays and Personalities*. New York: Duell, Sloan & Pearce, Inc., 1945, 309 pp.

————, *Plays for Americans: Thirteen New Non-Royalty Radio Plays*. New York: Rinehart & Company, Inc., 1942, 271 pp.

————, *This Freedom: Thirteen New Radio Plays*. New York: Random House, Inc., 1942, 239 pp.

———— and Stephen Longstreet, eds., *Free World Theatre: Nineteen New Radio Plays*. New York: Random House, Inc., 1944, 270 pp.

Wylie, Max, *Radio and Television Writing*. New York: Rinehart & Company, Inc., 1950, 635 pp.

ANTHOLOGIES OF GENERAL INTEREST

No listing of books is attempted here because of the wide distribution of cheap reprints. Any drugstore will have a wide selection of possible practice material in the twenty-five-cent reprint editions. The names and locations of the principal distributors of these reprints are given so that the student can write for a complete listing of current titles. From these lists he can find material to cater to any interest and to fit any need.

Ballantine Books. International Circulation Division of the Hearst Corporation, New York.

Bantam Books. Curtis Circulation Company, Philadelphia.

Gold Medal Books. Fawcett Publications, Inc., Greenwich, Conn.

Mentor Books. The New American Library of World Literature, Inc., New York.

Permabooks. Doubleday & Co., Inc., New York.

Pocket Books. Pocket Books, Inc., New York.

Rinehart Editions. Rinehart & Company, Inc., New York.

Signet Books. The New American Library of World Literature, Inc., New York.

· 14 ·

A List of

Practice Selections

❖⟫❖⟫❖⟫❖⟫❖⟫❖⟫❖⟫❖⟫❖⟫❖⟫❖⟫❖⟪❖⟪❖⟪❖⟪❖⟪❖⟪❖⟪❖⟪❖⟪❖

SELECTIONS FOR CHAPTER 2

Name of Selection	Author	Type of Selection	Type of Material
1. A Liberal Education	Thomas Huxley	Exposition	Teacher's
2. The Gifts of God	George Herbert	Exposition	Religious
3. Boyhood Memories	Mark Twain	Narration	General
4. The Ballad of William Sycamore	Stephen Vincent Benét	Narration	General
5. Maxwell House		Persuasion	Radio
6. A Hymn to God the Father	John Donne	Persuasion	Religious
7. Memoirs of a Banquet Speaker	James Thurber	Entertainment	General
8. The Family Fool	W. S. Gilbert	Entertainment	General
9. Organization of Material	Joseph Addison	Exposition	Teacher's
10. How the Greeks Lived	Hendrik Willem van Loon	Organization	Children's
11. The Financial Structure	Ellis Parker Butler	Organization	Business
12. What's a Flag	*New York Times*	Organization	Political
13. Who May Write	Henry Fielding	Organization	Teacher's
14. The Corporation and the Press	Ralph D. Paine	Organization	Business

Name of Selection	Author	Type of Selection	Type of Material
15. The Search for Wisdom	The Bible	Organization	Religious
16. A Cradle Song	Isaac Watts	Organization	Religious Poetry
17. Under the Capitol Dome	United Press	Organization	Radio News
18. Dickens the Actor	Hesketh Pearson	Organization	General
19. The Sentence	Henry David Thoreau	Sentences	Teacher's
20. Italics	H. W. Fowler	Sentences	Teacher's
21. Writer's Faults	Henry David Thoreau	Sentences	Teacher's
22. Grammar	Henry David Thoreau	Sentences	Teacher's
23. Punctuation	Edwin Duerr	Punctuation	Teacher's
24. Parentheses	Mark Twain	Punctuation	Teacher's
25. Semicolons	T. E. Lawrence	Punctuation	Teacher's
26. The Meaning of Words	John Ruskin	Words	Teacher's
27. Foreword, Preface	H. W. Fowler	Words	Teacher's
28. Didacticism	H. W. Fowler	Words	Teacher's
29. What Can Literature Do for Me?	C. Alphonso Smith	Understanding	Teacher's

SELECTIONS FOR CHAPTER 4

30. What to Do	John Mason Brown	Fellow Feeling	

SELECTIONS FOR CHAPTER 5

31. North Wind and Star Boy	Charles A. and Elaine Goodale Eastman	Phrasing	Children's
32. The Accounting Department	J. B. Galbraith	Phrasing	Business
33. Third Inaugural Address	F. D. Roosevelt	Phrasing	Political
34. America	Edmund Burke	Phrasing	Political
35. Roots	John G. Coulter	Phrasing	Teacher's
36. Roots Go Down	Lloyd Frankenberg	Phrasing	Teacher's
37. The Crime of Conspiracy	Harold R. Medina	Phrasing	Lawyer's

Name of Selection	Author	Type of Selection	Type of Material
38. My Sort of God	Heywood Broun	Phrasing	Religious
39. The Doc Quigg Story	United Press	Phrasing	Radio
40. The Hunter and His Wife	Russian Fairy Tales	Commas	Children's
41. Promoters of General Prosperity	Pope Pius XII	Commas	Business
42. Declaration of Independence	Thomas Jefferson	Commas	Political
43. Peace	Edmund Burke	Commas	Political
44. Civilization	T. S. Eliot	Commas	Teacher's
45. Prayer for Purim		Commas	Religious
46. Peace in the Atomic Era	Albert Einstein	Commas	Television
47. A Tale of Two Cities	Charles Dickens	Commas	General
48. Preparation of an Actor	Hesketh Pearson	Commas	General
49. The Commuter	E. B. White	Commas	General
50. On His Blindness	John Milton	Commas	Poetry
51. Rip Van Winkle	Washington Irving	Subordination	Children's
52. School Supplies	Robert Benchley	Subordination	General
53. Great Art	Roger Fry	Subordination	General
54. Sonnet	Sir Philip Sidney	Subordination	Poetry
55. Doing My Share	Mark Twain	Subordination	General
56. Nativity	The Bible	Subordination	Religious
57. Channel Crossing	United Press	Subordination	Radio
58. Voices	Oliver Wendell Holmes	Subordination	General
59. My Life Work	Thomas Huxley	Subordination	General
60. Superstition	Nathaniel Hawthorne	Subordination	General
61. Illness	Virginia Woolf	Subordination	General
62. Sleep	Thomas Dekker	Subordination	General
63. Voices II	Oliver Wendell Holmes	Subordination	General
64. Communicating Emotions	Roger Fry	Subordination	General
65. Throw-away Lines	Edwin Duerr	Subordination	General
66. Teaching	Ralph Waldo Emerson	Inflection	Teacher's
67. Constitutions	Edmund Burke	Inflection	Political
68. Roman Women	Agnes Repplier	Inflection	General
69. Laughter	Oliver Wendell Holmes	Inflection	General
70. Upon Westminster Bridge	William Wordsworth	Inflection	Poetry
71. Job	The Bible	Inflection	Religious
72. Works	The Bible	Inflection	Religious
73. Why So Pale and Wan?	Sir John Suckling	Inflection	Poetry
74. Farewell	Sir Thomas Wyatt	Inflection	Poetry
75. The Frog-Prince		Pauses	Children's

Name of Selection	Author	Type of Selection	Type of Material
76. University Days	James Thurber	Pauses	Teacher's
77. Folly	Oliver Goldsmith	Pauses	Poetry
78. Fishing	Robert Benchley	Pauses	General
79. Hammocks	Charles S. Brooks	Pauses	General
80. The Resurrection	The Bible	Pauses	Religious
81. Narcissus	Oscar Wilde	Pauses	General
82. Our Town	Thornton Wilder	Pauses	General
83. Silence	Edgar Lee Masters	Pauses	Poetry
84. Silence	Henry David Thoreau	Pauses	General
85. The Form of Solemnization of Matrimony		Pauses	Religious
86. Sauerkraut	United Press	Pauses	Radio
87. Our Town II	Thornton Wilder	Pauses	General
88. Dr. Faustus	Christopher Marlowe	Pauses	Poetry

SELECTIONS FOR CHAPTER 6

89. Tudor Plate	General Mills	Stress by Loudness	Radio
90. Hymns of All Churches	General Mills	Stress by Loudness	Radio
91. Profit in War	Edmund Burke	Stress by Pitch	Political
92. Gettysburg Address	Abraham Lincoln	Stress by Pitch	Political
93. The Three Billy-Goats Gruff		Stress by Quality	Children's
94. Anatomy of Sound	Norman Corwin	Variety in Loudness	Radio
95. The Very Bent Twig	Phyllis McGinley	Variety in Pitch	Poetry
96. The History of Bel	Apocrypha	Variety in Pitch	Religious
97. Regicide Peace	Edmund Burke	Variety in Pitch	Political
98. Savings Bonds		Variety in Pitch	Radio
99. The Collar	George Herbert	Variety in Pitch	Religious Poetry
100. The Abbey at Night	Logan Pearsall Smith	Variety in Pitch	General
101. On the Tombs in Westminster Abbey	Francis Beaumont	Variety in Pitch	Poetry
102. A Garage for Gabriel	Catherine Woolley	Variety in Pitch	Children's
103. The Night Has Been Long	W. S. Gilbert	Variety in Time	Poetry
104. Jehovah	Don Marquis	Variety in Time	General
105. The Golden Age	Kenneth Grahame	Variety in Time	General
106. Where Now?	Thomas Wolfe	Variety in Time	General
107. U. S. Graunt	Mark Twain	Variety in Time	General

Name of Selection	Author	Type of Selection	Type of Material
108. To the Terrestrial Globe	W. S. Gilbert	Variety in Time	Poetry
109. The Daily Miracle	Arnold Bennett	Variety in Time	Business
110. The Fair Catch	United Press	Variety in Time	Radio
111. Fight at the Bridge	Walter D. Edmonds	Variety in Time	General
112. The Mountain Whippoorwill	Stephen Vincent Benét	Variety in Time	Poetry

SELECTIONS FOR CHAPTER 7

113. Splendour of Words	Joseph Auslander	Words	General
114. These Names Are Words in Stone	V. O. Key, Jr.	Words	General
115. American Names	Stephen Vincent Benét	Words	General
116. British Names	R. G. Collingwood and J. N. L. Myres	Words	General
117. Jewish Worship		Words	Religious
118. Queen Mab	William Shakespeare	Words	Poetry
119. There Was a Child Went Forth	Walt Whitman	Images	Poetry
120. Ball of Fire	Amy Lowell	Images	General
121. My Uncle's Farm	Mark Twain	Images	General
122. The Poetry of Dress	Robert Herrick	Images	Poetry
123. The Gong	Lafcadio Hearn	Images	General
124. The Nightmare	Lafcadio Hearn	Images	General
125. The Twenty-third Psalm	The Bible	Images	Religious
126. Spring	James Boyd	Images	General
127. Sunrise	Mark Twain	Images	General
128. I Shall Not Care	Sara Teasdale	Images	Poetry
129. June	Bliss Perry	Images	General
130. The Landscape near an Aerodrome	Stephen Spender	Images	Poetry
131. Ploughing	Frank Norris	Images	General
132. The Golden World	Thomas Wolfe	Images	General
133. The Kitchen	Kenneth Roberts	Images	General
134. July Night	Henry David Thoreau	Images	General
135. Concert in the Park	E. B. White	Images	General
136. August	Elinor Wylie	Images	Poetry
137. August Third	Donald Culross Peattie	Images	General
138. Thanksgiving Day Proclamation	Governor Wilbur L. Cross	Images	Political

Name of Selection	Author	Type of Selection	Type of Material
139. October	Thomas Wolfe	Images	General
140. A Vagabond Song	Bliss Carman	Images	Poetry
141. September 15	Donald Culross Peattie	Images	General
142. October 24	Henry David Thoreau	Images	General
143. Ode to Autumn	John Keats	Images	Poetry
144. Fall	Lynn Riggs	Images	General
145. Music, When Soft Voices Die	Percy Bysshe Shelley	Mood	Poetry
146. Drinking Song	Richard Brinsley Sheridan	Mood	Poetry
147. Order for the Burial of the Dead		Mood	Religious
148. Aspects of the Earth	Amy Kelly	Mood	General
149. Sounds	Thomas Wolfe	Mood	General
150. Heat	Frank Norris	Mood	General
151. Mrs. Miniver	Columbia Broadcasting System	Mood	Radio
152. Colonel Rogers	Kenneth Roberts	Exaggeration	General
153. The Corpse Maker	Mark Twain	Exaggeration	General
154. This Is It	Oliver Wendell Holmes	Exaggeration	Poetry
155. Lutie	Margot Austin	Emotion	Children's
156. Hotspur's Reply	William Shakespeare	Emotion	Poetry
157. I Am a Lie	Nathaniel Hawthorne	Emotion	General
158. Preaching, Lecturing	Henry David Thoreau	Emotion	General
159. The Second Mrs. Burton	Martha Alexander	Emotion	Radio
160. Adventures of Ozzie and Harriet	Ozzie Nelson	Emotion	Radio
161. The World Is Too Much with Us	William Wordsworth	Emotion	Poetry

SELECTIONS FOR CHAPTER 12

162. Salut au Monde	Walt Whitman		Poetry
163. Ceremonies for Christmas	Robert Herrick		Poetry
164. The True Beauty	Thomas Carew		Poetry
165. Wishes	Richard Crashaw		Poetry
166. The Constant Lover	Sir John Suckling		Poetry
167. Go, Lovely Rose	Edmund Waller		Poetry
168. To Anthea	Robert Herrick		Poetry

Name of Selection	Author	Type of Selection	Type of Material
169. Forget Not Yet	Sir Thomas Wyatt		Poetry
170. Blame Not My Lute	Sir Thomas Wyatt		Poetry
171. Bolts of Melody	Emily Dickinson		Poetry
172. A Coffin Is a Small Domain	Emily Dickinson		Poetry
173. Bloom Is Result	Emily Dickinson		Poetry
174. Bees	Emily Dickinson		Poetry
175. Two Butterflies	Emily Dickinson		Poetry
176. Evening Hymn	Sir Thomas Browne		Religious Poetry
177. Peace	Henry Vaughan		Religious Poetry
178. Holy Sonnet	John Donne		Religious Poetry
179. Christ's Coming to Judgment	Thomas Dekker		Religious Poetry
180. On Psalm CXIX. 5	Francis Quarles		Religious Poetry
181. The Book	Henry Vaughan		Religious Poetry
182. The Twenty-fourth Psalm	The Bible		Religious Poetry
183. The Twenty-seventh Psalm	The Bible		Religious Poetry
184. The One Hundred and Fiftieth Psalm	The Bible		Religious Poetry
185. A Child's Grace	Robert Herrick		Religious Poetry
186. Parable of the Fig Tree	The Bible		Religious Prose
187. The Beatitudes	The Bible		Religious Prose
188. Bishops	The Bible		Religious Prose
189. Thanksgiving	Mark Twain		Humorous Prose
190. The Candy-Pull	Mark Twain		Humorous Prose

LONG SELECTIONS FOR EXAMINATION PURPOSES

191. The Happy Prince	Oscar Wilde	Children's
192. Guilty before Trial	Benjamin F. Fairless	Business
193. How Congress Makes a Law	Francis J. Myers	Teacher's
194. For the Glory of God	Ely E. Pilchik	Minister's
195. The American Economic System	U. S. Armed Forces Talk	Officer's

Name of Selection	Author	Type of Selection	Type of Material
196. Advocacy before the United States Supreme Court	Robert H. Jackson		Lawyer's
197. Where the People Stand	Elmo Roper		Radio
198. The Drainage Level	Walter D. Edmonds		General

· 15 ·

Practice Selections

❖➤❖➤❖➤❖➤❖➤❖➤❖➤❖➤❖➤ ❖❖❖❖❖❖❖❖❖❖❖❖

I · A Liberal Education

Suppose it were perfectly certain that the life and fortune of every one of us would, one day or other, depend upon his winning or losing a game of chess. Don't you think that we should all consider it to be a primary duty to learn at least the names and the moves of the pieces; to have a notion of a gambit, and a keen eye for all the means of giving and getting out of check? Do you not think that we should look with a disapprobation amounting to scorn, upon the father who allowed his son, or the state which allowed its members, to grow up without knowing a pawn from a knight?

Yet it is a very plain and elementary truth, that the life, the fortune, and the happiness of every one of us, and, more or less, of those who are connected with us, do depend upon our knowing something of the rules of a game infinitely more difficult and complicated than chess. It is a game which has been played for untold ages, every man and woman of us being one of the two players in a game of his or her own. The chess-board is the world, the pieces are the phenomena of the universe, the rules of the game are what we call the laws of Nature. The player on the other side is hidden from us. We know that his play is always fair, just, and patient. But also we know, to our cost, that he never overlooks a mistake, or makes the smallest allowance for ignorance. To the man who plays well, the highest stakes are paid, with that sort of overflowing generosity with which the strong shows delight in strength. And one who plays ill is check-mated—without haste, but without remorse.

My metaphor will remind some of you of the famous picture in which Retzsch has depicted Satan playing at chess with man for his soul.

Substitute for the mocking fiend in that picture, a calm, strong angel who is playing for love, as we say, and would rather lose than win—and I should accept it as an image of human life.

Well, what I mean by Education is learning the rules of this mighty game. In other words, education is the instruction of the intellect in the laws of Nature, under which name I include not merely things and their forces, but men and their ways; and the fashioning of the affections and of the will into an earnest and loving desire to move in harmony with those laws. For me education means neither more nor less than this. Anything which professes to call itself education must be tried by this standard, and if it fails to stand the test, I will not call it education, whatever may be the force of authority, or of numbers, upon the other side.

It is important to remember that, in strictness, there is no such thing as an uneducated man. Take an extreme case. Suppose that an adult man, in the full vigor of his faculties, could be suddenly placed in the world, as Adam is said to have been, and then left to do as he best might. How long would he be left uneducated? Not five minutes. Nature would begin to teach him, through the eye, the ear, the touch, the properties of objects. Pain and pleasure would be at his elbow telling him to do this and avoid that; and by slow degrees the man would receive an education, which, if narrow, would be thorough, real, and adequate to his circumstances, though there would be no extras and very few accomplishments.

And if to this solitary man entered a second Adam, or better still, an Eve, a new and greater world, that of social and moral phenomena, would be revealed. Joys and woes, compared with which all others might seem but faint shadows, would spring from the new relations. Happiness and sorrow would take the place of the coarser monitors, pleasure and pain; but conduct would still be shaped by the observation of the natural consequences of actions; or, in other words, by the laws of the nature of man.

To every one of us the world was once as fresh and new as to Adam. And then, long before we were susceptible of any other mode of instruction, Nature took us in hand, and every minute of waking life brought its educational influence, shaping our actions into rough accordance with Nature's laws, so that we might not be ended untimely by too gross disobedience. Nor should I speak of this process of education as past for any one, be he old as he may. For every man the world is as fresh as it was at the first day, and as full of untold novelties for him who has the eyes to see them. And Nature is still continuing her patient education of us in that great university, the universe, of which we are all members—Nature having no Test-Acts,

Those who take honours in Nature's university, who learn the laws which govern men and things and obey them, are the really great and successful men in this world. The great mass of mankind are the "Poll," who pick up just enough to get through without much discredit. Those who won't learn at all are plucked; and then you can't come up again. Nature's pluck means extermination.

Thus the question of compulsory education is settled so far as Nature is concerned. Her bill on that question was framed and passed long ago. But, like all compulsory legislation, that of Nature is harsh and wasteful in its operation. Ignorance is visited as sharply as wilful disobedience— incapacity meets with the same punishment as crime. Nature's discipline is not even a word and a blow, and the blow first; but the blow without the word. It is left to you to find out why your ears are boxed.

The object of what we commonly call education—that education in which man intervenes and which I shall distinguish as artificial education—is to make good these defects in Nature's methods; to prepare the child to receive Nature's education, neither incapably nor ignorantly, nor with wilful disobedience; and to understand the preliminary symptoms of her displeasure, without waiting for the box on the ear. In short, all artificial education ought to be an anticipation of natural education. And a liberal education is an artificial education, which has not only prepared a man to escape the great evils of disobedience to natural laws, but has trained him to appreciate and to seize upon the rewards, which Nature scatters with as free a hand as her penalties.

That man, I think, has had a liberal education, who has been so trained in youth that his body is the ready servant of his will, and does with ease and pleasure all the work that, as a mechanism, it is capable of; whose intellect is a clear, cold, logic engine, with all its parts of equal strength, and in smooth working order; ready, like a steam engine, to be turned to any kind of work, and spin the gossamers as well as forge the anchors of the mind; whose mind is stored with a knowledge of the great and fundamental truths of Nature and of the laws of her operations; one, who, no stunned ascetic, is full of life and fire, but whose passions are trained to come to heel by a vigorous will, the servant of a tender conscience; who has learned to love all beauty, whether of Nature or of art, to hate all vileness, and to respect others as himself.

Such an one and no other, I conceive, has had a liberal education; for he is, as completely as a man can be, in harmony with Nature. He will make the best of her, and she of him. They will get on together rarely; she as his ever beneficent mother; he as her mouth-piece, her conscious self, her minister and interpreter.

[1] Thomas Huxley, "A Liberal Education, and Where to Find It," *Collected Essays* (1893).

❖❖❖❖❖❖❖❖❖

2 · The Gifts of God

        When God at first made Man,
    Having a glass of blessings standing by;
    Let us (said He) pour on him all we can:
    Let the world's riches, which dispers'ed lie,
        Contract into a span.

        So strength first made a way;
    Then beauty flow'd, then wisdom, honour, pleasure:
    When almost all was out, God made a stay,
    Perceiving that alone, of all his treasure,
        Rest in the bottom lay.

        For if I should (said He)
    Bestow this jewel also on my creature,
    He would adore my gifts instead of me,
    And rest in Nature, not the God of Nature:
        So both should losers be.

        Yet let him keep the rest,
    But keep them with repining restlessness:
    Let him be rich and weary, that at least,
    If goodness lead him not, yet weariness
        May toss him to my breast.

2 George Herbert, "The Pulley," *The Temple* (1633).

❖❂❖❂❖❖❖❖❖❖❖

3 · Boyhood Memories

As I have said, I spent some part of every year at the farm until I was twelve or thirteen years old. The life which I led there with my cousins was full of charm, and so is the memory of it yet. I can call back the solemn twilight and mystery of the deep woods, the earthy smells, the faint odors of the wild flowers, the sheen of rain-washed foliage, the rattling clatter of drops when the wind shook the trees, the far-off hammering of woodpeckers and the muffled drumming of wood pheasants in the remoteness of the forest, the snapshot glimpses of disturbed wild creatures scurrying through the grass—I can call it all back and make it as real as it ever was, and as blessed. I can call back the prairie, and its loneliness and peace, and a vast hawk hanging motionless in the sky, with his wings spread wide and the blue of the vault showing through the fringe of their end feathers. I can see the woods in their autumn dress, the oaks purple, the hickories washed with gold, the maples and the sumachs luminous with crimson fires, and I can hear the rustle made by the fallen leaves as we plowed through them. I can see the blue clusters of wild grapes hanging among the foliage of the saplings, and I remember the taste of them and the smell. I know how the wild blackberries looked, and how they tasted, and the same with the pawpaws, the hazelnuts, and the persimmons; and I can feel the thumping rain, upon my head, of hickory nuts and walnuts when we were out in the frosty dawn to scramble for them with the pigs, and the gusts of wind loosed them and sent them down. I know the stain of blackberries, and how pretty it is, and I know the stain of walnut hulls, and how little it minds soap and water, also what grudged experience it had of either of them. I know the taste of maple sap, and when to gather it, and how to arrange the troughs and the delivery tubes, and how to boil down the juice, and how to hook the sugar after it is made, also how much better hooked sugar tastes than any that is honestly come by, let bigots say what they will. I know how a prize watermelon looks when it is sunning its fat rotundity among pumpkin vines and "simblins"; I know how to tell when it is ripe without "plugging" it; I know how inviting it looks when it is cooling itself in a tub of water under the bed, waiting; I know how it looks when it lies on the table in the sheltered great floor space between house and kitchen, and the children gathered for the sacrifice and their mouths watering; I know the crackling sound it makes when the carving knife enters its end, and I can see the split fly along in front of the blade as the knife cleaves its way to the other end; I can see its halves fall apart and display the rich red meat and the black seeds, and the heart standing up, a luxury fit for the elect; I know how a boy looks behind a yard-long slice of that melon, and I know how he feels; for I have been there. I know the taste of the watermelon which has been honestly come by, and I know the taste of the watermelon which has been acquired by art. Both taste good, but the experienced know which tastes best. I know the look of green apples and peaches and pears on the trees, and I know how entertaining they are when they are inside of a person. I know how ripe ones look when they are piled in pyramids under the trees, and how pretty they are and how vivid their colors. I know how a frozen apple looks, in a barrel down cellar in the wintertime, and how hard it is to bite, and how the frost makes the teeth ache, and yet how good it is, notwithstanding. I know the disposition of elderly people to select the specked apples for the children and I once knew ways to beat the game. I know the look of an apple that is roasting and sizzling on a hearth on a winter's evening, and I know the comfort that comes of eating it hot, along with some sugar and a drench of cream. I know the delicate art and mystery of so cracking hickory nuts and walnuts on a flatiron with a hammer that the kernels will be delivered whole, and I know how the nuts, taken in conjunction with winter apples, cider, and doughnuts, make old people's old tales and old jokes sound fresh and crisp and enchanting, and juggle an evening away before you know what went with the time. I know the look of Uncle Dan'l's kitchen as it was on the privileged nights, when I was a child, and I can see the white and black children grouped on the hearth, with the firelight playing on their faces and the shadows flickering upon the walls, clear back toward the cavernous gloom of the rear, and I can hear Uncle Dan'l telling the immortal tales which Uncle Remus Harris was to gather into his book and charm the world with, by and by; and I can feel again the creepy joy which quivered through me when the time for the ghost story was reached—and the sense of regret, too, which came over me, for it was always the last story of the evening and there was nothing between it and the unwelcome bed.

I can remember the bare wooden stairway in my uncle's house, and the turn to the left above the landing, and the rafters and the slanting roof over my bed, and the squares of moonlight on the floor, and the white cold world of snow outside, seen through the curtainless window. I can remember the howling of the wind and the quaking of the house on stormy nights, and how snug and cozy one felt, under the blankets, listening; and how the powdery snow used to sift in, around the sashes, and lie in little ridges on the floor and make the place look chilly in the morning and curb the wild desire to get up—in case there was any. I can remember how very dark that room was, in the dark of the moon, and how packed it was with ghostly stillness when one woke up by accident away in the night, and forgotten sins came flocking out of the secret chambers of the memory and wanted a hearing; and how ill chosen the time seemed for this kind of business; and how dismal was the hoo-hooing of the owl and the wailing of the wolf, sent mourning by on the night wind.

I remember the raging of the rain on that roof, summer nights, and how pleasant it was to lie and listen to it, and enjoy the white splendor of the lightning and the majestic booming and crashing of the thunder. It was a very satisfactory room, and there was lightning rod which was reachable from the window, an adorable and skittish thing to climb up and down, summer nights, when there were duties on hand of a sort to make privacy desirable.

[3] Samuel L. Clemens, *Mark Twain's Autobiography* (New York: Harper & Brothers, 1924), I, 109–115. Copyright, 1924, by Clara Gabrilowitsch. Copyright, 1952, by Clara Clemens Samossoud.

❧⟩⟨❧⟩⟨❧⟩❧⟨❧⟨❧⟨❧

4 · The Ballad of William Sycamore
(1790–1871)

My father, he was a mountaineer,
His fist was a knotty hammer;
He was quick on his feet as a running deer,
And he spoke with a Yankee stammer.

My mother, she was merry and brave,
And so she came to her labor,
With a tall green fir for her doctor grave
And a stream for her comforting neighbor.

And some are wrapped in the linen fine,
And some like a godling's scion;
But I was cradled on twigs of pine
In the skin of a mountain lion.

And some remember a white, starched lap
And a ewer with silver handles;
But I remember a coonskin cap
And the smell of bayberry candles.

The cabin logs, with the bark still rough,
And my mother who laughed at trifles,
And the tall, lank visitors, brown as snuff,
With their long, straight squirrel-rifles.

I can hear them dance, like a foggy song,
Through the deepest one of my slumbers,
The fiddle squeaking the boots along
And my father calling the numbers.

The quick feet shaking the puncheon-floor,
And the fiddle squealing and squealing,
Till the dried herbs rattled above the door
And the dust went up to the ceiling.

There are children lucky from dawn till dusk,
But never a child so lucky!
For I cut my teeth on "Money Musk"
In the Bloody Ground of Kentucky!

When I grew tall as the Indian corn,
My father had little to lend me,
But he gave me his great, old powder-horn
And his woodsman's skill to befriend me.

With a leather shirt to cover my back,
And a redskin nose to unravel
Each forest sign, I carried my pack
As far as a scout could travel.

Till I lost my boyhood and found my wife,
A girl like a Salem clipper!
A woman straight as a hunting-knife
With eyes as bright as the Dipper!

We cleared our camp where the buffalo feed,
Unheard-of streams were our flagons;
And I sowed my sons like the apple-seed
On the trail of the Western wagons.

They were right, tight boys, never sulky or slow,
A fruitful, a goodly muster.
The eldest died at the Alamo.
The youngest fell with Custer.

The letter that told it burned my hand.
Yet we smiled and said, "So be it!"
But I could not live when they fenced the land,
For it broke my heart to see it.

I saddled a red, unbroken colt
And rode him into the day there;
And he threw me down like a thunderbolt
And rolled on me as I lay there.

The hunter's whistle hummed in my ear
As the city-men tried to move me,
And I died in my boots like a pioneer
With the whole wide sky above me.

Now I lie in the heart of the fat, black soil,
Like the seed of a prairie-thistle;
It has washed my bones with honey and oil
And picked them clean as a whistle.

And my youth returns, like the rains of Spring,
And my sons, like the wild-geese flying;
And I lie and hear the meadow-lark sing
And have much content in my dying.

Go play with the towns you have built of blocks,
The towns where you would have bound me!
I sleep in my earth like a tired fox,
And my buffalo have found me.

[4] From *Ballads and Poems: 1915–1930*. Copyright, 1931, by Stephen Vincent Benét. Reprinted by permission of Rinehart & Company, Inc., Publishers.

❖⟩❖⟩❖⟨❖⟨⟨❖

5 · Maxwell House

Y'know, for all his talking, Father wouldn't think of doing without that paper. It's one of those things that mean so much to every day that comes along.

And something else we count on, you and I .... day in and day out .... is coffee. I mean really good coffee .... like our Maxwell House—coffee you sit down to and enjoy, cup after cup. That "Good to the Last Drop" flavor! You won't find it in any other coffee .... no coffee but Maxwell House. And as you'd expect—there's a very real reason why. It's a recipe. The only recipe there is, for that "Good to the Last Drop" flavor.

It's mighty important, that recipe of ours. Because the flavor of the coffee you enjoy depends on the blend .... the kind of coffees in it .... and how they're put together.

Now, coffee grows in many different varieties .... and you can blend them in all sorts of ways. But there's only one way .. one recipe .. for our famous Maxwell House flavor.

When all's said and done, it's this recipe of ours that makes the difference .... the big difference between just another coffee and the wonderfully good flavor of America's favorite brand.

It's a difference you'll taste for yourself .... the very first time you pour a cup of our Maxwell House Coffee. And I hope you will ... tomorrow—

Hope you'll start enjoying the coffee that's always
... "Good to the Last Drop."

5 Courtesy of General Foods Corporation, Maxwell House Coffee.

❖❖❖❖❖❖❖❖

6 · A Hymn to God the Father

Wilt Thou forgive that sin where I begun,
 Which was my sin, though it were done before?
Wilt Thou forgive that sin through which I run,
 And do run still though still I do deplore?
When Thou hast done, Thou hast not done,
 For I have more.

Wilt Thou forgive that sin which I have won
 Others to sin? and, made my sin their door?
Wilt Thou forgive that sin which I did shun
 A year, or two, but wallowed in, a score?
When Thou hast done, Thou hast not done,
 For I have more.

I have a sin of fear, that when I have spun
 My last thread, I shall perish on the shore;
But swear by Thyself, that at my death Thy Son
 Shall shine as He shines now, and heretofore;
And, having done that, Thou hast done,
 I fear no more.

6 John Donne, "A Hymn to God the Father," *Poems* (1633).

❖❖❖❖❖❖❖❖

7 · Memoirs of a Banquet Speaker
James Thurber

The sanity of the average banquet speaker lasts about two and a half
months; at the end of that time he begins to mutter to himself, and calls
out in his sleep. I am dealing here with the young banquet speaker, the
dilettante, who goes into it in quest of glamour. There is, he finds out too
late, no glamour at banquets—I mean the large formal banquets of big

associations and societies. There is only a kind of dignified confusion that gradually unhinges the mind.

Late in my thirty-fifth year, having tasted every other experience in life (except being rescued by Captain Fried), I decided to be a guest of honor at some glittering annual dinner in a big New York hotel. At first blush, you might think it would be difficult to be asked. It isn't. You don't, of course, have to be a member of an organization in order to address its annual banquet. In fact the organization doesn't even have to know who you are, and it almost never does. The names of the speakers are got out of newspapers and phone books, and from the better Christmas cards; sometimes a speaker is suggested to the entertainment committee by a woman named Mrs. Grace Voynton. That's all I know about her. She suggested me. I never saw her again. As a matter of fact, I never saw her at all. She phoned me one day and asked if I would address the annual banquet of a certain organization, the name of which, in the ensuing conversation, which was rather controversial, slipped my mind. I said I wouldn't address the banquet because my dinner pants were too tight. She was pleased to regard this as a pleasantry, and phoned me again the next day, as a woman will. Finally, I said I would make a short talk. I was told to be at the Commodore Hotel at seven-thirty on a certain Wednesday evening. It was only when I was in a taxi on my way to the hotel that I realized I didn't know the name, or the nature, of the organization I was going to talk to—let alone what I was going to talk about. So high is the courage of youth that the young banquet speaker is likely to dismiss this unfortunate ignorance too lightly. He has an idea that Mrs. Voynton will be at the hotel, or that the doorman will recognize him. Certainly, he thinks, it is going to be easy enough to find the banquet-room. It isn't going to be, though (the italics are mine). During the banquet season anywhere from three to eleven banquets are being held, simultaneously, at the average hotel on any given night. Not realizing this, the young guest of honor is almost sure to think that the first banquet table he spies is the one at which he belongs. There is only about one chance in ten that he is right.

I walked into the first banquet-room that I came to, on the mezzanine floor, after having been met by no one at all except a man who asked me where the ladies' dressing room was. I told him I didn't know and he walked over and told a lady who was with him that I didn't know. There is no reason in the world why a trivial incident like that should unnerve a banquet speaker; it leaves him, however, with a vague sense of insecurity; he begins to wonder where he is, and what night it is, and whether the whole thing may not possibly be a hoax.

In somewhat of a daze—the first warning of a bad mental state—I found myself seated at a long table on a dais, next to a lady who asked me, as soon as I had drunk a glass of ice water, if I understood the makeup and purposes of the organization we were about to address. She had also accepted over the phone, and had had a miserable connection. I told her facetiously—as one who whistles in the dark to keep his nerve up—that I was under the impression we were the guests of honor at the National Women's Bulb-Raising Association. This caused the man on her right to pale slightly. He drank a little water and whispered to me that, on the contrary, we were at the annual dinner of the North-Eastern States Meat-Handlers Association. I could see, however, that he was uncertain of himself on that point: He kept twisting his napkin. After the coffee and ice cream he was called upon for the first speech of the evening, and if ever a man touched lightly on the meat-handling situation he did. His nervous condition and incoherent remarks obviously upset the toastmaster who, all we speakers were instantly aware, was not absolutely sure that he was at the right banquet himself.

At this point, since I figured that several speakers were yet to come before I would be called on, I slipped from the table and made a hasty trip to the lobby to look up the sign which tells where the various conventions are being held. Seven were listed, and their locations were given merely as Ballroom A, Ballroom B, Second Assembly Hall, Jade Room, etc. It was impossible to identify these rooms in the short time at my disposal and so I simply hurried back to my seat. From the sign, however, I had discovered that there was a possibility I might be in the midst of the National Chassis-Builders Association, the Society for the Advancement of Electric Welding, the American Society of Syrup and Fondant Makers, or the Past Presidents and Active Officers of Ye Olde Record Binding Company.

As I sat in my chair, breathing heavily, I tried to think up a few words of greeting and appreciation which might apply equally to the aims and purposes of all the various organizations. This got me nowhere. Nor did I receive any help from the gentleman who was talking at the moment. His expression was the agonized expression of a man who hasn't the slightest idea what it is all about and wishes he were home. He told four stories, in a husky voice, and sat down. The toastmaster now arose and said that we were going to have the pleasure of listening to a man who knew more about the subject nearest to our hearts than anyone else in America, a man whose great authority in this field had been recognized by his being selected to write on the subject for the "Encyclopaedia Britannica" (I quote him more or less accurately—it was a little more involved than that.) Instead of naming his man at this juncture, the toastmaster told a story, and then reverted to the world's greatest authority on the subject nearest our hearts, repeating what he had already said and finally with a sweep of his hand, pronouncing the speaker's name—"Mr. Septimus R. Groves." As the toastmaster sat down, I lapsed back into my chair and applauded lightly. Nobody got up. All eyes then followed the toastmaster's—and rested finally on me. I knew now that I was at the wrong banquet. Vaguely, as I got to my feet, I wondered where Mr. Groves was, and on what subject he was so eminent an authority. I was received with tremendous applause. When it quieted down, I began to speak. I sketched briefly the advance of transportation, the passing of riveting, the improvement shown in the handling and distribution of meats, and the absolute reliance that one could place nowadays upon the bindings of old records. In conclusion I left with my audience the thought that in meat-handling, as in bulb-raising, chassis construction, electric welding, and binding old records it is Service and Cooperation that count. The speech was received with thunderous applause and a little stomping.

It was not until I got into a taxi that I realized my mind was already beginning to go. The driver asked me where to. I was surprised to hear myself tell him the Pennsylvania Hotel. There I registered as "Septimus R. Groves." "We already have a Septimus R. Groves registered here," said the clerk, with polite interest. "What's his name?" I asked. "Septimus R. Groves," he said. "He's attending the annual banquet of the Fish and Game Wardens." "Oh," I said, "There must be some mistake; the man you're thinking of is Horace R. Morgner—gypsum blocks and building laths." The clerk gave me my room key, albeit with a certain reluctance. It was a week before I went home. I don't mutter any longer, but I still cry out in my sleep.

⁷ By permission of the author. Copyright, 1930, The New Yorker Magazine, Inc.

❖❖❖❖ ❖❖❖❖

8 · The Family Fool

Oh! a private buffoon is a light-hearted loon,
    If you listen to popular rumour;
From the morn to the night he's so joyous and bright,
    And he bubbles with wit and good humour!
He's so quaint and so terse, both in prose and in verse;
    Yet though people forgive his transgression,
There are one or two rules that all family fools
    Must observe, if they love their profession.
        There are one or two rules,
          Half a dozen, may be,
       That all family fools,
         Of whatever degree,
Must observe, if they love their profession.

If you wish to succeed as a jester, you'll need
    To consider each person's auricular;

What is all right for B would quite scandalize C
    (For C is so very particular);
And D may be dull, and E's very thick skull
    Is as empty of brains as a ladle;
While F is F sharp, and will cry with a carp
    That he's known your best joke from his cradle!
        When your humour they flout,
            You can't let yourself go;
        And it *does* put you out
            When a person says, "Oh,
I have known that old joke from my cradle!"

If your master is surly, from getting up early
    (And tempers are short in the morning),
An inopportune joke is enough to provoke
    Him to give you, at once, a month's warning.
Then if you refrain, he is at you again,
    For he likes to get value for money;
He'll ask then and there, with an insolent stare,
    "If you know that you're paid to be funny?"
        It adds to the tasks
            Of a merryman's place
        When your principal asks,
            With a scowl on his face,
"If you know that you're paid to be funny?"

Comes a Bishop, maybe, or a solemn D.D.—
    Oh, beware of his anger provoking!
Better not pull his hair—don't stick pins in his chair;
    He don't understand practical joking.
If the jests that you crack have an orthodox smack,
    You may get a bland smile from these sages;
But should they, by chance, be imported from France,
    Half-a-crown is stopped out of your wages!
        It's a general rule,
            Though your zeal it may quench,
        If the family fool
            Tells a joke that's too French,
Half-a-crown is stopped out of his wages!

Though your head it may rack with a bilious attack,
    And your senses with toothache you're losing,
Don't be mopy and flat—they don't fine you for that,
    If you're properly quaint and amusing!
Though your wife ran away with a soldier that day,

> And took with her your trifle of money;
> Bless your heart, they don't mind—they're exceedingly kind—
> They don't blame you—as long as you're funny!
> It's a comfort to feel
> If your partner should flirt,
> Though *you* suffer a deal,
> They don't mind it a bit—
> They don't blame you—so long as you're funny!

[8] W. S. Gilbert, *The Yeoman of the Guard,* with music by Sir Arthur Sullivan (produced October 3, 1888).

❖⟩❖⟩❖◈❖◈◈◈

9 · Organization of Material

Irregularity and want of method, are only supportable in men of great learning or genius, who are often too full to be exact, and therefore chuse to throw down their pearls in heaps before the reader, rather than be at the pains of stringing them.

Method is of advantage to the work, both in respect to the writer and the reader. In regard to the first, it is a great help to his invention. When a man has planned his discourse, he finds a great many thoughts rising out of every head, that do not offer themselves upon the general survey of the subject. His thoughts are at the same time more intelligible, and better discover their drift and meaning, when they are placed in their proper lights, and follow one another in a regular series, than when they are thrown together without order and connexion. There is always an obscurity in confusion, and the same sentence that would have enlightened the reader in one part of the discourse, perplexes him in another. For the same reason likewise every thought in a methodical discourse shews itself in its greatest beauty, as the several figures in a piece of painting receive new grace from their disposition in the picture. The advantages of a reader from a methodical discourse, are correspondent with those of the writer. He comprehends everything easily, takes it in with pleasure, and retains it long.

Method is not less requisite in ordinary conversation than in writing, provided a man would talk to make himself understood. I, who hear a thousand coffee-house debates every day, am very sensible of this want of method in the thoughts of my honest countrymen. There is not one dispute in ten which is managed in those schools of politics, where, after the three first sentences, the question is not entirely lost. Our disputants put me in mind of the skuttle-fish, that, when he is unable to extricate himself, blackens all the water about him till he becomes invisible. The man who does not know how to methodize his thoughts, has always, to borrow a phrase from the *Dispensary, a barren superfluity of words;* the fruit is lost amidst the exuberance of leaves.

[9] Joseph Addison, Paper contributed to *The Spectator,* No. 476.

❖❭❖❭❖❖❖❰❖❰❖

10 · How the Greeks Lived

But how, you will ask, did the ancient Greeks have time to look after their families and their business if they were forever running to the market place to discuss affairs of state? In this chapter I shall tell you. In all matters of government, the Greek democracy recognized only one class of citizens—the freemen. Every Greek city was composed of a small number of free-born citizens, a large number of slaves and a sprinkling of foreigners.

At rare intervals (usually during a war, when men were needed for the army) the Greeks showed themselves willing to confer the rights of citizenship upon the "barbarians," as they called the foreigners. But this was an exception. Citizenship was a matter of birth. You were an Athenian because your father and your grandfather had been Athenians before you. But however great your merits as a trader or a soldier, if you were born of non-Athenian parents, you remained a "foreigner" until the end of time.

The Greek city, therefore, whenever it was not ruled by a king or a tyrant, was run by and for the freemen, and this would not have been possible without a large army of slaves who outnumbered the free citizens at the rate of five or six to one and who performed those tasks to which we modern people must devote most of our time and energy if we wish to provide for our families and pay the rent of our apartments.

The slaves did all the cooking and baking and candlestick-making of the entire city. They were the tailors and the carpenters and the jewelers and the schoolteachers and the bookkeepers and they tended the store and looked after the factory while the master went to the public meetings to discuss questions of war and peace or visited the theater to see the latest play of Aeschylus or hear a discussion of the revolutionary ideas of Euripides, who had dared to express certain doubts upon the omnipotence of the great god Zeus.

Indeed, ancient Athens resembled a modern club. All the free-born citizens were hereditary members and all the slaves were hereditary servants, and waited upon the needs of their masters, and it was very pleasant to be a member of the organization.

But when we talk about slaves, we do not mean the sort of people about whom you have read in the pages of *Uncle Tom's Cabin.* It is true that the position of those slaves who tilled the fields was a very unpleasant one, but the average freeman who had come down in the world and who had been obliged to hire himself out as a farm hand led just as miserable a life. In the cities, furthermore, many of the slaves were more prosperous than the poorer classes of the freemen. For the Greeks, who loved moderation in all things, did not like to treat their slaves after the fashion which afterward was so common in Rome, where a slave had as few rights as an engine in a modern factory and could be thrown to the wild animals upon the smallest pretext.

The Greeks accepted slavery as a necessary institution, without which no city could possibly become the home of a truly civilized people.

The slaves also took care of those tasks which nowadays are performed by the businessmen and the professional men. As for those household duties which take up so much of the time of your mother and which worry your father when he comes home from his office, the Greeks, who understood the value of leisure, had reduced such duties to the smallest possible minimum by living amidst surroundings of extreme simplicity.

To begin with, their homes were very plain. Even the rich nobles spent their lives in a sort of adobe barn, which lacked all the comforts which a modern workman expects as his natural right. A Greek home consisted of four walls and a roof. There was a door which led into the street but there were no windows. The kitchen, the living rooms and the sleeping quarters were built around an open courtyard in which there was a small fountain, or a statue and a few plants to make it look bright. Within this courtyard the family lived when it did not rain or when it was not too cold. In one corner of the yard the cook (who was a slave) prepared the meal and in another corner, the teacher (who was also a slave) taught the children the alpha beta gamma and the tables of multiplication and in still another corner the lady of the house, who rarely left her domain (since it was not considered good form for a married woman to be seen on the streets too often) was repairing her husband's coat with her seamstresses (who were slaves), and in the little office, right off the door, the master was inspecting the accounts which the overseer of his farm (who was a slave) had just brought to him.

When dinner was ready the family came together but the meal was a very simple one and did not take much time.

The Greeks seem to have regarded eating as an unavoidable evil and not a pastime, which kills many dreary hours and eventually kills many dreary people. They lived on bread and on wine, with a little meat and some green vegetables. They drank water only when nothing else was available because they did not think it very healthy. They loved to call on each other for dinner, but our idea of a festive meal, where everybody is supposed to eat much more than is good for him, would have disgusted them. They came together at the table for the purpose of a good talk and a good glass of wine and water, but as they were moderate people they despised those who drank too much.

The same simplicity which prevailed in the dining room also dominated their choice of clothes. They liked to be clean and well groomed, to have their hair and beards neatly cut, to feel their bodies strong with the exercise and the swimming of the gymnasium, but they never followed the Asiatic fashion which prescribed loud colors and strange patterns. They wore a long white coat and they managed to look as smart as a modern Italian officer in his long blue cape.

They loved to see their wives wear ornaments but they thought it very vulgar to display their wealth (or their wives) in public and whenever the women left their home they were as inconspicuous as possible.

In short, the story of Greek life is a story not only of moderation but also of simplicity. "Things," chairs and tables and books and houses and carriages, are apt to take up a great deal of their owners' time. In the end they invariably make him their slave and his hours are spent looking after their wants, keeping them polished and brushed and painted. The Greeks, before everything else, wanted to be "free," both in mind and in body. That they might maintain their liberty, and be truly free in spirit, they reduced their daily needs to the lowest possible point.

[10] From *The Story of Mankind,* by Hendrik Willem van Loon. Copyright, 1948, by Helen C. van Loon. Copyright, 1951, by Liveright Publishing Corporation.

❖⊰❖⊰❖⊱❖⊱❖

11 · The Financial Structure

Mrs. Jooks looked from the newspaper she was reading and asked, in that bland way that gets so many husbands into trouble:—

"Walter, dear, what is a 'financial structure'?"

"A what?"

"A financial structure. It says here: 'Now that the Oceanic Bank Company has secured 75 per cent of the stock of the Plethoric Title and Mortgage Company, its financial structure is complete. The Oceanic Bank Company own 100 per cent of the stock of the Oceanic Banking Company, 80 per cent of the stock of the Trans-Atlantic Oceanic Company, and all but the directors' qualifying shares of the International Trans-Atlantic Company. The Plethoric Title and Mortgage Company holds 90 per cent of the stock of the Balzac Trust Company, 100 per cent of the stock of the Premium Mortgage Company'—and a lot more of the same sort of thing, Walter. What does it mean?"

"Why that's simple, my dear. What you have just read me is the financial structure you asked me about. In this day, when great combinations of capital are required to swing the vast transactions that—"

"But I don't understand it."

"I can explain very easily, Jessie. Let us suppose that we buy a small place in the country—"

"Oh, I should love to!"

"I am just supposing. Suppose, then, we buy a small place in the country—ten acres, let us say. You and I and Dorothy put our money together and buy it. We call it the Jooks Farming and Dairy Company, and we each put in $3333.33 and pay $10,000 for the place. That is simple, isn't it?"

"You couldn't get much of a place for $10,000."

"That's just the point. You couldn't. But we do it anyway. So we go out there and start a garden. We have beets and spinach and beans and corn. So we get along for a year. At the end of the year I say to you, 'Jessie, I think I'll buy a cow'; so I take my own money and pay a hundred dollars for a cow, and I call it the Jooks Cow Company. So there are now two companies—the Farming and Dairy Company, and the Cow Company. You understand that?"

"Certainly."

"Good! We now have a cow. But we could use a pig, so you take your own money and pay fifty dollars for a pig, and you call it the Jooks Pig Company. There are now three companies."

"I can see that."

"But Dorothy thinks a chicken can pick up a living on the place, so she buys a chicken for two dollars."

"I don't think one chicken would be enough. I think one chicken would be too lonely."

"All right! All right! Make it ten chickens—ten chickens for twenty dollars."

"If you wouldn't mind, Walter, I would rather have the chickens—I always did want to have chickens."

"Then you have the chickens. I am only trying to explain what a financial structure is and—"

"And I'm sure Dorothy would rather not have the pig. Dorothy is always so dainty about things."

"All right! Let her have the cow. It makes no difference whatever. I'll have the pig, capital fifty dollars, and you have the chickens, capital twenty dollars, and Dorothy has the cow, capital one hundred dollars. So you call your chickens Mrs. Jooks Chicken Company. There are now four separate companies, all independent and good going concerns. But when we have been operating another year, we find we could do better if we had more land and more stock to raise, so we look around. Next door to us are Mr. and Mrs. Smith and their son."

"How old is the son? It would be nice for Dorothy if he was—"

"Never mind that. The Smiths have organized much as we have. They own eight acres, and they raise cucumbers and peas and squash and corn, calling it the Smith Farming and Culturing Company. They have two cows, two hundred dollars, called the Smith Cow Company. They have no pig. They have five chickens, ten dollars, called the Smith Chicken Company. They have nine rabbits, nine dollars, called the Smith Rabbit Company. The Smiths are getting along well enough, but none too well. Smith and his wife and their son——"

"What is the son's name?"

"Algernon."

"It's queer that they gave him a name like that. I should never call a boy Algernon."

"Please! Please, Jessie! I'm trying to explain what a financial structure is."

"Well, I'm listening, Walter. I think I have a right to know something about my neighbors, if I'm going to live next door to them."

"Yes? Well, please let me go on. These Smiths, next door to us, are up-to-date people. They see that combining allied interests is the modern financial trend, so one day at dinner Mr. Smith says, 'Folks, this thing of having a lot of separate companies is getting us nowhere. The Smith Farming and Culturing Company proposes to buy out the Smith Cow Company, the Smith Chicken Company, and the Smith Rabbit Company. How about it? I will sell the Smith Cow Company to the Farming and Culturing Company—100 per cent of it."

"So, then there is no more Smith Cow Company."

"But there is! Mr. Smith does not sell his cows; he keeps on running the cows; he remains Chairman of the Board of the Cow Company, and he only sells the stock of the Cow Company to the Smith Farming and Culturing Company. That is the way it is done, Jessie."

"I see."

"But when Mr. Smith turns to Mrs. Smith and Algernon, they look at each other queerly. Mrs. Smith says, 'John, I forgot to tell you, but Algernon needed money for some new rabbit hutches, and I bought 80 per cent of the stock of that Rabbit Company, and that stock is now owned by the Chicken Company."

"Wait a minute, Walter. There were nine rabbits and Algernon sold 80 per cent. That left him——"

"One and eight-tenths rabbits. But Mrs. Smith was fond of her chickens, and she did not want to part with them entirely to the Farming and Culturing Company, so she proposed to sell to it 90 per cent of the chickens and rabbits she now owned. For the Farming and Culturing Company, Mr. Smith accepted that offer, which included 90 per cent of Mrs. Smith's five chickens, and 90 per cent of 80 per cent of Algernon's nine rabbits. In other words,—let us see—Algernon now had one and eight-tenths rabbits, the Mrs. Smith Chicken Company had one-half a chicken and seventy-two one-hundredths of a rabbit, and the Smith Farming and Culturing Company has two cows, four and one-half chickens, and—wait a minute, yes, six and forty-eight one-hundredths rabbits. But, of course, the Cow and Rabbit Company now owned part of the Farm."

"Oh!"

"Which they got in exchange. And the Rabbit Company owned part of Mrs. Smith's chickens and part of Mrs. Smith's part of the Farm."

"Oh!"

"Mr. Smith now thought the financial structure was complete, but what do you think we had been doing all this while, my dear?"

"Farming,"—after a moment of deep thought.

"No. Yes—farming of course, but we have been building our financial structure in exactly the same way, Jessie. Financial structure building is the slogan of the day."

"I see I am going to lose some of my chickens. And I loved my chickens!"

"Oh come now! We must be progressive, my dear. We must follow the trend of the times. As a matter of fact, you were the first to propose a deal. You said to Dorothy, 'The Mrs. Jooks Chicken Company will sell you 80 per cent of its chickens for stock in your Cow Company,' and the deal was made. The Cow Company now had eight chickens and your Chicken Company retained two chickens."

"I hope one was a rooster."

"We will say it was. For our financial structure building that makes no difference. But what was I doing? I went to Dorothy and proposed to buy 90 per cent of the Cow Company. She agreed, and the deal was made. My Pig Company now owned nine-tenths of the cow, seven and two-tenths chickens, and the pig. But seeing that a farm could do better than a lot of separately managed concerns, the Jooks Farming and Dairy Company came to me—"

"You came to yourself?"

"I was President of the Farming Dairy Company, so I came to myself, as President of the Jooks Pig Company, and I bought 80 per cent of the Pig Company. I now owned, as the Farming and Dairy Company, seventy-two one-hundredths of a cow, five and seventy-six one-hundredths chickens, eight-tenths of a pig. You owned, as the Chicken Company—"

"Never mind, Walter, I see what is coming. You're going to buy 76 per cent of the Smith outfit—"

"Ninety per cent, to be exact. Ninety per cent, Jessie, thus bringing under one control—wait a minute! When the deal is completed, The Jooks Farming and Dairy Company would own—"

Late that night Mr. Jooks was still computing hundred-thousandths of rabbit, and tens of thousandths of a chicken, and saying, "No! Eight and nine hundred and seventy-six thousandths from eleven and eighty-four hundredths—no, that's not rabbits, that's cow—no, it couldn't be

w, there were only three cows, it's chickens. Hold on! I subtracted
bbits from pig here. Wait a minute, now—"

Mrs. Jooks had long since gone up to bed. At two o'clock Jooks
crumpled up his papers and put them in the fire-place. He stole upstairs
quietly and undressed as noiselessly as he could, but as he was putting on
his pyjamas Mrs. Jooks opened her eyes. She lay quiet for a moment,
getting awake.

"Walter?"

"Yes, my dear."

"Walter, I was thinking, before I went to sleep. I think fifty dollars is
too much to pay for a pig. I think I'd rather have a cheaper pig and more
chickens."

"Yes?"

"And Walter, I don't want to be in partnership with those Smiths.
I want to own my chickens myself."

She closed her eyes and a moment later, Mr. Jooks knew, by her
deep breathing, that she was asleep. She had left him only about 33 1/3
per cent of the bed. Very carefully, not to awaken her again and bring up
the matter of financial structures, Mr. Jooks got into bed. He drew over
himself 64 3/5 per cent of the bed covers. He fell asleep immediately,
for he was feeling exceptionally well satisfied with himself—he had
explained the higher finance to his wife.

[11] Ellis Parker Butler, "Snoops."

❖⋅⟫⋅⟩❖⋅⟨⋅⟨❖

12 · What's a Flag?

What's a flag? What's the love of country for which it stands? Maybe
it begins with love of the land itself. It is the fog rolling in with the tide
at Eastport, or through the Golden Gate and among the towers of San
Francisco. It is the sun coming up behind the White Mountains, over the
Green, throwing a shining glory on Lake Champlain and above the Adiron-
dacks. It is the *storied* Mississippi rolling swift and muddy past St. Louis,
rolling past Cairo, pouring down past the levees of New Orleans. It is
lazy noontide in the pines of Carolina; it is a sea of wheat rippling in
Western Kansas; it is the San Francisco peaks far north across the glowing
nakedness of Arizona; it is the Grand Canyon and a little stream coming
down out of a New England ridge, in which are trout.

It is men at work. It is the storm-tossed fishermen coming into
Gloucester and Provincetown and Astoria. It is the farmer riding his

great machine in the dust of harvest, the dairyman going to the barn before sunrise, the lineman mending the broken wire, the miner drilling for the blast. It is the servants of fire in the *murky* splendor of Pittsburgh, between the Allegheny and the Monongahela, the trucks rumbling through the night, the locomotive engineer bringing the train in on time, the pilot in the clouds, the riveter running along the beam a hundred feet in air. It is the clerk in the office, the housewife doing the dishes and sending the children off to school. It is the teacher, doctor and parson tending and helping body and soul, for small reward.

It is the small things remembered, the little corners of the land, the houses, the people that each one loves. We love our country because there was a little tree on a hill, and grass thereon, and a sweet valley below; because the hurdy-gurdy man came along on a sunny morning in a city street; because a beach or a farm or a lane or a house that might not seem much to others was once, for each of us, made magic. It is voices that are remembered only, no longer heard. It is parents, friends, the lazy chat of street and store and office, and the ease of mind that makes life tranquil. It is Summer and Winter, rain and sun and storm. These are flesh of our flesh, bone of our bone, blood of our blood, a lasting part of what we are, each of us and all of us together.

It is stories told. It is the Pilgrims dying in their first dreadful Winter. It is the minute-man standing his ground at Concord Bridge, and dying there. It is the army in rags, sick, freezing, starving at Valley Forge. It is the wagons and the men on foot going westward over Cumberland Gap, floating down the great rivers, rolling over the great plains. It is the settler hacking fiercely at the primeval forest on his new, his own lands. It is Thoreau at Walden Pond, Lincoln at Cooper Union, and Lee riding home from Appomattox. It is corruption and disgrace, answered always by men who would not let the flag lie in the dust, who have stood up in every generation to fight for the old ideals and the old rights, at risk of ruin or life itself.

It is a great multitude of people on pilgrimage, common and ordinary people, charged with the usual human failings, yet filled with such a hope as never caught the imaginations and the hearts of any nation on earth before. The hope of liberty. The hope of justice. The hope of a land in which a man can stand straight, without fear, without rancor.

The land and the people and the flag—the land of a continent, the people of every race, the flag a symbol of what humanity may aspire to when the wars are over and the barriers are down; to these each generation must be dedicated and consecrated anew, to defend with life itself, if need be, but, above all, in friendliness, in hope, in courage, to live for.

[12] Editorial in the New York *Times*, June 14, 1940.

◆⋙◆⋘◆

13 · Who May Write

Among other good uses for which I have thought proper to institute these several introductory chapters, I have considered them as a kind of mark or stamp, which may hereafter enable a very indifferent reader to distinguish what is true and genuine in this historic kind of writing, from what is false and counterfeit. Indeed, it seems likely that some such mark may shortly become necessary, since the favourable reception which two or three authors have lately procured for their works of this nature from the public, will probably serve as an encouragement to many others to undertake the like. Thus a swarm of foolish novels and monstrous romances will be produced, either to the great impoverishing of booksellers, or to the great loss of time and depravation of morals in the reader; nay, often to the spreading of scandal and calumny, and to the prejudice of the character of many worthy and honest people.

To prevent, therefore, for the future such intemperate abuses of leisure, of letters, and of the liberty of the press, especially as the world seems at present to be more than usually threatened with them, I shall here venture to mention some qualifications, every one of which are in a pretty high degree necessary to this order of historians.

The first is, genius, without a full vein of which no study, says Horace, can avail us. By genius I would understand that power, or rather those powers of the mind, which are capable of penetrating into all things within our reach and knowledge, and of distinguishing their essential differences. These are no other than invention and judgment; and they are both called by the collective name of genius, as they are of those gifts of nature which we bring with us into the world. Concerning each of which many seem to have fallen into very great errors; for by invention, I believe, is generally understood a creative faculty, which would indeed prove most romance writers to have the highest pretensions to it; whereas by invention is really meant no more (and so the word signifies) than discovery, or finding out; or to explain it at large, a quick and sagacious penetration into the true essence of all the objects of our contemplation. This, I think, can rarely exist without the concomitancy of judgment; for how we can be said to have discovered the true essence of two things, without discerning their difference, seems to me hard to conceive. Now this last is the undisputed province of judgment, and yet some few men of wit have agreed with all the dull fellows in the world in representing these two to have been seldom or never the property of one and the same person.

But though they should be so, they are not sufficient for our purpose, without a good share of learning; for which I could again cite the authority of Horace, and of many others, if any was necessary to prove that tools are of no service to a workman, when they are not sharpened by art, or when he wants rules to direct him in his work, or hath no matter to work upon. All these uses are supplied by learning; for nature can only furnish us with capacity; or, as I have chose to illustrate it, with the tools of our profession; learning must fit them for use, must direct them in it, and, lastly, must contribute part at least of the materials. A competent knowledge of history and of the belles-lettres is here absolutely necessary; and without this share of knowledge at least, to affect the character of an historian, is as vain as to endeavour at building a house without timber or mortar, or brick or stone. Homer and Milton, who, though they added the ornament of numbers to their works, were both historians of our order, were masters of all the learning of their times.

Again, there is another sort of knowledge, beyond the power of learning to bestow, and this is to be had by conversation. So necessary is this to the understanding the characters of men, that none are more ignorant of them than those learned pedants whose lives have been entirely consumed in colleges and among books; for however exquisitely human nature may have been described by writers, the true practical system can be learnt only in the world. Indeed the like happens in every other kind of knowledge. Neither physic nor law are to be practically known from books. Nay, the farmer, the planter, the gardener, must perfect by experience what he hath acquired the rudiments of by reading. How accurately soever the ingenious Mr. Miller may have described the plant, he himself would advise his disciple to see it in the garden. As we must perceive, that after the nicest strokes of a Shakespeare or a Jonson, or a Wycherly or an Otway, some touches of nature will escape the reader, which the judicious action of a Garrick, of a Cibber, or a Clive, can convey to him; so, on the real stage, the character shows himself in a stronger and bolder light than he can be described. And if this be the case in those fine and nervous descriptions which great authors themselves have taken from life, how much more strongly will it hold when the writer himself takes his lines not from nature, but from book? Such characters are only the faint copy of a copy, and can have neither the justness nor spirit of an original.

Now this conversation in our historian must be universal, that is, with all ranks and degrees of men; for the knowledge of what is called high life will not instruct him in low; nor *é converso,* will his being acquainted with the inferior part of mankind teach him in the manners of the superior. And though it may be thought that the knowledge of either may sufficiently enable him to describe at least that in which he hath been conversant, yet he will ever here fall greatly short of perfection; for the follies of either rank do in reality illustrate each other. For instance, the affectation of high life appears more glaring and ridiculous from the simplicity of the low; and again, the rudeness and barbarity of this latter, strikes with much stronger ideas of absurdity when contrasted with, and opposed to, the politeness which controls the former. Besides, to say the truth, the manners of our historians will be improved by both these conversations; for in the one he will easily find examples of plainness, honesty, and sincerity; in the other of refinement, elegance, and a liberality of spirits which last quality I myself have scarce ever seen in men of low birth and education.

Nor will all the qualities I have hitherto given my historian avail him, unless he have what is generally meant by a good heart, and be capable of feeling. The author who will make me weep, says Horace, must first weep himself. In reality, no man can paint a distress well which he doth not feel while he is painting it; nor do I doubt, but that the most pathetic and affecting scenes have been writ with tears. In the same manner it is with the ridiculous. I am convinced I never make my reader laugh heartily but where I have laughed before him; unless it should happen at any time, that instead of laughing with me he should be inclined to laugh at me. Perhaps this may have been the case at some passages in this chapter, from which apprehension I will here put an end to it.

[13] Henry Fielding, *Tom Jones* (1749).

❖❩❖❩❖ ❖❨❖❨❖

14 · The Corporation and the Press

. . . Mr. Bernard Baruch was asked not so long ago what he thought was the most pressing problem facing the people of the world today. The answer expected, of course, was atomic control or Russian aggression or some equally dread problem. The answer was much simpler. The most pressing problem of the World, said Mr. Baruch, was—making a living.

It was always so. But until the last century no one ever considered business, which for the most part is simply making a living, worthy of special public attention and discussion. One could assign a number of reasons for the emergence of a business press—the great achievements of industry, the great growth of industry, the great dependence upon industry—all of which would be quite valid. I'm going to suggest that you will cover more ground with another reason—the rise of the modern corporation.

We have had the corporation with us for a long time but I suspect that no one yet fully understands the role of the modern corporation in society. As we find it today, it is a wholly new institution. There's nothing quite like it in history.

FORTUNE had to invent a unique literary form to deal with this phenomenon, what we call the "Corporation Story." That is, a story not primarily about people, not primarily about things, but a story about an abstraction called a corporation.

For the sake of simplification, I am talking only about larger corporations, corporations which have achieved a distinct institutional character, a corporate personality of their own. They may be corporations with two thousand employees, or two hundred thousand employees. But they are publicly-owned and the managers are hired managers, not owners.

In the varying degrees the people who work for these corporations —and I include management—make their life in the corporation. The friends they see in their social life are more and more the friends of their corporate life. The corporation welcomes the employee's children at birth, looks after the family's health, often provides legal service when troubles arise, often banks the employee when he is in debt, gives him an education if he wants it, sometimes buries him when he dies, provides for his widow and may even give his children jobs. Companies, even large ones, constantly use the phrase, "family," the such and such family—which may or may not be a happy one.

The employee considers himself an American first and a company man second. After that he may be a Texan or a New Englander and then only very incidentally a member of his local community. His community *is* the corporation, for he may be ordered here or there, spending a few years in one place, a few years in another, finally in a suburb, a dormitory town, when he settles down for the last stretch in the home office. Only in the armed forces or the foreign service or in ecclesiastical orders will you find anything to parallel this acceptance of a discipline requiring one to uproot and move, family and all, wherever and whenever the corporation so orders.

This phenomenon of the corporation as a socio-economic institution has evoked the phrase "corporate feudalism" to describe what is going on. It is something far more significant than "paternalism," for there is undeniably a suggestion of the feudal relationship, the honorable exchange of fealty for care and protection, covering subtle and unspecified rights, duties, loyalties, privileges and responsibilities.

Of course the feudal analogy can easily be pushed to ridiculous extremes. The fact is that the big corporation is entirely without precedent.

It is quite clear that the modern corporation can and does exert an enormous force in modern society. We have a goodly number of giant companies, giant social-economic complexes, that can be compared only to whole sovereign countries. General Motors gross is larger than the gross product of Australia or of Sweden and its profits last year were as large as the total national budget of New Zealand or Norway. There are many benefits of bigness and many disadvantages. I'm not trying to strike any balance. I'm merely emphasizing that the managements of these vast enterprises wield power for good or for evil, and their actions are therefore of prime public interest.

It is of prime public interest not only in the social sense; their business policies are probably of considerably more importance to the country than their social policies. A serious error in business judgment throws men out of work, antagonizes the community and lowers the prestige of management in general. Above all let us have managements who can run business profitably. Like other dividends those beneficent, social dividends must be paid out of profits; no profits, no social goodies.

The odd thing about our present arrangement is that no one is quite sure where management fits into the general scheme of American society. The almost complete separation of ownership and management in the big modern corporation has left the managers with no clear definition of where their ultimate responsibilities lie. As we all know, the old lines of legal responsibility are growing more and more tenuous—the theoretical responsibility to the board of directors and through the directors to the stockholder-owners. In honest fact, the stockholder has to take what it pleases management to give them, and if they don't like it they have no recourse except to sell their shares.

In many respects, the modern corporation as I have described it is no longer business in the ordinary sense of the word. There are still many men who do run businesses as businesses, that is they spend their time making and selling goods with the idea of maximizing their profits and minimizing their losses.

Well, you may ask, doesn't everybody? No, I think there is some doubt about that, and I think you can find the same doubt in the minds of plenty of top managements. The corporation has to be profitable, that is, take in as much as it puts out with enough left to maintain its credit and to give heed to the future. But so does a co-operative or a so-called non-profit organization and for that matter so does the Russian economy as a whole.

If the corporation is no longer run primarily for the benefit of the stockholders, then what is it run for? The government? in a sense it is; it certainly takes several days of every corporate week to earn the taxes. For labor? Yes, a pretty good case can be made that the corporation today is indeed run for the benefit of labor. The consumer? Yes, again. The point is that if you add all this up you will find that the corporation is run not primarily for any one group; *the corporation is run for the corporation.*

The health and the continuity of the corporation itself has become management's ultimate responsibility. And by that token the condition of the corporation has become the only standard by which management can be fairly judged.

The condition of the corporation means much more than its financial condition. It may show satisfactory earnings and have half a billion in cash and government bonds, but if it is laggard in research, if the end of its raw materials is in sight, if it is short of young men, if it is failing to keep its share of the market, the corporate condition can hardly be said to be healthy. Some managements today, when thinking of the continuity of the corporation, have to think fifty to one hundred years ahead, literally.

Many of our managements with a philosophical turn of mind do indeed conceive their ultimate responsibility as a responsibility to the corporation. They see the corporation as an institution in which the interests of many groups must be harmonized for mutual benefit—stockholders, labor, customers, suppliers, the national interest and that most formidable thing called public opinion. The old triangular organization charts are becoming obsolete—stockholder-line-directors-line-president-line-vice presidents and so forth.

To get a proper picture today you do better with a chart approximating a solar system with management spinning in the center and all the other interested groups spinning around it in varying orbits, exercising varying gravitational pulls at various times. Successful management somehow keeps the whole system in tolerable order, and prevents at all costs a disastrous collision which would blow up the whole little universe.

[14] Excerpt from a speech by Ralph D. Paine, managing editor of *Fortune*.

❖❭❭❖❭❭❖❖❰❖❰❖❰❖

15 · The Search for Wisdom

Surely there is a mine for silver,
And a place for gold which they refine.
Iron is taken out of the earth,
And copper is molten out of the stone.
Man setteth an end to darkness,
And searcheth out, to the furthest bound,
The stones of obscurity and of thick darkness.
He breaketh open a shaft away from where men sojourn;
They are forgotten of the foot;
They hang afar from men, they swing to and fro.
As for the earth, out of it cometh bread;
And underneath it is turned up as it were by fire.
The stones thereof are the place of sapphires,
And it hath dust of gold.
That path no bird of prey knoweth,
Neither hath the falcon's eye seen it:
The proud beasts have not trodden it,
Nor hath the fierce lion passed thereby.
He putteth forth his hand upon the flinty rock;
He overturneth the mountains by the roots.
He cutteth out channels among the rocks;
And his eye seeth every precious thing.

He bindeth streams that they trickle not;
And the thing that is hid bringeth he forth to light.
But where shall wisdom be found?
And where is the place of understanding?
Man knoweth not the price thereof;
Neither is it found in the land of the living.
The deep saith, It is not in me;
And the sea saith, It is not with me.
It cannot be gotten for gold
Neither shall silver be weighed for the price thereof.
It cannot be valued with the gold of Ophir,
With the precious onyx, or the sapphire.
Gold and glass cannot equal it,
Neither can it be exchanged for jewels of fine gold.
No mention shall be made of coral or of crystal:
Yea the price of wisdom is above rubies.
The topaz of Ethiopia shall not equal it,
Neither shall it be valued with pure gold.
Whence then cometh wisdom
And where is the place of understanding?
Seeing it is hid from the eyes of all living,
And kept close from the birds of the heavens.
Destruction and death say,
We have heard a rumor thereof with our ears.
God understandeth the way thereof,
And he knoweth the place thereof.
For he looketh to the ends of the earth,
And seeth under the whole heaven;
To make a weight for the wind:
Yea, he meteth out the waters by measure.
When he made a decree for the rain,
And a way for the lightning of the thunder;
Then did he see it, and declare it;
He established it, yea, and searched it out.
And unto man he said,
Behold, the fear of the Lord, that is wisdom;
And to depart from evil is understanding.

[15] *The Holy Bible,* Job 28.

16 · A Cradle Song

Hush! my dear, lie still and slumber,
  Holy angels guard thy bed!
Heavenly blessings without number
  Gently falling on thy head.

Sleep, my babe; thy food and raiment,
  House and home, thy friends provide;
All without thy care or payment:
  All thy wants are well supplied.

How much better thou'rt attended
  Than the Son of God should be,
When from heaven He descended
  And became a child like thee!

Soft and easy is thy cradle:
  Coarse and hard thy Saviour lay,
When His birthplace was a stable
  And His softest bed was hay.

Blessèd babe! what glorious features—
  Spotless fair, divinely bright!
Must He dwell with brutal creatures?
  How could angels bear the sight?

Was there nothing but a manger
  Cursèd sinners could afford
To receive the heavenly stranger?
  Did they thus affront their Lord?

Soft, my child: I did not chide thee,
  Though my song might sound too hard;
'Tis thy mother sits beside thee,
  And her arms shall be thy guard.

Yet to read the shameful story
  How the Jews abused their King,
How they served the Lord of Glory,
  Makes me angry while I sing.

See the kinder shepherds round Him,
  Telling wonders from the sky!

Where they sought Him, there they found Him,
   With his Virgin mother by.

See the lovely Babe a-dressing;
   Lovely Infant, how He smiled!
When He wept, the mother's blessing
   Soothed and hush'd the holy Child.

Lo, He slumbers in His manger,
   Where the hornèd oxen fed:
Peace, my darling; here's no danger,
Here's no ox anear thy bed.

'Twas to save thee, child, from dying,
   Save my dear from burning flame,
Bitter groans and endless crying,
   That thy blest Redeemer came.
May'st thou live to know and fear Him,
   Trust and love Him all thy days;
Then go dwell forever near Him,
   See His face, and sing His praise!

[16] Isaac Watts, "A Cradle Song," quoted in *World's Classics, English Verse,* ed.
William Peacock (New York: London: Oxford University Press, 1930), III, 85.

❖⧘❖⧘❖⧨❖⧩⧪❖

17 · Under the Capitol Dome

Station (----) Presents:
"Under the Capitol Dome."
Five minutes of news from and about Washington.
Timely news, background, interpretation and comment
prepared by Robert J. Serling of the United press.
   The Navy and the Air Force still seem to be
feudin' as well as fightin'.
   A lot of it can be chalked up to natural rivalry.
But some of it stems from the Navy's deep conviction
that we may have gone overboard on this business of
long-range, strategic bombing.
   Over the weekend, Navy dive bombers attacked a
big railroad bridge at Seoul (sohl). The Navy planes
—with precision dive-bombing—scored eight direct
hits and knocked out the bridge. A Navy spokesman
rather pointedly reminded newsmen later this was the

same bridge Air Force B-29 bombers have been trying unsuccessfully to destroy for weeks.

This wasn't the only needle the Navy's been using on its brother service. In another incident last week, an Army unit and a Marine unit began a joint ground offensive. The Army unit was given regular air support by Air Force fighters. The Marines got a new type of air support furnished by Marine planes—with the Marine aircraft operating only fifty yards ahead of the advancing Leatherneck ground forces.

We won't go into the technical differences between the support furnished by the Air Force planes and that furnished by the Marine fighters. But after the attack was finished, the Marines pointed out their casualties were far lighter than those suffered by the Army troops.

The Air Force hasn't been winning many publicity victories in Korea. Even its most sensational operation was followed by criticism. This was the mass bombing of some 30-thousand Communist troops ready to move on Taegu. At first, it looked like one of the most brilliant accomplishments of the war. The North Koreans were reported stunned, disorganized and shattered. But two days later, they took off on their expected offensive against Taegu—about 30-thousand strong.

To Air Force critics, this was further proof that we've put too much faith into our heavy bombers— expecting them to be defense cure-alls. However, later information indicates the criticism may be as premature as were some of the optimistic claims made in the wake of that attack. Apparently, the North Koreans were able to start their Taegu drive only by drawing off strength from other sectors, because the Taegu concentration was so badly battered.

Anyway, the Air Force is rather bitter about the scoffing that went on after the B-29 raid apparently had failed in its objective. Airmen pointed out that B-29's aren't supposed to be used against ground forces, where the targets are too small and scattered.

This was shown in World War II, when about one thousand B-17 bombers carried out a similar mission against German troops. The Nazis, although pretty well smeared in the first few minutes, managed to pull back most of their forces in time and the effects of the raid were negligible.

This, of course, is just ammunition for Navy claims that we've overconcentrated on heavy bombers which can't do all the jobs a modern war requires. The Navy has been saying all along that heavy bombers are limited in their accuracy, and that ground-based fighters are limited by their range. And it points proudly to its own carrier-based bombers and fighters —claiming they're more mobile and more accurate in bombing missions against specific ground targets.

Thus far, the Navy argues, the Korean War has backed up these claims.

In a way, the Air Force hasn't had much of a chance to show its stuff in the Korean conflict. Industrial targets in Korea have been rather few.

The very lack of Korean industrial targets has been a propaganda liability. In bombing what few targets there are, the B-29's inevitably have killed civilians—something which the Communists scream loudly against. A few military experts say the tangible results of these raids haven't been worth the propaganda ammunition handed to the Russians. On the other hand, there undoubtedly is some military value to these behind-the-lines targets.

No one questions the tremendous need we'd have for heavy, long-range bombers in the event of war with Russia. But the Korean fighting has added a lot of supporters behind those advocating strong carrier-based air power—to do the precision-bombing job that heavy bombers can't do, and to furnish mobile floating airfields for planes which might otherwise have to operate from land bases too far away.

[17] EK&R736A8/22, United Press Radio, August 22, 1950.

❖❖❖❖❖❖❖❖❖

18 · Dickens the Actor

The fact that Dickens' first choice after making a success was to write for the stage reveals the most important feature of his character, which must now receive our attention: he was a born actor. As on the stage, so in real life, there are two main types of actor: there is the 'straight' actor who is only happy when appearing as himself, and there is the 'character' actor who is only at ease when disguised as someone else. Of performers in real life who concentrated on themselves, building up their own personalities until everything they said or did seemed to be characteristic of them, there were two excellent specimens in the nineteenth century: Benjamin Disraeli and Oscar Wilde. The most perfect example of the other kind, always imagining himself as someone else and constantly projecting his personality into any quantity of seemingly different parts, was Charles Dickens, a David Garrick in real life who might have been another Garrick on the stage and did become a super-Garrick on the platform. It was the great ambition of his early life to be a professional actor, and the great regret of his later life that he had not been one; but fortunately for us his histrionic genius went into the creation of fictional figures, most of which have a curiously theatrical flavour and are so vividly conceived that if their creator had impersonated half a dozen of them on the stage he would have been the greatest actor of his time. So entirely did he live the characters of his imagination that he never knew how much of his essential self he put into them, and thus we find bits of him in widely dissimilar parts which he went out of his way to make comically repulsive, not perceiving that their vitality was his, the source of his histrionic nature.

The born actor is a man who has all the ordinary human sensibilities in an exaggerated form and is tortured with the desire to exhibit them; he laughs more heartily, weeps more tearfully, reacts more quickly than other people to all forms of stimuli. In this important respect Dickens was unlike every other great novelist of the past. One thinks of Fielding or Smollett or Scott or Thackeray or Hardy or Wells as an actor, and one instantly dismisses the thought. But Dickens was an actor through and through. His characters, his comedy, his sentiment, are of the stage; he had the quick eye for human oddity, the photographic power of reproducing it and the love of repeating it, which is possessed by a Garrick or a Kean; he pours out his emotions as only an actor can; he describes a storm as a stage manager would like to produce it; his villains are melodramatic, his heroes and heroines are stagey, his scenes are of the theatre; and far more than any other novels, his have attracted both actors and dramatists. If he were alive today he would be the king of film writers, with Hollywood at his feet.

[18] Hesketh Pearson, *Dickens: His Character, Comedy, and Career* (New York: Harper & Brothers, 1949), p. 41.

❖⫸❖⫸❖⫷❖⫷❖⫷❖

19 · The Sentence

A perfectly healthy sentence, it is true, is extremely rare. For the most part we miss the hue and fragrance of the thought; as if we could be satisfied with the dews of the morning or evening without their colors, or the heavens without their azure. The most attractive sentences are, perhaps, not the wisest, but the surest and roundest. They are spoken firmly and conclusively, as if the speaker had a right to know what he says, and if not wise, they have at least been well learned. Sir Walter Raleigh might well be studied, if only for the excellence of his style, for he is remarkable in the midst of so many masters. There is a natural emphasis in his style, like a man's tread, and a breathing space between the sentences, which the best of modern writing does not furnish. His chapters are like English parks, or say rather like a Western forest, where the larger growth keeps down the underwood, and one may ride on horseback through the openings. All the distinguished writers of that period possess a greater vigor and naturalness than the more modern—for it is allowed to slander our own time,—and when we read a quotation from one of them in the midst of a modern author, we seem to have come suddenly upon a greener ground, a greater depth and strength of soil. It is as if a green bough were laid across the page, and we are refreshed as by the sight of fresh grass in midwinter or early spring. You have constantly the warrant of life and experience in what you read. The little that is said is eked out by implication of the much that was done. The sentences are verdurous and blooming as evergreen and flowers, because they are rooted in fact and experience, but our false and florid sentences have only the tints of flowers without their sap or roots. All men are really most attracted by the beauty of plain speech, and they even write in a florid style in imitation of this. They prefer to be misunderstood rather than to come short of its exuberance. Hussein Effendi praised the epistolary style of Ibrahim Pasha to the French traveler Botta, because of "the difficulty of understanding it; there was," he said, "but one person at Jidda who was capable of understanding and explaining the Pasha's correspondence." A man's whole life is taxed for the least thing well done. It is its net result. Every sentence is the result of a long probation. Where shall we look for standard English but to the words of a standard man? The word which is best said came nearest to not being spoken at all, for it is cousin to a deed which the speaker could have better done. Nay, almost it must have taken the place of a deed by some urgent necessity, even by some misfortune, so that the truest writer will be some captive knight, after all. And perhaps the fates had such a design, when, having stored Raleigh so richly with the substance of life and experience, they made him a fast prisoner, and compelled him to make his words his deeds, and transfer to his expression the emphasis and sincerity of his action.

Men have a respect for scholarship and learning greatly out of proportion to the use they commonly serve. We are amused to read how Ben Jonson engaged that the dull masks with which the royal family and nobility were to be entertained should be "grounded upon antiquity and solid learning." Can there be any greater reproach than an idle learning? Learn to split wood, at least. The necessity of labor and conversation with many men and things, to the scholar is rarely well remembered; steady labor with the hands, which engrosses the attention also, is unquestionably the best method of removing palaver and sentimentality out of one's style, both of speaking and writing. If he has worked hard from morning till night, though he may have grieved that he could not be watching the train of his thoughts during that time, yet the few hasty lines which at evening record his day's experience will be more musical and true than his freest but idle fancy could have furnished. Surely the writer is to address a world of laborers, and such therefore must be his own discipline. He will not idly dance at his work who has wood to cut and cord before nightfall in the short days of winter; but every stroke will be husbanded, and ring soberly through the wood; and so will the strokes of that scholar's pen, which at evening record the story of the day, ring soberly, yet cheerily, on the ear of the reader, long after the echoes of his axe have died away. The scholar may be sure that he writes the tougher truth for the calluses on his palms. They give firmness to the sentence. Indeed, the mind never makes a great and successful effort, without a corresponding energy of the body. We are often struck by the force and precision of style to which hard-working men, unpracticed in writing, easily attain when required to make the effort. As if plainness and vigor and sincerity, the ornaments of style, were better learned on the farm and in the workshop than in the schools. The sentences written by such rude hands are nervous and rough, like hardened thongs, the sinews of the deer, or the roots of the pine. As for the graces of expression, a great thought is never found in a mean dress; but though it proceed from the lips of the Woloffs, the nine Muses and the three Graces will have conspired to clothe it in fit phrase. Its education has always been liberal, and its implied wit can endow a college. The world, which the Greeks called Beauty, has been made such by being gradually divested of every ornament which was not fitted to endure. The Sibyl, "speaking with inspired mouth, smileless, inornate, and unperfumed, pierces through centuries by the power of the god." The scholar might frequently emulate the propriety and emphasis of the farmer's call to his team, and confess that if that were written it would surpass his labored sentences. Whose are the truly *labored* sentences? From the weak and flimsy periods of the politician and literary man, we are glad to turn even to the description of work, the simple record of the month's labor in the farmer's almanac, to restore our tone and spirits. A sentence should read as if its author, had he held a plough instead of a pen, could have drawn a furrow deep and straight to the end. The scholar requires hard and serious labor to give an impetus to his thought. He will learn to grasp the pen firmly so, and wield it gracefully and effectively, as an axe or a sword. When we consider the weak and nerveless periods of some literary men, who perchance in feet and inches come up to the standard of their race, and are not deficient in girth also, we are amazed at the immense sacrifice of thews and sinews. What! these proportions,—these bones,—and this their work! Hands which could have felled an ox have hewed this fragile matter which would not have tasked a lady's fingers! Can this be a stalwart man's work, who has a marrow in his back and a tendon

Achilles in his heel? They who set up the blocks of Stonehenge did somewhat, if they only laid out their strength for once, and stretched themselves.

[19] Henry David Thoreau, *A Week on the Concord and Merrimack Rivers.*

❖❖❖❖❖❖❖

20 · Italics

During the war many persons less conversant with the art of writing than with strategy or artillery or surgery or aeronautics or blockade law or food supply have, to our great advantage, occupied much space, instructively, in the magazines and newspapers. But a regrettable by-product of their activities has been a relapse into primitive methods of soliciting attention. Newspaper columns filled with a mosaic of roman and italic type that would have horrified the prewar editor have grown familiar. The practiced writer is aware that his business is to secure prominence for what he regards as the essence of his communication by so marshalling his sentences that they shall lead up to a climax, or group themselves round a centre, or be worded with different degrees of impressiveness as the need of emphasis varies; he knows too that it is an insult to the reader's intelligence to admonish him periodically by a change of type, like a bad teacher imploring his boys to attend for a moment, that he cannot safely go to sleep just now. But to those who, however competent on their special subject, have not had enough experience of writing to have learnt these rudiments it comes as natural to italicize every tenth sentence or so as it comes to the letter-writing schoolgirl to underline whatever she enjoys recording. These mosaics have on discreet readers exactly the repellent effect that interjections had on Landor: 'I read warily; and whenever I find the writings of a lady, the first thing I do is to cast my eyes along her pages to see whether I am likely to be annoyed by the traps and springguns of interjections, and if I happen to espy them I do not leap the paling'.

[20] H. W. Fowler, *A Dictionary of Modern English Usage* (Oxford: At the Clarendon Press, 1949), p. 304.

❖❖❖❖❖❖❖

21 · Writer's Faults

It is the fault of some excellent writers—DeQuincey's first impressions on seeing London suggest it to me—that they express themselves with too great fullness and detail. They give the most faithful, natural, and life-like account of their sensations, mental and physical, but they lack moderation and sententiousness. They do not affect us by an ineffectual earnestness and a reserve of meaning, like a stutterer; they say all they mean. Their sentences are not concentrated and nutty. Sentences which suggest far more than they say, which have an atmosphere about them, which do not merely report an old, but make a new, impression; sentences which suggest as many things and are as durable as a Roman aqueduct; to frame these, that is the *art* of writing. Sentences which are expensive, towards which so many volumes, so much life, went; which lie like boulders on the page, up and down or across; which contain the seed of other sentences, not mere repetition, but creation; which a man might sell his grounds and castles to build. If DeQuincey had suggested each of his pages in a sentence and passed on, it would have been far more excellent writing. His style is nowhere kinked and knotted up into something hard and significant, which you could swallow like a diamond, without (sic) digesting.

[21] Henry David Thoreau, *Journal*, August 22, 1851.

✦꙰✦꙰✦꙰✦꙰✦꙰

22 · Grammar

When I hear the hypercritical quarrelling about grammar and style, the position of the particles, etc., etc., stretching or contracting every speaker to certain rules of theirs,—Mr. Webster, perhaps, not having spoken according to Mr. Kirkham's rule,—I see that they forget that the first requisite and rule is that expression shall be vital and natural, as much as the voice of a brute or an interjection: first of all, mother tongue; and last of all, artificial or father tongue. Essentially your truest poetic sentence is as free and lawless as a lamb's bleat. The grammarian is often one who can neither cry nor laugh, yet thinks that he can express human emotions. So the posture-masters tell you how you shall walk,—turning your toes out, perhaps excessively,—but so the beautiful walkers are not made.

[22] Henry David Thoreau, *Journal*, January 2, 1859.

✦꙰✦꙰✦꙰✦꙰✦꙰

23 · Punctuation

Punctuation, to repeat purposely for emphasis, is primarily for the eye. People engaged in conversation are never aware of the punctuation marks in their speeches. They talk in images and ideas, not in perfect, discernible sentences. For that matter, there is no rule anywhere—although seemingly one was once set up by teachers—that says a speaker must always come to a full stop at each and every period mark. Radio actors give themselves away as either neophytes or grammarians when they come to full stops at all periods.

[23] Edwin Duerr, *Radio and Television Acting* (New York: Rinehart & Company, Inc., 1950), p. 111.

⋄⟫⋄⟫⋄⋄⟪⋄⟪⋄

24 · Parentheses

"Moreover" is a parenthesis, when interjected in that fashion; a parenthesis is evidence that the man who uses it does not know how to write English or is too indolent to take the trouble to do it; a parenthesis usually throws the emphasis upon the wrong word, and has done it in this instance; a man who will wantonly use a parenthesis will steal. For these reasons I am unfriendly to the parenthesis. When a man puts one into my mouth his life is no longer safe.

[24] Samuel L. Clemens, *Mark Twain's Autobiography* (New York: Harper & Brothers, 1924), I, 188. Copyright, 1924, by Clara Gabrilowitsch. Copyright, 1952, by Clara Clemens Samossoud.

⋄⟫⋄⟫⋄⋄⟪⋄⟪⋄

25 · Semicolons

The book so written passed in 1921 into proof: where it was fortunate in the friends who criticised it. Particularly it owes its thanks to Mr. and Mrs. Bernard Shaw for countless suggestions of great value and diversity: and for all the present semicolons.

[25] T. E. Lawrence, Prefatory Comment, *Seven Pillars of Wisdom* (New York: Doubleday & Co., Inc., 1935), p. 6.

⋄⟫⋄⟫⋄⋄⟪⋄⟪⋄

26 · The Meaning of Words

And, therefore, first of all, I tell you, earnestly and authoritatively, (I *know* I am right in this,) you must get into the habit of looking intensely at words, and assuring yourself of their meaning, syllable by syllable—nay, letter by letter. For though it is only by reason of the opposition of letters in the function of signs, to sounds in the function of signs, that the study of books is called "literature", and that a man versed in it is called, by the consent of nations, a man of letters instead of a man of books, or of words, you may yet connect with that accidental nomenclature this real principle:—that you might read all the books in the British Museum (if you could live long enough), and remain an utterly "illiterate" uneducated person; but that if you read ten pages of a good book, letter by letter,— that is to say, with real accuracy,—you are for evermore in some measure an educated person. The entire difference between education and non-education (as regards the merely intellectual part of it), consists in this accuracy. A well-educated gentleman may not know many languages,— may not be able to speak any but his own,—may have read very few books. But whatever language he knows, he knows precisely; whatever word he pronounces, he pronounces rightly; above all, he is learned in the *peerage* of words; knows the words of true descent and ancient blood, at a glance, from words of modern canaille; remembers all their ancestry—their inter-marriages, distantest relationships, and the extent to which they were admitted, and offices they held, among the national noblesse of words at any time, and in any country. But an uneducated person may know by memory any number of languages, and talk them all, and yet truly know not a word of any,—not a word even of his own. An ordinarily clever and sensible seaman will be able to make his way ashore at most ports; yet he has only to speak a sentence of any language to be known for an illiterate person; so also the accent, or turn of expression of a single sentence will at once mark a scholar. And this is so strongly felt, so conclusively admitted, by educated persons, that a false accent or a mistaken syllable is enough, in the parliament of any civilized nation, to assign to a man a certain degree of inferior standing for ever.

[26] John Ruskin, *Sesame and Lilies* (1863).

❖〉❖〉❖❖〈❖〈❖

27 · Foreword, Preface

FOREWORD, PREFACE. *F.* is a word invented fifty years ago as a Saxonism by anti-latinists, and caught up as a vogue-word by the people who love a new name for an old thing. *P.* has a 500-year history behind it in English, and far from being antiquated, is still *the* name for the thing. It is to be hoped that the vogue may pass, and the taste of the general public prevail over that of publishers and authors. A decent retirement might be found for *f.* if it were confined to the particular kind of preface that is supplied by some distinguished person for a book written by some-one else who feels the need of a sponsor.

But how one vogue-word drives out another! Here in 1924 comes a book on whose title-page is mention of neither preface nor foreword; instead, it is 'With a Prefatory Gesture by ————'. Poor old foreword! your vogue is past, your freshness faded; you are antiquated, vieux jeu, passé, démodé; your nose is out of joint. And, when *gesture* shall have followed you to limbo, we may hope to get back to *preface.*

²⁷ H. W. Fowler, *A Dictionary of Modern English Usage* (Oxford: At the Claren-don Press, 1949), p. 188.

⋗⋙⋙⋗⋖⋘⋖⋘⋖

28 · Didacticism

'No mortal but is narrow enough to delight in educating others into counterparts of himself'; the statement is from *Wilhelm Meister.* Men, especially, are as much possessed by the didactic impulse as women by the maternal instinct. Some of them work it off *ex officio* upon their chil-dren or pupils or parishioners or legislative colleagues, if they are blest with any of these; others are reduced to seizing casual opportunities, and practise upon their associates in speech or upon the world in print. The Anglo-Indian who has discovered that the suttee he read of as a boy is called *sati* by those who know it best is not content to keep so important a piece of knowledge to himself; he must have the rest of us call it *sati,* like the Hindoos (ah, no—Hindus) and himself; at any rate, he will give us the chance of mending our ignorant ways by printing nothing but *sati* and forcing us to guess what word known to us it may stand for. The orientalist whom histories have made familiar with the *Khalîf* is deter-mined to cure us of the delusion, implanted in our childish minds by hours with some bowdlerized *Arabian Nights,* that there was ever such a being as our old friend the Caliph. Literary critics saddened by our hazy notions of French do their best to lead us by example from *nom de plume* and *morale* to *nom de guerre* and *moral.* Dictionary devotees whose devotion extends to the etymologies think it bad for the rest of us to be connecting *amuck* with *muck,* and come to our rescue with *amok.* These and many more, in each of their teachings, teach us one truth that we could do as well with, and two falsehoods that are of some importance. The one truth is, for instance, that *Khalîf* has a greater resemblance to the Arabic than *Caliph;* is that of use to anyone who does not know it already? The two falsehoods are, the first that English is not entitled to give what form it chooses to foreign words that it has occasion to use;

and the second, that it is better to have two or more forms coexistent than to talk of one thing by one name that all can understand. If the first is not false, why do we say *Germany* and *Athens* and *Lyons* and *Constantinople* instead of *Deutschland* and the rest? or allow the French to insult us with *Londres* and *Angleterre?* That the second is false not even our teachers would deny; they would explain instead that their aim is to drive out the old wrong form with the new right one. That they are most unlikely to accomplish, while they are quite sure to produce confusion temporary or permanent; see Mahomet for a typical case.

Seriously, our learned persons and possessors of special information should not, when they are writing for the general public, presume to improve the accepted vocabulary; when they are addressing audiences of their likes, they may naturally use, to their hearts' content, the forms that are most familiar to writer and readers alike; but otherwise they should be at the pains to translate technical terms into English. And, what is of far greater importance, when they do forget this duty, we others who are unlearned, and naturally speak not in technical terms, but in English, should refuse to be either cowed by the fear of seeming ignorant, or tempted by the hope of passing for specialists, into following their bad example without their real though insufficient excuse.

[28] H. W. Fowler, *A Dictionary of Modern English Usage* (Oxford: At the Clarendon Press, 1949), p. 112.

❖)❖)❖)❖❖(❖(❖(❖

29 · What Can Literature Do for Me?

Do not approach literature, then from the fact-side, but from the heart-side. Strike first for what it has in common with yourself. See in it an outlet, not an inlet. Unfortunately it is still taught—you may be sure not learned—from the fact-side. I have before me three editions of *The Ancient Mariner*. They all have long introductions telling the facts about Coleridge's life, when and where the poem was written, when and where it was added to, what kind of line and stanza the poet used, what book or books he probably read before writing the poem, but not a word as to what the poem has in it for you and me or of you and me. Now the life of a poet, the date of his work, the kind of meter employed, all have something to do with a poem. But they are secondary, not primary. The first thing to do is to find yourself in the poem itself. When you do this, when the poem means something to you, when you see in it a reflection or extension of yourself, when it becomes a real outlet for you, you will want to know something about the writer. Seek first, however, yourself in the poem, and all these other things will be added unto you. You can no more learn literature from history of literature than you can learn arithmetic from the history of arithmetic.

[29] C. Alphonso Smith, *What Can Literature Do for Me?* (New York: Odyssey Press, Inc., 1913, 1924), pp. 8–9.

❖❖❖❖ ❖❖❖❖

30 · What to Do

No matter how calm or nervous, conscientious or inspired, a chairman may be, he or she still presents one problem to the speaker to which neither the introducer nor the audience ever gives much thought. That is, what to do, where to look, how to act, while you are being introduced. It seems simple enough from the front.

A chair—one of those chairs—is near the center of the stage. According to the protocol of the platform, the one nearer the entrance is usually yours. Supposedly all you have to do is to walk from the wings to that chair and then sit down on it and wait. But that walk of no more than ten or fifteen feet can seem an eternity. It is apt to be one of the unremembered interludes in the life of any person who has ever taken it. Twenty boards can unite to form a plank. You are in a trance, doing a conscious act unconsciously, driven forward only by the motor of your pounding heart. Matters are not helped by your knowing there is always the chance that the chairman may forget which of the seats he had agreed to occupy and the two of you may be caught playing "Going to Jerusalem" in public.

When in some manner unknown to you, you have at last reached your place, graver difficulties arise. The chair may be one of two kinds. Either its high back and its seat, though covered with petit point, may conceal boards so stiff that you are sure the committee must think your sacroiliac needs righting, or it is one of those low-set leather chairs which emits embarrassing noises as you sink down onto its air-filled cushions, and from the depths of which only a derrick can remove you. Once seated, you reach for the arms as if they were the hands of a long-lost friend. After you and the chairman have indulged in those preliminary whisperings, and both you and he have smiled broadly at jokes passed between you that neither of you has heard, the chairman rises to start his introduction.

Then your troubles begin in earnest. Even before he has finished saying "Ladies and Gentlemen," you are apt to have crossed, uncrossed, and recrossed your legs so many times that it must look from out front as if you were trying to dance the Highland fling sitting down. Suddenly realizing that poise is desirable, you quiet your shins by wrapping your feet around the far-sprung legs of the chair.

"We have with us tonight—" the chairman goes on. By now you have begun to do strange things with your hands. You have patted them together as if any moment you were about to applaud yourself. You have surveyed your fingers with a baby's wonder and an interest no manicurist has ever shown. You have bitten the knuckle of the right hand's middle finger until it is about to bleed. As the chairman continues, you have started that weird gesture known only to expectant lecturers, that act of public and dry libation in which you seem to wash the face (and every part thereof) with the hands but without benefit of soap and water.

These physical activities, these setting-down exercises, get you so warm before the real gymnastics of the evening have started that while the chairman is still trying to remember your occupation you have reached in despair for your handkerchief and begun waving it as if you were a morris dancer. Strangers in the rear of the auditorium have on occasion been so startled by what they have mistaken for friendly salutations that they have been known to wave back.

These are not the only betrayals of embarrassment which as a lecturer you try clumsily to control. There are others, and their causes are valid, very valid, indeed. When, for example, a frustrated biographer is at work on you, telling your life story in detail, should you appear as bored as the audience is? Or should you look surprised? When the place of your birth is mentioned, should your eyebrows arch with amazement into an "Is *that* so?" formation? When the college you remember slaving at is named, should you shake your head and whisper to yourself, "Well, well, well—do tell? So he went there? How very interesting"? When the introducer insists you are a dramatic critic, and says that you see plays on Broadway, should you make it clear that you are more astounded than anyone else by all this, and mutter audibly, "Fancy that, Hedda. Fancy that"? And if he goes so far as to mention some of your books, should you set a good example by crying, "Well, I'll be!" and whipping out a notebook and pencil to write down the titles?

On the rare occasions when the chairman gets his circulars mixed and has confused your case history with that of Eve Curie, John Mulholland, or Commander Byrd, is it or is it not forgivable for you to shake your head in gentle protest and indicate regretfully you have one, and only one, life to give to your country's lecture platform, and the introducer is taking it and someone else's in vain? Or should you play dead, exhibiting no more interest in the proceedings than a corpse does in the funeral oration he has provoked. When you are paid a compliment, every word of which drips with jasmine, honeysuckle, and unearned increment, and you feel diabetes sugaring your blood stream, should you show you have not forgotten *Veritas* was printed on your college shield by shouting, "No! No!"? Or should you meet kindness with kindness by crying, "A Daniel come to judgment! Yea, a Daniel!"?

Ought your eyes to be fixed on the footlights, the ceiling, the balcony, your wristwatch, or the introducer? And if upon the introducer, where? If he has struck a forensic attitude, should your eyes trace the outlines of his invisible toga? Or if she has struck a posture suggestive of Venus de Medici, should your face express gratitude that she is better dressed than the original?

If a giggling friend is winking at you in the fifth row, should you wink back? Or should you try to achieve that faraway look at which certain lecturers excel in their moments of being introduced, when they make it clear that their minds are in the clouds, that they are first cousins to yogis, that the affairs of this world do not interest them, and that—intellectually, at least—they have not as yet made their entrances.

No matter how much being introduced may embarrass you, you miss the introducer at those organizations where he does not appear. He may, by the very nature of his job and yours, develop in you a new sympathy for the criminal who must face the judge while his sentence is being read. Even during the Reign of Terror the people who faced the guillotine did not have to operate it. Confessors were near to hold their hands, and executioners to bow their heads. However awful their deaths may have been, they were not suicides.

It is when you are placed in solitary, and are waiting for the signal to be given, that you become the victim of worse fears than have ever paralyzed a chairman. It is after an experience of this sort that you are most apt to kneel down by your trundle at the hotel in the dark hours of night and thank God you are the kind of speaker who needs an introduction.

[30] From *Accustomed As I Am,* by John Mason Brown, pp. 35–40. Published by W. W. Norton & Co., Inc., 1942.

❖❱❱❱❖ ❖❰❖❰❖

31 · North Wind and Star Boy

In the very old day at the beginning of things, Star Boy went about in the world as a champion, defending all feeble folk against the attacks of their enemies.

The champion was so strong that he could not bend his bow of wood without breaking it; therefore he armed himself with a bone bow, a bone knife, and a stone war club.

One day, he came to the village of the Frogs, who poured out of their lodges to meet him and set before him food, but no water. "He who goes to the water," said they, "never returns. A great warrior lies there who has swallowed many of us alive, and now we are perishing of thirst!"

Star Boy himself was so thirsty that after he had eaten, he went down to the water, and was instantly swallowed by Tamahay, the Pickerel. But with his bone knife he slashed the Pickerel in the gills and escaped; after which he warned the big fish saying:

"Be careful how you wantonly destroy this people, for some day they will be used to destroy you!"

He then went on his way, as far as another village of Little People, who complained that they had no firewood.

"We dare not go to the wood any more," they said, "for there a fierce warrior lives who swoops down from above and devours us!"

Star Boy at once went to the wood, where he was attacked by Hinhan, the Owl. Him he easily conquered with his stone war club. "Because of your cruelty," he said to the Owl, "the sun shall blind you hereafter, so that you can hunt only in the dark, when the Mouse people are advised to take to their holes and hiding places."

Now Star Boy traveled northward, until he had reached the very northern-most country, and in that far land he found a people in great distress. This was because they feared Wazeya, the North Wind, who drove away the buffalo herds so that they had no meat. "And when he points his finger at one of us," said they, "that man dies!"

"Come let us hunt the buffalo!" said Star Boy to them; and although they were starving, they were afraid and unwilling to go. However, he made some of the men go out with him, and upon the open plain they met up with North Wind, who at once challenged the champion to do battle. The two rushed upon one another with great fury, and in the first onset Star Boy broke the bow of North Wind; but in the second, Star Boy was over-thrown and lay as one dead.

However, after a time he got up again, and they met for the third bout, when lo! neither could prevail against the other, so that in the midst of the fight they were obliged to sit upon a snowbank to rest. Star Boy sat upon his calf-skin and fanned himself with an eagle-wing, and immediately the snow began to melt, and the North Wind was forced to retreat. Before he went away, he made a treaty of peace with Star Boy, promising to come to earth for half the year only, and to give timely warning of his approach, so that the people might prepare for his coming and lay up food against the day of scarcity. By this means the winter and summer were established among us.

[31] *Wigwam Evenings,* pp. 213–217. Copyright, 1909, Little, Brown and Co. Copyright, 1937, Charles A. Eastman and Elaine Goodale Eastman.

❖❖❖❖ ❖❖❖❖

32 · The Accounting Department

I know that we seem to have more forms and reports than we have producing oil wells. But there is a reason for all this report work and I hope to give you a clearer understanding of the necessity for "paper work" in my remarks tonight.

Each one of us does some sort of personal "paper work" in the management of our own affairs. It may be paper work as simple as having a row of cans, each marked with a cost item, into which we divide our earnings each month; a can for rent into which we put so many dollars; a can for food; a can for clothing. Or our paper work may be our check-book-stub-report of expenses; it may be a family budget book. But, however we do it, all of us keep some sort of record of what we make and what we spend. That is really all there is to an accounting department—a place where a company keeps records of what it makes and what it spends. Of course, as the company grows larger, and its types of earning and spending grow more complicated the amounts of paper work grow.

For example, ———— here keeps the check book in his family. He knows where every cent is spent. But, let's say he opens a charge account and Mrs. ———— buys something and doesn't tell him about it. He no longer has a record of where every cent is spent. As soon as more than one person is authorized to make purchases the problem of keeping track of money becomes complicated. Right—? Imagine how complicated it could become if every person in Stanolind could go to the store and charge purchases to Stanolind. We would never know how much money we had. It's just because of the possibilities of complication that we have had to devise a system of purchase orders, invoices and accounting. It's just because of the possibility of complication you and I have to do "paper work."

If each of us carefully does the paper work connected with our job, the Stanolind Oil and Gas Company can operate efficiently and effectively for the betterment of us all. Your furnishing accurate and sufficient information on the reports you send to us will help us all to do our jobs in the efficient way necessary for continued growth.

Each of us here is a vital part of an aggressive and growing organization. As a company our growth in the future will be in direct proportion to the understanding, ability, efficiency and determination of us, the workers. We can achieve the "security" we all want by working "smarter" at our jobs.

Now that you see there is some sense to "paper work," let me explain my job and the function of your accounting department.

At the time a corporation such as Stanolind comes into being, the rules and regulations under which it is organized are carefully set out and written into its by-laws. These by-laws are not very interesting reading to anyone except lawyers, but somewhere in them it usually provides that the Comptroller will maintain accurate and complete records of all business transactions. The by-laws charge him to keep his records in such condition that at any time he can furnish the president and board of directors with evidence that the assets of the company are being safeguarded.

That's easy to say, but keeping all the necessary records turns into a tremendous job. Consider for a moment why record keeping of any kind is necessary. Most of our knowledge about business today—about science, about international relations, about so many things—is based upon our study of the written records left by the people who handled these things before our time. The history of any activity provides a guide for its proper management in the future.

Accounting is primarily the recording of the business history of a concern. As I have said, its main purpose is to collect and record the financial transactions of a business. And just as in any other history, the reason for it is to provide a guide for future activity—in this case, business activity.

The officers of a corporation have to consider many requirements in their day-to-day managing of the business. There are requirements of numerous laws, requirements made in contracts with other persons, and requirements of the stockholders which they must consider.

The many thousands of stockholders—the owners of the business—demand that the business be operated efficiently. To meet these requirements, company executives must be constantly advised of the condition of the business to control present operation and plan for the future—and it is here that the job of the accounting department begins.

The accountants summarize all the buying, selling and trading into an easily readable form. Only after they do this can the whole picture of a business be interpreted—interpreted by the company officers, stockholders, governmental agencies and the public.

[32] Excerpt from a speech by J. B. Galbraith. Reprinted by permission of the author.

❖⟩❖⟩❖◀⟨❖⟨❖

33 · Third Inaugural Address

On each national day of Inauguration since 1789, the people have renewed their sense of dedication to the United States.

In Washington's day the task of the people was to create and weld together a nation.

In Lincoln's day the task of the people was to preserve that nation from disruption from within.

In this day the task of the people is to save that nation and its institutions from disruption from without.

To us there has come a time, in the midst of swift happenings, to pause for a moment and take stock—to recall what our place in history has been, and to rediscover what we are and what we may be. If we do not, we risk the real peril of inaction.

Lives of nations are determined not by the count of years, but by the lifetime of the human spirit. The life of a man is three-score years and ten; a little more, a little less. The life of a nation is the fullness of the measure of its will to live.

There are men who doubt this. There are men who believe that democracy, as a form of government and a frame of life, is limited or measured by a kind of mystical and artificial fate—that, for some unexplained reason, tyranny and slavery have become the surging wave of the future—and that freedom is an ebbing tide.

But we Americans know that this is not true.

Eight years ago, when the life of this Republic seemed frozen by a fatalistic terror, we proved that this is not true. We were in the midst of shock—but we acted. We acted quickly, boldly, decisively.

These later years have been living years—fruitful years for the people of this democracy. For they have brought to us greater security and, I hope, a better understanding that life's ideals are to be measured in other than material things.

Most vital to our present and our future is this experience of a democracy which successfully survived crisis at home; put away many evil things; built new structures on enduring lines; and, through it all, maintained the fact of its democracy.

For action has been taken within the three-way framework of the Constitution of the United States. The coordinate branches of the government continue freely to function. The Bill of Rights remains inviolate. The freedom of elections is wholly maintained. Prophets of the downfall of American democracy have seen their dire predictions come to naught.

Democracy is not dying.

We know it because we have seen it revive—and grow.

We know it cannot die—because it is built on the unhampered initiative of individual men and women joined together in a common enterprise—an enterprise undertaken and carried through by the free expression of a free majority.

We know it because democracy alone, of all forms of government, enlists the full force of men's enlightened will.

We know it because democracy alone has constructed an unlimited civilization capable of infinite progress in the improvement of human life.

We know it because, if we look below the surface, we sense it still spreading on every continent—for it is the most humane, the most advanced, and in the end the most unconquerable of all forms of human society.

A nation, like a person, has a body—a body that must be fed and clothed and housed, invigorated and rested, in a manner that measures up to the objectives of our time.

A nation, like a person, has a mind—a mind that must be kept informed and alert, that must know itself, that understands the hopes and the needs of its neighbors—all the other nations that live within the narrowing circle of the world.

And a nation, like a person, has something deeper, something more permanent, something larger than the sum of all its parts. It is that something which matters most to its future—which calls forth the most sacred guarding of its present.

It is a thing for which we find it difficult—even impossible—to hit upon a single, simple word.

And yet we all understand what it is—the spirit—the faith of America. It is the product of centuries. It was born in the multitudes of those who came from many lands—some of high degree, but mostly plain people—who sought here, early and late, to find freedom more freely.

The democratic aspiration is no mere recent phase in human history. It *is* human history. It permeated the ancient life of early peoples. It blazed anew in the Middle Ages. It was written in Magna Carta.

In the Americas its impact has been irresistible. America has been the New World in all tongues, to all peoples, not because this continent was a new-found land, but because all those who came here believed they could create upon this new continent a new life—a life that should be new in freedom.

Its vitality was written into our own Mayflower Compact, into the Declaration of Independence, into the Constitution of the United States, into the Gettysburg Address.

Those who first came here to carry out the longings of their spirit, and the millions who followed, and the stock that sprang from them—all have moved forward constantly and consistently toward an ideal which in itself has gained stature and clarity with each generation.

The hopes of the Republic cannot forever tolerate either undeserved poverty or self-serving wealth.

We know that we still have far to go; that we must more greatly build the security and the opportunity and the knowledge of every citizen, in the measure justified by the resources and the capacity of the land.

But it is not enough to achieve these purposes alone. It is not enough to clothe and feed the body of this nation, and instruct and inform its mind. For there is also the spirit. And of the three, the greatest is the spirit.

Without the body and the mind, as all men know, the nation could not live.

But if the spirit of America were killed, even though the nation's body and mind, constricted in an alien world, lived on, the America we know would have perished.

That spirit—that faith—speaks to us in our daily lives in ways often unnoticed, because they seem so obvious. It speaks to us through the processes of governing in the sovereignties of forty-eight states. It speaks to us in our counties, in our cities, in our towns, and in our villages. It speaks to us from the other nations of the Hemisphere, and from those across the seas—the enslaved, as well as the free. Sometimes we fail to hear or heed these voices of freedom because to us the privilege of our freedom is such an old, old story.

The destiny of America was proclaimed in words of prophecy spoken by our first President in his first Inaugural in 1789—words almost directed, it would seem, to this year of 1941: "The preservation of the sacred fire of liberty and the destiny of the republican model of government are justly considered—deeply,—finally, staked on the experiment intrusted to the hands of the American people."

If we lose that sacred fire—if we let it be smothered with doubt and fear—then we shall reject the destiny which Washington strove so valiantly and so triumphantly to establish. The preservation of the spirit and faith of the nation does, and will, furnish the highest justification for every sacrifice that we may make in the cause of national defense.

In the face of great perils never before encountered, our strong purpose is to protect and to perpetuate the integrity of democracy.

For this we muster the spirit of America, and the faith of America.

We do not retreat. We are not content to stand still. As Americans, we go forward, in the service of our country, by the will of God.

[33] Third Inaugural Address, delivered by F. D. Roosevelt, January 20, 1941. *Vital Speeches of the Day*, VII, No. 8 (February 1, 1941), 226–227.

❖❂❖❂❖❖❂❂❖

34 · America

America, gentlemen say, is a noble object. It is an object well worth fighting for. Certainly it is, if fighting a people be the best way of gaining them. Gentlemen in this respect will be led to their choice of means by their complexions and their habits. Those who understand the military art will of course have some predilection for it. Those who wield the thunder of the state may have more confidence in the efficacy of arms. But I confess, possibly for want of this knowledge, my opinion is much more in favor of prudent management than of force; considering force not as an odious, but a feeble instrument for preserving a people so numerous, so active, so growing, so spirited as this, in a profitable and subordinate connection with us.

First, Sir, permit me to observe that the use of force alone is but temporary. It may subdue for a moment, but it does not remove the necessity of subduing again; and a nation is not governed which is perpetually to be conquered.

My next objection is its uncertainty. Terror is not always the effect of force, and an armament is not a victory. If you do not succeed, you are without resource; for, conciliation failing, force remains; but force failing, no further hope of reconciliation is left. Power and authority are sometimes bought by kindness; but they can never be begged as alms by an impoverished and defeated violence.

A further objection to force is, that you impair the object by your very endeavors to preserve it. The thing you fought for is not the thing which you recover; but depreciated, sunk, wasted, and consumed in the contest.

[34] Edmund Burke, *Conciliation with America* (1775).

❖⊃❖⊃❖ ❖⊂❖⊂❖

35 · Roots

Think of the delicate root of a young plant as it first begins to burrow into the soil. Pull it up gently, brush off the soil grains carefully, and you will find a tip as soft and tender as a baby's finger. Little here that suggests great power to dig! The smooth surface is broken only by a delicate fuzz of fine hairs. They are just behind the tip. Unless you have been very careful, these root-hairs have been broken off. This delicate root tip has a remarkable power. It has the power to penetrate stiff soil, to burrow deep below the surface. Sometimes even hard rocks are found broken by the gradual work of roots.

The structure and the position of roots suggest to us the things which they do. These principal functions of roots are to get from the soil those things necessary to the life of the plant which are found in the soil, and to hold the plant firm. The entire root system holds the plant firm, but only the young and tender parts do the work of absorption. By means of all its roots the plant is anchored so that its above-ground parts can grow up into the sunlight, and not be upset by the first breeze that comes along. By means of the tender tips of the roots and the hairs which they bear the plant absorbs materials which are to be used up there in the sunlight in the making of food. The older and tougher parts of the roots cannot do this work for the reason that, as they grow older, their surface became changed in such a way that it no longer admits water.

The amount of water which enters the roots of a plant is surprising. On a warm dry day more than a quart enters the roots of a sunflower of medium size. Think, then, of the thousand of gallons which enters the roots of a forest. All this water moves through the roots to the upper parts of the plant; the roots are the paths to the stem. So, to anchor the plant, to take in water, and to furnish the path to the stem are three functions of roots. Another comes to mind when we think of all the edible roots which find their way to our table. Of what advantage is a fleshy root to a radish? The advantage to us is plain enough, but what is the advantage to the radish? If left to itself the radish will use the food stored in its fleshy root to erect a stalk which will bear flowers and fruit. Similarly many other kinds of roots are used for the storage of food for later use. Thus a fourth function of roots is storage.

[35] John G. Coulter, *Plant Life and Plant Uses* (New York: American Book Company, 1913), pp. 46–47.

❖〉❖〉❖ ❖〈❖〈❖

36 · Roots Go Down

Roots go down
not as it is to drown—
falling through green fields of light farther and farther,
the green gone blue, gone purple and then black,
the black touchless plunging—
but at once under,
at once head-all-shovel lunging against the ground.

Neither is there any sound nor smell there. Or what is it
leads the roots onward through mazes of tryings and twistings?
Touch only? Is it all fingers
come alive in the live dark to be ears, eyes, nose and the
 taste and the crying?

As if the hand should open into the night,
flowering upon the darkness all around,
putting its fingers forth to feel out sight
to feel out sound;
to be all tongues for touching and tasting,
knuckle-sinuous and nailsharp against the dark;
to smell out ways;
to hark like hazel
the distant dripping of water wasting through clay.

[36] Lloyd Frankenberg, "Roots Go Down," *The Red Kite* (New York: Rinehart & Company, Inc., 1939).

❖〉❖〉❖ ❖〈❖〈❖

37 · The Crime of Conspiracy

Ladies and gentlemen of the jury you now approach the performance of one of the most sacred duties of citizenship, the meting out of justice. Just after you were sworn in as jurors I took occasion to make a few remarks which I shall now repeat in somewhat different form, as the thoughts I then expressed are peculiarly applicable to the period of your deliberations in order to reach a just and true verdict. I then told you to be patient and said that there are few qualities in life so important. I said that if you once get yourself in the frame of mind where you know that you have a task ahead and it has to be done carefully and it has to be done just right and you know that it will be wrong to let little things disturb you, then there comes a certain calm and peace of mind which are of the essence in the administration of justice. When you get yourself in that frame of mind you find not only that the task ahead becomes much easier, but in addition that the quality of your work in the administration of justice is of the quality that it should be. Justice does not flourish amidst emotional excitement and stress.

The rich and the poor, and persons of every race, creed, and condition stand alike before the bar of justice; and you must consider and weigh the evidence carefully, calmly and dispassionately, without the slightest trace of sympathy or prejudice for or against any party to the proceeding. The very importance of the case makes it all the more urgent that you heed these words of caution. In this connection you will bear in mind at all times that these 11 men are charged here as 11 individuals, the guilt or innocence of each of whom must be passed on by you separately, pursuant to and in accordance with the instructions which I am about to give you.

Never in all my long experience as a lawyer and in my brief experience as a judge have I seen a jury exhibit so much patience and pay such careful attention at all times to the testimony of the witnesses and the reading of exhibits, despite the prolonged duration of this trial. Let me express my sincere appreciation of the way in which you have performed your functions. You deserve special commendation and you are entitled to the gratitude of all citizens of the community for the sacrifice you have made and for the services you are rendering in the faithful performance of a public duty. And so I beg of you to continue on in the same spirit until the end.

The jury is composed of 12 men and women. While undoubtedly their verdict should represent the opinion of each individual juror, it by no means follows that opinions may not be changed by conference in the jury room. The very object of the jury system is to secure unanimity by a comparison of views and by arguments among the jurors themselves, provided this can be done reasonably and consistently with the conscientious convictions of the several jurors. Each juror should listen, with a disposition to be convinced, to the opinions and arguments of the others. It is not intended that a juror should go to the jury room with a fixed determination that the verdict shall represent his opinion of the case at that moment. Nor is it intended that he should close his ear to the arguments of other jurors who are equally honest and intelligent with himself.

The first thing I wish to make plain to you is the way in which our American system of jurisprudence defines the duties of the judge on the one hand and those of the jury on the other. It is exclusively my function clearly to set forth the rules of law which govern the case, with instructions as to their application. On these legal matters you must take the law as I give it to you; you are not at liberty to do otherwise. Thus I shall read the indictment and the statute applicable to the case and I shall construe the statute in those respects in which I think it requires construction and interpretation. I shall explain the function of the indictment, the presumption of innocence, the burden, resting upon the Government of proving its case to your satisfaction beyond a reasonable doubt and I shall give you the rules governing the trial of conspiracy cases, the rules to guide you in determining the credibility of witnesses and so on. My function is exclusively to instruct you on the law; and you must not permit any notions of your own or any matters referred to by counsel to obscure the fact that you must apply the law as I give it to you.

On the other hand, you are the sole judges of the facts and I shall refer to this circumstance again to impress it upon you. Just as you are not permitted to encroach upon my function in giving instructions on the law, so must I be careful not to encroach upon your function as the sole judges of the facts.

The relevant parts of the statute under the terms of which the indictment was drawn are as follows:

Sec. 2. (a) It shall be unlawful for (1) any person—to knowingly or wilfully advocate, * * * or * * * teach the duty, (or) necessity, * * * of overthrowing or destroying any government in the United States by force or violence, * * * ;

(3) to organize * * * any society, group, or assembly of persons who teach, (or) advocate, * * * the overthrow or destruction of any government in the United States by force or violence; * * * .

Sec. 2. (b) For the purpose of this section, the term 'government in the United States' means the Government of the United States, the government of any State, Territory, or possession of the United States, the government of the District of Columbia, or the government of any political subdivision of any of them.

Sec. 3. It shall be unlawful for any person * * * to conspire to commit, any of the acts prohibited by the provisions of this title.

[37] Excerpt from a speech by Harold R. Medina, delivered at the trial of the Communist leaders, New York, New York, October 13, 1949. *Vital Speeches of the Day,* XVI, No. 2 (November 1, 1949), 34–35.

38 · My Sort of God

I wish I could write it down. Of course, I can't. To define God is to limit him. Still it seems inevitable that man should do that in order to get some edge to which his mind may cling. All religion is concerned with this process of scaling down God into the realm of finite comprehension.

And so, although the various churches insist that the God confined in their own particular dogma is a Deity of absolute perfection, it seems to me that in every case there has been a minification. Perfection itself is a conception quite a bit beyond the range of mortal mind.

Orthodoxy has burdened Jehovah with human attributes. Anger and vengeance are attributed to Him because these are failings which we ourselves experience and can therefore understand.

And in the churches they also talk of God as all-powerful, but it does not seem to me that they quite mean that either. The conception of an all-powerful Deity has been decidedly qualified by the belief that His creature man got out of hand and could be saved from perdition only by the sacrifice of Christ, the son of God. An all-powerful God could have created Adam and Eve without sin and without the desire of sin. The existence of such a place as hell would be an indication of the fallibility of God. If souls were really lost it would be hard to acquit God of mislaying them.

But most of all I quarrel with the fundamentalist who insists that he "loves God." I don't believe him for a minute. Into love there must enter some slight solace of equality. Adoration and love I hold to be imperfect synonyms. No human being could possibly be at ease with the God of the dogmas. He could pray to such a God, but he could not explain, or argue, or have a joke. Fear tarnishes love. I could not love a God who held one hand behind His back and in that hand had hell. But, naturally, if I believed in such a God I would try very hard to feign love.

No, I do not think that man may ever expect to know God and to define Him. But there is an extraordinary something which happens now and again in the human spirit. There comes to the soul a second wind. A man gets the chance to say to himself, and to say truthfully, "This thing I have done is magnificent. I didn't know I had it in me."

The achievement need not be anything so tangible as the creation of music or poetry. It might be something which made people laugh. It could be a tingle, a taste, a hope, the sight of leaves in a wind, a caress. But in this moment there would be gusto. And the man upon whom the spell came would be for his little time valuable and important.

Something marching catches him up. Ahead are the banners and the bugles and we are all marching, marching away. Away—that's enough for anyone who feels the swing of it.

Oh, I can't define God, but I'm not an atheist.

Somebody may come along and say, "But you're not talking about God at all. You're talking about the will to live, or a good dinner, or a sunny day, or the subconscious."

I don't care what name is used because it really is God.

❖❖❖❖❖❖❖

39 · The Doc Quigg Story

Announcer: Station (---) presents ... "The Doc Quigg Story!" The diary of a distinguished United Press war correspondent. In today's episode, Reporter Quigg tells about the trials and tribulations he experienced in getting himself to the front to get shot at. Here's what happened:

Narrator: At 2 a.m. you get in a taxi in Tokyo and tell the driver Haneda Airport and hurry. "I'm in a hurry, mister," he replied, and tears off at a neat 20 miles an hour.

You drive through peaceful streets, honking night-going Japanese out of the way.

4:30 a.m. --- You weigh in your duffle bag and typewriter at the airport operations office. Only 58 pounds. The maximum allowed is 65. Other passengers for the trip to Korea arrive and you hear one G-I veteran of the fighting tell another: "Them South Koreans over there ain't got no guns. They use spears or anything to fight with."

5:30 a.m. --- The plane crew gives us yellow Mae West life preservers to put on. They help us strap parachutes on over the Mae Wests. Quite a warm ensemble in this hot climate.

"If we have to jump," the pilot says, "the crew chief will open the back door. Be sure to get out that door fast, because we'll be right behind you. And remember, don't pull the strings to inflate your Mae Wests until you're in the water. Otherwise, when you hit, it will fly up and knock you out."

6:30 a.m. --- We take off in a C-47 transport plane, the workhorse of the army in the last war. Mount Fuji's big volcanic cone looms off to the right, black and bare of snow in this summer season. The rough terrain of Japan slips by below, green rice paddies and terraced slopes between a mountain ridgework.

The rattle of the bare-walled army transport makes conversation difficult even with the man at your elbow. The strait-jacket effect of the Mae West-parachute combination makes it hard to twist around and look out the little windows.

We sit on long canvas benches slung along the sides of the plane's cabin, two rows of men facing each other, each man deep in thought.

Noon --- we stretch out on a concrete taxiway in the shade of our plane's wings and wait for it to be re-fueled.

At this airbase somewhere in Japan, the war comes at you at 600 miles an hour. Four silver F-80 jet fighters zip over the field in formation, peel off sharply one by one, land easily and then taxi back by us.

When they taxi, their jet engines squeal like tied-down fire sirens and heat waves billow from their blast-furnace tails.

There had been 11 big, red-topped refrigerator tanks of whole blood in our plane, lashed in the aisle with rope. Each can holds nine pints of blood. Now they are taken off and trucked to an evacuation hospital.

Just before we leave, a big hospital plane from Korea taxis up. The wounded, covered with blankets, are shoved on litters into ambulances.

2 p.m. --- We bounce onto an airstrip in Korea. Sweating soldiers carrying rifles pile aboard, and we're off again, rocking and bumping through the shaky air over the rugged Korean countryside.

Below are mountains with bare rock sides and now and then patches of green fuzz. Somehow, they look diseased. Now and then a shallow river winds between the mountains. We land at another strip, crowded with warplanes.

Twilight nears, and locusts buzz busily in the trees. A Korean woman next door bawls out her daughter with wild, hysterical shouts. The daughter had violated a taboo by taking a bath in the same room in which the family was eating dinner.

Another family digs a hole and buries its few pitiful possessions --- some wisps of cloth and pottery. To the west, artillery winks brightly among the darkening hills.

[39] FK217A9/1, United Press Radio, September 1, 1950.

❖⫸❖⫸❖⊰⫷⊰⫷⊰

40 · The Hunter and His Wife

Once upon a time there was a hunter who went every day into the forest to shoot game. He had a wife and two dogs. His wife was for ever scolding him, so that he was glad to get away from her into the forest. And she did not like dogs, and said they were always bringing dirt into the house with their muddy paws. So the dogs were glad to get away into the forest with the hunter.

One day the hunter and the two dogs wandered together through the deep woods, and never got a sight of a bird; no, they never even saw a hare. All day long they wandered on and saw nothing. The hunter had not fired a cartridge. He did not want to go home and have to answer all his wife's questions about why he had an empty bag, so he went deeper and deeper into the thick forest. And suddenly, as it grew towards evening, the sharp smell of burning wood floated through the trees, and the hunter, looking about him, saw the flickering of a fire. He made his way towards it, and found a clearing in the forest, and a wood pile in the middle of it, and it was burning so fiercely that he could scarcely come near it.

And this was the marvel, that in the middle of the blazing timbers was sitting a great snake, curled round and round upon itself and waving its head above the flames.

As soon as it saw the hunter it called out, in a loud hissing voice, to come near. The hunter went as near as he could, shading his face from the heat.

"My good man," says the snake, "pull me out of the fire, and you shall understand the talk of the beasts and the songs of the birds."

"I'll be happy to help you," says the hunter, "but how? for the flames are so hot that I cannot reach you."

"Put the barrel of your gun into the fire, and I'll crawl out along it."

The hunter put the barrel of his long gun into the flames, and instantly the snake wound itself about it, and so escaped out of the fire.

"Thank you, my good man," says the snake; "you shall know henceforward the language of all living things. But one thing you must remember. You must not tell any one of this, for if you tell you will die the death; and man only dies once, and that will be an end of your life and your knowledge."

Then the snake slipped off along the ground, and almost before the hunter knew it was going, it was gone.

Well, he went on with the two dogs, looking for something to shoot at; and when the dark night fell he was still far from home, away in the deep forest.

"I am tired," he thought, "and perhaps there will be birds stirring in the early morning. I will sleep the night here and try my luck at sunrise."

He made a fire of twigs and broken branches, and lay down beside it, together with his dogs. He had scarcely lain down to sleep when he heard the dogs talking together. He understood every word they said.

"Well, brother," says the first, "you sleep here and look after our master, while I run home to look after the house and yard. It will soon be one o'clock and when the master is away that is the time for thieves."

"Off with you, brother, and God be with you," says the second.

And the hunter heard the first dog go bounding away through the undergrowth, while the second lay still, with its head between its paws, watching its master and blinking at the fire.

Early in the morning the hunter was awakened by the noise of the dog pushing through the brushwood on its way back. He heard how the dogs greeted each other.

"Well, and how are you, brother?" says the first.

"Finely," says the second; "and how's yourself?"

"Finely too. Did the night pass well?"

"Well enough, thanks be to God. But with you, brother? How was it at home?"

"Oh, badly. I ran home, and the mistress, when she sees me, sings out, 'What the devil are you doing here without your master? Well, there's your supper'; and she threw me a crust of bread, burnt to a black cinder. I snuffed it and snuffed it, but as for eating it, it was burnt through. No dog alive could have made a meal of it. And with that she ups with a poker and beats me. Brother, she counted all my ribs and nearly broke each one of them. But at night, later on—just as I thought—thieves came into the yard, and were going to clear out the barn and the larder. But I let loose such a howl, and leapt upon them so vicious and angry, that they had little thought to spare for other people's goods, and had all they could do to get away whole themselves. And so I spent the night."

The hunter heard all that the dogs said, and kept it in mind. "Wait, a bit, my good woman," says he, "and see what I have to say to you when I get home."

That morning his luck was good, and he came home with a couple of hare and three or four woodcock.

"Good-day, mistress," says he to his wife, who was standing in the doorway.

"Good-day, master," says she.

"Last night one of the dogs came home," says he.

"It did," says she.

"And how did you feed it?" says he.

"Feed it, my love?" says she. "I gave it a whole basin of milk, and crumbled a loaf of bread for it."

"You lie, you old witch," says the hunter; "you gave it nothing but a burnt crust, and you beat it with the poker."

The old woman was so surprised that she let the truth out of her mouth before she knew. She says to her husband, "How on earth did you know all that?"

"I won't tell you," says the hunter.

"Tell me, tell me," begs the old woman, just like any woman when she wants to know too much.

"I can't tell you," says the hunter; "It's forbidden me to tell."

"Tell me, dear one," says she.

"Truly, I can't."

"Tell me, my little pigeon."

"If I tell you I shall die the death."

"Rubbish, my dearest, only tell me."

"But, I shall die."

"Just tell me that one little thing. You won't die for that."

And so, she bothered him and bothered him, until he thought, "There's nothing to be done if a woman sets her mind on a thing. I'd better die and get it over at once."

So he put on a clean white shirt, and lay down on the bench in the corner, under the sacred images, and made all ready for his death; and was just going to tell his wife the whole truth about the snake and the wood-pile, and how he knew the language of all living things. But just then there was a great clucking in the yard, and some of the hens ran into the cottage, and after them came the cock, pecking first one then another, and boasting,—

"That's the way to deal with you!"

So said the cock; and the hunter, lying there in his white shirt, ready to die, heard and understood every word.

"Yes," says the cock, as he drove the hens about the room, "you see I am not such a fool as our master here, who does not know how to keep a single wife in order. Why, I have thirty of you and more, and the whole lot of you hear from me sharp enough if you do not do as I say."

As soon as the hunter heard this he made up his mind to be a fool no longer. He jumped up from the bench, and took his whip and gave his wife such a beating that she never asked him another question to this day. And she has never yet learnt how it was that he knew what she did in the hut while he was away in the forest.

[40] Reprinted from *Russian Fairy Tales*, Peter Pauper Press, Mount Vernon, N. Y., with the permission of the publishers.

❖❖❖❖❖❖❖❖

41 · Promoters of General Prosperity

We have a great joy in receiving you here, representatives of the chambers of commerce from all over the world; you, who, in effect, represent the elite of the commercial world. We do not want to miss this occasion to tell you—in haste and in measure permitted by the extraordinary obligations of the Holy Year—a word of the Christian conception of your profession. Its role, its influence, its responsibilities are, in the present hour, of an importance and a gravity greater than ever. We believe it to be opportune that you crown your technical and juridical work by a serious moral consideration of its (commerce's) role and responsibilities.

It is not without impressive significance that mythology gave wings to Mercury (pagan god of commerce). Should we not see in that the symbol of the liberty that commerce needs to go and come across the borders of its own country? Certainly it is not a question—and none among you dreams of it—of claiming unlimited liberty, incompatible with the aims and needs of national economy, with the permanent care of material prosperity for all. But on the contrary, it is in view of this (national) prosperity that you aspire to a fuller liberty of commerce. And you have reason.

It is not enough, unfortunately, to have reason in the serene region of principles, as long as the most legitimate desires remain practically unrealizable because of purely political motives that continue to cramp the circulation and communication of persons and merchandise.

There are even countries where a system is erected, more or less absolute, that places all commerce in the hands of public authority. Let us affirm this clearly:

This is a tendency in opposition to the Christian conception of social economy. Commerce is fundamentally an activity of the individual and it is this private activity that gives him his first impulse and lights the flame of his enthusiasm.

Further, you will not obtain the goal you wish, which is the profit of general prosperity, without putting into its full light the personal exercise of commerce for the service of society's material well-being. The merchant, one will say, should be skilled without doubt; he must be a man of affairs, prudent more than sentimental, again, without doubt. But he must add to these strictly professional qualities a high concept of the ideal of his profession. As a businessman, he must also consider himself a servant of the community.

To have no other ambition but always to make more money and to enrich himself, he would betray his vocation, because one could well call by this name (vocation) the mission that God has assigned to him, above all in particularly difficult conditions as a merchant.

He would thus play the game of the malevolent, who strive to make of commerce a living vampire at the expense of all economic life. If, on the contrary, he aims and strives to circulate worldly goods, destined by God for the advantage of all, and takes them where they must serve and in a manner to make them serve well—then, indeed, the merchant is a good and true servant of society, a guarantee against misery, a promoter of general prosperity.

Nay, among other things, the concentration of commerce in the chambers of commerce and, perhaps one day, the constitution of these as representatives of all those linked with this profession, help maintain everywhere in its purity the ideals of the honest and, as is sometimes said, of the royally magnificent merchant.

But most important—because it is the solid basis of everything—is that this ideal bears the imprint of religion. Did not Our Lord Himself compare the Kingdom of Heaven to the precious gem that the wise merchant buys at the price of all his goods (Matthew 13, 45)? May this be the conviction of all of you; transmit it to your children, spread it among the young in your profession. Thus, you will bring upon yourselves, upon the good and healthy progress of your affairs and the whole world the most abundant divine favors, in pledge of which whole-heartedly We give you, your families, and those that you represent here Our Apostolic Benediction.

[41] Speech by Pope Pius XII, delivered to the representatives of the Chambers of Commerce, Vatican City, April 27, 1950. *Vital Speeches of the Day*, XVI, No. 16 (June 1, 1950), 483.

❖❖❖❖❖❖❖❖❖

42 · Declaration of Independence

When in the course of human events, it becomes necessary for one people to dissolve the political bands which have connected them with another, and to assume among the powers of the earth the separate and equal station to which the Laws of Nature and of Nature's God entitle them, a decent respect to the opinions of mankind requires that they should declare the causes which impel them to the separation.

We hold these truths to be self-evident, that all men are created equal, that they are endowed by their Creator with certain inalienable Rights, that among these are Life, Liberty and the pursuit of happiness. That to secure these rights, Governments are instituted among Men, deriving their just powers from the consent of the governed. That whenever any Form of Government becomes destructive of these ends, it is the Right of the People to alter or to abolish it, and to institute new Government, laying its foundation on such principles and organizing its powers in such form, as to them shall seem most likely to effect their Safety and Happiness. Prudence, indeed, will dictate that Governments long established should not be changed for light and transient causes; and accordingly all experience hath shown, that mankind are more disposed to suffer, while evils are sufferable, than to right themselves by abolishing the forms to which they are accustomed. But when a long train of abuses and usurpations, pursuing invariably the same Object, evinces a design to reduce them under absolute Despotism, it is their right, it is their duty, to throw off such Government, and to provide new Guards for their future security.

[42] Thomas Jefferson, *The Declaration of Independence.*

❖⟩❖⟩❖⟩❖⟨❖⟨❖⟨❖

43 · Peace

The proposition is peace. Not peace through the medium of war; not peace to be hunted through the labyrinth of intricate and endless negotiations; not peace to arise out of the universal discord fomented, from principle, in all parts of the Empire; not peace to depend on the juridical determination of perplexing questions, or the precise marking the shadowy boundaries of a complex government. It is simple peace; sought in its natural course, and in its ordinary haunts. It is peace sought in the spirit of peace, and laid in principles purely pacific. I propose, by removing the ground of the difference, and by restoring the former unsuspecting confidence of the Colonies in the Mother Country, to give permanent satisfaction to your people; and (far from a scheme of ruling by discord) to reconcile them to each other in the same act and by the bond of the very same interest which reconciles them to British government.

[43] Edmund Burke, *Conciliation with America* (1775).

❖⟩❖⟩❖ ❖⟨❖⟨❖

44 · Civilization

Mr. Laski is, or was convinced that the particular political and social changes which he desires to bring about, and which he believes to be advantageous for society, will, because they are so radical, result in a new civilization. That is quite conceivable: what we are not justified in concluding, with regard to his or any other changes in the social framework which anybody advocates, is that the "new civilization" is itself desirable. For one thing, we can have no notion of what the new civilization will be like: so many other causes operate than those we may have in mind, and the results of these and the others, operating together, are so incalculable, that we cannot imagine what it would *feel* like to live in that new civilization. For another thing, the people who live in that new civilization will, by the fact of belonging to it, be different from ourselves, and they will be just as different from Mr. Laski. Every change we make is tending to bring about a new civilization of the nature of which we are ignorant, and in which we should all of us be unhappy. A new civilization is, in fact, coming into being all the time: the civilization of the present day would seem very new indeed to any civilized man of the eighteenth century, and I cannot imagine the most ardent or radical reformer of that age taking much pleasure in the civilization that would meet his eye now. All that a concern for civilization can direct us to do, is to improve such civilization as we have, for we can imagine no other. On the other hand, there have always been people who have believed in particular changes as good in themselves, without worrying about the future of civilization, and without finding it necessary to recommend their innovations by the specious glitter of unmeaning promises.

[44] From *Notes toward the Definition of Culture,* p. 16. Copyright, 1949, by T. S. Eliot. Reprinted by permission of Harcourt, Brace and Company, Inc., and of Faber and Faber, Ltd.

❖⟩❖⟩❖◄(❖(◄❖

45 · Prayer for Purim

READER

Thou, O Lord, pleadest the cause of the just, and defeatest the devices of the cruel. The counsel of the heathen, Thou bringest to nought; the devices of the crafty, Thou makest of no effect.

We bless Thee, O Lord our God, that Thou hast sustained us in life and preserved the house of Israel unto this day. Thou didst work miracles for our fathers in the days of old, and hast enabled us to survive the enemies of Thy truth. When Haman rose up against us, Thou didst cause the devotion of Mordecai and the loving kindness of Esther to triumph over unjust wrath and hate. The righteous were delivered out of the hand of the wicked, and those who sought to destroy were themselves destroyed. Thou hast ever been Israel's salvation, our hope in every generation. None that trusts in Thee shall be put to shame.

We pray Thee, O Father, that in the presence of cruelty and wrong our hearts remain steadfast and true. When evil men plot against us and seek to uproot us, let not despair drain our strength nor fear chill our faith. Teach us to meet enmity with courage and hope, and to battle against adversity with resolute will and unyielding self-possession. Keep alive within us the vision of our higher purposes and nobler destiny, and renew our zeal for the divine tasks of life. Open our hearts to the cry of the persecuted and the despoiled. Hasten the day when hate and strife shall cease to divide the family of men, and justice and love reign supreme in the world.

SILENT PRAYER

Grant, O Heavenly Father, that we lie down to rest with a quiet mind, and rise again in health and strength, to take up the duties of the new day. Receive into Thy keeping our lives and the lives of our loved ones. May Thy protection be a shield around our homes during our sleeping hours. Preserve us from all evil, from the sword of the foe, from pestilence, famine and destruction. May we be freed from care and worry. May we readily forgive those who wrong us, and seek forgiveness of those whom we have wronged. So shall Thy blessing attend us, and Thy peace, O God, abide with us. Amen.

CHOIR

May the words of my mouth and the meditation of my heart be acceptable before Thee, O Lord, my Rock and my Redeemer.

[45] *The Union Prayerbook for Jewish Worship* (Cincinnati: The Central Conference of American Rabbis, 1940), p. 298.

❖❫❖❫❖❖❩❖❩❖❖

46 · Peace in the Atomic Era

I am grateful to you for the opportunity to express my conviction in this most important political question.

The idea of achieving security through national armament is, at the present state of military technique, a disastrous illusion. On the part of the United States this illusion has been particularly fostered by the fact that this country succeeded first in producing an atomic bomb. The belief seemed to prevail that in the end it were possible to achieve decisive military superiority.

In this way, any potential opponent would be intimidated, and security, so ardently desired by all of us, brought to us and all of humanity. The maxim which we have been following during these last five years has been, in short: security through superior military power, whatever the cost.

This mechanistic, technical-military psychological attitude had inevitable consequences. Every single act in foreign policy is governed exclusively by one viewpoint.

How do we have to act in order to achieve utmost superiority over the opponent in case of war? Establishing military bases at all possible strategically important points on the globe. Arming and economic strengthening of potential allies.

Within the country—concentration of tremendous financial power in the hands of the military, militarization of the youth, close supervision of the loyalty of the citizens, in particular, of the civil servants by a police force growing more conspicuous every day. Intimidation of people of independent political thinking. Indoctrination of the public by radio, press, school. Growing restriction of the range of public information under the pressure of military secrecy.

The armament race between the U.S.A. and the U.S.S.R., originally supposed to be a preventive measure, assumes hysterical character. On both sides, the means to mass destruction are perfected with feverish haste—behind the respective walls of secrecy. The H-bomb appears on the public horizon as a probably attainable goal. Its accelerated development has been solemnly proclaimed by the President.

If successful, radioactive poisoning of the atmosphere and hence annihilation of any life on earth has been brought within the range of technical possibilities. The ghostlike character of this development lies in its apparently compulsory trend. Every step appears as the unavoidable consequence of the preceding one. In the end, there beckons more and more clearly general annihilation.

Is there any way out of this impasse created by man himself? All of us, and particularly those who are responsible for the attitude of the U.S. and the U.S.R.R., should realize that we may have vanquished an external enemy, but have been incapable of getting rid of the mentality created by the war.

It is impossible to achieve peace as long as every single action is taken with a possible future conflict in view. The leading point of view of all political action should therefore be: What can we do to bring about a peaceful co-existence and even loyal cooperation of the nations?

The first problem is to do away with mutual fear and distrust. Solemn renunciation of violence (not only with respect to means of mass destruction) is undoubtedly necessary.

Such renunciation, however, can only be effective if at the same time a supra-national judicial and executive body is set up empowered to decide questions of immediate concern to the security of the nations. Even a declaration of the nations to collaborate loyally in the realization of such a "restricted world government" would considerably reduce the imminent danger of war.

In the last analysis, every kind of peaceful cooperation among men is primarily based on mutual trust and only secondly on institutions such as courts of justice and police. This holds for nations as well as for individuals. And the basis of trust is loyal give and take.

What about international control? Well, it may be of secondary use as a police measure. But it may be wise to overestimate its importance. The times of prohibition come to mind and give one pause.

[46] Speech by Dr. Albert Einstein, delivered at Princeton, N. J., for broadcast on a National Broadcasting Company television program, February 19, 1950. *Vital Speeches of the Day*, XVI, No. 10 (March 1, 1950), 302.

❖⟩❖⟩❖⟩❖⟨❖⟨❖⟨❖

47 · A Tale of Two Cities

It was the best of times, it was the worst of times, it was the age of wisdom, it was the age of foolishness, it was the epoch of belief, it was the epoch of incredulity, it was the season of Light, it was the season of Darkness, it was the spring of hope, it was the winter of despair, we had everything before us, we had nothing before us, we were all going direct to Heaven, we were all going direct the other way—in short, the period was so far like the present period, that some of its noisiest authorities insisted on its being received, for good or for evil, in the superlative degree of comparison only.

[47] Charles Dickens, *A Tale of Two Cities* (1859).

48 · Preparation of an Actor

. . . and, feeling a strong inclination to go on the stage, he took lessons in elocution and deportment from a professional actor, learnt a large number of parts, and spent hours before a mirror practising how to sit down on a chair, how to get up from it, how to enter and leave a room, how to bow and shake hands, how to express scorn, charm, love, hate, hope, despair, and all the other emotions.

[48] Hesketh Pearson, *Dickens: His Character, Comedy, and Career* (New York: Harper & Brothers, 1949), p. 15.

49 · The Commuter

The commuter is the queerest bird of all. The suburb he inhabits has no essential vitality of its own and is a mere roost where he comes at day's end to go to sleep. Except in rare cases, the man who lives in Mamaroneck or Little Neck or Teaneck, and works in New York, discovers nothing much about the city except the time of arrival and departure of trains and buses, and the path to a quick lunch. He is desk-bound, and has never, idly roaming in the gloaming, stumbled suddenly on Belvedere Tower in the Park, seen the ramparts rise sheer from the water of the pond, and the boys along the shore fishing for minnows, girls stretched out negligently on the shelves of the rocks; he has never come suddenly on anything at all in New York as a loiterer, because he has had no time between trains. He has fished in Manhattan's wallet and dug out coins. but has never listened to Manhattan's breathing, never awakened to its morning, never dropped off to sleep in its night. About 400,000 men and women come charging onto the Island each week-day morning, out of the mouths of tubes and tunnels. Not many among them have ever spent a drowsy afternoon in the great rustling oaken silence of the reading room of the Public Library, with the book elevator (like an old water wheel) spewing out books onto the trays. They tend their furnaces in Westchester and in Jersey, but have never seen the furnaces of the Bowery, the fires that burn in oil drums on zero winter nights. They may work in the financial district downtown and never see the extravagant plantings of Rockefeller Center—the daffodils and grape hyacinths, and birches and the flags trimmed to the wind on a fine morning in spring. Or they may work in a midtown office and may let a whole year swing round without sighting Governors Island from the sea wall. The commuter dies with tremendous mileage to his credit, but he is no rover. His entrances and exits are more devious than those in a prairie-dog village; and he calmly plays bridge while buried in the mud at the bottom of the East River. The Long Island Rail Road alone carried forty million commuters last year; but many of them were the same fellow retracing his steps.

❖⟩❖⟩❖◀⟨❖⟨❖

50 · On His Blindness

When I consider how my light is spent
    Ere half my days in this dark world and wide,
    And that one Talent which is death to hide
Lodged with me useless, though my soul more bent
To serve therewith my Maker, and present
    My true account, lest He returning chide,
    "Doth God exact day-labour, light denied?"
I fondly ask. But Patience, to prevent
That murmur, soon replies, "God doth not need
    Either man's work or his own gifts. Who best
        Bear His mild yoke, they serve Him best. His state
Is kingly: Thousands at his bidding speed,

And post o'er land and ocean without rest;
They also serve who only stand and wait."

[50] John Milton, "On His Blindness," *Milton's Complete Poetical Works,* ed. William Vaughn Moody (Cambridge: Houghton Mifflin Company, 1899), p. 77.

❧❧❧❧❧❧❧

51 · Rip Van Winkle

Whoever has made a voyage up the Hudson must remember the Kaatskill mountains. They are a dismembered branch of the great Appalachian family, and are seen away to the west of the river, swelling up to a noble height, and lording it over the surrounding country. Every change of season, every change of weather, indeed every hour of the day, produces some change in the magical hues and shapes of these mountains, and they are regarded by all the good wives, far and near, as perfect barometers. When the weather is fair and settled, they are clothed in blue and purple, and print their bold outlines on the clear evening sky; but sometimes when the rest of the landscape is cloudless, they will gather a hood of gray vapors about their summits, which, in the last rays of the setting sun, will glow and light up like a crown of glory.

At the foot of these fairy mountains, the voyager may have descried the light smoke curling up from a village, whose shingle-roofs gleam among the trees, just where the blue tints of the upland melt away into the fresh green of the nearer landscape. It is a little village, of great antiquity, having been founded by some of the Dutch colonists in the early times of the province, just about the beginning of the government of the good Peter Stuyvesant (may he rest in peace!), and there were some of the houses of the original settlers standing within a few years, built of small yellow bricks brought from Holland, having latticed windows and gable fronts, surmounted with weather-cocks.

In the same village, and in one of these very houses (which, to tell the precise truth, was sadly time-worn and weather-beaten), there lived, many years since, while the country was yet a province of Great Britain, a simple, good-natured fellow, of the name of Rip Van Winkle.

[51] Washington Irving, "Rip Van Winkle," *The Sketch Book* (1819).

❧❧❧❧❧❧❧

52 · School Supplies

I can remember the time (by pressing my temple very hard and holding my breath) when the opening of school meant simply buying a slate with a sponge tied to it and a box of colored crayons. No one, to my knowledge, ever used a slate and a sponge. They were simply a sentimental survival of an even earlier day which the man in the stationery store forced on children who were going to school. The colored crayons were, of course, for eating.

[52] Robert Benchley, *Chips off the Old Benchley* (New York: Harper & Brothers, 1949), p. 31.

❖⬗❖⬗❖⬗❖◀◆◀◆◀❖

53 · Great Art

. . . The greatest art has always been communal, the expression—in highly individualised ways, no doubt—of common aspirations and ideals.

[53] Roger Fry, *Vision and Design* (London: Chatto & Windus, 1929), p. 62. Reprinted with the permission of the author's executors and Chatto & Windus.

❖⬗❖⬗❖⬗ ◀◆◀◆◀❖

54 · Sonnet

Having this day my horse, my hand, my lance
Guided so well that I obtain'd the prize,
Both by the judgment of the English eyes
And of some sent from that sweet enemy France;
Horsemen my skill in horsemanship advance,
Town-folks my strength; a daintier judge applies
His praise to sleight which from good use doth rise;
Some lucky wits impute it but to chance;
Others, because of both sides I do take
My blood from them who did excel in this,
Think Nature me a man-at-arms did make.
How far they shot awry! the true cause is,
Stella look'd on, and from her heav'nly face
Sent forth the beams which made so fair my race.

[54] Sir Philip Sidney, *Astrophel and Stella* (1591).

❖⬗❖⬗❖⬗◀◆◀◆◀❖

55 · Doing My Share

My parents removed to Missouri in the early 'thirties; I do not remember just when, for I was not born then and cared nothing for such things. It was a long journey in those days, and must have been a rough and tiresome one. The home was made in the wee village of Florida, in Monroe County, and I was born there in 1835. The village contained a hundred people and I increased the population by 1 per cent. It is more than many of the best men in history could have done for a town. It may not be modest in me to refer to this, but it is true. There is no record of a person doing as much—not even Shakespeare. But I did it for Florida, and it shows that I could have done it for any place—even London, I suppose.

[55] Samuel L. Clemens, *Mark Twain's Autobiography* (New York: Harper & Brothers, 1924) I, 94. Copyright, 1924, by Clara Gabrilowitsch. Copyright, 1952, by Clara Clemens Samossoud.

❖⟩❖⟩❖❖❖❖❖

56 · Nativity

And it came to pass in those days, that there went out a decree from Caesar Augustus, that all the world should be taxed. (And this taxing was first made when Cyrenius was governor of Syria.) And all went to be taxed, every one into his own city. And Joseph also went up from Galilee, out of the city of Nazareth, into Judea, unto the city of David, which is called Bethlehem; (because he was of the house and lineage of David:) to be taxed with Mary his espoused wife, being great with child. And so it was, that, while they were there, the days were accomplished that she should be delivered. And she brought forth her first-born son, and wrapped him in swaddling clothes, and laid him in a manger; because there was no room for them in the inn. And there were in the same country shepherds abiding in the field, keeping watch over their flock by night. And, lo, the angel of the Lord came upon them, and the glory of the Lord shone round about them: and they were sore afraid. And the angel said unto them, Fear not: for, behold, I bring you good tidings of great joy, which shall be to all people. For unto you is born this day in the city of David a Saviour, which is Christ the Lord. And this shall be a sign unto you; Ye shall find the babe wrapped in swaddling clothes, lying in a manger. And suddenly there was with the angel a multitude of the heavenly host praising God, and saying, Glory to God in the highest, and on earth peace, good will toward men.

[56] *The Holy Bible,* Luke 2:1–14.

❖⟩❖⟩❖❖❖❖❖

57 · Channel Crossing

You could practically walk across the English
Channel this morning . . . if you didn't mind
stepping on a few heads.

The Channel hasn't been this crowded since the
evacuation of Dunquerque.

Nineteen — count 'em — 19 swimmers are in the
water, racing from Cap Gris Nez (kahp gree nay),
France, to Dover, England. And 70 — count them,
too — 70 boats are tagging along, loaded with
trainers, friends, newsmen, press-agents, cameras,
sponsors' products, and all the other paraphernalia
that goes with a dip in the big pond.

Twenty-four swimmers — 18 men and 6 women —
started the swim . . . dreamed up by the London Daily
Mail. The paper made it a race with the winner
getting 28-hundred dollars and his picture in the
paper. All those who finish get 700 dollars.

Five had to drop out. Four men and one woman.
One of the men was the only American contestant —
David Frank, a dress designer from New York City.

At the moment, an Egyptian who once was a body-
guard to the King of Egypt is in the lead. It's an
old hat to him —— since he's swum the channel in
both directions before this.

[57] S/RG507A8/22, United Press Radio, August 22, 1950.

❖)❖)❖❖((❖((❖

58 · Voices

Mingling with these inarticulate sounds in the low murmur of memory,
are the echoes of certain voices I have heard at rare intervals. I grieve to
say it, but our people, I think, have not generally agreeable voices. The
marrowy organisms, with skins that shed water like the backs of ducks,
with smooth surfaces neatly padded beneath, and velvet linings to their
singing-pipes, are not so common among us as that other pattern of
humanity with angular outlines and plane surfaces, arid integuments, hair
like the fibrous covering of a cocoa-nut in gloss and suppleness as well
as color, and voices at once thin and strenuous,—acidulous enough to
produce effervescence with alkalis, and stridulous enough to sing duets
with the katydids. I think our conversational soprano, as sometimes over-

heard in the cars, arising from a group of young persons, who may have taken the train at one of our great industrial centers, for instance,—young persons of the female sex, we will say, who have bustled in full-dress, engaged in loud strident speech, and who, after free discussion, have fixed on two or more double seats, which having secured, they proceed to eat apples and hand round daugerreotypes,—say, I think the conversational soprano, heard under these circumstances, would not be among the allurements the old Enemy would put in requisition, were he getting up a new temptation of St. Anthony.

[58] Oliver Wendell Holmes, *The Autocrat of the Breakfast Table* (1858).

❖❖❖❖❖ ❖❖❖❖❖

59 · My Life Work

The last thing that it would be proper for me to do would be to speak of the work of my life, or to say at the end of the day whether I think I have earned my wages or not. Men are said to be partial judges of themselves. Young men may be, I doubt if old men are. Life seems terribly foreshortened as they look back, and the mountain they set themselves to climb in youth turns out to be a mere spur of immeasurably higher ranges when, by failing breath, they reach the top. But if I may speak of the objects I have had more or less definitely in view since I began the ascent of my hillock, they are briefly these: To promote the increase of natural knowledge and to forward the application of scientific methods of investigation to all the problems of life to the best of my ability, in the conviction which has grown with my growth and strengthened with my strength, that there is no alleviation for the sufferings of mankind except veracity of thought and of action, and the resolute facing of the world as it is when the garment of make-believe by which pious hands have hidden its uglier features is stripped off.

It is with this intent that I have subordinated any reasonable, or unreasonable, ambition for scientific fame which I may have permitted myself to entertain to other ends; to the popularisation of science; to the development and organisation of scientific education; to the endless series of battles and skirmishes over evolution; and to untiring opposition to that ecclesiastical spirit, that clericalism, which in England, as everywhere else, and to whatever denomination it may belong, is the deadly enemy of science.

[59] Thomas Huxley, *Autobiography,* written in 1889.

❖❖❖❖❖ ❖❖❖❖❖

60 · Superstition

Nothing was more common, in those days, than to interpret all meteoric appearances, and other natural phenomena, that occurred with less regularity than the rise and set of sun and moon, as so many revelations from a supernatural source. Thus, a blazing spear, a sword of flame, a bow, or a sheath of arrows, seen in the midnight sky, prefigured Indian warfare. Pestilence was known to have been foreboded by a shower of crimson light. We doubt whether any marked event, for good or evil, ever befell New England, from its settlement down to Revolutionary times, of which the inhabitants had not been previously warned by some spectacle of this nature. Not seldom, it had been seen by multitudes. Oftener, however, its credibility rested on the faith of some lonely eye-witness, who beheld the wonder through the colored, magnifying, and distorting medium of his imagination, and shaped it more distinctly in his after-thought. It was, indeed, a majestic idea, that the destiny of nations should be revealed in these awful hieroglyphics, on the cope of heaven. A scroll so wide might not be deemed too expansive for Providence to write a people's doom upon. The belief was a favorite one with our forefathers, as betokening that their infant commonwealth was under a celestial guardianship of peculiar intimacy and strictness. But what shall we say, when an individual discovers a revelation, addressed to himself alone, on the same vast sheet of record! In such a case, it could only be the symptom of a highly disordered mental state, when a man, rendered morbidly self-contemplative by long, intense, and secret pain, had extended his egotism over the whole expanse of nature, until the firmament itself should appear no more than a fitting page for his soul's history and fate!

[60] Nathaniel Hawthorne, *The Scarlet Letter* (1850).

❖❩❧❩❖❖❧❪❖❪❖

61 · Illness

Considering how common illness is, how tremendous the spiritual change that it brings, how astonishing, when the lights of health go down, the undiscovered countries that are then disclosed, what wastes and deserts of the soul a slight attack of influenza brings to view, what precipices and lawns sprinkled with bright flowers a little rise of temperature reveals, what ancient and obdurate oaks are uprooted in us by the act of sickness, how we go down into the pit of death and feel the waters of annihilation close above our heads and wake thinking to find ourselves in the presence of the angels and the harpers when we have a tooth out and come to the surface in the dentist's armchair and confuse his "Rinse the mouth—rinse the mouth" with the greeting of the Deity stooping from the floor of Heaven to welcome us—when we think of this, as we are so frequently forced to think of it, it becomes strange indeed that illness has not taken its place with love and battle and jealousy among the prime themes of literature. Novels, one would have thought, would have been devoted to influenza; epic poems to typhoid; odes to pneumonia; lyrics to toothache. But no.

[61] From *The Moment and Other Essays,* by Virginia Woolf. Copyright, 1948, by Harcourt, Brace and Company, Inc.

❖❭❖❭❖❖❰❖❰❖

62 · Sleep

Do but consider what an excellent thing sleep is: it is so inestimable a jewel, that, if a tyrant would give his crown for an hour's slumber, it cannot be bought; of so beautiful a shape is it, that though a man lie with an Empress, her heart cannot beat quiet till he leaves her embracements to be at rest with the other; yea, so greatly indebted are we to this kinsman of death, that we owe the better tributary, half of our life to him; and there is good cause why we should do so; for sleep is that golden chain that ties health and our bodies together. Who complains of want? of wounds? of cares? of great men's oppressions? of captivity? whilst he sleepeth? Beggars in their beds take as much pleasure as kings; can we therefore surfeit on this delicate Ambrosia? Can we drink too much of that whereof to taste too little tumbles us into a churchyard, and to use it but indifferently throws us into Bedlam? No, No, look upon Endymion, the moon's minion, who slept three score and fifteen years, and was not a hair the worse for it.

[62] Thomas Dekker, *The Gull's Horn Book* (1609).

❖❭❖❭❖❖❰❖❰❖

63 · Voices II

Still, you hear noble voices among us,—I have known families famous for them,—but ask the first person you meet a question, and ten to one there is a hard, sharp, metallic, matter-of-business clink in the accents of the answer, that produces the effect of one of those bells which small tradespeople connect with their shop-doors, and which spring upon your ear with such vivacity, as you enter, that your first impulse is to retire at once from the precincts.

[63] Oliver Wendell Holmes, *The Autocrat of the Breakfast Table* (1858).

❖❖❖❖❖❖❖❖

64 · Communicating Emotions

He gives an example of what he means by calling art the means of communicating emotions. He says, let us suppose a boy to have been pursued in the forest by a bear. If he returns to the village and merely states that he was pursued by a bear and escaped, that is ordinary language, the means of communicating facts or ideas; but if he describes his state first of heedlessness, then of sudden alarm and terror as the bear appears, and finally of relief when he gets away, and describes this so that his hearers share his emotions, then his description is a work of art.

Now in so far as the boy does this in order to urge the villagers to go out and kill the bear, though he may be using artistic methods, his speech is not a pure work of art; but if of a winter evening the boy relates his experience for the sake of the enjoyment of his adventure in retrospect, or better still, if he makes up the whole story for the sake of the imagined emotions, then his speech becomes a pure work of art.

[64] Roger Fry, *Vision and Design* (London: Chatto & Windus, 1929), p. 28. Reprinted with the permission of the author's executors and Chatto & Windus.

❖❖❖❖❖❖❖❖

65 · Throw-away Lines

Closely related to subordinations are throw-away lines, lines that merely fill in, that serve as the mortar between one important thought and another. Noel Coward, in his biography, *Present Indicative,* wrote that the one important thing he learned from American acting was the art of throwing away a line—saying a line so that the audience could hear it and yet know that it was an unimportant one.

[65] Edwin Duerr, *Radio and Television Acting* (New York: Rinehart & Company, Inc., 1950), p. 144.

❖❖❖❖❖❖❖❖

66 · Teaching

The same reality pervades all teaching. The man may teach by doing, and not otherwise. If he can communicate himself he can teach, but not by words. He teaches who gives, and he learns who receives. There is no teaching until the pupil is brought into the same state or principle in which you are; a transfusion takes place; he is you and you are he; then is a teaching, and by no unfriendly chance or bad company can he ever quite lose the benefit. But your propositions run out of one ear as they ran in at the other. We see it advertised that Mr. Grand will deliver an oration on the Fourth of July, and Mr. Hand before the Mechanics' Association, and we do not go thither, because we know that these gentlemen will not communicate their own character and experience to the company. If we had reason to expect such a confidence we should go through all inconvenience and opposition. The sick would be carried in litters. But a public oration is an escapade, a noncommittal, an apology, a gag, and not a communication, not a speech, not a man.

A like Nemesis presides over all intellectual works. We have yet to learn that the thing uttered in words is not therefore affirmed. It must affirm itself, or no forms of logic or of oath can give it evidence. The sentence must also contain its own apology for being spoken.

[66] Ralph Waldo Emerson, "Spiritual Laws," *Essays,* 1841.

✦❭❭✦❭❭✦❬✦❬✦❬✦

67 · Constitutions

It is an obvious truth, that no constitution can defend itself. It must be defended by the wisdom and fortitude of men. These are what no constitution can give. They are the gifts of God; and he alone knows, whether we shall possess such gifts at the time we stand in need of them. Constitutions furnish the civil means of getting at the natural; it is all that in this case they can do.

[67] Edmund Burke, *Letters on a Regicide Peace* (1795–1797), Letter No. 4.

✦❭❭✦❭❭✦❬✦❬✦❬✦

68 · Roman Women

Rome was more concerned with the functions of motherhood than was Greece. She could not have endowed the world with her two great gifts, the sanctity of the family and the majesty of the law, she could not have given to it, as she did, a life morally worth the living, if she had not looked sharply after her women, emphasizing their duties rather than their privileges. But she was far from being a matriarchy like the United States. She was not a nation of husbands, but a nation of men. The foundation of the family was the father. He had undisputed authority, unshared responsibility, and often unlimited devotion.

[68] Agnes Repplier, *Eight Decades* (Boston: Houghton Mifflin Company, 1937), p. 54.

❖❖❖❖❖❖❖❖

69 · Laughter

. . . Well, I can't be savage with you for wanting to laugh, and I like to make you laugh, well enough, when I can. But then observe this: if the sense of the ridiculous is one side of an impressible nature, it is very well; but if that is all there is in a man, he had better have been an ape at once, and so have stood at the head of his profession. Laughter and tears are meant to turn the wheels of the same machinery of sensibility; one in wind-power, and the other water-power; that is all.

[69] Oliver Wendell Holmes, *The Autocrat of the Breakfast Table* (1858).

❖❖❖❖❖❖❖❖

70 · Upon Westminster Bridge

Earth has not anything to show more fair:
Dull would he be of soul who could pass by
A sight so touching in its majesty:
This City now doth like a garment wear

The beauty of the morning; silent, bare,
Ships, towers, domes, theatres, and temples lie
Open unto the fields, and to the sky;
All bright and glittering in the smokeless air.

Never did sun more beautifully steep
In his first splendour, valley, rock, or hill;
Ne'er saw I, never felt, a calm so deep!

The river glideth at his own sweet will:
Dear God! the very houses seem asleep;
And all that mighty heart is lying still!

[70] William Wordsworth, "Composed upon Westminster Bridge, September 3, 1802," *Poems in Two Volumes* (1807).

❖❖❖❖❖❖❖❖❖

71 · Job

Wherefore do the wicked live, become old, yea, are mighty in power?

Their seed is established in their sight with them, and their offspring before their eyes.

Their houses are safe from fear, neither is the rod of God upon them.

Their bull gendereth, and faileth not; their cow calveth, and casteth not her calf.

They send forth their little ones like a flock, and their children dance.

They take the timbrel and harp, and rejoice at the sound of the organ.

They spend their days in wealth, and in a moment go down to the grave.

Therefore they say unto God, Depart from us; for we desire not the knowledge of thy ways.

What is the Almighty, that we should serve him? and what profit should we have, if we pray unto him?

Lo, their good is not in their hand: the counsel of the wicked is far from me.

How oft is the candle of the wicked put out! and how oft cometh their destruction upon them! God distributeth sorrows in his anger.

They are as stubble before the wind, and as chaff that the storm carrieth away.

[71] *The Holy Bible,* Job 21:7–18.

❖❖❖❖❖❖❖❖❖

72 · Works

What doth it profit, my brethren, though a man say he hath faith, and have not works? can faith save him?

If a brother or sister be naked, and destitute of daily food,

And one of you say unto them, Depart in peace, be ye warmed and filled; notwithstanding ye give them not those things which are needful to the body; what doth it profit?

Even so faith, if it hath not works, is dead, being alone.

Yea, a man may say, Thou hast faith, and I have works; shew me thy faith without thy works, and I will shew thee my faith by my works.

Thou believest that there is one God; thou doest well: the devils also believe, and tremble.

But wilt thou know, O vain man, that faith without works is dead?

Was not Abraham our father justified by works, when he had offered Isaac his son upon the altar?

Seest thou how faith wrought with his works, and by works was faith made perfect?

And the scripture was fulfilled which saith, Abraham believed God, and it was imputed unto him for righteousness: and he was called the Friend of God.

Ye see then how that by works a man is justified, and not by faith only.

72 *The Holy Bible,* James 2:14–24.

❖❖❖❖❖ ❖❖❖❖❖

73 · Why So Pale and Wan?

Why so pale and wan, fond lover?
   Prythee, why so pale?
Will, if looking well can't move her,
   Looking ill prevail?
   Prythee, why so pale?

Why so dull and mute, young sinner?
   Prythee, why so mute?
Will, when speaking well can't win her,
   Saying nothing do't?
   Prythee, why so mute?

Quit, quit, for shame! this will not move,
   This cannot take her;
If of herself she will not love,
   Nothing can make her:
   The D——l take her!

73 Sir John Suckling, "Song," *Fragmenta Aurea* (1646).

❖❖❖❖❖❖❖❖❖

74 · Farewell

What should I say?
    Since faith is dead,
And truth away
    From you is fled,
    Should I be led
        With doubleness?
        Nay, nay, mistress!

I promised you,
    And you promised me,
To be as true
    As I would be.
    But since I see
        Your double heart,
        Farewell my part!

Though for to take
    It is not my mind
But to forsake,
    (One so unkind)
    And as I find
        So will I trust.
        Farewell, unjust!

Can ye say nay
    But you said
That I alway
    Should be obeyed,
    And thus betrayed
        Or that I wist?
        Farewell, unkist!

[74] Sir Thomas Wyatt, "A Revocation," *The Oxford Book of English Verse,* ed. Arthur Quiller-Couch (Oxford: At the Clarendon Press, 1948), pp. 66–67.

❖❩❧❩❧❖❦❦❖❦❖

75 · The Frog-Prince

    One fine evening a young Princess put on her bonnet and clogs and went out to take a walk by herself in a wood; and when she came to a cool spring of water that rose in the midst of it, she sat herself down to rest awhile. Now she had a golden ball in her hand, which was her favorite plaything; and she was always tossing it up into the air and catching it again as it fell. After a time she threw it up so high that she missed catching it as it fell; and the ball bounded away and rolled along upon the ground till at last it fell down into the spring. The Princess looked into the spring after the ball, but it was very deep, so deep that she could not see the bottom of it. Then she began to bewail her loss and said, "Alas! if I could only get my ball again, I would give all my fine clothes and jewels and everything that I have in the world."

Whilst she was speaking, a frog put its head out of the water and said, "Princess, why do you weep so bitterly?" "Alas!" said she, "What can you do for me, you nasty frog? My golden ball has fallen into the spring." The frog said, "I want not your pearls, and jewels and fine clothes; but if you will love me and let me live with you and eat from off your golden plate and sleep upon your bed, I will bring you your ball again." "What nonsense," thought the Princess, "this silly frog is talking! He can never even get out of the spring to visit me, though he may be able to get my ball for me, and therefore I will tell him he shall have what he asks." So she said to the frog, "Well, if you will bring me my ball, I will do all you ask." Then the frog put his head down and dived deep under the water; and after a little while he came up again with the ball in his mouth and threw it on the edge of the spring. As soon as the young Princess saw her ball, she ran to pick it up; and she was so overjoyed to have it in her hand again that she never thought of the frog, but ran home with it as fast as she could. The frog called after her, "Stay, Princess, and take me with you as you said." But she did not stop to hear a word.

The next day, just as the Princess had sat down to dinner, she heard a strange noise—tap, tap,—plash, plash,—as if something was coming up the marble staircase: and soon afterwards there was a gentle knock at the door, and a little voice cried out and said,

> "Open the door, my princess dear,
> Open the door to thy true love here!
> And mind the words that thou and I said
> By the fountain cool, in the greenwood shade."

Then the Princess ran to the door, and opened it, and there she saw the frog, whom she had quite forgotten. At this sight she was sadly frightened and, shutting the door as fast as she could, came back to her seat. The King, her father, seeing that something had frightened her, asked her what was the matter. "There is a nasty frog," said she, "at the door, that lifted my ball for me out of the spring this morning. I told him that he should live with me here, thinking that he could never get out of the spring; but there he is at the door, and he wants to come in."

While she was speaking the frog knocked again at the door and said,

"Open the door, my princess dear,
Open the door to thy true love here!
And mind the words that thou and I said
By the fountain cool, in the greenwood shade."

Then the King said to the young Princess, "As you have given your word you must keep it; so go and let him in." She did so, and the frog hopped into the room, and then straight on—tap, tap—plash, plash—from the bottom of the room to the top, till he came to the table where the Princess sat. "Pray lift me upon a chair," said he to the Princess, "and let me sit next to you." As soon as she had done this, the frog said, "Put your plate nearer to me, that I may eat out of it." This she did, and when he had eaten as much as he could, he said, "Now I am tired; carry me up stairs, and put me into your bed." And the Princess, though very unwilling, took him up in her hand and put him upon the pillow of her own bed, where he slept all night long. As soon as it was light he jumped up, hopped down stairs and went out of the house. "Now then," thought the Princess, "at last he is gone, and I shall be troubled with him no more."

But she was mistaken; for when night came again she heard the same tapping at the door; and the frog came once more and said.

"Open the door, my princess dear,
Open the door to thy true love here!
And mind the words that thou and I said
By the fountain cool, in the greenwood shade."

And when the Princess opened the door, the frog came in and slept upon her pillow as before, till the morning broke. And the third night he did the same. But when the Princess awoke on the following morning she was astonished to see, instead of the frog, a handsome Prince, gazing on her with the most beautiful eyes she had ever seen and standing at the head of her bed.

He told her that he had been enchanted by a spiteful fairy who had changed him into a frog; and that he had been fated so to abide till some princess should take him out of the spring and let him eat from her plate and sleep upon her bed for three nights. "You," said the Prince, "have broken this cruel charm, and now I have nothing to wish for but that you should go with me into my father's kingdom, where I will marry you, and love you as long as you live."

The young Princess, you may be sure, was not long saying "Yes," to all this; and as they spoke a gay coach drove up, with eight beautiful horses, decked with plumes of feathers and golden harness; and behind the coach rode the Prince's servant, faithful Heinrich, who had bewailed the misfortunes of his dear master during his enchantment so long and so bitterly that his heart had well-nigh burst.

They then took leave of the King and got into the coach with eight horses and all set out, full of joy and merriment, for the Prince's kingdom, which they reached safely; and there they lived happily a great many years.

❧❧❧❧❧❧❧❧

76 · University Days

Another course that I didn't like, but somehow managed to pass, was economics. I went to that class straight from botany class, which didn't help me in understanding either subject. I used to get them mixed up. But not as mixed up as another student in my economics class who came there direct from a physics laboratory. He was a tackle on the football team, named Bolenciecwcz. At that time Ohio State University had one of the best football teams in the country, and Bolenciecwcz was one of its outstanding stars. In order to be eligible to play it was necessary for him to keep up his studies, a very difficult matter, for while he was not dumber than an ox he was not any smarter. Most of his professors were lenient and helped him along. None gave him more hints, in answering questions, or asked him simpler ones than the economics professor, a thin timid man named Bassum. One day when we were on the subject of transportation and distribution, it came Bolenciecwcz's turn to answer a question. "Name one means of transportation," the professor said to him. No light came into the big tackle's eyes. "Just any means of transportation," said the professor. Bolenciecwcz sat staring at him. "That is," pursued the professor, "any medium, agency, or method of going from one place to another." Bolenciecwcz had the look of a man who is being led into a trap. "You may choose among steam, horse-drawn, or electrically propelled vehicles," said the instructor. "I might suggest the one which we commonly take in making long journeys across land." There was a profound silence in which everybody stirred uneasily, including Bolenciecwcz and Mr. Bassum. Mr. Bassum abruptly broke this silence in an amazing manner. "Choo-choo-choo," he said, in a low voice, and turned instantly scarlet. He glanced appealingly around the room. All of us, of course, shared Mr. Bassum's desire that Bolenciecwcz should stay abreast of the class in economics, for the Illinois game, one of the hardest and most important of the season, was only a week off. "Toot, toot, too-tooooooot!" some student with a deep voice moaned, and we all looked encouragingly at Bolenciecwcz. Somebody else gave a fine imitation of a locomotive letting off steam. Mr. Bassum himself rounded off the little show. "Ding, dong, ding, dong," he said hopefully. Bolenciecwcz was staring at the floor now, trying to think, his great brow furrowed, his huge hands rubbing together, his face red.

"How did you come to college this year, Mr. Bolenciecwcz?" asked the professor. *"Chuffa, chuffa, chuffa, chuffa."*

"M'father sent me," said the football player.

"What on?" asked Bassum.

"I git an 'lowance," said the tackle, in a low husky voice, obviously embarrassed.

"No, no," said Bassum. "Name a means of transportation. What did you *ride* here on?"

"Train."

The Illinois game was won.

[76] By permission. Copyright, 1933, by James Thurber. Originally published in the *New Yorker.*

❖❑❯❖❑❯❖❖❑❖❑❖

77 · Folly

When lovely woman stoops to folly,
And finds too late that men betray,—
What charm can soothe her melancholy,
What art can wash her guilt away?

The only art her guilt to cover,
To hide her shame from every eye,
To give repentance to her lover
And wring his bosom, is—to die.

[77] Oliver Goldsmith, "Woman," *The Vicar of Wakefield* (1766).

❖❑❯❖❑❯❖❖❑❖❑❖

78 · Fishing

Fishing is one of my favorite sports, and one of these days I expect to catch a fish. I have been at it fourteen years now and have caught everything else, including hell from the wife, a cold in the head, and up on my drinking. Next comes the fish.

[78] Robert Benchley, *Chips off the Old Benchley* (New York: Harper & Brothers, 1949), p. 165.

❖❑❯❖❑❯❖❖❑❖❑❖

79 · Hammocks

Hammocks were the fashion with open mesh and fringe and a stretcher at the end, and often they were slung in the back yard between the apple trees. And to sit with a young lady in a hammock was an intimacy denied upon a sofa. It seemed a device for sudden lovers, and sagged in the middle to an easy familiarity that loosened the heart upon a moonlit night. No lady could deny a hand, and even a freckled nose was boosted to a husband in such tight contagious circumstances.

79 Charles S. Brooks, *Like Summer's Cloud: A Book of Essays* (New York: Harcourt, Brace & Co., Inc., 1925).

❖❖❖❖❖❖❖❖

80 · The Resurrection

When the sabbath was past, Mary Magdalene, and Mary the Mother of James, and Salome, had bought sweet spices, that they might come and anoint him. And very early in the morning, the first day of the week, they came unto the sepulchre at the rising of the sun. And they said among themselves, Who shall roll us away the stone from the door of the sepulchre? And when they looked, they saw that the stone was rolled away: for it was very great. And entering into the sepulchre, they saw a young man sitting on the right side, clothed in a long white garment; and they were affrighted. And he said unto them, Be not affrighted: Ye seek Jesus of Nazareth, which was crucified: he is risen; he is not here: behold the place where they laid him. But go your way, tell his disciples and Peter that he goeth before you into Galilee: there shall ye see him, as he said unto you. And they went out quickly, and fled from the sepulchre; for they trembled and were amazed: neither said they any thing to any man; for they were afraid.

80 *The Holy Bible,* Mark 16:1–8.

❖❖❖❖❖❖❖❖

81 · Narcissus

When Narcissus died, the pool of his pleasure changed from a cup of sweet waters into a cup of salt tears, and the Oreads came weeping through the woodland that they might sing to the pool and give it comfort.

And when they saw that the pool had changed from a cup of sweet waters into a cup of salt tears, they loosened the green tresses of their hair, and cried to the pool, and said: "We do not wonder that you should mourn in this manner for Narcissus, so beautiful was he."

"But was Narcissus beautiful?" said the pool.

"Who should know better than you?" answered the Oreads. "Us did he ever pass by, but you he sought for, and would lie on your banks and look down at you, and in the mirror of your waters he would mirror his own beauty."

And the pool answered: "But I loved Narcissus because, as he lay on my banks and looked down at me, in the mirror of his eyes I saw my own beauty mirrored."

[81] *The Poems and Fairy Tales of Oscar Wilde* (New York: Modern Library, Inc., 1932).

❖❖❖❖❖❖❖❖❖❖

82 · Our Town

STAGE MANAGER: Three years have gone by.

Yes, the sun's come up over a thousand times.

Summers and winters have cracked the mountains a little bit more and the rains have brought down some of the dirt.

Some babies that weren't even born before have begun talking regular sentences already; and a number of people who thought they were right young and spry have noticed that they can't bound up a flight of stairs like they used to, without their heart fluttering a little.

Some older sons are sitting at the head of the table, and some people I know are having their meat cut up for them.—All that can happen in a thousand days.

Natures been pushing and contriving in other ways, too: a number of young people fell in love and got married. Yes, the mountain got bit away a few fractions of an inch; millions of gallons of water went by the mill; and here and there a new home was set up under a roof.

Almost everybody in the world gets married,—you know what I mean? In our town there aren't hardly any exceptions. Most everybody in the world climbs into their graves married.

. . .

So:

It's three years later. It's 1904. It's July 7th, just after High School Commencement. That's the time most of our young people jump up and get married. Soon as they've passed their last examinations in solid geometry and Cicero's Orations, looks like they suddenly feel themselves fit to be married.

❖❖❖❖❖ ❖❖❖❖❖

83 · Silence

I have known the silence of the stars and of the sea,
And the silence of the city when it pauses,
And the silence of a man and a maid,
And the silence for which music alone finds the word,
And the silence of the woods before the winds of spring begin,
And the silence of the sick
When their eyes roam about the room.
And I ask: For the depths
Of what use is language?
A beast of the field moans a few times
When death takes its young.
And we are voiceless in the presence of realities—
We cannot speak.

A curious boy asks an old soldier
Sitting in front of the grocery store,
"How did you lose your leg?"
And the old soldier is struck with silence,
Or his mind flies away
Because he cannot concentrate on Gettysburg.
It comes back jocosely
And he says, "A bear bit it off."
And the boy wonders, while the old soldier
Dumbly, feebly lives over
The flashes of guns, the thunder of cannon,
The shrieks of the slain,
And himself lying on the ground,
And the hospital surgeons, the knives,
And the long days in bed.
But if he could describe it all
He would be an artist.
But even if he were an artist there would be deeper wounds
Which he could not describe.

There is the silence of a great hatred,
And the silence of a great love,
And the silence of a deep peace of mind,
And the silence of embittered friendship,
There is the silence of spiritual crisis,
Through which your soul exquisitely tortured,
Comes with visions not to be uttered
Into a realm of higher life.
And the silence of the gods who understand each other
Without speech.
There is the silence of defeat.
There is the silence of those unjustly punished;
And the silence of the dying whose hand
Suddenly grips yours.
There is a silence between father and son,
When the father cannot explain his life,
Even though he be misunderstood for it.
There is the silence that comes between husband and wife.

There is the silence of those who have failed;
And the vast silence that covers
Broken nations and vanquished leaders.
There is the silence of Lincoln,
Thinking of the poverty of his youth.
There is the silence of Napoleon
After Waterloo.
And the silence of Jeanne d'Arc
Saying amid the flames, "Blessed Jesus"—
Revealing in two words all sorrow, all hope.
And there is the silence of age,
Too full of wisdom for the tongue to utter it
In words intelligible to those who have not lived
The great range of life.

And there is the silence of the dead.
If we who are in life cannot speak
Of profound experiences,
Why do you marvel that the dead
Do not tell you of death?
Their silence shall be interpreted
As we approach them.

[83] "Silence," from *Songs and Satires,* Edgar Lee Masters. Macmillan, New York, 1916. Permission granted by Ellen C. Masters.

84 · Silence

As the truest society approaches always nearer to solitude, so the most excellent speech finally falls into Silence. Silence is audible to all men, at all times, and in all places. She is when we hear inwardly, sound when we hear outwardly. Creation has not displaced her, but is her visible framework and foil. All sounds are her servants, and purveyors, proclaiming not only that their mistress is, but is a rare mistress, and earnestly to be sought after. They are so far akin to Silence that they are but bubbles on her surface, which straightway burst, an evidence of the strength and prolificness of the under-current; a faint utterance of Silence, and then only agreeable to our auditory nerves when they contrast themselves with and relieve the former. In proportion as they do this, and are heighteners and intensifiers of the Silence, they are harmony and purest melody.

Silence is the universal refuge, the sequel to all dull discourses and all foolish acts, a balm to our every chagrin as welcome after satiety as after disappointment; that background which the painter may not daub, be he master or bungler, and which, however awkward a figure we may have made in the foreground, remains ever our inviolable asylum, where no indignity can assail, no personality disturb us.

The orator puts off his individuality, and is then most eloquent when most silent. He listens while he speaks, and is a hearer along with his audience. Who has not hearkened to her infinite din? She is Truth's speaking-trumpet, the sole oracle, the true Delphi and Dodona, which kings and courtiers would do well to consult, nor will they be balked by an ambiguous answer. For through her all revelations have been made, and just in proportion as men have consulted her oracle within, they have obtained a clear insight, and their age has been marked as an enlightened one. But as often as they have gone gadding abroad to a strange Delphi and her mad priestess, their age has been dark and leaden. Such were garrulous and noisy eras, which no longer yield any sound, but the Grecian or silent and melodious era is ever sounding and resounding in the ears of men.

[84] Henry David Thoreau, *A Week on the Concord and Merrimack Rivers* (1849).

❧❧❧❧❦❦❦

85 · The Form of Solemnization of Matrimony

Dearly beloved, we are gathered together here in the sight of God, and in the face of this company, to join together this Man and this Woman

in holy Matrimony; which is an honourable estate, instituted of God, sig-
nifying unto us the mystical union that is betwixt Christ and his Church:
which holy estate Christ adorned and beautified with his presence and first
miracle that he wrought in Cana of Galilee, and is commended of Saint
Paul to be honourable among all men: and therefore is not by any to be
entered into unadvisedly or lightly; but reverently, discreetly, advisedly,
soberly, and in the fear of God. Into this holy estate these two persons
present come now to be joined. If any man can show just cause, why they
may not lawfully be joined together, let him now speak, or else hereafter
forever hold his peace.

I require and charge you both, as ye will answer at the dreadful day
of judgment when the secrets of all hearts shall be disclosed, that if either
of you know any impediment, why ye may not be lawfully joined together
in Matrimony, ye do now confess it. For be ye well assured, that if any
persons are joined together otherwise than as God's Word doth allow,
their marriage is not lawful.

[85] *The Book of Common Prayer* (New York: The Church Pension Fund, 1945),
p. 300.

⊱⊅⊱⊅⊱⊰⊰⊰⊱

86 · Sauerkraut

One of the good sources of Vitamin C --- sauerkraut --- can be served in a wide variety of meals.
The usual sauerkraut and wieners are just one
version.

Here's a simple recipe for escalloped sauerkraut
and tomatoes. It only calls for four ingredients --
one number two can of tomatoes, two and one-half cups
of sauerkraut, one cup of cracker or bread crumbs,
and two tablespoons of butter.

First drain the liquid from the tomatoes. Then
put alternate layers of tomatoes, sauerkraut, crumbs
and dots of butter in a well-greased baking dish.
Pour the liquid from the tomatoes over all the ingredients and top with buttered crumbs. Bake for 20
minutes in a moderately hot oven -- about 400
degrees. This recipe will make eight servings.

[86] EP243A8/22, United Press Radio, August 22, 1950.

⊱⊅⊱⊅⊱⊰⊰⊰⊱

87 · Our Town II

STAGE MANAGER:

This time nine years have gone by, friends—summer, 1913. Gradual changes in Grover's Corners. Horses are getting rarer. Farmers coming into town in Fords.

Chief difference is in the young people, far as I can see. They want to go to the moving pictures all the time. They want to wear clothes like they see there . . . want to be citified.

Everybody locks their house doors now at night. Ain't been any burglars in town yet, but everybody's heard 'bout 'em. But you'd be surprised though—on the whole, things don't change much at Grover's Corners.

Guess you want to know what all these chairs are here fur. Smarter ones have guessed it already. I don't know how you feel about such things; but this certainly is a beautiful place. It's on a hilltop—a windy hilltop—lots of sky, lots of clouds,—often lots of sun and moon and stars. You come up here on a fine afternoon and you can see range on range of hills—awful blue they are—up there by Lake Sunapee and Lake Winnapassaukee . . . and way up, if you've got a glass, you can see the White Mountains and Mt. Washington—where North Conway and Conway is. And, of course, our favorite mountain, Mt. Monadnock's, right here—and all around it lie these towns—Jaffrey, 'n East Jaffrey, 'n Peterborough, 'n Dublin and there, quite a ways down is Grover's Corners.

Yes, beautiful spot up here. Mountain laurel and li-lacks. I often wonder why people like to be buried in Woodlawn and Brooklyn when they might pass the same time up here in New Hampshire.

Over in that corner—are the old stones,—1670, 1680. Strong-minded people that come a long way to be independent. Summer people walk around there laughing at the funny words on the tombstones . . . it don't do any harm. And genealogists come up from Boston—get paid by city people for looking up their ancestors. They want to make sure they're Daughters of the American Revolution and of the *Mayflower* . . . . Well, I guess that don't do any harm either. Wherever you come near the human race, there's layers and layers of nonsense . . . .

Over there are some Civil War veterans too. Iron flags on their graves . . . New Hampshire boys . . . had a notion that the Union ought to be kept together, though they'd never seen more than fifty miles of it themselves. All they knew was the name, friends—the United States of America. The United States of America. And they went and died about it. This here is the new part of the cemetery. Here's your friend, Mrs. Gibbs. 'N let me see—Here's Mr. Stimson, organist at the Congregational Church. And over there's Mrs. Soames who enjoyed the wedding so—you remember? Oh, and a lot of others. And Editor Webb's boy, Wallace, whose appendix burst while he was on a Boy Scout trip to Crawford Notch.

Yes, an awful lot of sorrow has sort of quieted down up here. People just wild with grief have brought their relatives up to this hill. We all know how it is . . . and then time . . . and sunny days . . . and rainy days . . . 'n snow . . . tz-tz-tz. We're all glad they're in a beautiful place and we're coming up here ourselves when our fit's over. This certainly is an important part of Grover's Corners. A lot of thoughts come up here, night and day, but there's no post office.

Now I'm going to tell you some things you know already. You know'm as well as I do; but you don't take'm out and look at'm very often.

I don't care what they say with their mouths—everybody knows that *something* is eternal. And it ain't houses and it ain't names, and it ain't earth, and it ain't even the stars . . . everybody knows in their bones that *something* is eternal, and that something has to do with human beings. All the greatest people ever lived have been telling us that for five thousand years and yet you'd be surprised how people are always losing hold of it. There's something way down deep that's eternal about every human being.

[87] From *Our Town*, a Play by Thornton Wilder. Copyright, 1938, by Coward-McCann. Reprinted by permission. No performance whatsoever may be given of this play without written permission from Samuel French, 25 West 45th Street, New York 19, N. Y.

❖❙❫❙❫❖❖❪❪❖❪❪❖

88 · Doctor Faustus

Ah, Faustus,
Now hast thou one bare hour to live,
And then thou must be damned perpetually!
Stand still, you ever-moving spheres of Heaven,
That time may cease, and midnight never come;
Fair Nature's eye, rise, rise again and make
Perpetual day; or let this hour be but
A year, a month, a week, a natural day,
That Faustus may repent and save his soul!
O lente, lente, currite noctis equi!

The stars move still, time runs, the clock will strike,
The Devil will come, and Faustus must be damned.
O, I'll leap up to my God! Who pulls me down?
See, see where Christ's blood streams in the firmament!

One drop would save my soul—half a drop: ah, my Christ!
Ah, rend not my heart for naming of my Christ!
Yet will I call on him: O spare me, Lucifer!—
Where is it now? 'tis gone; and see where God
Stretcheth out his arm, and bends his ireful brows!
Mountain and hills come, come and fall on me,
And hide me from the heavy wrath of God!
No! No!
Then will I headlong run into the earth;
Earth gape! O no, it will not harbour me!
You stars that reigned at my nativity,
Whose influence hath allotted death and hell.
Now draw up Faustus like a foggy mist
Into the entrails of yon labouring clouds,
That when they vomit forth into the air,
My limbs may issue from their smoky mouths,
So that my soul may but ascend to Heaven.
          (*The clock strikes the half hour.*)
Ah, the half hour is past! 'twill all be past anon!
O God!
If thou wilt not have mercy on my soul,
Yet for Christ's sake whose blood hath ransomed me,
Impose some end to my incessant pain;
Let Faustus live in hell a thousand years—
A hundred thousand, and—at last—be saved!
O, no end is limited to damned souls!
Why wert thou not a creature wanting soul?
Or why is this immortal that thou hast?
Ah, Pythagoras' metempsychosis! were that true,
This soul should fly from me, and I be changed
Unto some brutish beast! all beasts are happy,
For when they die,
Their souls are soon dissolved in elements;
But mine must live, still to be plagued in hell.
Curst be the parents that engendered me!
No, Faustus: curse thyself: curse Lucifer
That hath deprived thee of the joys of Heaven.
          (*The clock strikes twelve.*)
O, it strikes! it strikes! Now, body, turn to air,
Or Lucifer will bear thee quick to hell.
          (*Thunder and Lightning.*)
O soul, be changed into little water-drops,
And fall into the ocean—ne'er be found.
          (*Enter Devils*)
My God! my God! look not so fierce on me!

Adders and serpents, let me breathe awhile!
Ugly hell, gape not! come not, Lucifer!
I'll burn my books!—Ah Mephistophilis!

[88] Christopher Marlowe, *The Tragical History of Doctor Faustus* (1604).

❖❀❁❀❁❀❮❀❮❀

89 · Tudor Plate

Announcer: Ladies, just think of it! Yours at no extra cost -- gleaming Tudor Plate teaspoons packed in twenty-five pound or larger sacks of Gold Medal "Kitchen-Tested" Enriched Flour. No, Ma'am, you don't pay one penny extra -- no cash to send in -- no waiting. Your Queen Bess pattern teaspoons are packed right in the large Gold Medal sacks -- one in the twenty-five pound sack ... TWO in the fifty pound sack ... FOUR in the one hundred pound sack.

Yes, Ma'am, now is the time to buy Gold Medal in large sack sizes --- and start saving for a complete silverware set, with sixteen different pieces, of lovely Queen Bess pattern silverware. This beautiful Queen Bess pattern was chosen by General Mills only after choices were expressed by sixteen thousand women. Remember, the teaspoons you get in the sack are an EXTRA BONUS, in addition to the regular silverware coupon you find in every sack of Gold Medal you buy.

You can depend on the uniform high quality of Gold Medal to give you wonderful results with everything you bake. Yes, because of its intensive pre-testing, General Mills guarantees that Gold Medal Flour will give completely satisfactory results or your money back.

Stop at your grocer's. Look for the Gold Medal Sacks that say: "Beautiful Queen Bess pattern teaspoons inside this bag." Offer good only while supplies last. This offer limited to the trading area of this station.

[89] Courtesy of General Mills, Inc.

❖❀❁❀❁❀❮❀❮❀

90 · Hymns of All Churches

Announcer: Welcome, friends and neighbors, to your program of Hymns of All Churches. General Mills, makers of Gold Medal "Kitchen-tested" Enriched Flour, is happy to bring you these broadcasts of the best-loved hymns of every faith, and all denominations.

(PAUSE)

You just don't know how GOOD biscuits can be till you've tried Betty Crocker's revolutionary, new STIR-N-ROLL Biscuit recipe! Just listen! The Betty Crocker Staff of General Mills agree that STIR-N-ROLL biscuits are richer, flakier, more beautifully golden-brown TOP and BOTTOM than any biscuits they've ever baked before!

What's more, the STIR-N-ROLL biscuit recipe is so amazingly easy that even beginners can make wonderful baking powder biscuits on their very first try. Real, old-fashioned, homemade biscuits -- the kind that have been the pride of good cooks for generations!

Here's all you do: Measure out -- into one cup -- Wesson Oil and milk. Add these two liquid ingredients all at once to a mixture of Gold Medal "Kitchen-tested" Enriched Flour, baking powder and salt. Stir lightly until dough cleans the side of the bowl. Press out with your hands or roll between waxed paper. Cut with unfloured biscuit cutter or drop dough from spoon and bake.

Like magic -- homemade biscuits so delicious that they invite comparison with any biscuits you've ever made with any other biscuit recipe!

Listen at the close of this program for complete details of how to get the STIR-N-ROLL biscuit recipe. Then -- just try it once. We know that you'll agree: It's THE ONE GREAT NEW BISCUIT RECIPE OF ALL TIME!

[90] Courtesy of General Mills, Inc.

❖❱❭❱❭❱❬❰❖❬❬❰❘

91 · Profit in War

The calculation of profit in all such wars is false. On balancing the account of such wars, ten thousand hogsheads of sugar are purchased at ten thousand times their price. The blood of man should never be shed but to redeem the blood of man. It is well shed for our family, for our friends, for our God, for our country, for our kind. The rest is vanity; the rest is crime.

[91] Edmund Burke, *Letters on a Regicide Peace* (1795–1797), Letter No. 1.

❖)❖)❖❖((❖((❖

92 · Gettysburg Address

Fourscore and seven years ago our fathers brought forth on this continent a new nation, conceived in liberty, and dedicated to the proposition that all men are created equal.

Now we are engaged in a great civil war, testing whether that nation, or any nation so conceived and so dedicated, can long endure. We are met on a great battlefield of that war. We have come to dedicate a portion of that field as a final resting place for those who here gave their lives that that nation might live. It is altogether fitting and proper that we should do this.

But, in a larger sense, we cannot dedicate—we cannot consecrate—we cannot hallow—this ground. The brave men, living and dead, who struggled here, have consecrated it, far above our poor power to add or detract. The world will little note nor long remember what we say here, but it can never forget what they did here. It is for us, the living, rather, to be dedicated here to the unfinished work which they who fought here have thus far so nobly advanced. It is rather for us to be here dedicated to the great task remaining before us,—that from these honored dead we take increased devotion to that cause for which they gave the last full measure of devotion; that we here highly resolve that these dead shall not have died in vain; that this nation, under God, shall have a new birth of freedom; and that government of the people, by the people, for the people, shall not perish from the earth.

[92] Abraham Lincoln, Gettysburg Address, delivered at the dedication of the National Cemetery, November, 1863.

❖)❖)❖❖((❖((❖

93 · The Three Billy-Goats Gruff

Once on a time there were three billy-goats, who were to go up to the hillside to make themselves fat, and the name of all three was "Gruff."

On the way up was a bridge over a burn they had to cross; and under the bridge lived a great ugly Troll, with eyes as big as saucers, and a nose as long as a poker.

So first of all came the youngest billy-goat Gruff to cross the bridge.

"Trip, trap; trip trap!" went the bridge.

"WHO'S THAT tripping over my bridge?" roared the Troll.

"Oh, it is only I, the tiniest billy-goat Gruff; and I'm going up to the hillside to make myself fat," said the billy-goat, with such a small voice.

"Now, I'm coming to gobble you up," said the Troll.

"Oh, no! pray don't take me. I'm too little, that I am," said the billy-goat; "wait a bit till the second billy-goat Gruff comes, he's much bigger."

"Well! be off with you," said the Troll.

A little while after came the second billy-goat Gruff to cross the bridge.

"Trip, Trap! Trip, Trap! Trip, Trap!" went the bridge.

"WHO'S THAT tripping over my bridge?" roared the Troll.

"Oh! it's the second billy-goat Gruff, and I'm going to the hillside to make myself fat," said the billy-goat, who hadn't such a small voice.

"Now, I'm coming to gobble you up," said the Troll.

"Oh, no! don't take me. Wait a little till the big billy-goat Gruff comes; he's much bigger."

"Very well! be off with you," said the Troll.

But just then up came the big billy-goat Gruff.

"TRIP, TRAP! TRIP, TRAP! TRIP, TRAP!" went the bridge, for the billy-goat was so heavy that the bridge creaked and groaned under him.

"WHO'S THAT tramping over my bridge?" roared the Troll.

"IT'S I! THE BIG BILLY-GOAT GRUFF," said the billy-goat, who had an ugly hoarse voice of his own.

"Now, I'm coming to gobble you up," roared the Troll.

> Well, come along! I've got two spears,
> And I'll poke your eyeballs out at your ears;
> I've got besides two curling-stones,
> And I'll crush you to bits, body and bones.

That was what the big billy-goat said; and so he flew at the Troll and poked his eyes out with his horns, and crushed him to bits, body and bones, and tossed him out into the burn, and after that he went up to the hillside. There the billy-goats got so fat they were scarce able to walk home again; and if the fat hasn't fallen off them, why they're still fat; and so:

> Snip, snap, snout,
> This tales told out.

[93] Sir George Webbe Dasent, *Popular Tales from the Norse* (New York: G. P. Putnam's Sons, 1908), pp. 264–265.

❧❧❧❧❧❧

94 · Anatomy of Sound

Woman: How would you like to get up before an
audience of five million people and introduce
yourself? Would you rap on the edge of a glass with
a spoon to get attention, like this?
(*Rapping on glass*)
Do you think that would quiet such an audience?
Would you clear your throat like this?
(*Clears throat*)
Or would you try to ride over their noise by shouting
through a public address system the traditional
salutation?
(*Over a public address amplifier, as though trying to stop a hubbub*)
Ladies and gentlemen!
(*Normal mike*)
And assuming you got the five million to quiet down,
how would you then proceed to introduce yourself?
You, standing alone on a stage with a battery of
lights turned on you as though you were a night
baseball game, only bigger.
Suppose some of your audience were playing bridge
and others arguing and still others reading newspapers? Would that terrify you? It would me, I
know -- except that at this moment when I am
addressing five million people and thousands of them
are playing bridge and talking across my voice and
riding in automobiles and reading things, I'm not at
all terrified. That's because there are four walls
of a radio studio around me, and I cannot see your
faces. I cannot see 246,197 cigarettes light up in
the dark across eight million square miles of
continent. And so it becomes relatively easy to get
on with perfect strangers. Seclusion has an etiquette
of its own. I will introduce myself to these
strangers after a token sound to separate an informal
prologue from a formal introduction.

[94] From *More by Corwin*, by Norman Corwin, p. 233. Reprinted by permission
of Henry Holt and Company, Inc. Copyright, 1944, by Norman Corwin.

❖❖❖❖❖❖❖

95 · The Very Bent Twig

When I was a lass in my teens,
   On looking Biology's plan up

I learned the importance of Genes
    In shaping a mouse or a man up.
The Genes and the Chromosomes, Science contended,
Ancestrally guarded, haphazardly blended,
Determined the whole
    Of all animate creatures,
From the shape of the soul
    To the tint of the features.

But now the psychologists tell us
    That Infancy settles our lots.
Are we happy or glum?
    Are we clever or slow?
It depends on the thumb
    That we sucked long ago
    When we first were susceptible tots.

Yoo-hoo, Heredity!
What's happened to Heredity?
We daren't thank Heredity
    For scholars or for scamps.
In the way that we develop
Family trees are little hel-op
We're the products of our Nannies,
    Not our Grannies or our Gramps.

If Junior can't learn to spell "cat"
    And looks at his books on the dour side,
Don't turn to your spouse with a flat
    "Observe how he takes after your side."
He probably suffered a setback material
From early excesses of kisses or cereal.
Conversely, if same's
    Full of honors and merits,
How sunk are your claims
    To the wit he inherits.

Away with Lombroso and Mendel.
    Their notions are worthless, though quaint.
It's the way we were frocked,
    Or the way we were bibbed,
Cuddled, sung to, or rocked,
    Or unfeelingly cribbed
    That decides what we are or we ain't.

Yoo-hoo, Environment!
We're nuts about Environment.
  It's training for the Toidy, now,
  It's dangling on the lap
That forms the lifelong habits
Of both Kallikaks and Cabots.
  (I don't know about the rabbits
  But it goes for Homo Sap.)

EPILOGUE

Still, don't you cry, Heredity. Just take the longer view.
They'll have another theory by 1952.

[95] Copyright, 1950, by Phyllis McGinley. Originally appeared in *The New Yorker*. Reprinted by permission of The Viking Press, Inc., New York, from *A Short Walk from the Station*, by Phyllis McGinley.

✦⟫✦⟫✦◆⟪◆⟪◆

96 · The History of Bel

The Babylonians had an idol called Bel, and there were spent upon him every day twelve great measures of fine flour, and forty sheep, and six vessels of wine. And the king worshipped it, and went daily to adore it; but Daniel worshipped his own God.

And the king said unto him: "Why dost not thou worship Bel?" Who answered and said: "Because I may not worship idols made with hands, but the living God, who hath created the heaven and the earth, and hath sovereignty over all flesh."

Then said the king unto him: "Thinkest thou not that Bel is a living God? Seest thou not how much he eateth and drinketh every day?" Then Daniel smiled, and said: "O King, be not deceived, for this is but clay within, and brass without, and did never eat or drink any thing."

So the king was wroth, and called for his priests and said unto them: "If ye tell me not who this is that devoureth these expences, ye shall die. But if ye can certify me that Bel devoureth them, then Daniel shall die, for he hath spoken blasphemously against Bel." And Daniel said unto the king, "Let it be according to thy word." Now the priests of Bel were three score and ten, besides their wives and children; and the king went with Daniel into the temple of Bel.

So Bel's priests said: "Lo, we go out, but thou, O King, set on the meat, and make ready the wine, and shut the door fast, and seal it with thine own signet. And tomorrow, when thou comest in, if thou findest not that Bel hath eaten up all, we will suffer death; or else Daniel that speaketh falsely against us."

And they little regarded; for under the table they had made a privy entrance, whereby they entered in continually, and consumed those things.

So when they were gone forth, the king set meats before Bel. Now Daniel had commanded his servants to bring ashes, and those they strewed throughout all the temple, in the presence of the king alone; then went they out, and shut the door, and sealed it with the king's signet, and so departed.

Now in the night came the priests with their wives and children (as they were wont to do), and did eat and drink up all.

In the morning betime the king arose, and Daniel with him. And the king said: "Daniel, are the seals whole?" And he said: "Yea, O King, they be whole." And as soon as he had opened the door, the king looked upon the table, and cried with a loud voice: "Great art thou, O Bel, and with thee is no deceit at all."

Then laughed Daniel, and held the king that he should not go in, and said: "Behold now the pavement, and mark well whose footsteps are these." And the king said: "I see the footsteps of men, women, and children."

And then the king was angry, and took the priests with their wives and children, who showed him the privy doors where they came in, and consumed such things as were upon the table.

Therefore the king slew them, and delivered Bel into Daniel's power, who destroyed him and his temple.

96 "The History of Bel," from the Apocrypha, in Dorothy Sayers, ed., *The Omnibus of Crime* (New York: Harcourt, Brace & Co., Inc., 1929), p. 51.

❖❖❖❖❖❖❖❖❖❖

97 · Regicide Peace

We are in a war of a peculiar nature. It is not with an ordinary community, which is hostile or friendly as passion or as interest may veer about; not with a State which makes war through wantonness, and abandons it through lassitude. We are at war with a system, which, by its essence, is inimical to all other Governments, and which makes peace or war, as peace and war may best contribute to their subversion. It is with an *armed doctrine* that we are at war. It has, by its essence, a faction of opinion, and of interest, and of enthusiasm, in every country. To us it is a Colossus which bestrides our channel. It has one foot on a foreign shore, the other upon British soil. Thus advantaged, if it can at all exist, it must finally prevail. Nothing can so completely ruin any of the old Governments, ours in particular, as the acknowledgment, directly or by implication, of any kind of superiority in this new power. This acknowledgment we make, if in a bad or doubtful situation of our affairs, we solicit peace; or if we yield to the modes of new humiliation, in which alone she is content to give us an hearing. By that means the terms cannot be of our choosing; no, not in any part . . . .

In one point we are lucky. The Regicide has received our advances with scorn. We have an enemy, to whose virtues we can owe nothing; but on this occasion we are infinitely obliged to one of his vices. We owe more to his insolence than to our own precaution. The haughtiness by which the proud repel us, has this good in it; that in making us keep our distance, they must keep their distance too.

. . . There is always an augury to be taken of what a peace is likely to be, from the preliminary steps that are made to bring it about. We may gather something from the time in which the first overtures are made; from the quarter whence they come; from the manner in which they are received. These discover the temper of the parties. If your enemy offers peace in the moment of success, it indicates that he is satisfied with something. It shews that there are limits to his ambition or his resentment. If he offers nothing under misfortune, it is probable, that it is more painful to him to abandon the prospect of advantage than to endure calamity. If he rejects solicitation, and will not give even a nod to the supplicants for peace, until a change in the fortune of the war threatens him with ruin, then I think it evident, that he wishes nothing more than to disarm his adversary to gain time. Afterwards a question arises, which of the parties is likely to obtain the greater advantages, by continuing disarmed and by the use of time.

With these few plain indications in our minds, it will not be improper to re-consider the conduct of the enemy together with our own, from the day that a question of peace has been in agitation. In considering this part of the question, I do not proceed on my own hypothesis. I suppose, for a moment, that this body of Regicide, calling itself a Republic, is a politick person, with whom something deserving the name of peace may be made. On that supposition, let us examine our own proceeding. Let us compute the profit it has brought, and the advantage that it is likely to bring hereafter. A peace too eagerly sought, is not always the sooner obtained. The discovery of vehement wishes generally frustrates their attainment; and your adversary has gained a great advantage over you when he finds you impatient to conclude a treaty. There is in reserve, not only something of dignity, but a great deal of prudence too. A sort of courage belongs to negotiation, as well as to operations of the field. A negotiator must often seem willing to hazard the whole issue of his treaty, if he wishes to secure any one material point.

[97] Edmund Burke, *Letters on a Regicide Peace* (1795–1797), Letter No. 1.

98 · Savings Bonds

OCTOBER – DECEMBER, 1949
U.S. Savings Bonds
10-SECOND LIVE ANNCT.
No. 4
(Prepared by Schwinner and
Scott)

ANNCR: <u>Smart</u> today -- Secure and happy tomorrow!
..... when you save for the future with
United States Savings Bonds. Join the
Payroll Savings Plan where you work ...
or the Bond-A-Month Plan when you bank!

❖❱❱❱❱❰❰❰❖

99 · The Collar

I struck the board, and cried, No more.
I will abroad.
What? shall I ever sigh and pine?
My lines and life are free; free as the road,
Loose as the wind, as large as store.
Shall I be still in suit?
Have I no harvest but a thorn
To let me blood, and not restore
What I have lost with cordial fruit?
Sure there was wine
Before my sighs did dry it: there was corn
Before my tears did drown it.
Is the year only lost to me?
Have I no bays to crown it?
No flowers, no garlands gay? all blasted?
All wasted?
Not so, my heart: but there is fruit,
And thou hast hands.
Recover all thy sigh-blown age
On double pleasures: leave thy cold dispute
Of what is fit and not; forsake thy cage,
Thy rope of sands,
Which petty thoughts have made, and made to thee

Good cable, to enforce and draw,
And be thy law,
While thou didst wink and would not see.
Away; take heed:
I will abroad.
Call in thy death's-head there: tie up thy fears.
He that forbears
To suit and serve his need,
Deserves his load.
But as I rav'd and grew more fierce and wild
At every word,
Methought I heard one calling, *Child;*
And I replied, *My Lord.*

[99] George Herbert, "The Collar," *The Temple* (1633).

❖❖❖❖❖❖

100 · The Abbey at Night

And as at night I went past the Abbey, saw its walls towering high and solemn among the Autumn stars, I pictured to myself the white population in the vast darkness of its interior—all that hushed people of Heroes—; not dead, I would think them, but animated with a still kind of life, and at last, after all their intolerable toils, the sounding tumult of battle, and perilous sea-paths, resting there, tranquil and satisfied and glorious, amid the epitaphs and allegorical figures of their tombs;—those high-piled, trophied, shapeless Abbey tombs, that long ago they toiled for, and laid down their gallant lives to win.

[100] Logan Pearsall Smith, *Trivia* (New York: Doubleday & Co., Inc., 1917), p. 60.

❖❖❖❖❖❖

101 · On the Tombs in Westminster Abbey

Mortality, behold and fear!
What a change of flesh is here!
Think how many royal bones
Sleep within these heaps of stones;
Here they lie, had realms and lands,
Who now want strength to stir their hands,

Where from their pulpits seal'd with dust
They preach, 'In greatness is no trust.'
Here's an acre sown indeed
With the richest royallest seed
That the earth did e'er suck in
Since the first man died for sin:
Here the bones of birth have cried—
'Though gods they were, as men they died!'
Here are sands, ignoble things,
Dropt from the ruin'd sides of kings:
Here's a world of pomp and state,
Buried in dust, once dead by fate.

101 Francis Beaumont, "On the Tombs in Westminster," *Poems* (1640).

❖❫❭❖❬❬❖❬❬❖

102 · A Garage for Gabriel

There was once a little car whose name was Gabriel.

Now poor Gabriel had no garage. He lived outdoors in a lot where they sold used cars. He wore a sign that said, "FOR SALE—CHEAP."

There were dents in his fenders. His paint was rusty. His doors sagged.

Every day Gabriel watched the shiny new cars roll by. But they never even looked at Gabriel.

"Oh," thought Gabriel, "how I should like to go whizzing right along. How I wish I were new and shiny!"

"But, specially," he thought sadly, "how I, *how* I wish I could have a garage!"

Well, one day two ladies came along.

They said to the man who sold cars, "Have you a small car?"

He pointed to Gabriel.

"We'll try it," they said. In they climbed.

"Now!" whispered Gabriel in great excitement. "I'll show them I can whiz right along. Then the ladies will buy me and give me a garage."

"*Whiz, whiz, whiz,*" went Gabriel around the block.

He was feeling mighty happy.

Round and round and round the block. *Whiz, whiz, whiz!*

"That will show them," he thought.

But the ladies cried, "Mercy, we don't want this car. It won't slow down at all."

Gabriel felt very sad.

Next day a college boy came.

"Here's a fine car," said the man.

"I'll try it," said the college boy.

"Oh, ho!" thought Gabriel. "This time I'll go very slowly, if that's what they want. Then the college boy will buy me and give me a garage."

So he went v-e-r-y, v—e—r—y, s——l——o——w——l——y.

But the college boy said, "That car's too slow!"

And off he marched.

Gabriel felt very sad.

But the next day a young lady came.

This time Gabriel was determined to do the right thing.

"I won't go too fast and I won't go too slow," he said. "But I'll show her I've got pep in my engine. Then she'll buy me and give me a garage."

The young lady started the engine.

"BANG!" shouted Gabriel. "BANG, BING, BANG, POP, POP!"

"My goodness!" cried the young lady. "This car's much too noisy!"

And off she hurried.

"Oh, dear!" cried poor Gabriel. "Won't *anyone* ever buy me and give me a garage? I'll never be so noisy again!"

So the next day when a man came and pressed the starter, Gabriel didn't make any noise. Not *any* noise.

"This car won't even start," said the man. He turned on his heel and left.

Well, Gabriel felt just awful. Now he was sure that he never would have a garage.

And then Jimmy and Jimmy's daddy came along.

"Have you a car for $50?" asked Jimmy's daddy.

The man was so *mad* at Gabriel, he said, "yes—*there's* a car for $50.

"Sold!" cried Jimmy's daddy.

They climbed right in.

Gabriel was so surprised that he never had time to show off. He just acted natural.

They drove up the street and stopped in front of a little yellow house.

Then Jimmy's daddy greased Gabriel's engine till it purred like a pussycat.

"I sound real quiet!" thought Gabriel.

Then Jimmy's daddy hammered out the dents in the fenders, and oiled the hinges and fixed the sagging doors.

"I feel real good!" whispered Gabriel.

And last of all, Jimmy's daddy gave Gabriel a coat of shiny red paint.

"I look FINE!" shouted Gabriel.

Then Jimmy and his daddy and mommy and Pooch, their cat, all went for a ride.

Every time they whizzed by another car, Gabriel bowed and smiled and the other cars bowed and smiled, too.

And when they came home, they whizzed right up the driveway into a little, yellow garage!

[102] Copyright, 1947, by American National Red Cross. Reprinted by permission of the author, Catherine Woolley.

❖⦚❖⦚❖⦚❖⦚❖

103 · The Night Has Been Long!

When you're lying awake with a dismal headache, and repose is
    taboo'd by anxiety,
I conceive you may use any language you choose to indulge in with-
    out impropriety;
For your brain is on fire—the bedclothes conspire of usual slumber
    to plunder you:
First your counterpane goes, and uncovers your toes, and your sheet
    slips demurely from under you;
Then the blanketing tickles—you feel like mixed pickles—so ter-
    ribly sharp is the pricking,
And you're hot, and you're cross, and you tumble and toss till there's
    nothing 'twixt you and the ticking.
Then your bedclothes all creep to the ground in a heap, and you pick
    'em all up in a tangle;
Next your pillow resigns and politely declines to remain at its usual
    angle.
Well, you get some repose in the form of a doze, with hot eye-balls
    and head ever aching,
But your slumbering teems with such horrible dreams that you'd very
    much better be waking.

. . .

You're a regular wreck, with a crick in your neck,
And no wonder you snore, for your head's on the floor,
And you've needles and pins from your soles to your shins,
And your flesh is a-creep, for your left leg's asleep,
And you've cramp in your toes, and a fly on your nose,
And some fluff in your lung, and a feverish tongue,
And a thirst that's intense, and a general sense
That you haven't been sleeping in clover.
But the darkness has passed, and it's daylight at last,
And the night has been long—ditto, ditto, my song—
And thank goodness, they're both of them over!

[103] W. S. Gilbert, *Iolanthe,* with music by Sir Arthur Sullivan (produced November 25, 1882).

❖⦚❖⦚❖⦚❖⦚❖

104 · Jehovah

JEHOVAH. Did I ever mention publicly how Hell got started? I don't
think I ever did. It was this way: I thought I'd do something nice for a lot
of the theologians who had, after all, been doing the best they could, according to their lights; so I gave them an enormous tract of Heaven to do what
they pleased with—set it apart for them to inhabit and administer. I didn't
pay any attention to it for a few thousand years, and when I looked at it
again, they'd made it into Hell.

104 Don Marquis, *Chapters for the Orthodox* (New York: Doubleday & Co., Inc.,
1934). Copyright, 1934, by Don Marquis, reprinted by permission of Doubleday &
Company, Inc.

105 · The Golden Age

The masterful wind was up and out, shouting and chasing, the lord
of the morning. Poplars swayed and tossed with a roaring swish; dead
leaves sprang aloft, and whirled into space; and all the clear-swept heaven
seemed to thrill with sound like a great harp. It was one of the first awak-
enings of the year. The earth stretched herself, smiling in her sleep; and
everything leapt and pulsed to the stir of the giant's movement.

105 Kenneth Grahame, *The Golden Age* (New York: John Lane Co., 1902), p. 11.

106 · Where Now?

"Where now?" Some quiet steps that came and passed along a leafy
nighttime street in summer in a little town down South long years ago;
a woman's voice, her sudden burst of low and tender laughter; then the
voices and the footsteps going, silence, the leafy rustle of the trees.

106 Thomas Wolfe, "The Story of a Novel," *Short Stories* (Baltimore: Penguin
Books, Inc., 1947), p. 128. Reprinted by permission of Charles Scribner's Sons.

107 · U. S. Graunt

After browsing among the stately ruins of Rome, of Baiae, of Pompeii, and after glancing down the long marble ranks of battered and nameless imperial heads that stretch down the corridors of the Vatican, one thing strikes me with a force it never had before: the unsubstantial, unlasting character of fame. Men lived long lives, in the olden time, and struggled feverishly through them, toiling like slaves, in oratory, in generalship, or in literature, and then laid them down and died, happy in the possession of an enduring history and a deathless name. Well, twenty little centuries flutter away, and what is left of these things? A crazy inscription on a block of stone, which snuffy antiquaries bother over and tangle up and make nothing out of but a bare name (which they spell wrong)—no history, no tradition, no poetry,—nothing that can give it even a passing interest. What may be left of General Grant's great name forty centuries hence? This—in the Encyclopedia for A.D. 5868, possibly.

"URIAH S. (or Z.) GRAUNT—popular poet of ancient times in the Aztec provinces of the United States of British America. Some authors say flourished about A.D. 742; but the learned Ah-ah Foo-foo states that he was a contemporary of Scharkspyre, the English poet, and flourished about A.D. 1328, some centuries *after* the Trojan war instead of before it. He wrote 'Rock me to Sleep, Mother.' "

These thoughts sadden me. I will to bed.

[107] Mark Twain, *The Innocents Abroad* (New York: Harper & Brothers, 1869), II, 53–54.

꘍꘍꘍꘍꘍

108 · To the Terrestrial Globe
(By a Miserable Wretch)

Roll on, thou ball, roll on!
Through pathless realms of Space
    Roll on!
What though I'm a sorry case?
What though I cannot meet my bills?
What though I suffer toothache's ills?
What though I swallow countless pills?
    Never *you* mind!
    Roll on!

Roll on, thou ball, roll on!
Through seas of inky air

Roll on!
It's true I've got no shirts to wear;
It's true my butcher's bill is due;
It's true my prospects all look blue—
But don't let that unsettle you!
Never *you* mind!
Roll on!
(*It rolls on.*)

[108] W. S. Gilbert, quoted in *The Home Book of Verse,* ed. B. E. Stevenson (New York: Henry Holt & Company, Inc., 1945), pp. 2075–2076.

❖❖❖❖❖❖❖❖

109 · The Daily Miracle

"Yes, he's one of those men that don't know how to manage. Good situation. Regular income. Quite enough for luxuries as well as needs. Not really extravagant. And yet the fellow's always in difficulties. Somehow he gets nothing out of his money. Excellent flat—half empty! Always looks as if he'd had the brokers in. New suit—old hat! Magnificent necktie—baggy trousers! Asks you to dinner, cut glass—bad mutton, or Turkish coffee—cracked cup! He can't understand it. Explanation simply is that he fritters his income away. Wish I had the half of it! I'd show him——"

So we have most of us criticized, at one time or another, in our superior way.

We are nearly all chancellors of the exchequer; it is the pride of the moment. Newspapers are full of articles explaining how to live on such and such a sum, and these articles provoke a correspondence whose violence proves the interest they excite. Recently, in a daily organ, a battle raged round the question whether a woman can exist nicely in the country on £85 a year. I have seen an essay, "How to live on eight shillings a week." But I have never seen an essay, "How to live on twenty-four hours a day." Yet it has been said that time is money. That proverb understates the case. Time is a great deal more than money. If you have time you can obtain money—usually. But though you have the wealth of a cloak-room attendant at the Carlton Hotel, you cannot buy yourself a minute more time than I have, or the cat by the fire has.

Philosophers have explained space. They have not explained time. It is the inexplicable raw material of everything. With it, all is possible; without it, nothing. The supply of time is truly a daily miracle, an affair genuinely astonishing when one examines it. You wake up in the morning, and lo! your purse is magically filled with twenty-four hours of the unmanufactured tissue of the universe of your life! It is yours. It is the most precious of possessions. A highly singular commodity, showered upon you in manner as singular as the commodity itself!

For remark! No one can take it from you. It is unstealable. And no one receives either more or less than you receive.

Talk about an ideal democracy! In the realms of time there is no aristocracy of wealth, and no aristocracy of intellect. Genius is never rewarded by even an extra hour a day. And there is no punishment. Waste your infinitely precious commodity as much as you will, and the supply will never be withheld from you. No mysterious power will say:—"This man is a fool, if not a knave. He does not deserve time; he shall be cut off at the meter." It is more certain than consols, and payment of income is not affected by Sundays. Moreover, you cannot draw on the future. Impossible to get into debt. You can only waste the passing moment. You cannot waste tomorrow; it is kept for you. You cannot waste the next hour; it is kept for you.

[109] Arnold Bennett, *How to Live on Twenty-four Hours a Day* (New York: Doubleday & Co., Inc., 1910), pp. 21–24.

❖❱❱❱❱❰❰❰❰❖

110 · The Fair Catch

Elimination of the Fair catch may make football a new game this year.

That's the prediction of Coach Bud Wilkinson of The University of Oklahoma. He held a press conference this afternoon in Oklahoma City.

Wilkinson is concerned about the effect of the new rule on his Sooners. He credits the Oklahoma's punt returns, together with fine out-of-bounds kicking, for the University's 21 straight victories including two Sugar Bowl games in the last two years.

Wilkinson told the newsmen that the punt return is a potent offensive weapon. In recent years there's been a tendency to kick out of bounds. If the safety man got his hands on the ball he could run it back or at the worst make the catch without any interference.

But the new rule will change all that, according to the youthful Sooner coach.

Now everybody will be trying for long, high boots that will cause the ball to land on its nose and bounce forward. The offensive team thus will have the weapon.

The fair catch rule protected the receiver from man-eating ends charging down on him. He could hold up his hand like a traffic cop and the tacklers couldn't do anything but pull up short.
    Under the new rule, a safety who holds up his hand will be lucky to get it back.

110 RB900P8/22, United Press Radio, August 22, 1950.

❖⫸⫸⊱⊰⫷❖

111 · The Fight at the Bridge

They had no time to think. They grabbed for the tent pegs and ran pell-mell to the bridgehead. They could see the rig coming at a gallop; it was coming from the west along the road they had just quit. It carried two lamps, and the vent holes sprayed light enough for Huguenine's little group to see the load of Burke's hyenas cramming the open box.

Chad tried to count them, a dozen anyway; they all looked tough. His mind went hastily over Huguenine's: four skinners, Huguenine made five, Fiero six, Pamplon seven, Ike eight, Shepley nine. But Burke's gang would all be fighters. It was just God that had put the bridge there, or maybe it was the canal commissioner, or the pig-headed farmer who had stood up for his rights, or the Democratic vote. It gave them a chance to make a stand. He felt a small cold spot in his smaller entrails enlarging rapidly. If they had had a minute more they could have ripped the planks out of the bridge.

But they had barely time to beat the gang to the top. Chad's feet pounded up the planks with Joe Duddy's and Bastock's. Huguenine, blowing in his wake, was crying, ... Then Budlong burst through them and hollered for room. He dropped his tent peg and took the light sledge in both hands, and as the opposing gang milled up the ramp roaring, he swung it from behind his calves, underhand, and let it go. It spun into their legs like a cartwheel lacking the rim. It mowed down three. They heard it cracking on shinbones, and an ugly shout burst from the men.

. . .

Budlong spat into his fist and grabbed his tent peg. The Burke men crashed into them. Chad was spun around by a glancing knock on his head; and he saw Fiero galloping away. Damn the Dago. Out of the mess a thick-built man materialized, jabbing at his guts with the end of his pole; he felt it and then a resounding hollow pumpkin sound from the man's head surprised him. He dropped the pole and covered his skull and Fred Shepley, white as fish belly, gave him a shove and the man's thick middle buckled uncannily and he went tail first through the rail, his splash shooting water nearly to the bridge floor.

The fight became completely snarled. It made no sense. A head showed up and you brought your peg down and as like as not you hit another head. Pamplon was dropped early. Chad tripped over him where he lay. He looked completely dead, but the blood was coming from his nose. He heard Ike yelping and then Joe Duddy bellowed just above him. He knew it was Joe from the size of his legs and the faint smell of Oscar on his shoes. He heaved himself up to see Joe and a red-faced mug wrestling for the same peg. Their faces were absorbed. They weren't doing any damage. They might as well have been counting cats. Chad swung his boot into the man's rear end with all his might and felt it bounce. The man belched like a steamboat, straightened and turned, and Joe Duddy brought the club down on the top of his head. The man fell against Chad and sat down hard. It was Walsh himself. To Chad it seemed beautiful. Then a stone hit him on the arm, and he saw Fiero poised on the bridge above, with rocks at his feet. His left leg was extended, his right hand back, head heaved, said, "Hah!" and let her come. Chad ducked. He heard Mr. Huguenine yelp, and whirled to see Shepley standing off two men.

Shepley had lost his peg and was using his fists. He was doing fine. But a third man hit him with the haft of a sledge and he went down like a post, full length. Chad took the rush of the three men. Budlong appeared with a bloody mouth and cracked one of them. He heard Joe Duddy's call for help. A great wet mass hit him in the back; he felt the weight like a bear's all over him and a pair of hairy arms took him round the waist, squeezing the juices in him, and he knew it was his thick-built antagonist climbed back from the canal. He butted backward with his head, and the man banged him on the planks and fell on top of him. They started rolling. Fiero shouted, "No rocks!" in a piercing voice and leaped for life. His splash coming up met Chad and the thick man going down and they all three tangled in the water. "Drink, bugger," grunted the thick man, jumping on Chad's neck. Chad ducked under water and clawed for his legs. He caught the waistband of the man's trousers and yanked. He felt the fly open and kept pulling. The trousers came down and Chad let go. The man stood there hobbled. He couldn't kick free. Chad reached out and pushed him over as easy as a rotted fence post. He went full length, mouth open, making a wide swell that lapped Chad's wishbone. Heaving a minute to get his wind back, Chad decided that he needn't bother about him. He could smell mud roiled from the bottom. As he started wading for the bank, the thick man rolled up through the water desperately hoisting his trousers and floundered towards the other shore.

111 Walter D. Edmonds, *Chad Hanna* (Boston: Little, Brown & Co., 1940), pp. 306–308. Copyright, 1940, by Walter D. Edmonds.

112 · The Mountain Whippoorwill
Or, How Hill-billy Jim Won the Great Fiddler's Prize
(A Georgia Romance)

Up in the Mountains, it's lonesome all the time,
(Sof' win' slewin' thu' the sweet-potatoe vine).

Up in the mountains, it's lonesome for a child,
(Whippoorwills a-callin' when the sap runs wild).

Up in the mountains, mountains in the fog,
Everythin's as lazy as an old houn' dog.

Born in the mountains, never raised a pet,
Don't want nuthin' an' never got it yet.

Born in the mountains, lonesome-born,
Raised runnin' ragged thu' the cockleburrs and corn.

Never knew my pappy, mebbe never should.
Think he was a fiddle made of mountain laurel-wood.

Never had a mammy to teach me pretty-please.
Think she was a whippoorwill, a-skitin' thu' the trees.

Never had a brother ner a whole pair of pants,
But when I start to fiddle, why, yuh got to start to dance!

Listen to my fiddle—Kingdom Come—Kingdom Come!
Hear the frogs a-chunkin' "Jug o' rum, Jug o' rum!"
Hear that mountain-whippoorwill be lonesome in the air,
An' I'll tell yuh how I traveled to the Essex County Fair.

Essex County has a mighty pretty fair,
All the smarty fiddlers from the South come there.

Elbows flyin' as they rosin up the bow
For the First Prize Contest in the Georgia Fiddlers' Show.

Old Dan Wheeling, with his whiskers in his ears,
King-pin fiddler for nearly twenty years.

Big Tom Sargent, with his blue wall-eye,
An' Little Jimmy Weezer that can make a fiddle cry.

All sittin' roun', spittin' high an' struttin' proud,
(*Listen, little whippoorwill, yuh better bug yore eyes!*)
Tun-a-tun tunin' while the jedges told the crowd
Them that got the mostest claps'd win the bestest prize.

Everybody waitin' for the first tweedle-dee,
When in comes a-stumblin'—hill-billy me!

Bowed right pretty to the jedges an' the rest,
Took a silver dollar from a hole inside my vest,

Plunked it on the table an' said, "There's my callin' card!
An' anyone that licks me—well, he's got to fiddle hard!"

Old Dan Wheeling, he was laughin' fit to holler,
Little Jimmy Weezer said, "There's one dead dollar!"

Big Tom Sargent had a yaller-toothy grin,
But I tucked my little whippoorwill spang underneath my chin,
An' petted it an' tuned it till the jedges said, "Begin!"

Big Tom Sargent was the first in line;
He could fiddle all the bugs off a sweet-potato vine.
He could fiddle down a possum from a mile-high tree.
He could fiddle up a whale from the bottom of the sea.

Yuh could hear hands spankin' till they spanked each other raw,
When he finished variations on "Turkey in the Straw."

Little Jimmy Weezer was the next to play;
He could fiddle all night, he could fiddle all day.

He could fiddle chills, he could fiddle fever,
He could make a fiddle rustle like a lowland river.

He could make a fiddle croon like a lovin' woman.
An' they clapped like thunder when he'd finished strummin'.

Then came the ruck of the bob-tailed fiddlers,
The let's go-easies, the fair-to-middlers.

They got their claps an' they lost their bicker,
An' settled back for some more corn-licker.

An' the crowd was tired of their no-count squealing,
When out in the center steps Old Dan Wheeling.

He fiddled high and he fiddled low,
(*Listen, little whippoorwill; yuh got to spread yore wings!*)
He fiddled with a cherrywood bow.
(*Old Dan Wheeling's got bee-honey in his strings.*)

He fiddled the wind by the lonesome moon,
He fiddled a most almighty tune.

He started fiddling like a ghost,
He ended fiddling like a host.

He fiddled north an' he fiddled south,
He fiddled the heart right out of yore mouth.

He fiddled here an' he fiddled there.
He fiddled salvation everywhere.

When he was finished, the crowd cut loose,
(*Whippoorwill, they's rain on yore breast.*)
An' I sat there wonderin', "What's the use?"
(*Whippoorwill, fly home to yore nest.*)

But I stood up pert an' I took my bow,
An' my fiddle went to my shoulder, so.

An—they wasn't no crowd to get me fazed—
But I was alone where I was raised.

Up in the mountains, so still it makes yuh skeered.
Where God lies sleepin' in his big white beard.

An' I heard the sound of the squirrel in the pine,
An' I heard the earth a-breathin' thu' the long night-time.

They've fiddled the rose an' they've fiddled the thorn,
But they haven't fiddled the mountain-corn.

They've fiddled sinful and fiddled moral,
But they haven't fiddled the breshwood-laurel.

They've fiddled loud, an' they've fiddled still,
But they haven't fiddled the whippoorwill.

I started off with a *dump-diddle-dump,*
(*Oh, Hell's broke loose in Georgia!*)
Skunk-cabbage growin' by the bee-gum-stump,
(*Whippoorwill, yo're singin' now!*)

Oh, Georgia booze is mighty fine booze,
The best yuh ever poured yuh,
But it eats the soles right offen yore shoes,
For Hell's broke loose in Georgia.

My mother was a whippoorwill pert,
My father, he was lazy,
But I'm Hell broke loose in a new store shirt
To fiddle all Georgia crazy.

Swing yore partners—up an' down the middle!
Sashay now—oh listen to that fiddle!
Flapjacks flippin' on a red-hot griddle,
An' hell broke loose,
Hell broke loose,
Fire on the mountains—snakes in the grass.
Satin's here a-bilin'—oh, Lordy, let him pass!
Go down Moses, set my people free,
Pop goes the weasel thu' the old Red Sea!
Jonah sittin' on a hickory-bough,
Up jumps a whale—an' where's yore prophet now?
Rabbit in the pea-patch, possum in the pot,
Try an' stop my fiddle, now my fiddle's gettin' hot!
Whippoorwill, singin' thu' the mountain hush,
Whippoorwill, shoutin' from the burnin' bush,
Whippoorwill, cryin' in the stable-door,
Sing to-night as yuh never sang before!
Hell's broke loose like a stompin' mountain-shoat,
Sing till yuh bust the gold in yore throat!
Hell's broke loose for forty miles aroun'
Bound to stop yore music if yuh don't sing it down.
Sing on the mountains, little whippoorwill,
Sing to the valleys, an' slap 'em with a hill,
For I'm struttin' high as an eagle's quill,
An' Hell's broke loose,
Hell's broke loose,
Hell's broke loose in Georgia!

They wasn't a sound when I stopped bowin',
(*Whippoorwill, yuh can sing no more.*)
But, somewhere or other, the dawn was growin',
(*Oh, mountain whippoorwill!*)

An' I thought, "I've fiddled all night an' lost.
Yo're a good hill-billy, but yuh've been bossed."

So I went to congratulate old man Dan,
—But he put his fiddle in my han'—
An' then the noise of the crowd began.

[112] From *Ballads and Poems: 1915–1930*. Copyright, 1931, by Stephen Vincent Benét. Reprinted by permission of Rinehart & Company, Inc., Publishers.

❖꞉❱❖꞉❱❖꞉❰❖꞉❰❖

113 · Splendour of Words

What virtue lingers in the sullen splendour
Of words! How can we covet words too highly!
The secret of some words will not surrender
To bribes or battles, that would step as shyly
As speckled young deer toward an outstretched hand
To nuzzle there with a delicious tingle
That stops the heart for breath; and some words stand
With high proud nostrils, that would sooner strangle
Than budge an inch of their uneasiness;
And some as ripe as fruit sunned in the south,
Fragrant with gold and eager to possess
A poet's passionate blood, his burning mouth;
And seldom, if at all, that perilous rhyme,
That ragged page ripped from the promptbook of Time.

[113] Joseph Auslander.

❖꞉❱❖꞉❱❖꞉❰❖꞉❰❖

114 · Those Names Are Words in Stone

We are not gathered to mourn the dead. Their passing has been marked by the tears of mothers and fathers. We can only see, not share that anguish. Nor do we gather to honor the dead. In death they achieved an honor which the living cannot embellish by word or by ceremony or by sign.

Peoples and institutions, above all colleges, live by their memories, their hopes, their faith. We are gathered to refresh our memories, to renew our hopes, to reaffirm our faith.

Names have been cut into marble and cast in bronze. Names, they are, one may say, which for a short moment are meaningful to classmates and to friends who soon depart, names which become quickly only anonymous lists at which the curious stare.

Yet architects and workmen wrote more than they knew. Between the lines in the lists, unwittingly, they etched our memories, our hopes, and our faith.

Adams, Bancroft, Bronson. Morrison, Otis, Porter. Such names, and there are many more, evoke memories of our country's long and honorable past, of old crises and tribulations, always surmounted. They remind us that we are the beneficiaries of a heritage bought not only by blood, but by the sweat and toil and devotion of generations, a heritage not to be accepted lightly but only with the hope that, by the fulfillment of our duty, it can be maintained unimpaired.

Adelman, Danowski, Levin. Andrews, Gallagher, O'Keefe. These cannot be read as but names. They symbolize the magic amalgam that is America. They remind us that we have drawn our strength from the corners of the earth; that the venturesome and unafraid have come to us and become of us; that oppressed men have sought here liberty and opportunity and that they have not been disappointed.

Biddle, Carey, Chickering. Rabinovitz, Scholtz, Siegel. Are these mere names? Not at all. They are words in stone which recall that we have lived, and now live, by a faith in liberty and equality. They remind us that our hopes, ever approached, never attained, are goals that give us courage and guidance. And they destroy the pretensions of those of little faith who would call the American dream only a mad fantasy.

Crawford, Hungerford, MacDougal. Frankenthal, McMullen, Randolph. What titles did they carry? Colonel and second lieutenant. Cadet and lieutenant-commander. Captain and machinist's mate. Apprentice seaman and private. We are reminded that we gain strength in the achievement of our great purposes by each contributing according to his ability; indeed, that it is the genius of a free people to clear the way for each to give his best to the common cause. And we recall that once the anger of debate is dissolved by decision we are accustomed to act together, united by the firm will of democratic discipline, be it a matter of war or peace.

Irwin, Morton, Schumann. Dugan, Newcomb, Waldman. Where did they fall? Aachen and the Argonne. Bremen and Subic Bay. Cambrai and New Caledonia. Chateau-Thierry and Corregidor. Tunisia and the Coral Sea. Verdun and Mindanao. Thus is written in stone our fearful power, a power pyramiding up from the mines of Minnesota, the arsenals of Connecticut, the fields of Nebraska, the refineries of Oklahoma, the furnaces of Pittsburgh, and the men and women of America. We recall that we command our destiny.

Architects and workmen wrote more than they knew. Little reveries etched imperceptibly into stone between the lines fade and form, gradually grow and transform themselves into a mighty epic.

Adams, Adelman, Biddle. Carey, Crawford, Danowski. Dugan, Gallagher, Hungerford. MacDougal, Morrison, O'Keefe. Porter, Randolph, Schumann—our memories, our hopes, our faith.

[114] Armistice Day address by V. O. Key, Jr., delivered at Yale University, New Haven, Connecticut, November 11, 1949. *Vital Speeches of the Day* (December 1, 1949), XVI, No. 4, 114–115.

❖⟩❖⟩❖⟨❖⟨❖

115 · American Names

I have fallen in love with American names,
The sharp names that never get fat,
The snakeskin-titles of mining-claims,
The plumed war-bonnet of Medicine Hat,
Tucson and Deadwood and Lost Mule Flat.

Seine and Piave are silver spoons,
But the spoonbowl-metal is thin and worn,
There are English counties like hunting-tunes
Played on the keys of a postboy's horn,
But I will remember where I was born.

I will remember Carquinez Straits,
Little French Lick and Lundy's Lane,
The Yankee ships and the Yankee dates
And the bullet-towns of Calamity Jane.
I will remember Skunktown Plain.

I will fall in love with a Salem tree
And a rawhide quirt from Santa Cruz,
I will get me a bottle of Boston sea
And a blue-gum nigger to sing me blues.
I am tired of loving a foreign muse.

Rue des Martyrs and Bleeding-Heart-Yard,
Senlis, Pisa, and Blindman's Oast,

It is a magic you guard
But I am sick for a newer ghost,
Harrisburg, Spartanburg, Painted Post.

Henry and John were never so
And Henry and John were always right?
Granted, but when it was time to go
And the tea and the laurels had stood all night,
Did they never watch for Nantucket Light?

I shall not rest quiet in Montparnasse.
I shall not lie easy at Winchelsea.
You may bury my body in Sussex grass,
You may bury my tongue at Champmedy.
I shall not be there. I shall rise and pass.
Bury my heart at Wounded Knee.

[115] From *Ballads and Poems: 1915–1930*. Copyright, 1931, by Stephen Vincent Benét. Reprinted by permission of Rinehart & Company, Inc., Publishers.

116 · British Names

The Stanegate is a road which runs from Carlisle along the north bank of the Eden by Low and High Crosby to Irthington, where it crosses the Irthing and passes close by a fort at Brampton Old Church; passing another fort at Easby, it travels up the left bank of the Irthing to another at Nether Denton and another at Throp, close to Gilsland, whence it climbs to the heights north of the Tyne valley to forts at Carvoran, Haltwhistle Burn, Chesterholm and Newbrough. After this its course is uncertain. It may cross the North Tyne near Chester; it may continue down the valley to Corbridge.

[116] *Roman Britain and the English Settlements,* by R. G. Collingwood and J. N. L. Myres. Reprinted by permission of Oxford University Press, Inc.

117 · Jewish Worship

READER
Hear, O Israel; The Lord our God, the Lord is One.

Praised be His name whose glorious kingdom is forever and ever.

(Congregation is seated)

CONGREGATION AND READER

Thou shalt love the Lord, thy God, with all thy heart, with all thy soul, and with all thy might. And these words, which I command thee this day, shall be upon thy heart. Thou shalt teach them diligently unto thy children, and shalt speak of them when thou sittest in thy house, when thou walkest by the way, when thou liest down, and when thou risest up. Thou shalt bind them for a sign upon thy hand, and they shall be for frontlets between thine eyes. Thou shalt write them upon the doorposts of thy house and upon thy gates: That ye may remember and do all My commandments and be holy unto your God.

RESPONSIVE READING

READER

True and enduring is Thy Word which Thou hast spoken through Thy prophets.

CONGREGATION

Thou art the living God, Thy words bring life and light to the soul.

Thou art the strength of our life, the rock of our salvation; Thy kingdom and Thy trust abide forever.

Thou hast been the help of our fathers in time of trouble and art our refuge in all generations.

Thou art the first and the last, and besides Thee there is no redeemer nor helper.

As Thou hast saved Israel from Egyptian bondage, so mayest Thou send Thy help to all who are oppressed.

May Thy law rule in the hearts of all Thy children, and Thy truth unite them in bonds of fellowship.

May the righteous of all nations rejoice in Thy grace and triumph by Thy power.

O God, who art our refuge and our hope, we glorify Thy name now as did our fathers in ancient days:

CHOIR

Who is like unto Thee, O Lord? Who is like unto Thee, glorious in Holiness, awe-inspiring, working wonders?

READER

A new song the redeemed sang unto Thy name.

They proclaimed Thy sovereignty and said:

CHOIR

The Lord shall reign forever and ever.

READER

O Rock of Israel, redeem those who are oppressed and deliver those who are persecuted. Praised be Thou, our Redeemer, the Holy One of Israel.

CHOIR

Amen.

[117] *The Union Prayerbook for Jewish Worship* (Cincinnati: The Central Conference of American Rabbis, 1940), p. 316.

❖❖❖❖❖❖❖

118 · Queen Mab

O, then, I see Queen Mab hath been with you.
She is the fairies' midwife, and she comes
In shape no bigger than an agate-stone
On the fore-finger of an alderman,
Drawn with a team of little atomies
Athwart men's noses as they lie asleep:
Her wagon-spokes made of long spinners' legs;
The cover of the wings of grasshoppers,
The traces of the smallest spider's web,
The collars of the moonshine's watery beams,
Her whip of cricket's bone, the lash of film,
Her waggoner a small grey-coated gnat,
Not half so big as a round little worm
Prick'd from the lazy finger of a maid,
Her chariot is an empty hazel-nut
Made by the joiner squirrel, or old grub,
Time out o' mind the fairies' coachmakers.
And in this state she gallops night by night
Through lovers' brains, and then they dream of love;
O'er courtiers' knees, that dream on curt'sies straight;
O'er lawyers' fingers, who straight dream on fees;
O'er ladies' lips, who straight on kisses dream,
Which oft the angry Mab with blisters plagues
Because their breaths with sweetmeats tainted are.
Sometimes she gallops o'er a courtier's nose,
And then dreams he of smelling out a suit;
And sometimes comes she with a tithe-pig's tail,
Tickling a parson's nose as a' lies asleep,
Then he dreams of another benefice.
Sometimes she driveth o'er a soldier's neck,
And then dreams he of cutting foreign throats,

Of breaches, ambuscadoes, Spanish blades,
Of healths five-fathom deep; and then anon
Drums in his ear, at which he starts and wakes,
And, being thus frighted, swears a prayer or two,
And sleeps again.

118 William Shakespeare, *Romeo and Juliet.*

❖❖❖❖❖❖❖❖

119 · There Was a Child Went Forth

There was a child went forth every day,
And the first object he look'd upon, that object he became,
And that object became part of him for the day or a certain part
of the day,
Or for many years or stretching cycles of years.

The early lilacs became part of this child,
And grass and white and red morning-glories, and white and red
clover, and the song of the phoebe-bird,
And the Third-month lambs and the sow's pink-faint litter, and
the mare's foal and cow's calf,
And the noisy brood of the barnyard or by the mire of the pond-
side,
And the fish suspending themselves so curiously below there,
and the beautiful curious liquid,
And the water-plants with their graceful flat heads, all became
part of him.

The field-sprouts of Fourth-month and Fifth-month became part
of him,
Winter-grain sprouts and those of the light-yellow corn, and the
esculent roots of the garden,
And the apple-trees cover'd with blossoms and the fruit afterward, and wood-berries, and the commonest weeds by the
road,
And the old drunkard staggering home from the outhouse of the
tavern whence he had lately risen,
And the schoolmistress that pass'd on her way to the school,
And the friendly boys that pass'd, and the quarrelsome boys,
And the tidy and fresh-cheek'd girls, and the barefoot negro boy
and girl,

And all the changes of city and country wherever he went.

His own parents, he that had father'd him and she that had con-
ceiv'd him in her womb and birth'd him,

They gave this child more of themselves than that,

They gave him afterward every day, they became part of him.

The mother at home quietly placing the dishes on the supper-
table,

The mother with mild words, clean her cap and gown, a wholesome odor falling off her person and clothes as she walks by

The father, strong, self-sufficient, manly, mean, anger'd, unjust,

The blow, the quick loud word, the tight bargain, the crafty lure,

The family usages, the language, the company, the furniture, the
yearning and swelling heart,

Affection that will not be gainsay'd, the sense of what is real, the
thought if after all it should prove unreal,

The doubts of day-time and the doubts of night-time, the curious
whether and how,

Whether that which appears so is so, or is it all flashes and
specks?

Men and women crowding fast in the streets, if they are not
flashes and specks what are they?

The streets themselves and the facades of houses, and goods in
the windows,

Vehicles, teams, the heavy-plank'd wharves, the huge crossing
at the ferries,

The village on the highland seen from afar at sunset, the river
between,

Shadows, aureola and mist, the light falling on roofs and gables
of white or brown two miles off,

The schooner near by sleepily dropping down the tide, the little
boat slack-tow'd astern,

The hurrying tumbling waves, quick-broken crests, slapping,

The strata of color'd clouds, the long bar of maroon-tint away
solitary by itself, the spread of purity it lies motionless in,

The horizon's edge, the flying sea-crow, the fragrance of salt
marsh and shore mud,

These became part of that child who went forth every day, and
who now goes, and will always go forth every day.

[119] Walt Whitman, "There Was a Child Went Forth," *Leaves of Grass* (1855).

❖⫸⫸⫸❖⊰⊰❖⊰❖

120 · A Ball of Fire

A ball of fire falls on the lead of the roof, and the sky tears apart on a spike of flame. Up the spire, behind the lacings of stone, zigzagging in and out of the carved tracings, squirms the fire. It spouts like yellow wheat from the gargoyles, coils around the head of Saint John, and aureoles him in light. It leaps into the night and hisses against the rain. The Cathedral is a burning stain on the white, wet night.

. . . Quivering, spearing, thrusting, lapping, streaming, run the flames. Over roofs, and walls, and shops, and stalls. Smearing the gold on the sky, the fire dances, lances itself through the doors, and lisps and chuckles along the floors . . . . The little red lips of flame creep along the ceiling beams.

[120] Amy Lowell, *Men, Women, and Ghosts* (Boston: Houghton Mifflin Company, 1916), pp. 231–233

❖⊃❖⊃❖◅《◅❖《◅❖

121 · My Uncle's Farm

It was a heavenly place for a boy, that farm of my uncle John's. The house was a double log one, with a spacious floor (roofed in) connecting it with the kitchen. In the summer the table was set in the middle of that shady and breezy floor, and the sumptuous meals—well, it makes me cry to think of them. Fried chicken, roast pig; wild and tame turkeys, ducks, and geese; venison just killed; squirrels, rabbits, pheasants, partridges, prairie-chickens; biscuits, hot batter cakes, hot buckwheat cakes, hot "wheat bread," hot rolls, hot corn pone; fresh corn boiled on the ear, succotash, butter-beans, string-beans, tomatoes, peas, Irish potatoes, sweet potatoes; buttermilk, sweet milk, "clabber"; watermelons, muskmelons, cantaloupes—all fresh from the garden; apple pie, peach pie, pumpkin pie, apple dumplings, peach cobbler—I can't remember the rest.

[121] Samuel L. Clemens, *Mark Twain's Autobiography* (New York: Harper & Brothers, 1924), I, 96. Copyright, 1924, by Clara Gabrilowitsch. Copyright, 1952, by Clara Clemens Samossoud.

❖⊃❖⊃❖◅《◅❖《◅❖

122 · The Poetry of Dress

A sweet disorder in the dress
Kindles in clothes a wantoness—

A lawn about the shoulders thrown
Into a fine distraction,—
An erring lace, which here and there
Enthrals the crimson stomacher,—
A cuff neglectful, and thereby
Ribbands to flow confusedly—

A winning wave, deserving note,
In the tempestuous petticoat,—
A careless shoe-string, in whose tie
I see a wild civility,—
Do more bewitch me, than when art
Is too precise in every part.

[122] Robert Herrick, "Delight in Disorder," *Hesperides* (1648).

✧⟩✦⟩✦⬗⟨⬖⟨⬖⟨✦

123 · The Gong

The gong glimmered pale and huge and yellow, like the moon rising over a southern swamp. My friend tapped its ancient face with a muffled drum-stick, and it commenced to sob, like waves upon a low beach. He tapped it again and it moaned like the wind in a mighty forest of pines. Again, and it commenced to roar, and with each tap the roar grew deeper and deeper, till it seemed like thunder rolling over an abyss in the Cordilleras, or the crashing of Thor's chariot wheels. It was awful, and astonishing as awful. I assure you I did not laugh at it at all. It impressed me as something terrible and mysterious. I vainly sought to understand how that thin, thin disk of trembling metal could produce so frightful a vibration.

[123] Elizabeth Bisland, ed., *Life and Letters of Lafcadio Hearn* (Boston: Houghton Mifflin Company, 1906), I, 172.

✧⟩✦⟩✦⬗⟨⬖⟨⬖⟨✦

124 · The Nightmare

The night stifled;—the air seemed to be coagulating. The single large window, overlooking a garden, had been left open,—but there was no movement in that atmosphere. Bats—very large bats,—flew soundlessly in and out;—one actually fanning my face with its wings as it circled over the bed. Heavy scents of ripe fruit—nauseously sweet—rose from the garden, where palms and plantains stood still as if made of metal. From the woods above the town stormed the usual night-chorus of tree-frogs, insects, and nocturnal birds,—a tumult not to be accurately described by any simile, but suggesting, through numberless sharp tinkling tones, the fancy of a wide slow cataract of broken glass. I tossed and turned on the hot hard bed, vainly trying to find one spot a little cooler than the rest. Then I rose, drew a rocking-chair to the window and lighted a cigar. The smoke hung motionless; after each puff, I had to blow it away. My man had ceased to snore. The bronze of his naked breast—shining with moisture under the faint light of the shrine-lamp, showed no movement of respiration. He might have been a corpse. The heavy heat seemed always to become heavier. At last, utterly exhausted, I went back to bed, and slept.

It must have been well after midnight when I felt the first vague uneasiness,—*the suspicion,*—that precedes a nightmare. I was half-conscious, dream-conscious of the actual,—knew myself in that very room, wanted to get up. Immediately the uneasiness grew into terror, because I found that I could not move. Something unutterable in the air was mastering will. I tried to cry out, and my utmost effort resulted only in a whisper too low for any one to hear. Simultaneously I became aware of a Step ascending the stair,—a muffled heaviness; and the real nightmare began,—the horror of the ghastly magnetism that held voice and limb,— the hopeless will-struggle against dumbness and impotence. The stealthy Step approached,—but with lentor malevolently measured,—slowly, slowly, as if the stairs were miles deep. It gained the threshold,—waited. Gradually then, and without sound, the locked door opened; and the Thing entered, bending as it came,—a thing robed,—feminine,—reaching to the roof,— not to be looked at! A floor-plank creaked as It neared the bed;— and then—with a frantic effort—I woke, bathed in sweat; my heart beating as if it were going to burst. The shrine-light had died; in the blackness I could see nothing; but I thought I heard that Step retreating. I certainly heard the plank creak again. With the panic still upon me, I was actually unable to stir. The wisdom of striking a match occurred to me, but I dared not yet rise. Presently, as I held my breath to listen, a new wave of black fear passed through me; for I heard moanings,—long nightmare moanings;—moanings that seemed to be answering each other from two different rooms below. And then, close to me, my guide began to moan,— hoarsely, hideously.

[124] Lafcadio Hearn, *Exotics and Retrospectives* (Boston: Little, Brown & Co., 1919), pp. 281–283.

❧❧❧❧❧❧

125 · The Twenty-third Psalm

The Lord is my shepherd; I shall not want.

He maketh me to lie down in green pastures: he leadeth me beside the still waters.

He restoreth my soul: he leadeth me in the paths of righteousness for his name's sake.

Yea, though I walk through the valley of the shadow of death, I will fear no evil: for thou art with me; thy rod and thy staff they comfort me.

Thou preparest a table before me in the presence of mine enemies: thou anointest my head with oil; my cup runneth over.

Surely goodness and mercy shall follow me all the days of my life: and I will dwell in the house of the Lord for ever.

125 *The Holy Bible,* Psalm 23.

❖❖❖❖❖❖❖

126 · Spring

Spring came; the pines thrust brilliant new green spray above the sober old green leaves, the last cones fell softly bouncing to the ground, slim white candle blossoms reached up to the sun; below, the dogwood opened in a silver mist, songsparrows bustled and twittered in the thorns. Vixens, heavy with cub, withdrew to the dark swamps. The first young rabbits frolicked in the dusk. The vulture now hung interminably against the blue, peering in vain for signs of death in a land where life was now renewed and beauty born again.

126 James Boyd, *Drums* (New York: Charles Scribner's Sons, 1925), p. 40.

❖❖❖❖❖❖❖

127 · Sunrise

I had myself called with the four-o'clock watch, mornings, for one cannot see too many summer sunrises on the Mississippi. They are enchanting. First, there is the eloquence of silence; for a deep hush broods everywhere. Next, there is the haunting sense of loneliness, isolation, remoteness from the worry and bustle of the world. The dawn creeps in stealthily; the solid walls of black forest soften to gray, and vast stretches of the river open up and reveal themselves; the water is glass-smooth, gives off spectral little wreaths of white mist, there is not the faintest breath of wind, nor stir of leaf; the tranquility is profound and infinitely satisfying. Then a bird pipes up, another follows, and soon the pipings develop into a jubilant riot of music. You see none of the birds; you simply move through an atmosphere of song which seems to sing itself. When the light has become a little stronger, you have one of the fairest and softest pictures imaginable. You have the intense green of the shade in front of you; upon the next projecting cape, a mile off or more, the tint has lightened to the tender young green of spring; the cape beyond that one has almost lost color, and the furthest one, miles away under the horizon, sleeps upon the water a mere dim vapor, and hardly separable from the sky above it and about it. And all this stretch of river is a mirror, and you have the shadowy reflections of the leafage and the curving shores and the receding capes pictured in it. Well, that is all beautiful; soft and rich and beautiful; and when the sun gets well up, and distributes a pink flush here and a powder of gold yonder and a purple haze where it will yield the best effect, you grant that you have seen something that is worth remembering.

[127] Samuel L. Clemens, *Life on the Mississippi* (New York: Harper & Brothers, 1907), pp. 258–259.

❖❖❖❖❖❖❖❖

128 · I Shall Not Care

When I am dead and over me bright April
    Shakes out her rain-drenched hair,
Though you should lean above me broken-hearted,
    I shall not care.

I shall have peace, as leafy trees are peaceful
    Where rain bends the bough;
And I shall be more silent and cold-hearted
    Than you are now.

[128] From Sara Teasdale, *Rivers to the Sea*. Copyright, 1915, by The Macmillan Company and used with their permission.

❖❖❖❖❖❖❖❖

129 · June

June was my favorite month at the farm, for there was a great crested flycatcher's nest in the apple tree by the pond, red roses from Colchester, Connecticut, were in blossom by the old cellar hole where they had been planted a hundred years earlier, red-winged blackbirds nested in the rushes, red-fins darted in the tiny brook, and east of the Stone Hill road, in a grove where Williams students now hunt for golf balls sliced from the first tee, there was then a nest of the very rare yellow-billed cuckoo. There would be young partridges on Stone Hill by June, and always the chance of seeing a fox.

[129] Bliss Perry, *And Gladly Teach* (Boston: Houghton Mifflin Company, 1935), p. 18.

130 · The Landscape near an Aerodrome

More beautiful and soft than any moth
With burring furred antennae feeling its huge path
Through dusk, the air-liner with shut-off engines
Glides over suburbs and the sleeves set trailing tall
To point the wind. Gently, broadly, she falls
Scarcely disturbing charted currents of air.

Lulled by descent, the travellers across sea
And across feminine land indulging its easy limbs
In miles of softness, now let their eyes trained by watching
Penetrate through dusk the outskirts of this town
Here where industry shows a fraying edge.
Here they may see what is being done.

Beyond the winking masthead light
And the landing-ground, they observe the outposts
Of work: chimneys like lank black fingers
Or figures frightening and mad: and squat buildings
With their strange air behind trees, like women's faces
Shattered by grief. Here where few houses
Moan with faint light behind their blinds
They remark the unhomely sense of complaint, like a dog
Shut out and shivering at the foreign moon.

In the last sweep of love, they pass over fields
Behind the aerodrome, where boys play all day
Hacking dead grass: whose cries, like wild birds,
Settle upon the nearest roofs
But soon are hid under the loud city.

Then, as they land, they hear the tolling bell
Reaching across the landscape of hysteria
To where, larger than all the charcoaled batteries
And imaged towers against that dying sky,
Religion stands, the church blocking the sun.

[130] Stephen Spender, *Poems,* pp. 55–56. Reprinted by permission of Random House, Inc. Copyright, 1934, by Modern Library, Inc. Reprinted also by permission of Faber and Faber, Ltd.

❖❖❖❖❖❖❖❖❖

131 · Ploughing

The ploughs, thirty-five in number, each drawn by its team of ten, stretched in an interminable line, nearly a quarter of a mile in length . . . . A prolonged movement rippled from team to team, disengaging in its passage a multitude of sounds—the click of buckles, the creak of straining leather, the subdued clash of machinery, the cracking of whips, the deep breathing of nearly four hundred horses, the abrupt commands and cries of the drivers, and, last of all, the prolonged, soothing murmur of the thick brown earth turning steadily from the multitude of advancing shears . . . .

The ploughing, now in full swing, enveloped him in a vague, slow-moving whirl of things. Underneath him was the jarring, jolting, trembling machine; not a clod was turned, not an obstacle encountered, that he did not receive the swift impression of it through all his body, the very friction of the damp soil, sliding incessantly from the shiny surface of the shears, seemed to reproduce itself in his finger-tips and along the back of his head. He heard the horse-hoofs by the myriads crushing down easily, deeply, into the loam, the prolonged clinking of trace-chains, the working of the smooth brown flanks in the harness, the clatter of wooden hames, the champing of bits, the click of iron shoes against pebbles, the brittle stubble of the surface ground crackling and snapping as the furrows turned, the sonorous, steady breaths wrenched from the deep, laboring chests, strap-bound, shining with sweat, and all along the line the voices of the men talking to the horses. Everywhere there were visions of glossy brown backs, straining, heaving, swollen with muscle; harness streaked with specks of froth, broad, cup-shaped hoofs, heavy with brown loam, men's faces red with tan, blue overalls spotted with axle-grease; muscled hands, the knuckles whitened in their grip on the reins, and through it all the ammoniacal smell of the horses, the bitter reek of perspiration of beasts and men, the aroma of warm leather, the scent of dead stubble—and stronger and more penetrating than everything else, the heavy, enervating odour of the upturned, living earth.

[131] Frank Norris, *The Octopus* (New York: Doubleday & Co., Inc., 1930), pp. 122–125.

❖❱❱❱❱❱❖❰❰❖❰❰❖

132 · The Golden World

He had heard already the ringing of remote church bells over a countryside on Sunday night; had listened to the earth steeped in the brooding symphony of dark, and the million-noted little night things; and he had heard thus the far retreating wail of a whistle in a distant valley, and faint thunder on the rails; and he felt the infinite depth and width of the golden world in the brief seductions of a thousand multiplex and mixed mysterious odors and sensations, weaving, with a blinding interplay and aural explosions, one into the other.

He remembered yet the East India Tea House at the Fair, the sandal-wood, the turbans, and the robes, the cool interior and the smell of India tea; and he had felt now the nostalgic thrill of dew-wet mornings in Spring, the cherry scent, the cool clarion earth, the wet loaminess of the garden, the pungent breakfast smells and the floating snow of blossoms.

[132] Thomas Wolfe, *Look Homeward, Angel* (New York: Charles Scribner's Sons, 1929), p. 84

❖❱❱❱❱❱❖❰❰❖❰❰❖

133 · The Kitchen

Off to the westward, as I climbed, the roof of our own house came into sight, short in front, long in back to make room for the kitchen. I could smell that kitchen now—the odor of shoe-blacking in one corner, where the four-legged hinged box had stood, covered with old carpeting, harsh on the knuckles, on which we brushed our muddy shoes; the smell of pine and birch wood from another corner, where a door, covered with gray gauze to keep out flies, led to the woodshed, grape arbor and barn; the scent of spices, cookies and new bread from the third corner, where a door opened into the pantry—that dangerous and delicious room rich in crocks filled with doughnuts and cookies, pans of milk topped with yellow cream, jugs of maple syrup, jars of mincemeat, and a sugar barrel with a scoop that held a mouthful of sugar—if one had as large a mouth as mine.

[133] Kenneth Roberts, *Oliver Wiswell* (New York: Doubleday & Co., Inc., 1940), p. 812.

❖⟩❖⟩❖❖❖❖❖

134 · July Night

Now at least the moon is full, and I walk alone, which is best by night, if not by day always. Your companion must sympathize with the present mood. The conversation must be located where the walkers are, and vary exactly with the scene and events and the contour of the ground. Farewell to those who will talk of nature unnaturally, whose presence is an interruption . . . .

I start a sparrow from her three eggs in the grass, where she had settled for the night. The earliest corn is beginning to show its tassels now, and I scent it as I walk,—its peculiar dry scent. (This afternoon I gathered ripe blackberries, and felt as if the autumn had commenced.) Now perchance many sounds and sights only remind me that they once said something to me, and are so by association interesting. I go forth to be reminded of a previous state of existence, if perchance any memento of it is to be met with hereabouts. I have no doubt that Nature preserves her integrity. Nature is in as rude health as when Homer sang. We may at last by our sympathies be well. I see a skunk on Bear Garden Hill stealing noiselessly away from me, while the moon shines over the pitch pines, which send long shadows down the hill. Now, looking back, I see it shining on the south side of farmhouses and barns with a weird light, for I pass here half an hour later than last night. I smell the huckleberry bushes. I hear a human voice,—some laborer singing after his day's toil,—which I do not often hear. Loud it must be, for it is far away. Methinks I should know it for a white man's voice. Some strains have the melody of an instrument. Now I hear the sound of a bugle in the 'Corner,' reminding me of poetic wars; a few flourishes and the bugler has gone to rest. At the foot of the Cliff hill I hear the sound of the clock striking nine, as distinctly as within a quarter of a mile usually, though there is no wind. The moonlight is more perfect than last night; hardly a cloud in the sky,—only a few fleecy ones. There is more serenity and more light. I hear that sort of throttled or chuckling note as of a bird flying high, now from this side, then from that. Methinks when I turn my head I see Wachusett from the side of the hill. I smell the butter-and-eggs as I walk. I am startled by the rapid transit of some wild animal across my path, a rabbit or a fox,—or you hardly know if it be not a bird. Looking down from the cliffs, the leaves of the tree-tops shine more than ever by day. Here and there a lightning-bug shows his greenish light over the tops of the trees.

As I return through the orchard, a foolish robin bursts away from his perch unnaturally, with the habits of man. The air is remarkably still and unobjectionable on the hill-top, and the whole world below is covered as with a gossamer blanket of moonlight. It is just about as yellow as a blanket. It is a great dimly burnished shield with darker blotches on its surface. You have lost some light, it is true, but you have got this simple and magnificent stillness, brooding like genius.

[134] Henry David Thoreau, *Journal,* July 12, 1851.

❧❧❧❧❧❧❧❧

135 · Concert in the Park

Another hot night I stop off at the Goldman Band concert in the Mall in Central Park. The people seated on the benches fanned out in front of the band shell are attentive, appreciative. In the trees the night wind stirs, bringing the leaves to life, endowing them with speech; the electric lights illuminate the green branches from the under side, translating them into a new language. Overhead a plane passes dreamily, its running lights winking. On the bench directly in front of me, a boy sits with his arm around his girl; they are proud of each other and are swathed in music. The cornetist steps forward for a solo, begins, "Drink to me only with thine eyes . . . ." In the wide, warm night the horn is startlingly pure and magical. Then from the North River another horn solo begins—the *Queen Mary* announcing her intentions. She is not on key; she is a half tone off. The trumpeter in the bandstand never flinches. The horns quarrel savagely, but no one minds having the intimation of travel injected into the pledge of love. "I leave," sobs Mary. "And I will pledge with mine," sighs the trumpeter. Along the asphalt paths strollers pass to and fro; they behave considerately, respecting the musical atmosphere. Popsicles are moving well. In the warm grass beyond the fence, forms wriggle in the shadows, and the skirts of the girls approaching on the Mall are ballooned by the breeze, and their bare shoulders catch the lamplight. "Drink to me only with thine eyes." It is a magical occasion, and it's all free.

[135] E. B. White, *Here Is New York* (New York: Harper & Brothers, 1949), p. 35. Copyright, 1949, by The Curtis Publishing Company.

❧❧❧❧❧❧❧❧

136 · August

Why should this Negro insolently stride
Down the red noonday on such noiseless feet?
Piled in his barrow, tawnier than wheat,
Lie heaps of smouldering daisies, sombre-eyed,
Their copper petals shrivelled up with pride,
Hot with a superfluity of heat,
Like a great brazier borne along the street
By captive leopards, black and burning pied.

Are there no water-lillies, smooth as cream,
With long stems dripping crystal? Are there none
Like those white lillies, luminous and cool,
Plucked from some hemlock-darkened northern stream
By fair-haired swimmers, diving where the sun
Scarce warms the surface of the deepest pool?

[136] Reprinted from *Collected Poems of Elinor Wylie*. By permission of Alfred A.
Knopf, Inc. Copyright, 1921, 1932, by Alfred A. Knopf, Inc.

❖⟫❖⟫❖❖❰❖❰❖

137 · August Third

Those there are who are annoyed or repelled (or they affect to be),
by what they call lush or extravagant beauty. They will enjoy nothing
but the bleakest of New England scenery—a few hard-bitten pastures,
a rocky wall, a moth-eaten hill that is neither a bold mountain nor a
stirring plain, and a stern and paintless old house.

Of this company I do not make one. If it is shallow not to be able
to see beauty in the austere, it is monkish, parsimonious and timid to
despise the lavish and complex beauty of life reaching its full expression.
I liked what little I ever saw of the tropics, and the fact that I was born
in a region where Nature was economical of her colors and form begets
in me no sentimental feelings about such scenes.

I love the southern landscape, and I love it in summer only a little
less than in spring. The South, in winter, is mild enough, but it is little
more; it is simply not itself. You probably do not know Labrador until
you have lived a winter in it, and to taste the undiluted wine of a hot
country, you should see it through a summer. I live in that intemperate
zone that is icy in winter and flaming in summer; it blends the tastes of
north and south.

And in summer the tropical element in it comes out. Now the heat shimmers above the marshes; it dances over the hills in a haze, engulfs the cool old houses as if they were islands on the landscape. Everywhere the deep blue green of heavy foliage is in full summer splendor; on all the pools the jade green sargassos of the duckweed stretch away across the stagnant water; in the breathless nights the whippoorwill complains, it has been said, that "It is so still, so still, so still!"

[137] From *An Almanac for Moderns,* by Donald Culross Peattie. Copyright, 1935, by Donald Culross Peattie. Courtesy of G. P. Putnam's Sons.

138 · Thanksgiving Day Proclamation

As the colors of Autumn stream down the wind, scarlet in sumach and maple, spun gold in the birches, a splendor of smoldering fire in the oaks along the hill, and the last leaves flutter away, and dusk falls briefly about the worker bringing in from the field a late load of its fruit, and Arcturus is lost to sight and Orion swings upward that great sun on his shoulder, we are stirred once more to ponder the Infinite Goodness that has set apart for us, in all this moving mystery of creation, a time of living and a home. In such a spirit I appoint Thursday, the twenty-fourth of November, a day of Public Thanksgiving. In such a spirit I call upon the people to acknowledge heartily, in friendly gathering and house of prayer, the increase of the season nearing now its close; the harvest of earth, the yield of patient mind and faithful hand, that have kept us fed and clothed and have made for us a shelter even against the storm. It is right that we whose arc of sky has been darkened by no war hawk, who have been forced by no man to stand and speak when to speak was to choose between death and life, should give thanks also for the further mercies we have enjoyed, beyond desert or any estimation, of Justice, Freedom, Loving-kindness, Peace-resolving, as we prize them, to let no occasion go without some prompting or some effort worthy in a way however humble of those proudest among man's ideals which burn, though it may be like candles fitfully in our gusty world, with a light so clear we name its source divine.

[138] Governor Wilbur L. Cross, "Proclamation for a Day of Public Thanksgiving," *Collier's,* Vol. 102, No. 21 (November 19, 1938).

139 · October

October is the richest of the seasons: the fields are cut, the granaries are full, the bins are loaded to the brim with fatness, and from the cider-press the rich brown oozings of the York Imperials run. The bee bores to the belly of the yellowed grape, the fly gets old and fat and blue, he buzzes loud, crawls slow, creeps heavily to death on sill and ceiling, the sun goes down in blood and pollen across the bronzed and mown fields of old October.

The corn is shocked: it sticks out in hard yellow rows upon dried ears, fit now for great red barns in Pennsylvania, and the big stained teeth of crunching horses. The indolent hooves kick swiftly at the boards, the barn is sweet with hay and leather, wood and apples—this, and the clean dry crunching of the teeth is all: the sweat, the labor, and the plow is over. The late pears mellow on a sunny shelf; smoked hams hang to the warped barn rafters; the pantry shelves are loaded with 300 jars of fruit. Meanwhile the leaves are turning, turning, up in Maine, the chestnut burrs plop thickly to the earth in gusts of wind, and in Virginia the chinkapins are falling.

There is a smell of burning in small towns in afternoon, and men with buckles on their arms are raking leaves in yards as boys come by with straps slung back across their shoulders. The oak leaves, big and brown, are bedded deep in yard and gutter: they make deep wadings to the knee for children in the streets. The fire will snap and crackle like a whip, sharp acrid smoke will sting the eyes, in mown fields the little vipers of the flame eat past the black coarse edges of burned stubble like a line of locusts. Fire drives a thorn of memory in the heart.

The bladed grass, a forest of small spears of ice, is thawed by noon: summer is over but the sun is warm again, and there are days throughout the land of gold and russet. But summer is dead and gone, the earth is waiting, suspense and ecstasy are gnawing at the hearts of men, the brooding prescience of frost is there. The sun flames red and bloody as it sets, there are old red glintings on the battered pails, the great barn gets the ancient light as the boy slops homeward with warm foaming milk. Great shadows lengthen in the fields, the old red light dies swiftly, and the sunset barking of the hounds is faint and far and full of frost: there are shrewd whistles to the dogs, and frost and silence—this is all. Wind stirs and scuffs and rattles up the old brown leaves, and through the night the great oak leaves keep falling.

Trains cross the continent in a swirl of dust and thunder, the leaves fly down the tracks behind them: the great trains cleave through gulch and gully, they rumble with spoked thunder on the bridges over the powerful brown wash of mighty rivers, they toil through hills, they skirt the rough brown stubble of shorn fields, they whip past empty stations in the little towns and their great stride pounds its even pulse across America. Field and hill and lift and gulch and hollow, mountain and plain and river, a wilderness with fallen trees across it, a thicket of bedded brown and twisted undergrowth, a plain, a desert, and a plantation, a mighty landscape with no fenced niceness, an immensity of fold and convolution that can never be remembered, that can never be forgotten, that has never been described—weary with harvest, potent with every fruit and ore, the immeasurable richness embrowned with autumn, rank, crude, unharnessed, careless of scars or beauty, everlasting and magnificent, a cry, a space, an ecstasy!—American earth in old October.

And the great winds howl and swoop across the land: they make a distant roaring in great trees, and boys in bed will stir in ecstasy, thinking of demons and vast swoopings through the earth. All through the night there is the clean, the bitter rain of acorns, and the chestnut burrs are plopping to the ground.

And often in the night there is only the living silence, the distant frosty barking of a dog, the small clumsy stir and feathery stumble of the chickens on limed roosts, and the moon, the low and heavy moon of autumn, now barred behind the leafless poles of pines, now at the pinewoods' brooding edge and summit, now falling with ghost's dawn of milky light upon rimed clods of fields and on the frosty scurf on pumpkins, now whiter, smaller, brighter, hanging against the steeple's slope, hanging the same way in a million streets, steeping all the earth in frost and silence.

Then a chime of frost-cold bells may peal out on the brooding air, and people lying in their beds will listen. They will not speak or stir, silence will gnaw the darkness like a rat, but they will whisper in their hearts:

"Summer has come and gone, has come and gone. And now—?" But they will say no more, they will have no more to say: they will wait listening, silent and brooding as the frost, to time, strange ticking time, dark time that haunts us with the briefness of our days. They will think of men long dead, of men now buried in the earth, of frost and silence long ago, of a forgotten face and moment of lost time, and they will think of things they have no words to utter.

And in the night, in the dark, in the living sleeping silence of the towns, the million streets, they will hear the thunder of the fast express, the whistles of great ships upon the river.

What will they say then? What will they say?

[139] Reprinted from *Of Time and the River*, by Thomas Wolfe. Copyright, 1935, by Charles Scribner's Sons. Used by permission of the publishers.

❖❖❖❖❖❖❖❖

140 · A Vagabond Song

There is something in the autumn that is native to my blood—
Touch of manner, hint of mood;
And my heart is like a rhyme,
With the yellow and the purple and the crimson keeping time.

The scarlet of the maples can shake me like a cry
Of bugles going by.
And my lonely spirit thrills
To see the frosty asters like a smoke upon the hills.

There is something in October sets the gypsy blood astir;
We must rise and follow her,
When from every hill of flame
She calls and calls each vagabond by name.

[140] Reprinted by permission of Dodd, Mead & Company from Bliss Carman's *Poems*. Copyright, 1929, by Bliss Carman.

❖⋙⋙❖⋘⋘❖

141 · September 15

Autumn at first is no more than a freshening of morning and evening, a certain sweet and winy odor in the air that blows upon the cheek as one steps out of doors in the morning, or opens the window at night to lean out a moment and look at the stars, before turning at last to sleep.

Autumn is the blooming of the goldenrod all through the oak woods and across the fields. Autumn is the cricket's cry, the swarming of the monarch and the storms of the Lisa butterfly. It is the odor of leaf fires, the smell of crushed marigold leaves, of tansy leaves and the sharp terebinthine scent of walnut husks that look so apple green and leave so brown a stain.

Autumn is the end of vacation, the beginning of school, the gathering of grackles, the dropping of ripe plums, the swarming of yellow hornets in the pear orchards. It is the ripening of the wild rice, the meeting together of bobolink hordes, the first hint of scarlet in the sumac leaf and the dewberry cane. It is the end of one more year's experiment. Now Nature dismantles her instruments and lays them away.

[141] From *An Almanac for Moderns*, by Donald Culross Peattie. Copyright, 1935, by Donald Culross Peattie. Courtesy of G. P. Putnam's Sons.

❖⋙⋙❖⋘⋘❖

142 · October 24

The brilliant autumnal colors are red and yellow and the various tints, hues, and shades of these. Blue is reserved to be the color of the sky, but yellow and red are the colors of the earth flower. Every fruit, on ripening, and just before its fall, acquires a bright tint. So do the leaves; so the sky before the end of the day, and the year near its setting. October is the red sunset sky, November the later twilight. Color stands for all ripeness and success. We have dreamed that the hero should carry his color aloft, as a symbol of the ripeness of his virtue. The noblest feature, the eye, is the fairest-colored, the jewel of the body. The warrior's flag is the flower which precedes his fruit. He unfurls his flag to the breeze with such confidence and brag as the flower its petals. Now we shall see what kind of fruit will succeed.

The very forest and herbage, the pellicle of the earth as it were, must acquire a bright color, an evidence of its ripeness, as if the globe itself were a fruit on its stem, with ever one cheek toward the sun.

Our appetites have commonly confined our views of ripeness and its phenomena—color and mellowness and perfectness—to the fruits which we eat, and we are wont to forget that an immense harvest which we do not eat, hardly use at all, is annually ripened by nature. At our annual cattle-shows and horticultural exhibitions we make, as we think, a great show of fair fruits, destined, however, to a rather ignoble fate, fruits not worshipped for this chiefly; but round about and within our towns there is annually another show of fruits, on an infinitely grander scale, fruits which address our taste for beauty alone.

[142] Henry David Thoreau, *Journal,* October 24, 1858.

❖⫶❖⫶❖⫸❖◄⫷❖◄⫷❖

143 · Ode to Autumn

Season of mists and mellow fruitfulness!
Close bosom-friend of the maturing sun;
Conspiring with him how to load and bless
With fruit the vines that round the thatch-eaves run;
To bend with apples the moss'd cottage-trees,
And fill all fruit with ripeness to the core;
To swell the gourd, and plump the hazel shells
With a sweet kernel; to set budding more
And still more, later flowers for the bees,
Until they think warm days will never cease;
For Summer has o'erbrimm'd their clammy cells.

Who hath not seen Thee oft amid thy store?
Sometimes whoever seeks abroad may find

Thee sitting careless on a granary floor,
Thy hair soft-lifted by the winnowing wind;
Or on a half-reap'd furrow sound asleep,
Drowsed with the fume of poppies, while thy hook
Spares the next swath and all its twined flowers;
And sometime like a gleaner thou dost keep
Steady thy laden head across a brook;
Or by a cider-press, with patient look,
Thou watchest the last oozings, hours by hours.

Where are the songs of Spring? Ay, where are they?
Think not of them,—thou hast thy music too,
While barréd clouds bloom the soft-dying day
And touch the stubble-plains with rosy hue;
Then in a wailful choir the small gnats mourn
Among the river-sallows, borne aloft
Or sinking as the light wind lives or dies;
And full-grown lambs loud bleat from hilly bourn;
Hedge-crickets sing, and now with treble soft
The redbreast whistles from a garden-croft,
And gathering swallows twitter in the skies.

[143] John Keats, "To Autumn," *Lamia, Isabella, The Eve of St. Agnes, and Other Poems* (1820).

❖❖❖❖❖❖❖❖❖

144 · Fall

LAUREY (*with real passion*) If we ever had to leave this here place, Aunt Eller, I'd shore miss it. I like it. I like that thicket down by the branch whur the 'possums live, don't you? And the way we set around in the evenings in thrashin' time, a-eatin' mushmelons and singin', and oh! Lots of things! Runnin' to the cellar in a storm, and them yeller trumpet tomaters even, you make jam out of, and the branch and the pond to skate on—They's only one thing I don't to say *like*. And that's Sunday in fall, when it's windy, and the sun shines, and the leaves pile up thick agin the house. I'm afraid of my life to go from here to the kitchen—like sump'n was gonna ketch me!

[144] Lynn Riggs, *Green Grow the Lilacs* (Samuel French, Inc., 1931).

❖❖❖❖❖❖❖❖❖

145 · Music, When Soft Voices Die

Music, when soft voices die,
Vibrates in the memory—
Odours when sweet violets sicken,
Live within the sense they quicken.

Rose leaves, when the rose is dead,
Are heap'd for the beloved's bed;
And so thy thoughts, when thou art gone,
Love itself shall slumber on.

145 Percy Bysshe Shelley, "To ——," *Posthumous Poems* (1824).

❖❱❱❖❱❖❖❰❖❰❰❖

146 · Drinking Song

Here's to the maiden of bashful fifteen,
  Here's to the widow of fifty,
Here's to the flaunting extravagant queen,
  And here's to the housewife that's thrifty.

    Let the toast pass,
    Drink to the lass,
I'll warrant she'll prove an excuse for the glass.

Here's to the charmer, whose dimples we prize,
  And now to the maid who has none, sir,
Here's to the girl with a pair of blue eyes,
  And here's to the nymph with but one, sir.

    Let the toast pass,
    Drink to the lass,
I'll warrant she'll prove an excuse for the glass.

Here's to the maiden with a bosom of snow,
  And to her that's as brown as a berry;
Here's to the wife with a face full of woe,
  And now to her that is merry.

    Let the toast pass,
    Drink to the lass,
I'll warrant she'll prove an excuse for the glass.

For let 'em be clumsy, or let 'em be slim,
   Young or ancient, I care not a feather;
So fill a pint bumper quite up to the brim,
   And let us e'en toast them together.

      Let the toast pass,
      Drink to the lass,
I'll warrant she'll prove an excuse for the glass.

[146] Richard Brinsley Sheridan, *The School for Scandal.*

❧❧❧❧❧❧

147 · The Order for the Burial of the Dead

I am the resurrection and the life, saith the Lord: he that believeth in me, though he were dead, yet shall he live: and whosoever liveth and believeth in me, shall never die.

I know that my redeemer liveth, and that he shall stand at the latter day upon the earth: and though this body be destroyed, yet shall I see God: whom I shall see for myself, and mine eyes shall behold, and not as a stranger.

We brought nothing into this world, and it is certain we can carry nothing out. The Lord gave, and the Lord hath taken away; blessed be the name of the Lord.

[147] *The Book of Common Prayer* (New York: The Church Pension Fund, 1945), p. 324

❧❧❧❧❧❧

148 · Aspects of the Earth

The eternal aspect of her earth, unchanged by all the ravages of conflict, must have renewed its patient poetry and solace. Beyond the rivers that moated the ancient high place of the Poitevin counts the land ebbed away, nursing on its bosom here a hamlet, there a mill, yonder a priory. The immemorial toil of ox and colon went forward in the field, and the tireless magpie skimmed the furrow. The chestnuts bloomed again. In the busy commune all about the palace were heard the creak of wheels, the slithering of horses' hoofs upon the cobblestones, the drumming of hammers, the rasp of the stonecutter's adz, the voices of housewives, and the cries of children; and over all the other sound the dissolving resonance of bells—the bells of Saint Pierre, Saint Radigonde, Saint Porchaire, and Notre-Dame la Grande, proclaiming the office and the calendar of the everlasting church.

[148] Reprinted by permission of the publishers from Amy Kelly's *Eleanor of Aquitaine and the Four Kings* (Cambridge, Mass: Harvard University Press, 1950).

❖〉❖〉❖◄〈◄〈◄

149 · Sounds

I know the sound of a milk wagon as it entered an American street just at the first gray of the morning, the slow and lonely clopping of the hoof upon the street, the jink of bottles, the sudden rattle of a battered old milk can, the swift and hurried footsteps of the milkman, and again the jink of bottles, a low word spoken to his horse, and then the great, slow, clopping hoof receding into silence, and then quietness and a bird song rising in the street again. Or it would be a little wooden shed out in the country two miles from my home where people waited for the streetcar, and I could see and feel again the dull and rusty color of the old green paint and see and feel all of the initials that had been carved out with jackknives on the planks and benches within the shed, and smell the warm and sultry smell so resinous and so thrilling, so filled with a strange and nameless excitement of an unknown joy, a coming prophecy, and hear the streetcar as it came to a stop, the moment of brooding, drowsing silence; a hot thrum and drowsy stitch at three o'clock; the smell of grass and hot sweet clover; and then the sudden sense of absence, loneliness and departure when the streetcar had gone and there was nothing but the hot and drowsy stitch at three o'clock again.

[149] Thomas Wolfe, *The Story of a Novel* (New York: Charles Scribner's Sons, 1936).

❖〉❖〉❖◄〈◄〈◄

150 · Heat

It was high noon, and the rays of the sun, that hung poised directly overhead in an intolerable white glory, fell straight as plummets upon the roofs and streets of Guadalajara. The adobe walls and sparse brick sidewalks of the drowsing town radiated the heat in an oily, quivering shimmer. The leaves of the eucalyptus trees around the Plaza drooped motionless, limp and relaxed under the scorching, searching blaze. The shadows of these trees had shrunk to their smallest circumference, contracting close about the trunks. The shade had dwindled to the breadth of a mere line. The sun was everywhere. The heat exhaling from brick and plaster and metal met the heat that steadily descended blanket-wise and smothering from the pale, scorched sky. Only the lizards . . . remained without, motionless, as if stuffed, their eyes closed to mere slits, basking, stupefied with heat. At long intervals the prolonged drone of an insect developed out of the silence, vibrated a moment in a soothing, somnolent, long note, then trailed slowly into the quiet again.

[150] Frank Norris, *The Octopus* (New York: Doubleday & Co., Inc., 1930), p. 265.

❖❐❖❐❖❖❖❖❖❖❖

151 · Mrs. Miniver

(Dramatic narrative—you are furthering the action of a story—you contribute to its mood.)

The stars have gone and only a thin ghost of a moon rides the rim of the night. There is no breeze — just darkness and silence. Mrs. Miniver stands by the window. Downstairs she can hear Clem bolting the door. He will be up soon, tired, asleep before he touches the pillow. The search was long and fruitless. And the telephone — the telephone has remained stricken and mute. No word of Vin. Somewhere in the darkness of the land a boy is hiding. Somewhere in the emptiness of the sky, a few clouds are torn where Vin might have passed. In Mrs. Miniver's own mind these thoughts persist. If she could only sleep .... if she could only sleep.

[151] Announcer Audition No. 4, Columbia Broadcasting System. Radio adaptation of *Mrs. Miniver*. Copyright, 1940, by Jan Struther.

❖❐❖❐❖❖❖❖❖❖❖

152 · Colonel Rogers

We watched the French day and night. They never made a move but what we knew about it and told Johnson. We killed their Indians and sunk their boats and burned their crops and took prisoners; and after we'd been at it a month, the French would 'a' paid five thousand pounds, hard money, for Rogers' scalp. The next year Rogers had two companies of Rangers, and the next year he had four, and now he's got eight, not counting his Stockbridge Indians; and if the English win this war, it'll be because of what Rogers and his Rangers have done for 'em, by God! Why, this fellow Rogers, he'll march fifty-sixty miles in a day, with three feet of snow on the ground and the glass down to thirty below, or he'll march the same distance when it's up to a hundred and twenty, like a furnace, and he'll take the britches and the hides off any Frenchman and Indians that get in his way! He's a hell-roarer and a caution, that's what he is! There aint a soldier anywhere, French or English, colonel or general, that can hold a candle to him! The English know it, too! The best man they had, young Lord Howe, he went to school to Rogers, so to learn how to fight a battle the way it ought to be fought in this country; but before he learned his lesson, he got killed fighting the English way, and there never was a damneder shame!

152 Kenneth Roberts, *Northwest Passage* (New York: Doubleday & Co., Inc., 1946), p. 75.

+:):+:):+<(<+(<+

153 · The Corpse Maker

"Whoo-oop! I'm the old original iron-jawed, brass-mounted, copper-bellied corpse-maker from the wilds of Arkansaw! Look at me! I'm the man they call Sudden Death and General Desolation! Sired by a hurricane, dam'd by an earthquake, half-brother to the cholera, nearly related to the smallpox on the mother's side! Look at me! I take nineteen alligators and a bar'l of whisky for breakfast when I'm in robust health, and a bushel of rattlesnakes and a dead body when I'm ailing. I split the everlasting rocks with my glance, and I squench the thunder when I speak! Whoo-oop! Stand back and give me room according to my strength! Blood's my natural drink, and the wails of the dying is music to my ear. Cast your eye on me, gentlemen! and lay low and hold your breath, for I'm 'bout to turn myself loose!"

All the time he was getting this off, he was shaking his head and looking fierce, and kind of swelling around in a little circle, tucking up his wristbands, and now and then straightening up and beating his breast with his fist, saying, "Look at me, gentlemen!" When he got through, he jumped up and cracked his heels together three times, and let off a roaring "Whoo-oop! I'm the bloodiest son of a wildcat that lives!"

Then the man that had started the row tilted his old slouch hat down over his right eye; then he bent stooping forward, with his back sagged and his south end sticking out far, and his fists a-shoving out and drawing in in front of him, and so went around in a little circle about three times, swelling himself up and breathing hard. Then he straightened, and jumped up and cracked his heels together three times before he lit again (that made them cheer), and he began to shout like this:

"Whoo-oop! bow your neck and spread, for the kingdom of sorrow's a-coming! Hold me down to the earth, for I feel my powers a-working! whoo-oop! I'm a child of sin, *don't* let me get a start! Smoked glass, here, for all! Don't attempt to look at me with the naked eye, gentlemen! When I'm playful I use the meridians of longitude and parallels of latitude for a seine, and drag the Atlantic Ocean for whales! I scratch my head with the lightning and purr myself to sleep with the thunder! When I'm cold, I bile the Gulf of Mexico and bathe in it; when I'm hot I fan myself with an equinoctial storm; when I'm thirsty I reach up and suck a cloud dry like a sponge; when I range the earth hungry, famine follows in my tracks! Whoo-oop! Bow your neck and spread! I put my hand on the sun's face and make it night in the earth; I bite a piece out of the moon and hurry the seasons; I shake myself and crumble the mountains! Contemplate me through leather—*don't* use the naked eye! I'm the man with a petrified heart and biler-iron bowels! The massacre of isolated communities is the pastime of my idle moments, the destruction of nationalities the serious business of my life! The boundless vastness of the great American desert is my inclosed property, and I bury my dead on my own premises!" He jumped up and cracked his heels together three times before he lit (they cheered him again), and as he came down he shouted out: "Whoo-oop! bow your neck and spread, for the Pet Child of Calamity's a-coming!"

[153] Samuel L. Clemens, *Life on the Mississippi* (New York: Harper & Brothers, 1917), pp. 21–22.

≻⫶≻⫶≻⫸⫷⫶⫷⫶

154 · This Is It

A Prologue? Well, of course the ladies know;—
I have my doubts. No matter,—here we go!
What is a Prologue? Let our Tutor teach:
Pro means beforehand; *logos* stands for speech.
'Tis like the harper's prelude on the strings,
The prima donna's courtesy ere she sings.
Prologues in meter are to other *pros*
As worsted stockings are to engine-hose.

"The world's a stage,"—as Shakespeare said, one day;
The stage a world—was what he meant to say.
The outside world's a blunder, that is clear;

The real world that Nature meant is here.
Here every foundling finds its lost mamma;
Each rogue, repentant, melts his stern papa;
Misers relent, the spendthrift's debts are paid,
The cheats are taken in the traps they laid;
One after one the troubles all are past
Till the fifth act comes right side up at last,
When the young couple, old folks, rogues, and all,
Join hands, *so* happy at the curtain's fall.
—Here suffering virtue finds relief,
And black-browed ruffians always come to grief.
—When the lorn damsel, with a frantic screech,
And cheeks as hueless as a brandy-peach,
Cries, "Help, kyind Heaven!" and drops upon her knees
On the green—baize,—beneath the (canvas) trees,—
See to her side avenging Valor fly:—
"Ha! Villain! Draw! Now, Terraitorr, yield or die!"
—When the poor hero flounders in despair,
Some dear lost uncle turns up millionaire,—
Clasps the young scapegrace with paternal joy,
Sobs on his neck, *"My boy!* My Boy!! MY BOY!!!"

Ours, then, sweet friends, the real world to-night
Of love that conquers in disaster's spite.
Ladies, attend! While woful cares and doubt
Wrong the soft passion in the world without,
Though fortune scowl, though prudence interfere,
One thing is certain: Love will triumph here!

Lords of creation, whom your ladies rule,—
The world's great masters, when you're out of school,—
Learn the brief moral of our evening's play:
Man has his will,—but woman has her way!
While man's dull spirit toils in smoke and fire,
Woman's swift instinct threads the electric wire,—
The magic bracelet stretched beneath the waves
Beats the black giant with his score of slaves.
All earthly powers confess your sovereign art
But that one rebel,—woman's wilful heart,
All foes you master; but a woman's wit
Lets daylight through you ere you know you're hit.
So, just to picture what her art can do,
Hear an old story made as good as new.

Rudolph, professor of the headsman's trade,
Alike was famous for his arm and blade.

One day a prisoner Justice had to kill
Knelt at the block to test the artist's skill.
Bare-armed, swart-visaged, gaunt, and shaggy-browed,
Rudolph the headsman rose above the crowd.
His falchion lighted with a sudden gleam,
As the pike's armor flashes in the stream.
He sheathed his blade; he turned as if to go;
The victim knelt, still waiting for the blow.
"Why strikest not? Perform thy murderous act,"
The prisoner said. (His voice was slightly cracked.)

"Friend, I *have* struck," the artist straight replied;
"Wait but one moment, and yourself decide."
He held his snuff-box,—"Now then, if you please!"
The prisoner sniffed, and, with a crashing sneeze,
Off his head tumbled,—bowled along the floor,—
Bounced down the steps;—the prisoner said no more!

Woman! thy falchion is a glittering eye;
If death lurks in it, oh, how sweet to die!
Thou takest hearts as Rudolph took the head;
We die with love, and never dream we're dead!

[154] Oliver Wendell Holmes, *The Autocrat of the Breakfast Table* (1858).

❖❱❖❱❖❰❖❰❖❰❖

155 · Lutie

Once there was a little mountain boy named Lutie.
Come fall, Lutie had to go to school.
"Never *been* to school," said Lutie.
"Don't *want* to go to school.
"Don't *want* to leave old cat Meat.
"Don't *want* to leave old dog Gone.
"Don't *want* to leave old horse Hyde.
"Going to carry on," cried Lutie. "Going to jump up and down and act mighty *awful!*

"Don't want to leave this old mountain, even!" shouted Lutie, jumping up and down.

"Or my apple orchard either," hollered Lutie, jumping up and down even faster.

"A'going to carry on something powerful!" shouted Lutie, throwing himself on the ground. "A'going to make a dreadful scene!!"

And Lutie did.

"Sure is bad," sighed cat Meat, "when Lutie takes on the way he's doing."

"Yuss," agreed dog Gone. "Sure is *bad.*"

"In all my nine old lives," shouted cat Meat, "I've never seen sech a pity. I *can't* stand these here scenes at all. I'm a'going to run up the path a piece and climb me a tree!"

And cat Meat did.

"Schooling must be something hateful the way our Lutie takes to it," shuddered dog Gone. "It's most the wust plaguing that ever came on hereabouts."

"Uh-huh," agreed horse Hyde. "What has our Lutie ever done to deserve such a right cruel punishing?"

"I dunno," said dog Gone, "but I'm going to get me to where there's a patch of peace and quiet!"

And he did.

"I could use me a patch of peace and quiet, too," mumbled old horse Hyde. "So I'll jest up my heels and make myself real scarce on this here landscape!"

And horse Hyde did.

So Lutie was left alone in the apple orchard.

And Lutie carried on until he got tired of it.

"Now that I've had my fill of taking on," said Lutie, pulling himself together, "I've come to change my mind.

"I'm off to school come hail or high water!!"

So Lutie grabbed his book and marched along until he spied cat Meat hiding up a tree.

"I spy you, cat," cried Lutie, pointing his finger. "You're going to be a mighty lonesome old cat without me. No one to scratch your ears! No one to fetch you catnip! Expect you'll feel so bad you'll waste away to a shadow!"

"Waste away to a *shadow,*" thought cat Meat. "Well, I'd better come down this here tree and act real friendly."

"Too bad for you," said Lutie, looking hard at cat Meat. "Still, I've made up my mind to get me some fancy book learning.

"So good-by!" said Lutie, turning down the path that led to the school house.

"Too bad for me is right!" gasped cat Meat. "I *might* waste away to a shadow!

"I *won't* be left behind," cried cat Meat. "I'll be quiet like a clam, and I'll follow along right behind Lutie!"

And he did.

"I spy you, too," hollered Lutie when he came to where dog Gone was hiding.

"Come out from under that briar bush!"

"You're a'going to miss me something pitiful," shouted Lutie, pointing at dog Gone. "You'll be the lonesomest old dog in all these mountains. You'll feel so bad you'll take to pining, and piny dogs can't eat down supper."

"Take to *pining*," gasped dog Gone. "I'd better come out and shine up friendly."

"It's a *pity!*" said Lutie, looking stern at dog Gone, "*but,* I must be off to get my fancy learning. So good-by!

"Good-by, old dog Gone!"

"Miss my supper!" howled dog Gone, watching Lutie winding down the path that led to school.

"Take to pining and neglect my supper. *I should guess not!*" yelped dog Gone. "I'll follow Lutie, too. I'll follow right behind cat Meat."

Next Lutie met up with old horse Hyde.

"I spy you, horse Hyde!" cried Lutie. "You're going to miss me something awful *too!*

"You'll feel so bad," said Lutie, "when I'm off to learn reading and writing and arithmetic that you'll get a cruel pain from a' grieving. And I won't be here to give you a dose of Dr. Pony's-Pain-Killer."

"Pains!!" moaned horse Hyde. "I hate pains! And I hates pains even wuss when there's no Pony's-Pain-Killer on hand to ease me."

"It's a shame," said Lutie. "Still I must get along to my learning.

"So good-by, horse Hyde," said Lutie, starting on his way to school again.

"I've got horse sense even if I ain't got no learning," grumbled horse Hyde. "I ain't a' going to be left behind without no Pony's-Pain-Killer to ease my grieving.

"I'm jest a' going to plod along right after the others," decided horse Hyde. "Even though I do smell rain!"

So old horse Hyde plodded along after the others in the gathering gloom.

Then the storm broke!

"I knowed it, I knowed it," said horse Hyde to dog Gone. "I felt it in my poor old bones!"

"*I* feel it, too," cried dog Gone. "I feel hail big as eggs hitting on my back!"

"Forget the hail," gasped cat Meat. "It's a' turning to *rain!* And I hates rain wuss than anything. We'd best step fast and catch up to Lutie!"

So cat Meat, dog Gone and horse Hyde started to run.

"It's well nigh dark like night time," cried Lutie. "Never did I see such a rain before!"

Then lightning flashed!

"I'm afeared," hollered Lutie. "I wish I were back in the orchard with Meat, Gone and Hyde!"

Then black clouds thundered like cannon!

"Learning can wait," cried Lutie. "I'm a' going to run for home and get me under my cot bed!!"

So Lutie turned and banged *smack* into cat Meat, dog Gone and horse Hyde who had just caught up to him.

"In my hour of need," gasped Lutie, "I find you with me!

"Now, I'm not afeared. I'm brave as bobcats!

"We'll all take the path to learning!

"So follow me!" shouted Lutie, facing into the rain.

"Rain's a coming down harder than ever!" complained horse Hyde.

"Rain's covered up the path!" cried dog Gone.

"Rain's up to my *toes!*" shouted cat Meat. "I'm a' going to get me to a high spot!"

"Tarnation!" hollered Lutie. "It's still a'coming! We'll all be a'floating soon!"

"It's most up to *my* ankles now," wailed dog Gone.

"It's about up to *my* old heels," groaned horse Hyde.

"And it would be up to my *waist,*" smirked cat Meat, "if I hadn't climbed up on Lutie's head already!"

"We'll never get to school at all," sighed Lutie, "if I don't think of how to save us *quick!*"

"If Lutie doesn't think of how to save *me* quick," yowled cat Meat, "it'll be too late. I'll go home!

"I don't care if I do waste away to a shadow!

"I can't stand this rain much longer!"

"Tarnations," shouted Lutie. "This here's a'getting some deeper. It's up to dog Gone's knees, and it's over old Hyde's heels.

"And *now,*" cried Lutie, "it's even up to my shinbones!

"No time for wasting," yelled Lutie.

"This fine heating stove that's a'going by will save cat Meat, and keep my neck from kinking!

"Get in, cat Meat!" cried Lutie, brushing cat Meat off his head and pushing him into the stove.

"Collect yourself and rest easy, cat! Look out the door and take in the scenery," said Lutie, grabbing hold of the stove pipe. "And now we're off to school again!"

So they splashed along till the rain crept up to dog Gone's waistline.

"I don't mind rain as a rule," complained dog Gone. *"Never* have been one to mind rain much. But this here is different! It's most up to my ears! If Lutie doesn't save me quick, *too,* I'll go home and start in at pining!"

"Rain's getting wicked," cried Lutie. "The time has come to save dog Gone!

"So pounce up on this writing desk and be saved," shouted Lutie, pushing dog Gone onto a big old desk that came bobbing by.

But dog Gone just slid off the other side and was wet to the bone!

"Pounce up and be saved again," panted Lutie, pushing dog Gone onto the desk once more, "for I have me a right smart idea.

"With these a'holding down your ears, dog," said Lutie, pinning Gone's ears to the desk with a pair of big book ends, "your troubles will be ended."

And they were.

Then Lutie tied the desk to the stove with one of his handkerchiefs.

"Now we're off for school again!" said Lutie, taking hold of the desk and splashing along until horse Hyde began to shake like an aspen leaf.

"My joints are creaking something painful," shuddered horse Hyde. "I could sure use me a dose of Pony's-Pain-Killer right now!

"If Lutie doesn't aid *me* shortly, I can't hardly count on horse sense no longer. I'd rather go home and start to work on grieving!"

"Horse Hyde," shouted Lutie, "cease your shaking and prepare to be saved!

"Step up, horse Hyde," cried Lutie, catching hold of a pair of steps that came whirling by.

"Step up these steps and be saved from the shivers!"

"Seems a queer way to ease the shivers," grumbled horse Hyde, "but maybe it's some better than nothing!"

So old horse Hyde stumbled up the steps and onto the floor that went with them.

And he was saved.

"Rest your bones, old Hyde," said Lutie, "while I tie your steps to the writing desk with my *other* handkerchief.

"And now," gasped Lutie feebly, "we would be off to school again, *if* this rain weren't well-nigh over *my* ears!

"So it's time to save me," decided Lutie, "else I never will get learning!

"I'd crawl in the stove with cat Meat," cried Lutie, "but the stove won't fit me!

"I'd climb on the desk with dog Gone," hollered Lutie, "only there's no book ends to spare.

"Or I'd step up with horse Hyde," yelled Lutie, "if he weren't already so crowded.

"Tarnation," cried Lutie. "If I can't think of something to save me quick *I'll go home!* I'll get me under my cot bed and forget about learning!"

Then just as the rain was *almost* over his ears, Lutie thought he heard a ringing.

"I'm hearing bells," gasped Lutie. "Bells!

"Salvation is at hand!" hollered Lutie, grabbing a rope that hung from a great bell that came swinging by on a roof.

"Saved!!" shouted Lutie.

"Rain's stopping," said Lutie, putting his hand out from under the big bell.

"Sure is," thought cat Meat, sticking his nose out the stove door.

"Dark clouds are well nigh gone," smiled Lutie, peering out at the sky.

"Sure thing," agreed dog Gone, looking up from his book ends.

"And the sun shines bright," cried Lutie, squinting into the sunshine.

"Sure does," mumbled horse Hyde. "Bright sun's mighty good for my shivers."

"So," said Lutie, crawling out from under the big bell, "the time has come to have me a look around."

And Lutie did.

Lutie stood up and saw him a sight!

"Tarnation," gasped Lutie. "It's a round man a'sitting on top of a world!

"What's he a'doing out there, a'bobbing along like a cork and a'reading a big old geography book?

"He's plumb sure to roll over," cried Lutie. "Right sudden!"

"He should cast aside that old reading book and prepare to be saved," cried Lutie, tolling the big bell so loud that the round man nearly jumped off the world!"

"Great snakes and little fishes," sputtered the round man. "Where am I?

"What strange place have I come to?" cried he, blinking at Lutie, "where folks live on roofs, and horses sit on steps, and dog's ears have bookends and cats nest in stoves? I can't find such a place in my big geography!"

"You've no time for reading geography books," shouted Lutie, throwing the round man the end of the bell rope. "So collect yourself to be saved!"

"I *am* collected," cried the round man, catching the bell rope.

"Then be saved," cried Lutie, pulling so hard on the rope that he pulled the round man right off the world.

"Queer way to be saved," cried Lutie when the round man landed plop in a little puddle that was all that was left of the rain.

"Queer indeed," gasped the round man, still holding the bell rope and clutching his geography book.

"You didn't hardly need no saving at all," said Lutie. "This here rain has went away—"

"Gone away," corrected the round man. "Continue!"

"Gone away," continued Lutie, "so swift that we're about left high and dry!"

"How right you are!" agreed the round man, blinking about him. "I'm *quite* high and dry except in places!"

"Then," said Lutie, sliding down the bell rope, "I'd best get me down to earth, too.

"Tarnation!" shouted Lutie when he was down to earth again.

"This here rain has took me right back to where I started from! And I don't need no geography books to tell me!

"It's took me and cat Meat and dog Gone and horse Hyde right plumb back to my *own* big old apple orchard, and I never got to school at all!

"I'll *never* get to learn reading and writing and arithmetic," howled poor Lutie. "I'll never get no learning nohow!"

"Tisk, tsk, tsk," said the round man, shaking his finger at Lutie. "We *must* mind our grammar."

"I can't heed grammar!" shouted Lutie, "because I just feel something awful!

"I feel *so* bad," hollered Lutie, "that I've got to carry on!

"A' going to carry on something *fierce*," yelled Lutie, jumping up and down. "A' going to make a *terrible* scene again!"

And Lutie did.

"Lutie sure is at it again," gulped cat Meat.

"Only *wusser!*" gasped dog Gone, pulling his ears out from under the book ends.

"After what *I've* been through," went on cat Meat, struggling out of the heating stove, "I can't take no more. I'm going to find me a tall tree and get me up it!"

"Cat Meat sure is right," cried dog Gone, rolling off the desk to the ground. "And *I* can't stand no more either!

"I'll run for a brier bush!"

"I'll pick up my heels, too," mumbled horse Hyde, scrambling to his feet and plodding down the steps. "I'll jest make a big piece of space between me and here!"

So Lutie was left alone in the orchard with the round man.

But the round man paid no heed to Lutie at all.

The round man was busy as a beetle in a biscuit! He was pushing the steps, pulling the roof, tugging the desk, toting the world and dragging the stove until they all went together.

"Now," said Lutie when he was tired of taking on, "I have me another right smart idea.

"I won't go to school at all!" declared Lutie. "I'm all through with seeking this here fancy learning!"

"Tsk, tsk," smiled the round man at Lutie. *"Do* take notice of what *I've* put together!"

"Tarnation!" hollered Lutie. "It's the school house!!"

"How right you are," beamed the round man.

"And I'm the school master!"

"Tarnation alive," yelled Lutie. "I never knowed it else I'd have acted some different!"

"No doubt, no doubt," chuckled the school master.

"But since I *didn't,*" yelled Lutie, "I'm a'going to make myself real scarce on this here old mountain!"

And away went Lutie.

So the school master was left all alone in the old apple orchard.

But not for long!

"I spy you," cried the school master when his short legs had caught him up to where Lutie was hiding in an apple tree.

"I spy you," cried the school master pointing his finger at Lutie.

"So you see," beamed the school master, starting up after Lutie, "you *are* going to school after all.

"Right in your own apple orchard."

"He's a looking right proud," said cat Meat, peering through the school house door at Lutie.

"That he is," replied dog Gone. "Schooling sure is something Lutie's taken him a fancy to."

"Tsk, tsk, tsk," said old horse Hyde to the others.

"We must mind our grammar!"

155 *Lutie,* by Margot Austin. Published and copyright, 1944, by E. P. Dutton & Co., Inc., New York.

❧❧❧❧❧❧

156 · Hotspur's Reply

My liege, I did deny no prisoners.
But I remember, when the fight was done,
When I was dry with rage and extreme toil,
Breathless and faint, leaning upon my sword,
Came there a certain lord, neat, and trimly dress'd,
Fresh as a bridegroom; and his chin new reap'd
Show'd like a stubble-land at harvest home;
He was perfumed like a milliner;
And 'twixt his finger and his thumb he held
A pouncet-box, which ever and anon
He gave his nose and took't away again;
Who therewith angry, when it next came there,
Took it in snuff; and still he smiled and talk'd;
And as the soldiers bore dead bodies by,
He call'd them untaught knaves, unmannerly,
To bring a slovenly unhandsome corpse
Betwixt the wind and his nobility.

With many a holiday and lady terms
He question'd me; amongst the rest, demanded
My prisoners in your majesty's behalf.
I then, all smarting with my wounds being cold,
To be so pester'd with a popinjay,
Out of my grief and impatience,
Answer'd neglectingly, I know not what—
He should, or he should not; for he made me mad
To see him shine so brisk and smell so sweet,
And talk so like a waiting gentlewoman
Of guns and drums and wounds—God save the mark!—
And telling me the sovereign'st thing on earth
Was parmaceti for an inward bruise;
And that it was a pity, so it was,
This villanous salt-petre should be digg'd
Out of the bowels of the harmless earth,
Which many a good tall fellow had destroy'd
So cowardly: and but for these vile guns
He would himself have been a soldier.
This bald unjointed chat of his, my lord,
I answer'd indirectly, as I said;
And I beseech you, let not his report
Come current for an accusation
Betwixt my love and your high majesty.

[156] William Shakespeare, *The First Part of King Henry the Fourth.*

❖❱❱❱❱❱❰❰❰❰❰❖

157 · I Am a Lie

I whom you behold in these black garments of the priesthood, I, who ascend the sacred desk, and turn my pale face heavenward, taking upon myself to hold communion, in your behalf, with the Most High Omniscience, I, in whose daily life you discern the sanctity of Enoch, I, whose footsteps, as you suppose, leave a gleam along my earthly track, whereby the pilgrims that shall come after me may be guided to the regions of the blest, I, who have laid the hand of baptism upon your children, I, who have breathed the parting prayer over your dying friends, to whom the Amen sounded faintly from a world which they had quitted, I, your pastor, whom you so reverence and trust, am utterly a pollution and a lie!

[157] Nathaniel Hawthorne, *The Scarlet Letter* (1850).

❖❱❱❱❱❱❰❰❰❰❰❖

158 · Preaching, Lecturing

Preaching? Lecturing? Who are ye that ask for these things? What do ye want to hear, ye puling infants? A trumpet-sound that would train you up to mankind, or a nurse's lullaby? The preachers and lecturers deal with men of straw, as they are men of straw themselves. Why, a free-spoken man, of sound lungs, cannot draw a long breath without causing your rotten institutions to come toppling down by the vacuum he makes. Your church is a baby-house made of blocks, and so of the state. It would be a relief to breathe one's self occasionally among men. If there were any magnanimity in us, any grandeur of soul, anything but sects and parties undertaking to patronize God and keep the mind within bounds, how often we might encourage and provoke one another by a free expression! I will not consent to walk with my mouth muzzled, not till I am rabid, until there is danger that I shall bite the unoffending and that my bite will produce hydrophobia.

Freedom of speech! It hath not entered into your hearts to conceive what those words mean. It is not leave given me by your sect to say this of that; it is when leave is given to your sect to withdraw. The church, the state, the school, the magazine, think they are liberal and free! It is the freedom of a prison-yard. I ask only that one fourth part of my honest thoughts be spoken aloud. What is it you tolerate, you church to-day? Not truth, but a life long hypocrisy. Let us have institutions framed not out of our rottenness, but out of our soundness. This factitious piety is like stale gingerbread. I would like to suggest what a pack of fools and cowards we mankind are. They want me to agree not to breathe too hard in the neighborhood of their paper castles. If I should draw a long breath in the neighborhood of these institutions, their weak and flabby sides would fall out, for my own inspiration would exhaust the air about them. The church! It is eminently the timid institution, and the heads and pillars of it are constitutionally and by principle the greatest cowards in the community. The voice that goes up from the monthly concerts is not so brave and so cheering as that which rises from the frog-ponds of the land. The best 'preachers,' so called, are an effeminate class; their bravest thoughts wear petticoats. If they have any manhood they are sure to forsake the ministry, though they were to turn their attention to baseball. Look at your editors of popular magazines. I have dealt with two or three the most liberal of them. They are afraid to print a whole sentence, a *round* sentence, a free-spoken sentence. They want to get thirty thousand subscribers, and they will do anything to get them. They consult the D.D.'s and all the letters of the alphabet before printing a sentence. I have been into many of these cowardly New England towns where they *profess* Christianity,—invited to speak, perchance,—where they were trembling in their shoes at the thought of the things you might say, as if they knew their weak side,—that they were weak on all sides. The devil they have covenanted with is a timid devil. If they would let their sores alone they might heal, and they could to the wars again like men; but instead of that they get together in meeting-house cellars, rip off the bandages and poultice them with sermons.

It is no compliment to be invited to lecture before the rich Institutes and Lyceums. The settled lecturers are as tame as the settled ministers. The audiences do not want to hear any prophets; they do not wish to be stimulated and instructed, but entertained. They, their wives and daughters, go to the Lyceum to suck a sugar-plum. The little of medicine they get is disguised with sugar. It is never the reformer they hear there, but a faint and timid echo of him only. They seek a pass-time merely. Their greatest guns and sons of thunder are only wooden guns and great-grandsons of thunder, who give them smooth words well pronounced from manuscripts well punctuated,—they who have stolen the little fire they have from prophets whom the audience would quake to hear. They ask for orators that will entertain them and leave them where they found them.

They want all of a man but his truth and independence and manhood.

[158] Henry David Thoreau, *Journal,* November 16, 1858.

❖⫷❖⫷❖⫸❖⫸❖

159 · Second Mrs. Burton

TERRY: (*sotto*)

A simple matter of choice. You take or you give.
You love or you're loved. Simple. Nothing to it.
Man's greatest gift. Choice. "Which hand do you
take?" They start us early — making choices.
Teaching us how it's done. You can't have both.
That's your trouble, Terry, old girl. You want both.
That isn't the way the game's played. You know that.
But nobody ever explained to you why the rules <u>had</u>
to be the way they are. That's the trouble. You
want what's in both hands. And why not? That's
what they forget to tell you. It's the same way
with that "You can't have your cake and eat it, too"
business. All right — you can't have <u>all</u> your
cake at a special given moment if you've just eaten
<u>all</u> your cake. But why can't you have a slice now
and then and save some — and when your supply begins
to get low — take another one? That's what nobody
ever bothered to explain. Why can't you — "take"
sometimes — and "give" sometimes? Why do you have

to stay on one side or the other? Why can't you —
love and be loved? Isn't life big enough — and
strong enough — to hold that much love all at once?
Sure, it is. It's happened. What about — Abelard
and Heloise? Well — they didn't turn out so well.
But — what about Elizabeth Barrett and Robert
Browning? They turned out all right. They thrived.
So that proves it. It can happen.
(*beat*)

But — I guess it takes a special breed of people.
Poets maybe. Maybe it can only happen to poets —
who don't care about — money and — the old Burton
Store — and things like that. Maybe — I should
have married a poet. Because — I don't think
there's much chance that Stan and I — will ever go
down as one of the great romances of history. If
heaven's our destination — we'll have to slip
through another entrance.
(*bitterly*)

And it'll probably say "Burton Store" over the door.
(*slight pause*)

Elizabeth Miller's right. Stan doesn't need me. I
knew she was right when she said it — but I couldn't
tell her so. Why couldn't I? Why did I resent it
— when I already knew it was the truth? Why didn't
I come right out and say, "Yes, I know. I've thought
about it myself?" I don't suppose it's "my secret."
Probably everybody in Dickston has thought about it
— one time or another. I don't feel guilty about
it. I'm sorry. I wish he did. But I can't help
it if he doesn't. I just haven't got the things he
needs. I'm not even good luck for him. He was
better off in every way before he knew me. I guess
I'm actually — "bad luck" for him. Everything he
values — he had more of before he knew me. Hmf!
A fine help-mate I turned out to be.
(*beat*)

What did I do wrong? Where'd I go off? I wanted
so much to — to be good for him.
(*deep breath*)

But nothing's been the way I thought it would be. I
guess — maybe — nothing ever is. You can't have
your cake and eat it, too. Maybe you — can't have
your dream and live it too.

[159] Martha Alexander, *The Second Mrs. Burton.* Reproduced through the courtesy of the author. *The Second Mrs. Burton* is sponsored by General Foods Corporation.

❧❧❧❧❧❧❧

160 · The Adventures of Ozzie and Harriet

ANNOUNCER: (*excited*)

How do you do, ladies and gentlemen. This is Vern Smith speaking to you from the vacant lot at the corner of Rogers Road and Elm Street and bringing you a play-by-play description of the great annual football classic between the Rogers Road Pelicans and the Gardner Street Tigers. There's an enthusiastic crowd here this afternoon — must be twenty-five people. It's the second quarter of the game, and the Rogers Road Pelicans are leading by a scant six points. Score: Gardner Street Tigers 66 — Rogers Road Pelicans 72.

There's a slight delay out there on the field at the moment, but fortunately the situation is in the capable hands of that well-known football expert — that master of gridiron strategy — Ozzie Nelson. At the start of the game Ozzie was merely a spectator . . . but not for long. Knowing of his inexhaustible fund of football know-how and cunning, the kids have asked him to help out. Yes, folks, Ozzie is going to referee!

(*whistle*)

There's time in . . . . The Tigers are into the huddle . . . . up to the line . . . it's a three man line, eight quarterbacks in the backfield. Ricky Nelson getting ready to center the ball. He's doing a great job out there — playing center for both sides. The ball is snapped . . . it's going to be a pass . . . . No, he's going to run with it. . . . He changed his mind . . . . He changed it again . . . . He's going to throw it . . . . It's a long high spiral . . . . There goes Ozzie . . . . He's got his eye on the ball. Look out, Ozzie! Ouch!

(*he groans*)

Right in the eye! He got his eye a little too close. There's going to be a penalty. He's calling the ball back. Oh-oh, the Tiger rooting section doesn't like it. Fifteen yards for unnecessary roughness, Ozzie says. There's an argument out there. Oh-oh! He's reversed his decision. The play was good. The Tigers get a twenty yard gain. Oh-Oh! The Pelican's rooting section doesn't like that. Another argument out there . . . Ozzie is right in the middle of it. Wait a minute . . . there's another decision. Ozzie says take the play over. Oh-oh! The crowd doesn't

like that either. They're still arguing out there.
And here's another substitution. . . . Ozzie Nelson
is coming out of the game!

160 By Ozzie Nelson and staff. Reproduced through the courtesy of Ozzie Nelson.

❖꘎꘎꘎꘎

161 · The World Is Too Much with Us

The World is too much with us; late and soon,
Getting and spending, we lay waste our powers;
Little we see in Nature that is ours;
We have given our hearts away, a sordid boon!

This Sea that bares her bosom to the moon,
The winds that will be howling at all hours
And are up-gather'd now like sleeping flowers,
For this, for everything, we are out of tune;

It moves us not.—Great God! I'd rather be
A Pagan suckled in a creed outworn,—
So might I, standing on this pleasant lea,
Have glimpses that would make me less forlorn;
Have sight of Proteus rising from the sea;
Or hear old Triton blow his wreathèd horn.

161 William Wordsworth, "The World Is Too Much with Us," *Poems in Two
Volumes* (1807).

❖꘎꘎꘎꘎

162 · Salut au Monde!

What do you hear, Walt Whitman?
I hear the workman singing and the farmer's wife singing,
I hear in the distance the sounds of children and of animals early
    in the day,
I hear emulous shouts of Australians pursuing the wild horse,
I hear the Spanish dance with castanets in the chestnut shade, to
    the rebeck and guitar,
I hear continual echoes from the Thames,
I hear fierce French liberty songs,

I hear of the Italian boat-sculler the musical recitative of old poems,

I hear the locusts in Syria as they strike the grain and grass with the showers of their terrible clouds,

I hear the Coptic refrain toward sundown, pensively falling on the breast of the black venerable vast mother the Nile,

I hear the chirp of the Mexican muleteer, and the bells of the mule,

I hear the Arab muezzin calling from the top of the mosque,

I hear the Christian priests at the altars of their churches,

I hear the responsive bass and soprano,

I hear the cry of the Cossack, and the sailor's voice putting to sea at Okotsk,

I hear the wheeze of the slave-coffle as the slaves march on, as the husky gangs pass on by twos and threes, fastened together with wrist chains and ankle chains,

I hear the Hebrew reading his records and psalms,

I hear the rhythmic myths of the Greeks, and the strong legends of the Romans,

I hear the tale of the divine life and bloody death of the beautiful God the Christ,

I hear the Hindoo teaching his favorite pupil the loves, wars, adages, transmitted safely to this day from poets who wrote three thousand years ago.

[162] Walt Whitman, "Salut au Monde!" *Leaves of Grass* (1855).

❖❖❖❖❖❖❖❖

163 · Ceremonies for Christmas

Come, bring with a noise,
My merry merry boys,
The Christmas log to the firing;
While my good dame, she
Bids ye all be free,
And drink to your heart's desiring.

With the last year's brand
Light the new block, and
For good success in his spending,
On your psaltries play,
That sweet luck may
Come while the log is a-teending.

> Drink now the strong beer,
> Cut the white loaf here;
> The while the meat is a-shredding
> For the rare mince-pie,
> And the plums stand by
> To fill the paste that's a-kneading.

163 Robert Herrick, "Ceremonies for Christmas," *Hesperides* (1648).

❖❖❖❖❖❖❖

164 · The True Beauty

> He that loves a rosy cheek,
> Or a coral lip admires,
> Or from star-like eyes doth seek
> Fuel to maintain his fires;
> As old Time makes these decay,
> So his flames must waste away.
>
> But a smooth and steadfast mind,
> Gentle thoughts and calm desires,
> Hearts with equal love combined,
> Kindle never-dying fires.
> Where these are not, I despise
> Lovely cheeks or lips or eyes.

164 Thomas Carew, "Disdain Returned," *Poems* (1640).

❖❖❖❖❖❖❖

165 · Wishes

> Whoe'er she be,
> That not impossible She
> That shall command my heart and me;
>
> Where'er she lie,
> Lock'd up from mortal eye,
> In shady leaves of destiny:
>
> Till that ripe birth
> Of studied Fate stand forth,
> And teach her fair steps to our earth;

Till that divine
Idea take a shrine
Of crystal flesh, through which to shine:

—Meet you her, my Wishes,
Bespeak her to my blisses,
And be ye call'd, my absent kisses.

I wish her beauty
That owes not all its duty
To gaudy tire, or glist'ring shoe-tie:

Something more than
Taffeta or tissue can,
Or rampant feather, or rich fan.

A face that's best
By its own beauty drest,
And can alone command the rest:

A face made up
Out of no other shop
Than what Nature's white hand sets ope.

. . .

Days, that need borrow
No part of their good morrow
From a fore-spent night of sorrow:

Days, that in spite
Of darkness, by the light
Of a clear mind are day all night.

. .

Life, that dares send
A challenge to his end,
And when it comes, say, 'Welcome, friend.'

Sydneian showers
Of sweet discourse, whose powers
Can crown old Winter's head with flowers.

Soft silken hours,
Open suns, shady bowers;
'Bove all, nothing within that lowers.

Whate'er delight
Can make day's forehead bright
Or give down to the wings of night.

. . .

I wish her store
Of worth may leave her poor
Of wishes; and I wish—no more.

—Now, if Time knows
That Her, whose radiant brows
Weave them a garland of my vows;

. . .

Her that dares be
What these lines wish to see:
I seek no further, it is She.

'Tis She, and here
Lo! I unclothe and clear
My wishes' cloudy character.

. . .

Such worth as this is
Shall fix my flying wishes,
And determine them to kisses.

Let her full glory,
My fancies, fly before ye:
Be ye my fictions:—but her story.

₁₆₅ Richard Crashaw, "Wishes to His Supposed Mistress," *Steps to the Temple, Sacred Poems, with The Delights of the Muses* (1648).

❖⟩❖⟩❖◆⟨❖⟨❖

166 · The Constant Lover

Out upon it, I have loved
　　Three whole days together!
And am like to love three more,
　　If it prove fair weather.

Time shall moult away his wings
　　Ere he shall discover
In the whole wide world again
　　Such a constant lover.

But the spite on't is, no praise
   Is due at all to me:
Love with me had made no stays,
   Had it any been but she.

Had it any been but she,
   And that very face,
There had been at least ere this
   A dozen dozen in her place.

[166] Sir John Suckling, "The Constant Lover," *The Last Remains* (1659).

❖⊃❖⊃❖⊰⟨❖⟨⟨⊰

167 · Go, Lovely Rose

Go, lovely Rose!
Tell her, that wastes her time and me,
   That now she knows,
When I resemble her to thee,
How sweet and fair she seems to be.

   Tell her that's young
And shuns to have her graces spied,
   That hadst thou sprung
In deserts, where no men abide,
Thou must have uncommended died.

   Small is the worth
Of beauty from the light retired:
   Bid her come forth,
Suffer herself to be desired,
And not blush so to be admired.

   Then die! that she
The common fate of all things rare
   May read in thee:
How small a part of time they share
That are so wondrous sweet and fair!

[167] Edmund Waller, "Song," *Poems* (1664).

❖⊃❖⊃❖⊰⟨❖⟨⟨⊰

168 · To Anthea

Bid me to live, and I will live
Thy Protestant to be:
Or bid me love, and I will give
A loving heart to thee.

A heart as soft, a heart as kind,
A heart as sound and free
As in the whole world thou canst find,
That heart I'll give to thee.

Bid that heart stay, and it will stay,
To honour thy decree:
Or bid it languish quite away,
And't shall do so for thee.

Bid me to weep, and I will weep
While I have eyes to see:
And having none, yet I will keep
A heart to weep for thee.

Bid me despair, and I'll despair,
Under that cypress tree:
Or bid me die, and I will dare
E'en Death, to die for thee.

Thou art my life, my love, my heart,
The very eyes of me,
And hast command of every part,
To live and die for thee.

[168] Robert Herrick, "To Anthea, Who May Command Him Anything," *Hesperides* (1648).

❖)▷❖)▷❖(❖(❖(❖❖

169 · Forget Not Yet

Forget not yet the tried intent
Of such a truth as I have meant,
My great travail, so gladly spent,
Forget not yet.

Forget not yet when first began
The weary life ye know, since whan
The suit, the service none tell can,
   Forget not yet.

Forget not yet the great assays,
The cruel wrong, the scornful ways;
The painful patience in denays,
   Forget not yet.

Forget not yet, forget not this,
How long ago hath been, and is
The mind that never meant amiss,—
   Forget not yet.

Forget not then thine own approved,
The which so long hath thee so loved,
Whose steadfast faith yet never moved,
   Forget not this.

[169] Sir Thomas Wyatt, "Forget Not Yet," *Additional Ms.* 17492.

❖❱❖❱❱❖❰❰❖❰❰❖

170 · Blame Not My Lute

Blame not my lute, for he must sound
  Of this and that as liketh me;
For lack of wit the lute is bound
  To give such tunes as pleaseth me.
Though my songs be somewhat strange,
And speaks such words as touch thy change,
   Blame not my lute.

My lute, alas, doth not offend,
  Though that perforce he must agree
To sound such tunes as I intend
  To sing to them that heareth me;
Then though my songs be somewhat plain
And toucheth some that use to feign,
   Blame not my lute.

My lute and strings may not deny,
But as I strike they must obey;
Break not them, then so wrongfully,
But wreak thyself some wiser way;
And though the songs which I endite
To quit thy change with rightful spite,
Blame not my lute.

Spite asketh spite, and changing change,
And falséd faith must needs be known;
The fault so great, the case so strange,
Of right it must abroad be blown:
Then since that by thine own desert
My songs do tell how true thou art,
Blame not my lute.

Blame but thyself that hast misdone
And well deservéd to have blame;
Change thou thy way so evil begun,
And then my lute shall sound that same:
But if till then my fingers play,
By thy desert, their wonted way,
Blame not my lute.

Farewell, unknown, for though thou break
My strings in spite with great disdain,
Yet have I found out for thy sake
Strings for to string my lute again.
And if perchance this silly rhyme
Do make thee blush at any time,
Blame not my lute.

170 Sir Thomas Wyatt, "Blame Not My Lute," *Additional Ms.* 17492.

>:)>:)>:(:(:<

171 · Bolts of Melody

I would not paint a picture.
I'd rather be the one
Its bright impossibility
To dwell delicious on,
And wonder how the fingers feel
Whose rare celestial stir

Evokes so sweet a torment,
Such sumptuous despair.

I would not talk like cornets.
I'd rather be the one
Raised softly to horizons
And out, and easy on
Through villages of ether,
Myself endued balloon
By but a lip of metal,
The pier to my pontoon.

Nor would I be a poet.
It's finer own the ear,
Enamored, impotent, content
The license to revere—
A privilege so awful
What would the dower be
Had I the art to stun myself
With bolts of melody!

❖⫸⫸⫸❖⫷⫷❖⫷⫷

172 · A Coffin Is a Small Domain

A coffin is a small domain
Yet able to contain
A rudiment of paradise
In its diminished plane.

A grave is a restricted breadth
Yet ampler than the sun
And all the seas he populates
And lands he looks upon,

To him who on its low repose
Bestows a single friend—
Circumference without relief,
Or estimate, or end.

⫸⫸⫸❖⫷⫷❖⫷⫷

173 · Bloom Is Result

Bloom is result. To meet a flower
And casually glance
Would cause one scarcely to suspect
The minor circumstance

Assisting in the bright affair
So intricately done,
Then offered as a butterfly
To the meridian.

To pack the bud, oppose the worm,
Obtain its right of dew,
Adjust the heat, elude the wind,
Escape the prowling bee,

Great nature not to disappoint
Awaiting her that day—
To be a flower is profound
Responsibility!

173 From *Bolts of Melody,* by Emily Dickinson, edited by Mabel Loomis Todd and Millicent Todd Bingham. Copyright, 1945, by Millicent Todd Bingham.

❖⟩❖⟩❖⟨❖⟨❖

174 · Bees

Bees are black with gilt surcingles,
Buccaneers of buzz,
Ride abroad in ostentation
And subsist on fuzz,

Fuzz ordained, not fuzz contingent,
Marrows of the hill,
Jugs a universe's fracture
Could not jar or spill.

174 From *Bolts of Melody,* by Emily Dickinson, edited by Mabel Loomis Todd and Millicent Todd Bingham. Copyright, 1945, by Millicent Todd Bingham.

❖⟩❖⟩❖⟨❖⟨❖

175 · Two Butterflies

Two butterflies went out at noon
And waltzed upon a farm,
And then espied circumference
And caught a ride with him;

Then lost themselves and found themselves
In eddies of the sun,
Till rapture missed her footing
And both were wrecked in noon.

To all surviving butterflies
Be this biography,
Example, and monition
To entomology.

175 From *Bolts of Melody,* by Emily Dickinson, edited by Mabel Loomis Todd and Millicent Todd Bingham. Copyright, 1945, by Millicent Todd Bingham.

⊹⊱⊹⊱⊹⊹⊰⊹⊰⊰⊹

176 · Evening Hymn

The night is come like to the day,
Depart not Thou, great God, away;
Let not my sins, black as the night,
Eclipse the lustre of Thy light.
Keep still in my horizon, for to me
The sun makes not the day, but Thee.
Thou whose nature cannot sleep,
On my temples sentry keep;
Guard me 'gainst those watchful foes,
Whose eyes are open while mine close.
Let no dreams my head infest,
But such as Jacob's temples blest.
While I do rest, my soul advance,
Make my sleep a holy trance:
That I may, my rest being wrought,
Awake into some holy thought.
And with as active vigour run
My course, as doth the nimble sun.
Sleep is a death, O make me try

By sleeping what it is to die.
And as gently lay my head
On my grave, as now my bed.
Now ere I rest, great God, let me
Awake again at last with Thee.
And thus assured, behold I lie
Securely, or to wake or die.
These are my drowsy days, in vain
I do now wake to sleep again.
O come that hour, when I shall never
Sleep again, but wake for ever!

176 Sir Thomas Browne.

❖❱❱❱❱❭❭❰❰❰❖

177 · Peace

My soul, there is a country
    Far beyond the stars,
Where stands a wingéd sentry
    All skilful in the wars,
There above noise and danger
    Sweet Peace sits crown'd with smiles,
And One born in a manger
    Commands the beauteous files.
He is thy gracious Friend,
    And (O my soul, awake!)
Did in pure love descend
    To die here for thy sake,
If thou canst get but thither,
    There grows the flower of Peace,
The Rose that cannot wither,
    Thy fortress, and thy ease;
Leave then thy foolish ranges;
    For none can thee secure,
But One, who never changes,
    Thy God, thy life, thy cure.

177 Henry Vaughan, "Peace," *Poems* (1646).

❖❱❱❱❱❭❭❰❰❰❖

178 · Holy Sonnet

Death be not proud, though some have called thee
Mighty and dreadful, for, thou art not so,
For, those, whom thou think'st, thou dost overthrow,
Die not, poor death, nor yet canst thou kill me.
From rest and sleep, which but thy pictures be,
Much pleasure, then from thee, much more must flow,
And soonest our best men with thee do go,
Rest of their bones, and soul's delivery.
Thou art slave to Fate, Chance, kings, and desperate men,
And dost with poison, war, and sickness dwell,
And poppy, or charms can make us sleep as well,
And better than thy stroke; why swell'st thou then?
One short sleep past, we wake eternally,
And death shall be no more; death, thou shalt die.

[178] John Donne, "Holy Sonnets, X," *Divine Poems* (1635).

179 · Christ's Coming to Judgment

As in a royal army, led by a king,
After the cannon's sulphurous thundering;
Horror on all side roaring; wings here flying
At winds, like armed eagles; here, troops dying;
A butcherous execution through the field,
Bellowing with fiend-like threats, where yet none yield;
Though death stalks up and down, ghastly and pale,
The victor's wreath lying in a doubtful scale;—
The king himself, safeguarded on a hill,
Seeing this black day, yet stirring not until
He finds fit time to strike; then down, amain,
Worrying he comes—a glorious, dreadful train
Of high heroic spirit circling him round,
Who with swift vengeance do their foes confound,
And, slave-like, drag them at proud chariot-wheels,
Whilst miseries worse than death tread on their heels:—
So, but with greater terror, state and wonder,
Heaven's Supreme Monarch—one hand gripping thunder;

The other, storms of hail, whirlwinds and fire—
(Ensigns of his hot-burning, quenchless ire,)
When the world's buildings smothered lay in smoke,
With sparkling eyes majestically broke
Out of his palace, ne'er set ope before,
And stood like a triumphant conqueror,
Trampling on Death and Hell. About him round,
Like petty viceroys, spirits, methought all crown'd,
Show'd as if none but kings had been his guard;
Whole hierarchies of saints were then preferred,
With principalities, powers and dominations,
Thrones, angels, and archangels, all at once
Filling the presence; then, like heaven-born twins,
Flew fiery cherubins and seraphins;
Whilst the old patriarchs, clothed all in white,
Were rapt with joy, to see beams far more bright,
About the prophets and the apostles run,
Than those whose flames were kindled at the sun.
Martyrs, methought, with self-same lustre shined
As gold which seven times was by fire refined;
Virgins, whose souls in life from lust liv'd clear,
Had silver robes, and on their heads did wear
Coronets of diamonds . . .
God's heir-apparent (here, once, made away)
Triumphed in this, his coronation-day,
In which heaven was his kingdom, mercy his throne,
Justice his sceptre, a communion
Of sanctified souls the courtly peers,
And his star-chamber lords; who now had years
Which never turned them grey by time's rough weather:
Greatness was now no more called fortune's feather,
Nor honour held a fruitless, golden dream,
Nor riches a bewitching swallowing stream,
Nor learning laughed at, as the beggar's dower,
Nor beauty's painted cheek a summer flower;
No, no: life endless was, yet without loathing,
Honour and greatness were immortal clothing,
Riches were subject to no base consuming,
Learning burnt bright without contentious fuming,
Beauty no painting brought, but still renew'd:
Each one had here his full beatitude.
    That face, whose picture might have ransomed kings,
Yet put up spittings, bafflings, buffetings,—
That head, which could a crown of stars have worn,
Yet spitefully was wrenched with wreaths of thorn,—

Those hands and feet, where purest stamps were set,
Yet nail'd up like pieces counterfeit,—
Those lips, which, though they had command o'er all,
Being thirsty, vinegar had to drink, and gall,—
That body, scourged and torn with many a wound,
That his dear blood, like balm, might leave us sound,—
The well of life, which with a spear being tried,
Two streams mysterious gushed out from his side;—
Messias, great Jehovah, God on high,
Yet hail'd King of the Jews in mockery,—
The manger-cradled babe, the beggar born,
The poorest worm on earth, the height of scorn;—
That Lord, by his own subjects crucified,
Lo, at this grand assize, comes glorified,
With troops of angels, who his officers are,
To call by sound of triumph his foes to a bar.
Thus stood he armed—justice his breastplate was,
Judgement his helmet, stronger far than brass;
On his right arm truth's shield he did advance:
And turned his sharpened wrath into a lance;
Out of his mouth a two-edged sword did fly,
To wound body and soul eternally:
Armed cap-a-pie thus, who 'gainst him durst fight?
There was no ground for strength nor yet for flight.
        At this, methought, all graves that ever held
Dead corse, yawn'd wide open, and compell'd
The bones of dead men up, with flesh, to rise;
Yea, those on whom the seas did tyrannize,
And drown'd in wrecks, and which were piece-meal eaten,
With lively bodies to the shores were beaten;
Whom sword or fire, gibbets, or wheels had torn,
Had their own limbs again, and were new born;
From the first man God made to the last that died,
The names of all were here exemplified:
Emperors and kings, patriarchs, and tribes forgotten,
The conquerors of the world—moulder'd and rotten—
Lords, beggars, men and women, young and old,
Up, at a bar set forth, their hands did hold.
The Judge being set, in open court were laid
Huge books, at sight of which all were dismay'd,
Would fain have shrunk back, and fell down with fear;
In sheets of brass all stories written were
(Which those great volumes held) charactered deep
With pens of steel, eternal files to keep
Of every nation since the world began,

And every deed, word, thought, of every man.
Sins hatched in caves, or such whose bawd was night,
The minutes of the act, were here set right;
Great men, whose secret, damn'd sins vizards wore
So close, that none upon their brows could score
The least black-line—because none durst—had here
A bill of items in particular,
What their souls owed for sin to death and hell;
Or, if it happened that they e'er did well,
In these true journals it at large was found,
And with rich promise of reward was crown'd.

179 Thomas Dekker.

❖❖❖❖❖❖❖❖

180 · On Psalm CXIX. 5

Where shall I seek a guide? where shall I meet
    Some lucky hand to lead my trembling paces?
What trusty lantern will direct my feet
    To scape the danger of these dangerous places?
        What hopes have I to pass without a guide?
Where one gets safely through, a thousand fall beside.

An unrequested star did gently slide
    Before the Wise Men to a greater Light;
Backsliding Israel found a double guide;
    A pillar, and a cloud; by day, by night:
        Yet in my desperate dangers, which be far
More great than theirs, I have nor pillar, cloud, nor star.

O that the pinions of a clipping dove
    Would cut my passage through the empty air;
Mine eyes being sealed, how would I mount above
    The reach of danger and forgotten care!
        My backward eyes should ne'er commit that fault,
Whose lasting guilt should build a monument of salt.

Great God, that art the flowing Spring of light,
    Enrich mine eyes with Thy refulgent ray:
Thou art my path; direct my steps aright;
    I have no other light, no other way:

I'll trust my God, and Him alone pursue;
His Law shall be my path; His heavenly light my clue.

[180] Francis Quarles, "On Psalm cxix. 5," *Emblems* (1635).

❖❖❖❖❖❖❖❖

181 · The Book

Eternal God! Maker of all
That have lived here, since the Man's fall;
The Rock of Ages! in whose shade
They live unseen, when here they fade.

Thou knew'st this paper, when it was
Mere seed, and after that but grass;
Before 'twas drest or spun, and when
Made linen, who did wear it then:
What were their lives, their thoughts and deeds
Whether good corn, or fruitless weeds.
Thou knew'st this tree, when a green shade
Cover'd it, since a cover made,
And where it flourish'd, grew, and spread,
As if it never should be dead.

Thou knew'st this harmless beast, when he
Did live and feed by Thy decree
On each green thing; then slept (well-fed)
Clothed with this skin, which now lies spread
A covering o'er this aged book,
Which makes me wisely weep and look
On my own dust; mere dust it is,
But not so dry and clean as this.
Thou knew'st and saw'st them all and though
Now scatter'd thus, dost know them so.

O knowing, glorious Spirit! when
Thou shalt restore trees, beasts and men,
When Thou shalt make all new again,
Destroying only death and pain,
Give him amongst Thy works a place,
Who in them loved and sought Thy face!

[181] Henry Vaughan, "The Book," *Silex Scintillans* (1650).

❖❖❖❖❖❖❖❖

182 · The Twenty-fourth Psalm

The earth is the Lord's, and the fulness thereof; the world, and they that dwell therein.

For he hath founded it upon the seas, and established it upon the floods.

Who shall ascend into the hill of the Lord? or who shall stand in his holy place?

He that hath clean hands, and a pure heart; who hath not lifted up his soul unto vanity, nor sworn deceitfully.

He shall receive the blessing from the Lord, and righteousness from the God of his salvation.

This is the generation of them that seek him, that seek thy face, O, Jacob. Selah.

Lift up your head, O ye gates; and be ye lift up, ye everlasting doors; and the King of glory shall come in.

Who is this King of glory? The Lord strong and mighty, the Lord mighty in battle.

Lift up your heads, O ye gates; even lift them up, ye everlasting doors; and the King of glory shall come in.

Who is this King of glory? The Lord of host, he is the King of glory. Selah.

182 *The Holy Bible,* Psalm 24.

◆◗◆◗◆◆◆◆◆◆◆

183 · The Twenty-seventh Psalm

The Lord is my light and my salvation; whom then shall I fear? the Lord is the strength of my life; of whom then shall I be afraid?

. . .

One thing have I desired of the Lord, which I will require; even that I may dwell in the house of the Lord all the days of my life, to behold the fair beauty of the Lord, and to visit his temple.

For in the time of trouble he shall hide me in his tabernacle; yea, in the secret place of his dwelling shall he hide me, and set me up upon a rock of stone.

And now shall he lift up mine head above mine enemies round about me.

Therefore will I offer in his dwelling an oblation, with great gladness: I will sing and speak praises unto the Lord.

Hearken unto my voice, O Lord, when I cry unto thee; have mercy upon me, and hear me.

My heart hath talked of thee, Seek ye my face: Thy face, Lord, will I seek.

O hide not thou thy face from me, nor cast thy servant away in displeasure.

Thou hast been my succour; leave me not, neither forsake me, O God of my salvation.

. . .

I should utterly have fainted, but that I believe verily to see the goodness of the Lord in the land of the living.

O tarry thou the Lord's leisure; be strong, and he shall comfort thine heart; and put thou thy trust in the Lord.

[183] *The Holy Bible,* Psalm 27. (Coverdale Bible, 1535)

184 · The One Hundred and Fiftieth Psalm

Praise ye the Lord. Praise God in his sanctuary; praise him in the firmament of his power.

Praise him for his mighty acts; praise him according to his excellent greatness.

Praise him with the sound of the trumpet; praise him with the psaltery and harp.

Praise him with the timbrel and dance; praise him with stringed instruments and organs.

Praise him upon the loud cymbals; praise him upon the high sounding cymbals.

Let everything that hath breath praise the Lord. Praise ye the Lord.

[184] *The Holy Bible,* Psalm 150.

185 · A Child's Grace

Here a little child I stand,
Heaving up my either hand;
Cold as paddocks though they be,
Here I lift them up to Thee,

For a benison to fall
On our meat, and on us all. Amen.

185 Robert Herrick, "Another Grace for a Child," *Hesperides* (1648).

>)>)>:(:(:

186 · Parable of the Fig Tree

And Jotham went and stood on the top of Mount Gerizim, and lifted up his voice, and cried, and said unto them, Hearken unto me, ye men of Shechem, that God may hearken unto you.

The trees went forth on a time to anoint a king over them; and they said unto the olive tree, Reign thou over us.

But the olive tree said unto them, Should I leave my fatness, wherewith by me they honor God and man, and go to be promoted over the trees?

And the trees said to the fig tree, Come thou, and reign over us.

But the fig tree said unto them, Should I leave my sweetness, and my good fruit, and go to be promoted over the trees?

Then said the trees unto the vine, Come thou, and reign over us.

And the vine said unto them, Should I leave my new wine, which cheereth God and men, and go to be promoted over the trees?

Then said all the trees unto the bramble, Come thou and reign over us.

And the bramble said unto the trees, If in truth ye anoint me king over you, then come and put your trust in my shadow; and if not, let fire come out of the bramble, and devour the cedars of Lebanon.

186 *The Holy Bible,* Judges 9:7–15.

>)>)>:(:(:

187 · The Beatitudes

Blessed are the poor in spirit: for theirs is the kingdom of heaven.

Blessed are they that mourn: for they shall be comforted.

Blessed are the meek: for they shall inherit the earth.

Blessed are they which do hunger and thirst after righteousness: for they shall be filled.

Blessed are the merciful: for they shall obtain mercy.

Blessed are the pure in heart: for they shall see God.

Blessed are the peacemakers: for they shall be called the children of God.

Blessed are they which are persecuted for righteousness' sake: for theirs is the kingdom of heaven.

[187] *The Holy Bible,* Matthew 5:3–9.

❖❂❖❂❖❂❖❂❖

188 · Bishops

This is a true saying, if a man desire the office of a bishop, he desireth a good work.

A bishop then must be blameless, the husband of one wife, vigilant, sober, of good behavior, given to hospitality, apt to teach;

Not given to wine, no striker, not greedy of filthy lucre; but patient, not a brawler, not covetous;

One that ruleth well his own house, having his children in subjection with all gravity;

(For if a man know not how to rule his own house, how shall he take care of the church of God?)

Not a novice, lest being lifted up with pride he fall into the condemnation of the devil.

Moreover he must have a good report of them which are without; lest he fall into reproach and the snare of the devil.

Likewise must the deacons be grave, not double-tongued, not given to much wine, not greedy of filthy lucre;

Holding the mystery of the faith in a pure conscience.

And let these also first be proved; then let them use the office of a deacon, being found blameless.

. . .

For they that have used the office of a deacon well purchase to themselves a good degree, and great boldness in the faith which is in Christ Jesus.

[188] *The Holy Bible,* I Timothy 3:1–10, 13.

❖❂❖❂❖❂❖❂❖

189 · Thanksgiving

My seventieth birthday arrived recently—that is to say, it arrived on the 30th of November, but Colonel Harvey was not able to celebrate it on that date because that date had been pre-empted by the President to be used as the usual and perfunctory Thanksgiving Day, a function which originated in New England two or three centuries ago when those people recognized that they really had something to be thankful for—annually, not oftener—if they had succeeded in exterminating their neighbors, the Indians, during the previous twelve months instead of getting exterminated by their neighbors, the Indians. Thanksgiving Day became a habit, for the reason that in the course of time, as the years drifted on, it was perceived that the exterminating had ceased to be mutual and was all on the white man's side, consequently on the Lord's side; hence it was proper to thank the Lord for it and extend the usual annual compliments. The original reason for a Thanksgiving Day has long ago ceased to exist—the Indians have long ago been comprehensively and satisfactorily exterminated and the account closed with the Lord, with the thanks due. But, from old habit, Thanksgiving Day has remained with us, and every year the President of the United States and the Governors of all the several states and territories set themselves the task, every November, to hunt up something to be thankful for, and then they put those thanks into a few crisp and reverent phrases, in the form of a proclamation, and this is read from all the pulpits in the land, the national conscience is wiped clean with one swipe, and sin is resumed at the old stand.

[189] Samuel L. Clemens, *Mark Twain's Autobiography* (New York: Harper & Brothers, 1924), I, 291. Copyright, 1924, by Clara Gabrilowitsch. Copyright, 1952, by Clara Clemens Samossoud.

❖❖❖❖❖❖❖❖❖

190 · The Candy-Pull

It is to this kind that untoward things happen. My sister gave a "candy-pull" on a winter's night. I was too young to be of the company, and Jim was too diffident. I was sent up to bed early, and Jim followed of his own motion. His room was in the new part of the house and his window looked out on the roof of the ∟ annex. That roof was six inches deep in snow, and the snow had an ice crust upon it which was as slick as glass. Out of the comb of the roof projected a short chimney, a common resort for sentimental cats on moonlight nights—and this was a moonlight night. Down at the eaves, below the chimney, a canopy of dead vines spread away to some posts, making a cozy shelter, and after an hour or two the rollicking crowd of young ladies and gentlemen grouped themselves in its shade, with their saucers of liquid and piping-hot candy disposed about them on the frozen ground to cool. There was a joyous chaffing and joking and laughter—peal upon peal of it.

About this time a couple of old, disreputable tomcats got up on the chimney and started a heated argument about something; also about this time I gave up trying to get to sleep and went visiting to Jim's room. He was awake and fuming about the cats and their intolerable yowling. I asked him, mockingly, why he didn't climb out and drive them away. He was nettled, and said overboldly that for two cents he *would*.

It was a rash remark and was probably repented of before it was fairly out of his mouth. But it was too late—he was committed. I knew him; and I knew he would rather break his neck than back down, if I egged him on judiciously.

"Oh, of course you would! Who's doubting it?"

It galled him, and he burst out, with sharp irritation, "Maybe *you* doubt it!"

"I? Oh no! I shouldn't think of such a thing. You are always doing wonderful things, with your mouth."

He was in a passion now. He snatched on his yarn socks and began to raise the window, saying in a voice quivering with anger:

"*You* think I dasn't—you do! Think what you blame please. *I* don't care what you think. I'll show you!"

The window made him rage; it wouldn't stay up.

I said, "Never mind, I'll hold it."

Indeed, I would have done anything to help. I was only a boy and was already in a radiant heaven of anticipation. He climbed carefully out, clung to the window sill until his feet were safely placed, then began to pick his perilous way on all-fours along the glassy comb, a foot and a hand on each side of it. I believe I enjoy it now as much as I did then; yet it is nearly fifty years ago. The frosty breeze flapped his short shirt about his lean legs; the crystal roof shone like polished marble in the intense glory of the moon; the unconscious cats sat erect upon the chimney, alertly watching each other, lashing their tails and pouring out their hollow grievances; and slowly and cautiously Jim crept on, flapping as he went, the gay and frolicsome young creatures under the vine canopy unaware, and outraging these solemnities with their misplaced laughter. Every time Jim slipped I had a hope; but always on he crept and disappointed it. At last he was within reaching distance. He paused, raised himself carefully up, measured his distance deliberately, then made a frantic grab at the nearest cat—and missed it. Of course he lost his balance. His heels flew up, he struck on his back, and like a rocket he darted down the roof feet first, crashed through the dead vines, and landed in a sitting position in fourteen saucers of red-hot candy, in the midst of all that party—and dressed as *he* was—this lad who could not look a girl in the face with his clothes on. There was a wild scramble and a storm of shrieks, and Jim fled up the stairs, dripping broken crockery all the way.

[190] Samuel L. Clemens, *Mark Twain's Autobiography* (New York: Harper & Brothers, 1924), I, 135–138. Copyright, 1924, by Clara Gabrilowitsch. Copyright, 1952, by Clara Clemens Samossoud.

➤➤➤➤◆◀◀◀◀

191 · The Happy Prince

High above the city, on a tall column, stood the statue of the Happy Prince. He was gilded all over with thin leaves of fine gold, for eyes he had two bright sapphires, and a large red ruby glowed on his sword-hilt.

He was very much admired, indeed. "He is as beautiful as a weather-cock," remarked one of the Town Councillors who wished to gain a reputation for having artistic tastes; "only not quite so useful," he added, fearing lest people should think him unpractical, which he really was not.

"Why can't you be like the Happy Prince?" asked a sensible mother of her little boy who was crying for the moon. "The Happy Prince never dreams of crying for anything."

"I am glad there is someone in the world who is quite happy," muttered a disappointed man as he gazed at the wonderful statue.

"He looks just like an angel," said the Charity Children as they came out of the cathedral in their bright scarlet cloaks, and their clean white pinafores.

"How do you know?" said the Mathematical Master, "you have never seen one."

"Ah! but we have, in our dreams," answered the children; and the Mathematical Master frowned and looked very severe, for he did not approve of children dreaming.

One night there flew over the city a little Swallow. His friends had gone away to Egypt six weeks before, but he had stayed behind, for he was in love with the most beautiful Reed. He had met her early in the spring as he was flying down the river after a big yellow moth, and had been so attracted by her slender waist that he had stopped to talk to her.

"Shall I love you?" said the Swallow, who liked to come to the point at once, and the Reed made him a low bow. So he flew round and round her, touching the water with his wings, and making silver ripples. This was his courtship, and it lasted all through the summer.

"It is a ridiculous attachment," twittered the other Swallows, "she has no money, and far too many relations"; and, indeed, the river was quite full of Reeds. Then, when the autumn came, they all flew away.

After they had gone he felt lonely, and began to tire of his lady-love. "She has no conversation," he said, "and I am afraid that she is a coquette, for she is always flirting with the wind." And certainly, whenever the wind blew, the Reed made the most graceful curtsies. "I admit that she is domestic," he continued, "but I love travelling, and my wife, consequently, should love travelling also."

"Will you come away with me?" he said finally to her; but the Reed shook her head, she was so attached to her home.

"You have been trifling with me," he cried. "I am off to the Pyramids. Good-bye!" and he flew away.

All day long he flew, and at night-time he arrived at the city. "Where shall I put up?" he said; "I hope the town has made preparations."

Then he saw the statue on the tall column. "I will put up there," he cried; "it is a fine position with plenty of fresh air." So he alighted just between the feet of the Happy Prince.

"I have a golden bedroom," he said softly to himself as he looked round, and he prepared to go to sleep; but just as he was putting his head under his wing a large drop of water fell on him. "What a curious thing!" he cried, "there is not a single cloud in the sky, the stars are quite clear and bright, and yet it is raining. The climate in the north of Europe is really dreadful. The Reed used to like the rain, but that was merely her selfishness."

Then another drop fell.

"What is the use of a statue if it cannot keep the rain off?" he said; "I must look for a good chimney-pot," and he determined to fly away.

But before he had opened his wings, a third drop fell, and he looked up, and saw—Ah! what did he see?

The eyes of the Happy Prince were filled with tears, and tears were running down his golden cheeks. His face was so beautiful in the moonlight that the little Swallow was filled with pity.

"Who are you?" he said.

"I am the Happy Prince."

"Why are you weeping then?" asked the Swallow; "you have quite drenched me."

"When I was alive and had a human heart," answered the statue, "I did not know what tears were, for I lived in the Palace of Sans Souci, where sorrow is not allowed to enter. In the daytime I played with my companions in the garden, and in the evening I led the dance in the Great Hall. Round the garden ran a very lofty wall, but I never cared to ask what lay beyond it, everything about me was so beautiful. My courtiers called me the Happy Prince, and happy indeed I was, if pleasure be happiness. So I lived, and so I died. And now that I am dead they have set me up here so high that I can see all the ugliness and all the misery of my city, and though my heart is made of lead yet I cannot choose but weep."

"What, is he not solid gold?" said the Swallow to himself. He was too polite to make any personal remarks out loud.

"Far away," continued the statue in a low, musical voice, "far away in a little street there is a poor house. One of the windows is open, and through it I can see a woman seated at a table. Her face is thin and worn, and she has coarse red hands, all pricked by the needle, for she is a seamstress. She is embroidering passion-flowers on a satin gown for the loveliest of the Queen's maids-of-honor to wear at the next Court-ball. In a bed in the corner of the room her little boy is lying ill. He has a fever, and is asking for oranges. His mother has nothing to give him but river water, so he is crying. Swallow, Swallow, little Swallow, will you not bring her the ruby out of my sword-hilt? My feet are fastened to this pedestal and I cannot move."

"I am waited for in Egypt," said the Swallow. "My friends are flying up and down the Nile, and talking to the large lotus-flowers. Soon they will be going to sleep in the tomb of the great King. The King is there himself in his painted coffin. He is wrapped in yellow linen, and enbalmed with spices. Round his neck is a chain of pale green jade, and his hands are like withered leaves."

"Swallow, Swallow, little Swallow," said the Prince, "will you not stay with me for one night, and be my messenger? The boy is so thirsty, and the mother so sad."

"I don't think I like boys," answered the Swallow. "Last summer, when I was staying on the river, there were two rude boys, the miller's sons, who were always throwing stones at me. They never hit me, of course; we swallows fly far too well for that, and besides, I come of a family famous for its agility; but still, it was a mark of disrespect."

But the Happy Prince looked so sad that the little Swallow was sorry. "It is very cold here," he said; "but I will stay with you for one night, and be your messenger."

"Thank you, little Swallow," said the Prince.

So the Swallow picked out the great ruby from the Prince's sword, and flew away with it in his beak over the roofs of the town.

He passed by the cathedral tower, where the white marble angels were sculptured. He passed by the palace and heard the sound of dancing. A beautiful girl came out on the balcony with her lover. "How wonderful the stars are," he said to her, "and how wonderful is the power of love!" "I hope my dress will be ready in time for the State-ball," she answered; "I have ordered passion-flowers to be embroidered on it; but the seam-stresses are so lazy."

He passed over the river, and saw the lanterns hanging to the masts of the ships. He passed over the Ghetto, and saw the old Jews bargaining with each other, and weighing out money in copper scales. At last he came to the poor house and looked in. The boy was tossing feverishly on his bed, and the mother had fallen asleep, she was so tired. In he hopped, and laid the great ruby on the table beside the woman's thimble. Then he flew gently round the bed, fanning the boy's forehead with his wings. "How cool I feel," said the boy, "I must be getting better"; and he sank into a delicious slumber.

Then the Swallow flew back to the Happy Prince and told him what he had done. "It is curious," he remarked, "but I feel quite warm now, although it is so cold."

"That is because you have done a good action," said the Prince. And the little Swallow began to think, and then he fell asleep. Thinking always made him sleepy.

When day broke he flew down to the river and had a bath. "What a remarkable phenomenon," said the Professor of Ornithology as he was passing over the bridge. "A swallow in winter!" And he wrote a long letter about it to the local newspaper. Every one quoted it, it was full of so many words that they could not understand.

"To-night I go to Egypt," said the Swallow, and he was in high spirits at the prospect. He visited all the public monuments, and sat a long time on the top of the church steeple. Wherever he went the sparrows chirruped, and said to each other, "What a distinguished stranger!" so he enjoyed himself very much.

When the moon rose he flew back to the Happy Prince. "Have you any commissions for Egypt?" he cried. "I am just starting."

"Swallow, Swallow, little Swallow," said the Prince, "will you not stay with me one night longer?"

"I am waited for in Egypt," answered the Swallow. "To-morrow my friends will fly up to the Second Cataract. The river-horse couches there among the bulrushes, and on a great granite throne sits the God Memmon. All night long he watches the stars, and when the morning star shines he utters one cry of joy, and then he is silent. At noon the yellow lions come down to the water's edge to drink. They have eyes like green beryls, and their roar is louder than the roar of the cataract."

"Swallow, Swallow, little Swallow," said the Prince, "far away across the city I see a young man in a garret. He is leaning over a desk covered with papers, and in a tumbler by his side there is a bunch of withered violets. His hair is brown and crisp, and his lips are red as a pomegranate, and he has large and dreamy eyes. He is trying to finish a play for the Director of the Theatre, but he is too cold to write any more. There is no fire in the grate, and hunger has made him faint."

"I will wait with you one night longer," said the Swallow, who really had a good heart. "Shall I take him another ruby?"

"Alas! I have no ruby now," said the Prince; "my eyes are all that I have left. They are made of rare sapphires, which were brought out of India a thousand years ago. Pluck out one of them and take it to him. He will sell it to the jeweller, and buy food and firewood, and finish his play."

"Dear Prince," said the Swallow, "I cannot do that;" and he began to weep.

"Swallow, Swallow, little Swallow," said the Prince, "do as I command you."

So the Swallow plucked out the Prince's eye, and flew away to the student's garret. It was easy enough to get in, as there was a hole in the roof. Through this he darted, and came into the room. The young man had his head buried in his hands, so he did not hear the flutter of the bird's wings, and when he looked up he found the beautiful sapphire lying on the withered violets.

"I am beginning to be appreciated," he cried; "this is from some great admirer. Now I can finish my play," and he looked quite happy.

The next day the Swallow flew down to the harbour. He sat on the mast of a large vessel and watched the sailors hauling big chests out of the hold with ropes. "Heave a-hoy!" they shouted as each chest came up. "I am going to Egypt!" cried the Swallow, but nobody minded, and when the moon rose he flew back to the Happy Prince.

"I am come to bid you good-bye," he cried.

"Swallow, Swallow, little Swallow," said the Prince, "will you not stay with me one night longer?"

"It is winter," answered the Swallow, "and the chill snow will soon be here. In Egypt the sun is warm on the green palm-trees, and the crocodiles lie in the mud and look lazily about them. My companions are building a nest in the Temple of Baalbec, and the pink and white doves are watching them, and cooing to each other. Dear Prince, I must leave you, but I will never forget you, and next spring I will bring you back two beautiful jewels in place of those you have given away. The ruby shall be redder than a red rose, and the sapphire shall be as blue as the great sea."

"In the square below," said the Happy Prince, "there stands a little match-girl. She has let her matches fall in the gutter, and they are all spoiled. Her father will beat her if she does not bring home some money, and she is crying. She has no shoes or stockings, and her little head is bare. Pluck out my other eye, and give it to her, and her father will not beat her."

"I will stay with you one night longer," said the Swallow, "but I cannot pluck out your eye. You would be quite blind then."

"Swallow, Swallow, little Swallow," said the Prince, "do as I command you."

So he plucked out the Prince's other eye, and darted down with it. He swooped past the match-girl, and slipped the jewel into the palm of her hand. "What a lovely bit of glass," cried the little girl; and she ran home, laughing.

Then the Swallow came back to the Prince. "You are blind now," he said, "so I will stay with you always."

"No, little Swallow," said the poor Prince, "you must go away to Egypt."

"I will stay with you always," said the Swallow, and he slept at the Prince's feet.

All the next day he sat on the Prince's shoulder, and told him stories of what he had seen in strange lands. He told him of the red ibises, who stand in long rows on the banks of the Nile, and catch gold fish in their beaks; of the Sphinx, who is as old as the world itself, and lives in the desert, and knows everything; of the merchants, who walk slowly by the side of their camels, and carry amber beads in their hands; of the King of the Mountains of the Moon, who is as black as ebony, and worships a large crystal; of the great green snake that sleeps in a palm-tree, and has twenty priests to feed it with honey-cakes; and of the pygmies who sail over a big lake on large flat leaves, and are always at war with the butterflies.

"Dear little Swallow," said the Prince, "you tell me of marvellous things, but more marvellous than anything is the suffering of men and of women. There is no Mystery so great as Misery. Fly over my city, little Swallow, and tell me what you see there."

So the Swallow flew over the great city, and saw the rich making merry in their beautiful houses, while the beggars were sitting at the gates. He flew into dark lanes, and saw the white faces of starving children looking out listlessly at the black streets. Under the archway of a bridge two little boys were lying in one another's arms to try and keep themselves warm. "How hungry we are!" they said. "You must not lie here," shouted the Watchman, and they wandered out into the rain.

Then he flew back and told the Prince what he had seen.

"I am covered with fine gold," said the Prince, "you must take it off, leaf by leaf, and give it to my poor; the living always think that gold can make them happy."

Leaf after leaf of the fine gold the Swallow picked off, till the Happy Prince looked quite dull and grey. Leaf after leaf of the fine gold he brought to the poor, and the children's faces grew rosier, and they laughed and played games in the street. "We have bread now!" they cried.

Then the snow came, and after the snow came the frost. The streets looked as if they were made of silver, they were so bright and glistening; long icicles like crystal daggers hung down from the eaves of the houses, everybody went about in furs, and the little boys wore scarlet caps and skated on the ice.

The poor little Swallow grew colder and colder, but he would not leave the Prince, he loved him too well. He picked up crumbs outside the baker's door when the baker was not looking, and tried to keep himself warm by flapping his wings.

But at last he knew that he was going to die. He had just strength to fly up to the Prince's shoulder once more. "Good-bye, dear Prince!" he murmured, "will you let me kiss your hand?"

"I am glad that you are going to Egypt at last, little Swallow," said the Prince, "you have stayed too long here; but you must kiss me on the lips, for I love you."

"It is not to Egypt that I am going," said the Swallow. "I am going to the House of Death. Death is the brother of Sleep, is he not?"

And he kissed the Happy Prince on the lips, and fell down dead at his feet.

At that moment a curious crack sounded inside the statue, as if something had broken. The fact is that the leaden heart had snapped right in two. It certainly was a dreadfully hard frost.

Early the next morning the Mayor was walking in the square below in company with the Town Councillors. As they passed the column he looked up at the statue: "Dear me! how shabby the Happy Prince looks!" he said.

"How shabby indeed!" cried the Town Councillors, who always agreed with the Mayor, and they went up to look at it.

"The ruby has fallen out of his sword, his eyes are gone, and he is golden no longer," said the Mayor; "in fact, he is little better than a beggar!"

"Little better than a beggar," said the Town Councillors.

"And here is actually a dead bird at his feet!" continued the Mayor. "We must really issue a proclamation that birds are not to be allowed to die here." And the Town Clerk made a note of the suggestion.

So they pulled down the statue of the Happy Prince. "As he is no longer beautiful he is no longer useful," said the Art Professor at the University.

Then they melted the statue in a furnace, and the Mayor held a meeting of the Corporation to decide what was to be done with the metal. "We must have another statue, of course," he said, "and it shall be a statue of myself."

"Of myself," said each of the Town Councillors, and they quarrelled. When I last heard of them they were quarrelling still.

"What a strange thing," said the overseer of the workmen at the foundry. "This broken lead heart will not melt in the furnace. We must throw it away." So they threw it on a dust heap where the dead Swallow was also lying.

"Bring me the two most precious things in the city," said God to one of His Angels; and the Angel brought Him the leaden heart and the dead bird.

"You have rightly chosen," said God, "for in my garden of Paradise this little bird shall sing for evermore, and in my city of gold the Happy Prince shall praise me."

[191] Oscar Wilde, *The Happy Prince and Other Tales* (1888).

✤❭✦❭❱✦❰✦❰✦

192 · Guilty before Trial

It is a pleasure and a privilege to be here today and to take part in this great jubilee that the Boston Chamber of Commerce is staging. I am particularly happy to see assembled in this room such a representative cross-section of American enterprise. Here at a table in front of me I see some of my old friends from the Smaller Business Association of New England, and at other tables throughout the room are many of the outstanding business and industrial leaders from almost every section of the country.

Believe me, gentlemen, I am proud indeed to stand in the company of men who have done so much to give the American people the most bountiful standard of living this world has ever seen. It is reassuring to know that success in business is not yet regarded as a disgrace in this great land of ours, and that fruitful enterprise is not without honor, except, perhaps, in some parts of our national capital.

However, I must confess that I am a little surprised at the boldness of the Boston Chamber of Commerce in arranging this celebration at all. Now I wouldn't say, of course, that you are boasting or bragging about your city, because I realize fully that no true Bostonian would ever permit himself to take more than a modest and becoming pride even in Boston's most spectacular achievements. But I will say that you are certainly making no secret whatever of the fact that Boston is big and important and rich and successful.

Perhaps you gentlemen have forgotten that Boston is an incorporated city, and that no corporate entity today can safely possess the characteristics to which you are pointing with such natural and pardonable pride. So I think I should warn you that down along the banks of the Potomac, the wise and prudent businessman speaks of these things only in apologetic whispers and the motto that he follows is: "Grow Slow."

I do not wish to convey the impression, however, that this antipathy towards bigness and success is universally entertained in Washington. It isn't. There are Government officials who, I feel sure, look with high favor upon big business and good profits; and it is a great pleasure to have one of these Washington friends with us today. I refer, of course, to the distinguished Assistant Secretary of the Treasury, Mr. Graham. He has my deepest sympathy for he has to meet what I suppose is the largest payroll in the world—the Federal payroll. On the other hand, I am certain that he must be very grateful indeed to all of us businessmen for the help we give him. I do not know, of course, how well he makes out with the rest of you gentlemen; but as far as U.S. Steel is concerned, the tax collectors are getting two and a quarter times as much out of our business as the stockholders are.

So I think we have a right to assume that we are all among friends, and that the long-range interests of the Government and of business are really the same things after all. How could it be otherwise when Government is wholly dependent upon the success of business and industry; when business and industry are equally dependent upon successful Government and when the American people are dependent upon both? So any development which threatens the welfare of business or of Government is—and ought to be—a matter of immediate concern to both.

And that is why I want to talk with you today about a problem that President Truman discussed in a special message which he sent to Congress two weeks ago—a message on small business. It was a temperate, reasoned, non-political exposition of his views on the subject; and it is in this same temperate, reasoned and wholly non-political vein that I propose to comment upon it.

After saying a few guardedly kind words about big business, the President pointed out that—great and successful as this economic system of ours has been—it still is not as good as he—or as any of us for that matter—would want it to be. He said that it is not providing jobs for all the men and women who want work, and that—if it is ever to provide full employment—more new businesses, and more small businesses, must be established. He recommended therefore that Congress pass legislation designed to provide these new, small businesses with capital and with technical assistance.

Now gentlemen, I have noticed that whenever our Government officials set out, these days, to be helpful to some segment of our economy, they think almost automatically in terms of money—of financial aids, or subsidies. These are governmental crutches which may serve well enough to support an economic invalid, but—of themselves—they can do nothing to cure his basic affliction. Unless the Government contemplates going into the crutch business permanently, therefore, the day must come when these businesses will be able to stand squarely on their own feet. So I can't help wondering if the President, in his program, has really probed down to the roots of the trouble.

Certainly we must recognize the fact that for more than 300 years, our American economic system has provided employment for our people as our Nation has grown. Of course, there have been temporary periods of depression and famine—the "lean years" that have always beset both the agricultural and industrial advances of mankind since the days of Joseph and the Pharaohs. But over the centuries, generally, there have been jobs in America for all.

Now if what the President says is true—if our system is no longer fulfilling our employment needs in this day and hour when we are enjoying a relatively high peak of prosperity—then, somewhere, there is a monkey wrench in the machinery. And since all of us here in this room are intimately acquainted with the working parts of our industrial economy, it seems to me that it's up to us to find the monkey wrench before it is too late.

Let's look around. Here we are in Boston, the birthplace of American manufacturing and one of the Nation's great centers of investment capital.

More than 125 new manufacturing enterprises are established here in Greater Boston every year. So, clearly, we do have new businesses. Moreover, Massachusetts has more investors in proportion to its population than any other State in the Union, and the savings deposits in Boston's banks are nearly three times the national average on a per capita basis. Clearly, therefore, there is available capital for business here.

Why is it then that we do not have more new businesses? Why are investors unwilling to risk more of their savings? Or, why are our people unwilling to seek more of this capital and to set themselves up in business?

Gentlemen, as a mechanic who has had some slight experience with this great industrial machine of ours, it is my professional opinion that we will do well to look for that misplaced monkey wrench in the Washington gear box. In fact, it would not surprise me if we were to find several monkey wrenches there.

We shall certainly find tax laws that discourage investment and that encourage small businessmen to sell out, and to cash in on their capital gains.

We shall find widespread antagonism towards profits and a reluctance to recognize the facts of inflation. Everybody realizes that a worker who earned $30 a week in 1939 now has to get $51 in order to have the same amount of purchasing power. Yet few people seem to understand t'at the stockholder who got a $6 dividend in 1939, now has to get $10.20 on that same investment, just to break even in terms of our present-day, sixty-cent greenbacks.

We shall find other laws and attitudes that will certainly tend to discourage even the most venturesome newcomer to the field of business, but the biggest monkey wrench of all—the greatest single drawback to the effective operation of our modern economic system—is the amazing but undeniable fact that the minute any man successfully establishes himself in any business nowadays, he automatically becomes a potential jailbird.

Yes, the truth is that we have on our Federal statute books today a complete hodge-podge of so-called "anti-trust" laws which have been allowed to grow, like Topsy, for sixty years, and which cannot be reconciled even with each other. And the only way a businessman can be sure of obeying them all is just to go broke.

Now gentlemen, I am not a lawyer and I'm not going to ask you to take my word for that. I shall merely read you a comment written by Supreme Court Justice Jackson when he was the head of the Anti-Trust Division in the Department of Justice. He said:

> It is impossible for a lawyer to determine what business conduct will be pronounced lawful by the Courts. This situation is embarrassing to businessmen wishing to obey the law and to Government officials attempting to enforce it.

In other words, gentlemen, nobody in business, in Government, or anywhere else, knows what the law is except the Supreme Court of the United States, and sometimes even the members of the Court don't seem to be too sure about it. In fact, the present judicial attitude towards our anti-monopoly laws reminds me of a quotation from Ralph Waldo Emerson which is carved in large letters on the side of the new Hunter College building in New York, but which might be equally appropriate if chiseled on the marble walls of the Supreme Court building in Washington. It says:

> We are of different opinions at different hours; but we always may be said to be, at heart, on the side of truth.

Now that is a very commendable philosophy. An enlightened willingness to change one's mind from hour to hour may be a fine thing in the academic atmosphere of any College or of any Court, but speaking as a practical businessman, I can only say, "It's a helluva way to run a railroad."

So we come face to face with the fact that laws governing business are not really written in Congress, but in the Courts, and what five members of the Supreme Court say the law is, may be something vastly different from what Congress intended the law to be.

Again I do not ask you to take my word for it. I refer you to a quotation cited by United States Supreme Court Justice Burton in his dissenting opinion in the Cement Case. There it was pointed out that the basing point system had been in use by industry for half a century, and that Congress—after repeated study—had steadfastly refused to pass any of the bills proposing to outlaw it. Then it was said:

> We know of no criticism so often and so forcibly directed at the Courts—particularly the Federal Courts—as their propensity for usurping the functions of Congress. If this pricing system which Congress, over the years, has steadfastly refused to declare illegal, is now to be outlawed by the Courts, it will mark the high tide in judicial usurpation.

Yet the Court, as you know, did outlaw the selling methods used in the cement industry. The result was that the heads of more than 100,000 American businesses—men who had been conducting their affairs in a perfectly law-abiding manner—were suddenly confronted by the possibility of being classed as criminals.

Gentlemen, I don't have to tell you that if we persist in that kind of a system of law—and if we enforce it impartially against all offenders—virtually every business in America, big and small, is going to have to be run from Atlanta, Sing Sing, Leavenworth, or Alcatraz.

And that is no mere personal opinion on my part either. One of the severest critics of this legalistic merry-go-round we live on is Chairman Lowell Mason of the Federal Trade Commission, whose duty it is to enforce many of these laws, and who can therefore be regarded as one of the Nation's outstanding authorities on the subject.

He says:

> American business is being harassed, bled and even blackjacked under a preposterous crazyquilt system of laws, many of which are unintelligible, unenforceable and unfair. There is such a welter of laws governing interstate commerce that the Government literally can find some charge to bring against any concern it chooses to prose-

cute. I say that this system is an outrage, and that it's time the Government did something sensible about bringing its own operations up to the same standard of ethics that it expects of business.

Now those are strong words, coming from a member of the Federal Trade Commission and from a man who was appointed to that office by President Truman. Unfortunately, they are also true words.

The unhappy fact is that once a man goes into business, anything he does is wrong. We don't need a lawyer to tell us that. Most of us know it from our own personal experience. Let's take the question of competition, for example:

To a practical businessman—and stripped of a lot of legalistic gobbledygook—competition is a very simple thing. It exists when two or more companies are trying to sell similar products to the same customer. But when the businessman of today tries to compete in the open market, what happens?

If his product is of approximately the same quality as that of his competitor, if each competitor provides the same service, and if both enjoy equally good reputations for dependability and integrity, it is perfectly obvious that both are going to have to offer their wares at the same price in order to keep in the running.

But if both quote the same price, that fact alone is construed to be evidence of collusion and a violation of the Sherman Anti-Trust Law.

So our businessman cuts his price, tries to undersell his competitor, and thinks he's staying safely on the right side of the Sherman Act. Don't ever try that, my friends, because then you're in *real* trouble under the Robinson-Patman Act. Look what happened to Minneapolis-Honeywell, and to Standard Oil of Indiana when they tried to cut *their* prices to meet their competition. The A. & P. has been accused—among other things— of consistently *underselling* its competitors. And one of the charges in the suit that the Department of Justice has brought against Du Pont is that the company *lowered* the price of cellophane twenty-one times.

So if our businessman obeys the Sherman Law he is probably violating the Robinson-Patman Act, and if he obeys the Robinson-Patman Act he is almost sure to be violating the Sherman Anti-Trust Law. He can't lower his price safely, and he can't leave it where it is; so the only thing left for him to do is to *raise* it. There's no law against that, of course, except the law of supply and demand.

If he raises his price, and his competitors don't, he goes out of business. If his competitors do follow his lead and raise their prices too, he can stay in business, but he's right back where he started so far as the anti-trust laws are concerned, and in addition to that he is almost certain to get an "invitation"—or a subpoena—from Senator O'Mahoney and Congressman Celler. Whatever he does, he's sunk.

It's no wonder people are reluctant to rush in and start new businesses today. The only mystery to me is that any new businesses are started at all.

But that is only a part of the story. The laws governing competition and prices have been changed frequently. Mr. Mason puts it this way.

> In 1932 we put a pants presser in jail if he conspired to fix prices. In 1933 we put him in jail if he didn't. Next year, vice versa again.
>
> Later on, if he went into the coal business we assessed a heavy penalty against him if he didn't charge a fixed price. That is, of course, if the coal was soft. If it was hard—vice versa.
>
> Then take the meat packers. We made them get out of the retail chain store business in 1920. But now there are half a dozen big retail chains in the meat packing business. I guess the meat packers just went into the wrong business first.

Is it any wonder, gentlemen, that a businessman gets discouraged these days when not even his lawyer can figure out which end is up? But that's not the end of his troubles either. In 1941, in the Rigid Conduit Case, the Federal Trade Commission's staff came up with a wonderful new theory. It decided that it didn't even have to go to the trouble of finding a businessman guilty of any transgression of the law. His personal guilt—or lack of it—didn't matter. If the Commission felt that there was a social danger involved, it could issue an order against him anyway.

Lowell Mason, in a recent speech before the American Steel Warehouse Association in Texas, pointed out that this interesting theory of justice—whereby a man could be penalized without being found guilty of anything—was introduced in Russia by Commissar Krylenko. "It is not clear," he says, "whether the Federal Trade Commission got the idea from Krylenko, or whether Krylenko got it from the Commission."

In any event, he observes, Krylenko has since been liquidated; but the American authors of the same philosophy within the Commission have not.

These, then, are a few of the hurdles that confront the intrepid soul who would venture into the business world today—but they are only a few. A compilation of the orders already issued by the Federal Trade Commission shows that there are more than 2,200 different business practices that have been held to be illegal. So our newcomer in the field would, of course, do well to memorize this list with painstaking care before he even unlocks the door of his own office.

Gentlemen, I shall not belabor the point further. I merely submit that when every businessman in America can be found guilty of violating the law, then there is something wrong with the law—and not with the businessman. From our theorists in Washington today, we hear a great deal about "tightening the loopholes" in our anti-monopoly legislation.

In heaven's name, gentlemen, what loopholes?

What we need is not a tightening of the laws, or a loosening of them, but a complete redefinition of lawful business conduct. To quote one final thought-provoking sentence from Lowell Mason: "The Comintern loves it when the men of America who govern, pit themselves against the men of America who produce, and it's time that the Government and business stopped playing cops and robbers with each other."

To that, I think all of us here will utter a profound "Amen."

It takes a man of real courage to go into business today, knowing that he must satisfy the conflicting demands of his workers, his stockholders, and his customers. Any man who can do that deserves to succeed for he is performing a great public service. And if he is willing to take such risks, it seems to me that he is entitled to look to his Government for aid—not in the form of loans, or grants, or subsidies—but in the form of clean-cut, understandable rules which clearly mark the boundaries of good and lawful business practice.

The defining of those boundaries should not be left to those who hate business, to those who seek personal or political power over it, nor to theorists who want to experiment with it. It is not a job for irresponsible underlings in Federal bureaus. It is a job which requires the highest skills of Government officials who understand the problems of business, and of businessmen who understand the problems of Government. It is a job— in short—for men who have a mutual respect for the rights of each other, and a common devotion to the welfare of America.

If the realistic and informed men of Government will ever sit down with reasonable and experienced men of business and make up their collective mind as to what monopoly really is, what competition is, what business conduct is ethical and proper, and what business conduct is injurious and wrong, I think we will find fewer monkey wrenches in the machinery, and the Government will be able to get out of the crutch business in short order. I believe we need then have no fears about our economic system. It will continue—as it has for these past 330 years—to provide us with the jobs we need and the abundance of goods and services that has made America the wealthiest, happiest, and most secure nation in the world.

But all this is not just going to happen of its own accord. It is not going to happen at all unless we do something about it. As Americans we take pride in this historic city and in this historic State—in Faneuil Hall, the cradle of our precious liberties, and in the Bill of Rights which was forever to protect us from the petty tyrannies of thoughtless and indifferent government.

I can think of no more appropriate surroundings therefore in which to dedicate ourselves here and now to the task of winning from our Congress at Washington the one remaining right that today is unjustly denied to every businessman in America and to every man in America who may wish to go into business.

That is the right to be right!

192 An address by Benjamin F. Fairless, President of the United States Steel Corporation, at the Boston Jubilee of 1950, Mid-Century Celebration of Progress, Boston, Massachusetts, May 18, 1950.

❖⟩❖⟩❖⟨❖⟨❖

193 · How Congress Makes a Law

I have intended in one of these regular radio reports to the people of Pennsylvania to paint, in broad strokes, a picture of the way a piece of legislation is born, and the fashion in which it ultimately grows up to become a public law.

Of course, to those of us who are Members of the House of Representatives, or the Senate, knowledge of this sort is part of our stock-in-trade, but I have often been surprised, in reading over my mail, or in talking to Pennsylvanians who come to see me, when I realize that relatively little is understood about the way Congress operates.

Let us suppose that a matter comes to my attention with the indication that it would be desirable to pass a law relating to it. The first step, naturally, involves quite a bit of research into the existing laws we already have on the books to make absolutely certain that there is no legislative provision which covers the situation. When I am satisfied that no suitable legislation exists, the next step is one of collecting all of the factual background I can possibly get in order that I may be sure the proposal has merit.

In gathering these facts, it is frequently necessary to call upon experts in Pennsylvania who are acquainted with the matter, and who can explain what this will mean to the people of our State. It is also necessary, quite frequently to call upon representatives of the local, or the state, or the Federal Government, for their comments and recommendations regarding the proposal.

Then, with all the facts before me, I go over the various means which have been suggested for accomplishing the desired result. Then follows the job of drawing up a bill, which, in appropriate legal terms, will carry out the intended purpose of the law. Members of the Senate are assisted in drafting this legal language by an official group known as the Legislative Counsel, a body of skilled lawyers, who are expert in drawing up legislation.

The steps I have enumerated thus far may, in the case of comprehensive legislation, consume weeks, or even months, before I am satisfied that we have come up with a proposal suitable for the purpose at hand. On the other hand, of course, there are occasions where the facts are clear from the start, where the remedy needed is a simple one that may be accomplished with the passage of a short, concise piece of legislation.

In any event, once the bill is drafted, the rules of the Senate permit any Member to introduce a bill at any time, or at least there are very few occasions in the Senate when we may not interrupt debate long enough to introduce a piece of proposed legislation. This is accomplished by rising from your chair on the Senate floor and being recognized by the Presiding Officer, explaining that you wish to submit a bill.

Only under the most unusual circumstances does the Senate proceed immediately to consider and vote on the proposal at the time it is introduced. Instead, the Presiding Officer of the Senate refers the proposal to one of the standing legislative committees.

Now let me explain to you just what these legislative committees do. We have, in the Senate, a total of fifteen such committees, and I will name each of them now in order that you can see the type of legislation which each of these considers. We have a Committee on Agriculture and Forestry, a Committee on Appropriations, on Armed Services, on Banking and Currency, a Committee on the District of Columbia, on Expenditures in the Executive Departments, on Finance, a Committee on Foreign Relations, and then on Interior and Insular Affairs, a Committee on Interstate and Foreign Commerce, and on the Judiciary, a Committee on Labor and Public Welfare, and one on Post Office and Civil Service, another on Public Works, and on Rules and Administration.

With the exception of the Appropriations Committee, each of these fifteen Committees is composed of thirteen of the 96 Members of the Senate. As a general practice, every Senator serves on two such legislative committees. I, for example, am a member of the Finance Committee and the Senate Committee on Interstate and Foreign Commerce. In the 81st Congress, in which, as you know, the Democrats outnumber the Republicans in both houses, there are usually 8 Democrats and 5 Republicans to make up the 13 members of the committees, since this ratio is approximately proportional to the ratio of Democrats to Republicans in the Senate.

When you stop to think about it, it is obvious why we must have a committee system in the Congress. Let me illustrate this by pointing out that 2,675 separate bills were introduced by the 96 Members of the Senate in the first session of the 81st Congress. It's obvious that no Member of the Senate could be familiar with all of the provisions of all of these bills. It's obvious, too, that there may be three or four, or sometimes as many as fifteen or twenty, bills introduced by different Senators, all of which deal with aspects of the same problem.

So the primary purpose of our legislative committees is to provide the Senate with a relatively small group which becomes expert, say, in matters of the Armed Services. All of the bills that relate to the Armed

Services are referred to that Committee. It is the Committee's duty to examine them all. The Committee may decide it would be preferable to group a number of bills together, consider them all at once and report out a single piece of legislation which covers all of the situations visualized by those separate measures. On the other hand, the Committee may have before it only one bill which relates to a given proposal, and in that event, the measure will be considered separately.

It is surprising how few of the bills referred to any committee are controversial. And under these circumstances, the Committee will examine the merits of the proposal and perhaps vote to report the original bill pretty much in the form it was submitted, recommending at the same time that the Senate act favorably upon it.

Where a number of bills are considered at the same time, however, where the matters involved are steeped in controversy over the way the situation should be handled, the usual practice of the Committee is to appoint a subcommittee and conduct public hearings. To these hearings are invited the representative of groups interested in the legislation being considered. These witnesses explain to the Committee why they favor or oppose the various proposals under discussion. Particularly when the subject matter is comprehensive in its scope and controversial in its nature, Committee hearings may go on for months and months in an endeavor to put all of the facts of the case before the sub-committee.

When at last the Committee is satisfied that no new facts will be brought to light, the hearings are brought to a close, and the Members go into what is known as Executive Session. Here they debate among themselves all the various proposals, rejecting those that are clearly unsuitable, and attempting to work out provisions upon which all the Members can agree.

During the course of executive sessions, efforts are made to draft a single bill containing the proposals agreed to, and ultimately the 13 Members vote to recommend the new bill to the Senate. Such a Committee vote may produce any number of results. All 13 Members may agree unanimously to the bill as it then stands. This has been especially true in the field of foreign policy, where Republicans and Democrats alike on that Committee have agreed down to the last comma on virtually every measure reported from that Committee. Unanimous agreement by the 13 Members characterizes the vote in most Committees on most legislation.

There are, of course, the few occasions—occasions that are always given tremendous publicity—in which a Committee divides right down the middle and votes squarely along party lines, the Democrats voting one way, the Republicans the other. As I say, this doesn't happen often among the experts who know most about the legislation before them. When a Committee does vote 8 to 5 to report a bill in a particular form, the 5 minority Members almost invariably write a dissenting report, and you can generally count on a fight when such a measure hits the Senate floor.

I will say a brief word about the reports which accompany each bill as it is voted out of Committee and sent to the Senate. These reports usually outline the provisions of the bill, and summarize the Committee's reasons for recommending passage of the measure. A minority report points a finger at the provisions in the bill which the minority does not endorse, and gives the reasons for its opposition.

There is a final possibility that may result from a Committee vote. The Committee may vote to report out no legislation at all, thus bottling a bill up in Committee and, in effect, killing any chance that the Senate might consider it at all.

When this happens, about the only way in which the Senate may bring the issue to a vote is through the extraordinary tactic of the Senate itself voting to discharge the Committee of further consideration of the bill. You may recall that this tactic was proposed late last summer as a means of bringing the Displaced Persons bill out to the Senate floor. Before that tactic had been attempted, however, the Judiciary Committee did vote to report out the bill.

Once a bill has been reported out of Committee, it is placed upon the calendar of the Senate. The calendar is simply a list of bills upon which the Committee work has been completed and that are all ready for action.

It may surprise many of you, but almost all the bills passed by the Senate are passed with the unanimous consent of the entire body. This is accomplished by what we refer to as "calling the calendar." When this is done, we read down the list of bills, and if no objection is heard to the bill at the time its number is called, the measure is passed by unanimous consent. However, if only one Senator opposes a bill, he may enter an objection when the number is called, and the bill is held over to be brought up later for debate, and ultimately to be voted upon.

Once a bill has been objected to and passed over, it remains on the Senate calendar. Thereafter, it becomes the duty of the majority policy committee of the Senate to determine the time at which the measure will be brought up for debate. In my capacity as the Assistant Majority Leader of the Senate, or the "Whip," as the job is otherwise known, I am one of the eight Democratic Senators who serve on the majority policy committee. Our job, as I've already indicated, is first, to determine the sequence in which the legislation is brought up for debate. The policy committee has the further function of mapping the general strategy which will be used in guiding the legislative program of the Administration.

When the policy committee met shortly before the first day of this Session of the 81st Congress, we decided to bring up the oleo bill as the initial measure the Senate would consider.

Once a measure has been selected for debate, the efforts to obtain passage of the bill are usually assumed by the Senators who serve on the Committee which processed the legislation, since they are the real experts on the measure, and the Senate necessarily must rely on their special knowledge of the facts. The Committee Members are, of course, assisted by the Senate leaders, and for that matter, by any other Senators who wish to participate in the debate.

The bill, as you realize, must be agreed to in every respect by both the House and the Senate before it can be sent to the President for his signature, making it a public law. So, if the Senate is the first to pass the bill, it is referred then to the House of Representatives for consideration. If, on the other hand, the House has already passed the measure, but in a slightly different form from the Senate version, a conference committee, composed of a few Representatives and a few Senators, is appointed, and the compromise agreement is ultimately sent back to each house for its approval before sending it to the President.

Thus it is that a law is passed by the Congress. I hope you have enjoyed this broadcast, and that you will join me again in two weeks.

[193] Address by Francis J. Myers, transcribed and broadcasted over eighteen Pennsylvania radio stations, week end of January 20–22, 1950. *Vital Speeches of the Day,* XVI, No. 12 (April 1, 1950), 382–384.

❧❧❧❧❧❧❧

194 · For the Glory of God

Hear All You Who Labor and Bleed and Die That America Shall Live:

In the beginning God created the Heaven and Earth. On the sixth day the Almighty breathed life into man, the crown of his creation. The heavens are the abode of God, the earth He bequeathed to man.

Now the earth was filled with the bounty of God. From its bosom man drew coal to keep him warm, iron with which to make things, oil to enable him to traverse the length and breadth of this earth, and all manner of minerals to serve man and to enrich his days. Upon its face the earth grew grain from which man could make bread, and timber out of which man could build a home, and cotton from which man could weave clothes, and all manner of fruits and vegetables that man might prosper. Flocks grazed and strayed upon the fields of the earth, fish played in earth's sylvan stream, and from these man derived food and strength. What a magnificent heritage God bequeathed to man, this good mother earth. Eternal Thanksgiving to God!

How happily man could have lived upon this bountiful earth. But man heeded not the teachings of his creator. Man became quarrelsome, he divided himself into many groups and many nations. Man waxed greedy and tore the crumbs of bread out of the mouth of his brother—strife again.

Barriers sprang up between men; religious, geographical, economic. And man drew the iron from the bosom of the earth, not to make of it the useful plough and pruning-hook but the destructive sword and spear. Man slew his brother. Mother earth, once so beautifully green with life was stained with the red blood of violence. There was chaos and confusion, and there was cold and hunger, and the crown of God's creation was tarnished. For man heeded not the teachings of his Creator.

But lo in later centuries a great miracle occurred upon this sinful earth. It was as if the Almighty gave man another chance. A new continent was discovered—a rich and resourceful continent, America they called it. And to it flocked many children of man to begin life anew, to try living once again in accordance with God's will. They came from many lands, spoke many tongues, worshipped the same God in several ways. They were dreamers of dreams and weavers of hopes, they poured into this new land their strength and their joy and their sorrow. They brought forth a new nation, conceived in liberty and dedicated to the proposition that all men are created equal. Indeed they even believed that all men were endowed by their creator with certain inalienable rights, and among these were life, liberty, the pursuit of happiness. It was the kind of land that God had intended to have upon this earth. America they called it. Eternal Thanksgiving to God!

Among the many peoples who landed on these shores were the Jews— an old people, a bruised people, a people eternally dedicated to God. There were some who called them "God's chosen people," but they were really a *God-choosing people*. These people had sprung from a glorious land, Palestine they called it—a land where men seemed to draw nearer to God, a land that nurtured God-intoxicated men, a Moses and a Jesus, and a Mohammed. The Jewish people was born in freedom, weaned on the Ten Commandments, lullabied by the Psalmist, disciplined by the seer. But the Jewish people were not to hoard their spiritual treasures, they were to be the carriers of the ethics of Moses and the songs of David and the prophecies of Jeremiah, to all mankind. For the blessings of God, spiritual as well as material, are not the possessions of one group but are to be shared by all the children of God.

And so the Jewish people taught their ethics and songs and prophecies from generation to generation and from father to son, and many people were persuaded by their mission. Among the Jewish people was one named Joshua of Bethlehem, whom the Greeks called Jesus, and another named Saul of Tarsus, whom the Greeks called Paul. And these God-imbued saw God in a somewhat different light, and thus Mother Judaism gave birth to a Daughter, Christianity. And mother and daughter lived side by side for many centuries, sometimes disputing as members of a family will, but more often loving and respecting one another, for after all both sought the same God. And in the golden land of America especially, Judaism and Christianity lived together in peace and worked together in concord for the Glory of God, for the dignity of man, and for devotion to country. Eternal Thanksgiving to God!

Those who found God through Christianity were many in this America, and those who found Him through Judaism were few. The many and the few engaged in the common task giving their all proportionate to their number.

Among Christopher Columbus' intrepid little band of mariners were several Jewish seamen including Rodrigo de Triana and Luis De Torres.

Once this land was discovered no time was lost in erecting sanctuaries to God. The Christians were many in number and so they built their first church in the early sixteenth century. The Jews were a handful and so they waited until 1683 to build their first synagogue on old Mill Street in New York.

To this land came the pioneers of Jamestown and pilgrims of Plymouth Rock. They began to plant and build. Our American forefathers were a godly people and they were steeped in the teachings of the Old Testament, and they named their young by Biblical names. There are those who say "Hebraic mortar cemented the foundations of American democracy."

And the thirteen colonies had complaints against the mother-country. Bravely they proclaimed a Declaration of Independence. This was revolution, this was war. A mere 3,000 Jews lived in America during the Revolutionary War, 300 of them served in the militia and the regular army; and among them were Lieut. Colonel Isaac Franks and Major David Franks, and Major Benjamin Nones—staff officer under George Washington. And Haym Salomon, who gave all his possessions and his very life that the Continental Army might continue the campaign.

Christian and Jew, each according to this number, served in the Revolution. It was won. A new nation salutes the sun—the United States of America, founded on a constitution, buttressed by the Bill of Rights. Eternal Thanksgiving to God!

No longer say, General Washington, say now, President Washington. The founder and the first president wrote several letters to the Americans of Jewish faith. To the Congregation in Newport, Rhode Island, he wrote:

> The citizens of the United States have a right to applaud themselves for having given to mankind examples of an enlarged and liberal policy worthy of imitation. All possess alike liberty of conscience and immunities of citizenship. It is now no more, that toleration is spoken of as if it were by indulgence of one class of people that another enjoyed the exercise of their inherent natural right, for happily, the government of the United States which gives to *bigotry no sanction, to persecution no assistance,* requires only that they who live under its protection shall demean themselves as good citizens in giving it on all occasions their effectual support. May the children of the stock of Abraham continue to merit and enjoy the good will

of the other inhabitants, while every one shall sit in safety under his own vine and fig tree, and there shall be none to make him afraid.

And the young Republic grew and it flourished and it prospered. For it had found favor in God's eyes and He smiled beneficence upon it. And when there was war again, as in 1812, Christians and Jews, according to their number, gave their all. And among those who fought valiantly in this war was Commodore Uriah P. Levy, United States Navy, and Captain Mordecai Myers, United States Army. The war was won. And the Republic continued to grow and to prosper and its name became honored in the lands across the seas. Eternal Thanksgiving to God!

And more people came to these shores. Christians and Jews from every land. For they were refugees from the ravages of political and economic and social and religious persecutions in the Old World. They came here and joined hands with the builders of the New World.

Behold, grievances are multiplying among the states of the Union. Differences of opinion, quarrels, skirmishes, the nation splits—war between the states! And about this time there were some 200,000 of Jewish faith in America—6,000 served on the side of the North and 1,200 on the side of the South. Many fell, Christians and Jews, but that Nation of the people, by the people, and for the people, did not perish from the earth. Eternal Thanksgiving to God!

And the war-torn nation buried its dead, fulfilled its days of mourning and with malice toward none and charity toward all, bound up its wounds and resumed its growth.

And now more people came from across the seas. Christians and Jews from many lands. As these immigrants entered New York Harbor they beheld with prayerful gratitude the benevolent figure of the Statue of Liberty. And they noticed that upon her bosom was engraved these lines written by an American woman of Jewish faith, Emma Lazarus:

"Keep, ancient lands, your storied pomp!" cries she
    With silent lips. "Give me your tired, your poor
Your huddled masses yearning to breathe free,
    The wretched refuse of your teeming shore,
Send these, the homeless, tempest-tost to me.
    I lift my lamp beside the golden door."

And the tired and the poor and the tempest-tost swarmed to this land. And they tilled this soil and they erected these buildings, and they spanned this continent with road and rail. Christians and Jews from many lands, according to their number gave to America their brain and brawn. Both looked heavenward in prayer, and the Almighty looked down upon them and smiled as though to say, "This is as it should be, my children, bless you."

And now it was the twentieth century. Men across the seas began to quarrel for more colonies and for trade. Fiercely they competed with each other and then an explosion, the World War. Once again misery and sorrow cloaked the earth. Those in battle respected neither the property nor person of neutral America. War-hating America, peace-loving America, enters the war not for conquest and gain but for the Glory of God, for the dignity of man, for devotion to country and for the living principle of democracy.

Christian and Jew, each according to his number, participated under the American flag during World War I. More than 200,000 of Jewish faith were in the American armed forces; 3,000 of them fell on the battle-field, 10,000 were injured. When the war was won, the nation rose from its dead, bound up its wounds and resumed its mission of building a land worthy of God's presence. Eternal Thanksgiving to God!

A decade passes, then another—and again there is discord. The war to end wars fell short of its goal. The people across the seas failed to recognize the spark of the divine in man. They failed to respect the dignity of humanity. They would not believe that all men are endowed by their Creator with certain inalienable rights, and that among these were life, liberty, and the pursuit of happiness. They dealt treacherously each man against his brother. The law of the jungle became the law of the land. The mailed fist of the strong smote the jaw of the weak and the iron heel of the tyrant ground into the dust the defenseless. Woe to the few! Woe to the Jews—that handful of God-choosing people who had settled the shores of Europe in early days and had given their best, their all, in every land. The enemy who rejected God sought to erase Christianity from the face of the earth. But he well knew that he must first anni-hilate Judaism, the corner-stone of Christianity. The anti-Christ always destroys those who gave Jesus to the world before proceeding to demolish all that Jesus taught.

Horrifying facts emerge from the lands dominated by the Monster of the Twentieth Century. Two, yea three, millions of Jews annihilated in but a few years. These are the facts recounted by the United States Department of State, by the Vatican, and by the governments in exile resident in London. Behold, 4,000,000 more are now supplicating the heavens with their cry, "My God, My God, Why Hast Thou Forsaken Me."

And there were some who arose and said, "Would that the nations of the world gave these millions a refuge, a chance at life." Where? Why not in the land of their forefathers? Years ago men began asking why the Holy Land remained neglected. For the land flowing with milk and honey had become a depopulated wilderness, the habitat of the jackal and the asp. The homeland of the teachers of religion, the cradle of the three great faiths had been forsaken. Then a new movement began, designed to re-settle and rebuild and restore the Holy Land. Under the banner of this new movement gathered hundreds of young pioneers of Jewish faith from Poland and Russia and Germany. After the fashion of the Pilgrim fathers who came to America, they journeyed to Palestine and they began building and sowing and planting. And now within twenty years the wilderness that had been Palestine was miraculously transformed. Again it is a land flowing with milk and honey. Farms, factories, cities, spring up—the land of the ancient religious teachers has been reclaimed, it is alive once more. Some 600,000 Jews have found homes there. And now they help supply our Allies. In their new hospitals they minister to our American soldiers; indeed they house and feed our next door neighbors. All this in fulfillment of the prophecies of Isaiah and Jeremiah and Ezekiel. Eternal Thanksgiving to God!

Behold, America has been treacherously attacked. Once again we find ourselves engaged in a great war testing whether our way of life under God shall long endure. Even, as yesterday, our aims in this war are not conquest nor gain . . . our aims had been proclaimed in ages past by the prophets. Today America has emblazoned these prophetic ideals upon her shield:

Freedom of Speech—"These are the things that ye shall do: Speak every man the truth with his neighbor—," the prophet taught. And America heeds his words and replies, God granted to every man a glorious faculty—speech. Man everywhere shall have the right to speak in accordance with the dictates of his heart; let him only remember to keep his tongue from speaking evil and his lips from uttering guile—let him speak truth!

Freedom of Religion—"My house shall be a house of prayer for all people," the prophet taught. And America heeds his words and replies, is not God's house the whole wide earth? Every man, everywhere shall have the right to worship at the altar of his choosing!

Freedom from Want—"Is it not to deal thy bread to the hungry, and that thou bring the poor that are cast out to thy house, where thou seest the naked, that thou cover him, and that thou hide not thyself from thine own flesh," the prophet taught. And America heeds his words and replies, no man any where shall starve. Every man everywhere shall have a roof over his head and a garment to wear and the opportunity to earn a livelihood!

Freedom from Fear—"And they shall beat their swords into ploughshares and their spears into pruning-hooks. Nation shall not lift up sword against nation nor shall they learn war any more. But they shall sit every man under his vine and under his fig tree and none shall make them afraid," the prophet taught. And America heeds his word and replies, no man anywhere shall have fear. Every man, everywhere shall have peace!

For these we labor and bleed and die, we of Jewish faith, side by side with our Christian brothers, for devotion to country, for the dignity of man, for the Glory of God.

[194] Rabbi Ely E. Pilchik, *For the Glory of God, for the Dignity of Man, for Devotion to Country* (1943). An address, reprinted by permission of the author.

195 · The American Economic System

Today we shall talk about our country's economic system—as distinct from its government—and we shall consider the relationship of the individual citizen to that system.

What is an economic system? It is more than just the way in which money is issued and regulated, or the way in which business is organized and conducted. It is the entire process by which the people of a country provide themselves with jobs, incomes, food, clothing, shelter, and other material needs. It grows out of a people's way of looking at things. It is a part of a nation's social system; it reflects its principles of government. A series of talks on American citizenship would not be complete without a consideration of the American economic system.

What is a Capitalist Economy?

Before we can go very far in thinking about the economic life of either the whole United States or a single American community, we must understand the term "capitalism." Like many words in economics and politics, it is used by different people to mean all kinds of things. Let's pin it down.

Capitalism is an economic system which encourages individuals to own property and to use that property to produce or acquire more property. It's a way of life in which people get money by producing goods or providing services that other people want, and then use the money to buy what they want. Buying and selling, wages, and credit are essential to the system, and its foundation rests on the bedrock of private ownership of property.

A nation is capitalist—as contrasted to socialist or communist—when it entrusts its economic welfare and processes largely to individual citizens and groups of citizens who own, privately, most of the means of producing wealth. An individual is a capitalist if he owns a factory, a mine, a store, a farm, or anything else with which he produces wealth. (Wealth is an economist's word for anything which has value in money.) If you own a house for which someone pays you rent, you are a capitalist. If you own a share of stock in a corporation—as millions of Americans do—for the dividend you get from it, you are a capitalist. If you have put money into an interest-bearing bank account, you are a capitalist. If you own War Bonds or United States Savings Bonds on which you will draw interest, you are a capitalist. If you have an insurance policy, you are a capitalist. In all of these ways, and in many others, you and I constantly are using what we own to obtain something else—money or goods—to own. In all of these ways, we are capitalists.

People who own and manage businesses often are called "capitalists" to distinguish them from the "laborers" to whom they pay wages. When using the term "capitalist" in this sense, however, we should beware of falling into the communist fallacy of assuming that capitalists are a "class," completely separate from the "working class" and opposed to their employees' interests. Most individual wage-earners are capitalists also in one or more of the ways we have mentioned. And today's wage-earner frequently is an employer tomorrow.

What Does "Free Enterprise" Mean?

The American way of carrying on economic activities sometimes is described by another term—"free enterprise"—which has almost the same meaning as "capitalism." Capitalism is the economic system; free enterprise is the way in which business usually operates in a capitalist system.

The dictionary defines "enterprise" as "a project undertaken or to be undertaken—especially one that requires boldness or energy." Under *free enterprise,* private individuals or groups, owning their own property, undertake business ventures on their own initiative and at their own risk, carry them on in their own way, and enjoy the profits, or suffer the losses, that result.

The United States, as a Nation, encourages the free enterprise of its citizens. Obviously, such a system can exist only under a government which guarantees other individual freedoms also. Enterprise cannot be free if individuals are not free.

How did we come to have the free enterprise system? Our early settlers did not bring it with them. They had lived under a system in which trade and industry were heavily regulated by government. They had not looked upon freedom to choose a vocation as a natural right. Their few liberties had been granted reluctantly by their rulers. Many colonists were indentured servants, bound to their masters for a certain period in return for their oversea passage. Although the early New Englanders fled from *religious* persecution, they apparently were not consciously dissatisfied with their *economic* lot in the mother country.

However, as time passed, individualism developed. It grew partly out of conditions of frontier life, in which every man was more or less on his own, and partly from the adventurous spirit of the colonists; but it came about most of all because life in the colonies was so different, and so far away, from that of England that resistance to the mother country's attempts to regulate colonial activities grew strong. . . . Abusive regulation of colonial industry and trade was a major cause of the American Revolution, and was so stated in the Declaration of Independence.

But the Declaration of Independence was more than a document of rebellion. It expressed a new philosophy—that the rights of free men were more important than the authority of government. We have seen that this philosophy underlay the freedoms written into the Bill of Rights. It became a cornerstone of our political thinking and it underlies our free economy—our freedom of enterprise.

What Are the Principles of Free Enterprise?

1. The first principle of free enterprise is the principle of *reward* or *compensation*—commonly called the *profit motive*. This principle holds that the hope of personal financial gain, sufficient to make the effort and risk of business worth while, is a strong and proper incentive. The principle holds further that, without this incentive, individuals are not likely to undertake business ventures freely.

2. The second principle of free enterprise is the principle of *private ownership*. This principle holds that an individual is entitled to own and keep the reward of his enterprise, whether money or property of other kinds. It holds that, without private ownership, the individual cannot enjoy permanently the full reward of his effort; that, without the possibility of ownership, the individual will not work any more, or any harder, than necessary for his immediate needs unless he is forced to do so by authority; and that force does not produce the efficiency that voluntary effort produces.

Part of private ownership is the right of an individual to sell what he owns and also to make gifts or bequests, to pass along to other persons of his choice portions of the accumulated rewards of his enterprise.

3. The third principle of free enterprise is the principle of *competition*. This principle holds that business and industrial activities will be carried on most efficiently and to the greatest good of all, when competition between individuals and organizations in the production and selling of goods is substantially unrestricted. It holds that free competition urges the individual on to make a better product or render better service, at a lower price, in order to do more business and thereby accumulate a larger reward.

It holds, further, that, if competition essentially is unrestricted, the public will be assured of the volume of goods and services it needs, or wants, through the operation of the law of supply and demand. If manufacturers, in their competitive zeal, produce a larger supply of goods than the public demands, the price of the goods tends to sink below the point where it is profitable to produce them. If manufacturers produce less than the public demands, prices go up for a while; but in the long run more competitors enter the field to fill the demand. When it is filled, prices drop. If they fall below the level of profit, some of the less efficient competitors may be forced out of the field. Thus, competition helps to regulate not only the supply of goods, but their price and quality.

4. The fourth principle of free enterprise is the principle of *validity of contracts*. This principle holds that an individual is entitled to be assured that a business agreement is sacred and that it will be enforced by the courts if necessary. Without valid, enforceable contracts, our whole system would fall.

. . .

How Free Is Free Enterprise?

Under the American system of free enterprise, the individual citizen or group of citizens in business may operate with relative freedom but not with absolute freedom. Since human nature is variable, not all businessmen—or all of any other kind of men—can be depended upon to act always for the public good. Therefore, reasonable regulation has been undertaken by business itself and by the Government in order to safeguard the public welfare and business as a whole.

Businesses, for example, have their trade associations and their codes of approved business practices. Almost every town and city of size has its Better Business Bureau, organized by businessmen for the protection of the public and the correction of unethical business practices. Some regulating is done by Government in the interest of the public and through agencies authorized by the people's elected representatives. When local public services (such as gas, electricity, and bus lines) are owned privately, communities usually set up commissions to fix rates, approve changes in service, and perform other regulatory functions to protect the public against excessive charges or abuses of other kinds. State legislatures fix the maximum rates of interest that loan companies may charge. Courts will not uphold a contract to do an illegal thing or to perform an act against the public interest. Private property may be taken over by the local, State, or Federal Government, at a fair price, if the public interest demands that it be used for a public purpose—as the route of a highway, for example. There are laws intended to prevent business agreements that stifle competition instead of encouraging it. The Constitution gives the Federal Government authority to regulate business that operates across State lines. Many Federal laws that regulate business in the public interest are based on this authority. Typical agencies created by Congress for this purpose are the Interstate Commerce Commission, the Civil Aeronautics Board and Administration, the Securities and Exchange Commission, and the Coal Mines Inspection Service. Agencies like these protect the public against fraud, unfair practices, and excessive prices, and the workers against unsafe conditions.

On the other hand, not all of our laws regarding business and industry regulate and restrict them. Many protect and encourage them. Among the first of such laws was the Tariff Act of 1828, designed to protect many of our young and struggling industries against foreign competition by taxing goods brought in from other countries. Since then, tariff laws of many types have been enacted—some increasing the taxes on imports, some decreasing them. Recently, we have been entering into trade agreements with other nations under which import duties on certain products are lowered by both countries, in order to establish two-way international trade and to restore a balance of imports and exports.

Other laws in the early days gave public lands to companies to encourage the building of railroads, and to individuals to encourage the settlement of the West. The Federal Government has given financial help (subsidies) to business ventures like the merchant marine and the ship-building industry, that meet important needs at financial risks so great that private companies hesitate to assume them alone. Indirect aid or subsidy, without which the aviation industry could not have developed to its present position of prominence, has been given in the form of municipal and federally-owned airports and navigation facilities. The Government also helps business enterprise through loans and guarantees of credit. The Reconstruction Finance Corporation is one such loan agency. The Farm Credit Administration is another. The Veterans' Administration, under the G.I. Bill of Rights, guarantees a certain portion of loans made by private banks and lending agencies to World War II veterans who want to start businesses or buy homes or farms.

How Do Workers Benefit under Free Enterprise?

In the course of our history, the American workingman has thrived and prospered under free enterprise. He enjoys freedoms and benefits undreamed of in many countries. His standard of living is unsurpassed. He may choose the place where he wants to live and work. He may change his occupation. He is not required to work for any employer against his will or under conditions he is unwilling to accept. He may organize. He may strike, except when the President or the courts decree that a specific strike endangers the national health and safety. He may seek and accept the job paying the highest wages. He may increase his wages by increasing his skill. He may go into business for himself and employ others. Powerful labor unions, like powerful corporations, sometimes have used their size or strategic position to gain advantages. One of today's great legislative problems is how to strike an even balance between employers and employees in industry, so that neither takes advantage of the other and so that the interests of the country will be served.

Can You Answer the Critics of the American System?

Capitalism and our system of free enterprise have their critics. Some of the criticisms are misleading, but others point to real difficulties which Americans in general believe they are capable of handling.

1. One of these criticisms is that, under free enterprise, some businessmen are so intent upon immediate profit that they waste the country's natural resources with no thought for the future. As evidence, the critics point to our depleted reserves of oil, coal, and iron and to our greatly reduced forest lands.

In our early history, when forests were cut down without regard for replanting, and mines were worked for the most productive ore and then abandoned, these charges were no doubt just. In those days, waste probably would have occurred under any economic system, for men could see no end to the land's resources. Now, however, we have developed national conservation programs in which Government and industry cooperate to protect our forests, minerals, soils, and fisheries, and these programs are in operation.

2. Another charge is that keen competition makes some companies abuse their freedoms and exploit the consumer. Glowing advertisements for useless products are cited as evidence. However, the regulatory agencies already mentioned, along with others, are guarding the rights of the consumer constantly. And each State has its commissions on weights and measures, interest rates, health, and factors in which the practices of business may need regulating.

3. With respect to national defense, the criticism is made that, under our economic system, the Nation is slow to get under way when war comes. It should be noted, however, that the apparent advantage of dictatorships in preparing for war comes from their starting the war when they feel ready to fight. Once the United States began to produce for World War II, it amassed more and better military equipment than the Axis powers had, although the enemy nations had been preparing for many years. Both World Wars proved that free enterprise can out-produce a regimented economy, even though totalitarian aggressors can get a temporary advantage. Our security against war lies in "keeping our guard up"—in maintaining defenses strong enough to make an attack upon us a grave risk.

4. A fourth criticism sometimes brought against the system of free enterprise is that it produces "big business." This charge implies that, through its very size, a large business organization tends to stifle competition, and further, that it tends to "fix" prices and force small businesses to conform or be pushed to the wall.

Some business enterprises in the United States have grown to tremendous size. About one-sixth of our three million businesses are corporations, large and small, and about half of the value of all of these corporations' plants, machinery, and other assets are owned by about a thousand of them. In the main, these thousand large concerns are our "big business." They have become big because they have been able to produce larger quantities of goods and to lower costs and prices. But large businessess are not typical of American business as a whole. Ninety percent of our businesses, including small corporations, are small enterprises; 85 percent of all retail establishments are small; 80 percent of our manufacturing establishments are single-unit businesses; and 98 percent of them employ 250 persons or less.

Size, in itself, is not an evil. Some types of business can be carried on more efficiently by large organizations; others, by small ones. The manufacture of steel, automobiles, airplanes, and many other products, is a large-scale operation, engaged in by large corporations. The manufacture of many kinds of clothing is carried on mainly by small concerns. When a business can be operated more efficiently by a large organization, or when the unit cost of production of the product can be lowered by large-scale production, the public benefits. When a small business can operate in a specific field more efficiently and economically than a large one, the public likewise benefits, and the attempts of large concerns to compete will fail. A business, large or small, is good or bad for the public interest according to the way it operates. A small company that violates the Pure Food and Drugs Act is just as bad as a large one whose product is impure. At times, large organizations have limited the supply of a product, restrained trade, and otherwise operated as monopolies. Then they are *abusing* the system of free enterprise, and they run afoul of the Sherman Antitrust Act of 1890 and the Clayton Act of 1914, enacted to curb practices which "substantially lessen competition."

5. Another and very basic criticism of free enterprise is that it has failed to prevent extreme hardships due to cycles of "boom and bust." Whether periods of inflation and deflation can be prevented remains an unanswered question. Our country has not been wrecked by either, though it has been put to the test by both. Much has been done to ease the shock of "hard times." The depression of the 1930's led to the enactment of a series of laws designed to protect the Nation against the worst aspects of any future depression. Among these laws are the Securities and Exchange Act, regulating dealings in stocks and bonds; Federal insurance of bank deposits up to $5,000; Federal insurance of home mortgages; a "floor" under farm prices; and the provisions of the Social Security Act. In addition, under the provisions of the Full Employment Act of 1946, Congress is kept constantly and accurately informed about our economic situation, so that it may take prompt steps to take up the employment slack in private industry if necessary.

6. Still another criticism of free enterprise is that it brings about unequal distribution of wealth and income. We cannot dispute this. However, most Americans do not conceive of an ideal society as one in which everybody has the same amount of wealth. Rather, they want everybody to have a fair chance to engage in profitable competition, or to get and hold a job that brings him an income that will give him and his family a decent living and allow him to make the most of his life. To help bring this about, we have a minimum wage law, unemployment and old-age insurance, and other Government-sponsored programs. Many private industries provide pension plans, welfare funds, low-cost housing, and insurance against seasonal unemployment. High wages and short work weeks have come hand-in-hand. Things that used to be luxuries are now everyday necessities. Nowhere else does the so-called "common man" live as well as in the United States.

The Federal Government enters into contracts with private firms in many communities to keep up the necessary types of ship-building, research, and manufacturing which otherwise are unattractive to private enterprise in peacetime. Many private nonprofit groups do basic research useful to national defense. Thus, although our giant industrial network does not convert to war overnight, it is so geared to the possible needs of national defense that it can get under way with assurance.

The basic answer to criticisms of the American economic system is that, under our form of representative government, we are equipped to cope with whatever problems experience reveals. The individual citizen, through his elected representatives, is at the controls.

Summary

Many criticisms have been leveled against free enterprise, but most Americans believe in it and support it staunchly. Just as they do not believe that our Government is perfect, so they do not believe that our economic system is perfect, but they hold that failures of the American system of free enterprise are primarily the result of human frailties. They believe that our system of government is best able to cope with and compensate for such frailties.

They believe that the Government should aid and encourage free enterprise. They believe that the public welfare requires a limited amount of governmental regulation of the practices of business and labor. The nature and extent of this regulation are prescribed by the people's elected representatives.

In the changeover from an agricultural to an industrial civilization, the United States, under its system of free enterprise, has achieved the highest standard of living that the world ever has known. But, even if this were not true, it is probable that most Americans would prefer to live under that system, because it is based upon the same principles of individual freedom that underlie our system of government, and distinguish it from the regimented totalitarianism that characterizes some other parts of the world.

[195] From Armed Forces Talk No. 302, Armed Forces Information and Education Division, Office of the Secretary of Defense, for the Chief, Armed Forces Information and Education Division.

❖❖❖❖❖❖❖❖❖

196 · Advocacy before the United States Supreme Court

Ladies and Gentlemen of the California Bar:

The invitation to deliver this lecture is a signal honor, and the temptation is to respond with a discourse upon some tempestuous issue of worldwide reverberations. But it will encounter less competition and be more useful to the profession to choose a workaday subject on which I have some experience to support my opinions and you have personal experience to warrant criticising them. Let us consider together the problems which confront a lawyer when his case reaches its journey's end in the Supreme Court of the United States.

More than ten years ago, Mr. John W. Davis, in a wise and stimulating lecture on "The Argument of an Appeal," shared with our profession the lessons of his own rich experience. He suggested, however, that such a lecture should come from a judge—from one who is to be persuaded, rather than from an advocate. With characteristic felicity, he said: "Who would listen to a fisherman's weary discourse on fly-casting . . . if the fish himself could be induced to give his views on the most effective method of approach?" I cannot add to the available learning on this subject—I can only offer some meditations by one of the fish.

Let me confess that, when dangling bait before judges, I have not always practiced what I now preach. Many lessons that I pass on to you were learned the hard way in the years when I was intensively occupied with presentation of government litigations to the Court. And if I appear to overrate trifles, remember that a multitude of small perfections helps to set mastery of the art of advocacy apart from its counterfeit—mere forensic fluency.

Is Oral Argument Decisive?

Lawyers sometimes question the value of the relatively short oral argument permitted in the Nation's highest Court. They ask whether it is not a vestigial formality with little effect on the result. In earlier times with few cases on its docket, the Court could and did hear arguments that lasted for days, from such advocates as Webster, Pinkney, and Luther Martin. Over the years the time allotted for hearing has been shortened, but its importance has not diminished. The significance of the trend is that the shorter the time, the more precious is each minute.

I think the Justices would answer unanimously that now, as traditionally, they rely heavily on oral presentations. Most of them form at least a tentative conclusion from it in a large percentage of the cases. This is not to say that decisions are wholly at the peril of first impressions. Indeed, deliberation never ceases and there is no final commitment until decision actually is announced. It is a common experience that a Justice is assigned to write an opinion for the Court in accordance with a view he expressed in conference, only to find from more intensive study that it was mistaken. In such circumstances, an inadequate argument would have lost the case, except that the writing Justice rescues it. Even then, his change of position may not always be persuasive with his colleagues and loss of a single vote may be decisive. The bar must make its preparations for oral argument on the principle that it always is of the highest, and often of controlling, importance.

Who Should Present the Argument?

If my experiences at the bar and on the bench unite in dictating one imperative, it is: Never divide between two or more counsel the argument on behalf of a single interest. Sometimes conflicting interests are joined on one side and division is compelled, but otherwise it should not be risked.

When two lawyers undertake to share a single presentation, their two arguments at best will be somewhat overlapping, repetitious and incomplete and, at worst, contradictory, inconsistent and confusing. I recall one misadventure in division in which I was to open the case and expound the statute involved, while counsel for a government agency was to follow and explain the agency's regulations. This seemed a natural place to sunder the argument. But the Court perversely refused to honor the division. So long as I was on my feet, the Justices were intensely interested in the regulations, which I had not expected to discuss. By the time my associate took over, they had developed a lively interest in the statute, which was not his part of the case. No counsel should be permitted to take the floor in any case who is not willing to master and able to present every aspect of it. If I had my way, the Court rules would permit only one counsel to argue for a single interest. But while my colleagues think such a rule would be too drastic, I think they all agree that an argument almost invariably is less helpful to us for being parceled out to several counsel.

Selection of leading counsel often receives a consideration after the case arrives at the high Court that would have been more rewarding before the trial. But when the case is docketed in Supreme Court, the question is, shall counsel who conducted the case below conduct its final review? If not, who shall be brought in?

Convincing presentations often are made by little-known lawyers who have lived with the case through all courts. However, some lawyers, effective in trial work, are not temperamentally adapted to less dramatic appellate work. And sometimes the trial lawyer cannot forego bickering over petty issues which are no longer relevant to aspects of the case reviewable by the Supreme Court. When the trial attorney lacks dispassionate judgment as to what is important on appeal, a fresh and detached mind is likely to be more effective.

No lawyer, otherwise fairly equipped for his profession, need hesitate to argue his own case in Supreme Court merely because he has not appeared in that Court before. If he will conform his argument to the nature of its review and his preparation to the habits of the Court, he has some advantages over a lawyer brought in at that late stage. Sometimes even his handicap will work out to his advantage. Some years ago, a country lawyer arguing a tax case gleaned from baffling questions from the bench that his case was not going well. He closed by saying, "I hope you will agree with me, because if you don't, I certainly am in wrong with my best client." Such a plea is not enough to win a decision, but its realism would assure a most sympathetic hearing from any judge who can still remember what it is to face and explain to a defeated client.

Many litigants, and not a few lawyers, think it is some advantage to have their case sponsored by a widely known legal reputation. If such counsel is selected because of his professional qualifications, I have nothing to say against that. Experience before the Supreme Court is valuable, as is experience in any art. One who is at ease in its presence, familiar with its practice, and aware of its more recent decisions and divisions, holds some advantage over the stranger to such matters. But it is a grave mistake to choose counsel for some supposed influence or the enchantment of political reputation, and, above all, avoid the lawyer who thinks he is so impressively eminent that he need give no time to preparation except while he is on a plane going to Washington. Believe me when I say that what impresses the Court is a lawyer's argument, not his eminence.

On your first appearance before the Court, do not waste your time, or ours, telling us so. We are likely to discover for ourselves that you are a novice but will think none the less of you for it. Every famous lawyer had his first day at our bar, and perhaps a sad one. It is not ingratiating to tell us you think it is an overwhelming honor to appear, for we think of the case as the important thing before us, not the counsel. Some attorneys use time to thank us for granting the review, or for listening to their argument. Those are not intended as favors and it is good taste to accept them as routine performance of duty. Be respectful, of course, but also be self-respectful, and neither disparage yourself nor flatter the Justices. We think well enough of ourselves already.

. . .

What Aids to Delivery of the Argument Are Appropriate?

The manner of delivery must express the talents and habits of the advocate. No one method is indispensable to success, and practice varies widely. Few lawyers are gifted with memory and composure to argue a case without papers of any kind before them. It is not necessary to try. The memorized oration, or anything stilted and inflexible, is not appropriate. Equally objectionable is the opposite extreme—an unorganized, rambling discourse, relying on the inspiration of the moment. If one's oral argument is simply reading his printed brief aloud, he could as well stay at home. Almost as unsatisfying is any argument that has been written out and is read off to us, page after page. We like to meet the eye of the advocate, and sometimes when one starts reading his argument from a manuscript he will be interrupted, to wean him from his essay; but it does not often succeed. If you have confidence to address the Court only by reading to it, you really should not argue there.

The first step in preparation for all exigencies of argument is to become filled with your case—to know every detail of the evidence and findings, to weigh fairly every contention of your adversary, and to review not only the rule of law applicable to the specific issue but the body of law in its general field. You never know when some collateral or tangential issue will suddenly come up.

My practice was to prepare notes, consisting of headings and catch-words rather than of details, to guide the order of argument and prevent important items from being overlooked. Such notes help to get back on the track if one is thrown off by interruptions. They will tend to limit rambling and irrelevance, give you some measure of confidence, and at the same time let you frequently meet your judges eye to eye.

Do not think it beneath you to rehearse for an argument. Not even Caruso, at the height of his artistic career, felt above rehearsing for a hundredth performance, although he and the whole cast were guided and confined by a libretto and a score. Of course, I do not suggest that you should declaim and gesture before a mirror. But if you have an asso-ciate, try out different approaches and thrash out every point with him. Answer the questions that occur to another mind. See what sequence of facts is most effective. Accustom yourself to your materials in different arrangements. Argue the case to yourself, your client, your secretary, your friend, and your wife if she is patient. Use every available anvil on which to hammer out your argument.

If one is not familiar with the Court and its ways, it may be helpful to arrive a day or two early to observe its procedure, to see how the Court deals with counsel and how counsel gets on with the Court.

When the day arrives, shut out every influence that might distract your mind. An interview with an emotional client in difficulty may be upsetting. Friends who bear bad news may unintentionally disturb your poise. Hear nothing but your case, see nothing but your case, talk nothing but your case. If making an argument is not a great day in your life, don't make it; and if it is, give it everything in you.

By all means leave at home the associate who feels constantly im-pelled to tug at your coattails, to push briefs in front of you, or to pass up unasked-for suggestions while you are speaking. These well-meant but ill-conceived offerings distract the attention of the Court, but they are even more embarrassing and confusing to counsel. The offender is an unmitigated pest, and even if he is the attorney who employed you, sup-press him.

I doubt whether it is wise to have clients or parties in interest attend the argument if it can be avoided. Clients unfortunately desire, and their presence is apt to encourage, qualities in an argument that are least admired by judges. When I hear counsel launch into personal attacks on the opposition or praise of a client, I instinctively look about to see if I can identify the client in the room—and often succeed. Some counsel have become conspicuous for the gallery that listens to their argument and, when it is finished, ostentatiously departs. The case that is argued to please a client, impress a following in the audience, or attract notice from the press, will not often make a favorable impression on the bench. An argument is not a spectacle.

You should be warned that, in accoustical properties, the Supreme Court chamber is wretched. If your voice is low, it burdens the hearing, and parts of what you say may be missed. On the other hand, no judge likes to be shouted at as if he were an ox. I know of nothing you can do except to bear the difficulty in mind, watch the bench and adapt your delivery to avoid causing apparent strain.

The time allotted to you will be one hour ordinarily, and half of that if the case is on summary docket. Time is sometimes, though rarely, extended in advance if the case appears to require it, but seldom do we find extended time of much help to the Court. In any event, do not waste time complaining that you do not have enough time. That is a confession of your own inadequacy to handle the case as the Court's experience indicates it should be. Keep account of your own time or, if you cannot, have an assistant do so. Some lawyers ask, and some even ask several times, how much time they have left and wait for it to be calculated. Why will a lawyer interrupt his effort to hold the attention of a Court to his argument in order to divert its mind to the clock? Successful advocacy will keep the Justice's minds on the case, and off the clock.

This, above all, remember: Time has been bestowed upon you, not imposed upon you. It will show confidence in yourself and in your case, and good management of your argument, if you finish before the signal stops you. On the other hand, if the warning that your time has expired catches you in the middle of an argument, the chances are that you have not made good economy of your time.

To Be, or Not to Be, Questioned from the Bench?

The Supreme Court, more than most tribunals, is given to questioning counsel. Since all of the Justices gave the case preliminary consideration when certiorari was granted or jurisdiction was noted, tentative opinions or inquiries are apt to linger in their minds.

Questions usually seek to elicit information or to aid in advancing or clarifying the argument. A question argumentative in form should not be attributed to hostility, for oftentimes it is put, not to overbear counsel, but to help him sharpen his position. Now and then, of course, counsel may be caught in a cross-fire of questions between differing Justices, each endeavoring to bring out some point favorable to his own view of the law. That tests the agility and diplomacy of counsel.

Some lawyers feel an ill-concealed resentment at questions from the bench. It is not hard to see that if they had the wit they have the will to respond as did a British barrister in an incident related to me by Sir Arthur Goodhart: The Judge said, "I have been listening to you now for four hours and I am bound to say I am none the wiser." The barrister replied: "Oh, I know that, my Lord, but I had hoped you would be better informed."

A Justice may abruptly indicate conclusions which tempt a lawyer to reply as one did long ago in a local court in the country where I practiced. He had barely stated his contention when the judge said: "There is nothing to your proposition—just nothing to it." The lawyer drew himself up and said: "Your Honor, I have worked on this case for six weeks and you have not heard of it twenty minutes. Now, Judge, you are a lot smarter man than I am, but there is not that much difference between us."

But I always feel that there should be some comfort derived from any question from the bench. It is clear proof that the inquiring Justice is not asleep. If the question is relevant, it denotes he is grappling with your contention, even though he has not grasped it. It gives you opportunity to inflate his ego by letting him think he has discovered an idea for himself.

When I was at the bar, it seemed to me that I could make no better use of my time than to answer any doubt which a judge would do me the favor to disclose. Experience in the Court teaches that a lawyer's best points are sometimes made by answers to pertinent and penetrating questions. A lively dialogue may be a swifter and surer vehicle to truth than a dismal monologue. The wise advocate will eagerly embrace the opportunity to put at rest any misconception or doubt which, if the judge waited to raise it in the conference room, counsel would have no chance and perhaps no one present would have the information to answer.

Some lawyers complain that questioning is overdone; and sometimes colloquy between Court and counsel is undoubtedly carried too far. If cases were uniformly well presented, perhaps the best results would be obtained if few questions were asked. Generally, an argument that from its very outset shows that it will be well-organized and thorough tends to ward off questions. At all events, nothing tests the skill of an advocate or endangers his position more than his answer to questions, and in nothing is experience, poise, and a disciplined mind a greater asset.

I advise you never to postpone answer to a question for, that always gives an impression of evasion. It is better immediately to answer the question, even though you do so in short form and suggest that you expect to amplify and support your answer later.

Counsel should be prepared to deal with any relevant question, but, if he is not, he ventures less by a frank admission that he does not know the answer than by a guess. Counsel need not fear that he will be prejudiced by declining to be drawn into a discussion of some proposition that is irrelevant to his case. To refuse might seem like a rebuff to the inquirer, but it may delight eight colleagues.

How Should Counsel Be Attired?

It may seem a trivial matter, but I am told that one of the questions most frequently addressed to the Clerk's Office concerns the apparel in which counsel must, or should, appear. Formal dress is traditional and I understand once was required.

Some amusing stories of those days linger among Court attaches. It is said that Chief Justice Taft once refused admission to the bar to a candidate who appeared without necktie or waistcoat, with the suggestion that he renew his application when properly attired. The Marshal's Office kept in active service, and still keeps in moth balls, one or two cutaway coats to lend to counsel in need. Apparently he is expected to be equipped with his own trousers.

Those days have passed away, but the tradition remains that appearance before the Court is no ordinary occasion. Government lawyers and many others, particularly older ones, adhere to the custom of formal morning dress. The Clerk's Office advises that either this or a dark business suit is appropriate. But the informality which permeates all official life has penetrated the Court. It lays down no rule for its bar.

No toleration, however, can repeal the teaching of Polonius that "The apparel oft proclaims the man." You will not be stopped from arguing if you wear a race-track suit or sport a rainbow necktie. You will just create a first impression that you have strayed in at the wrong bar. For raiment of counsel, like the robe of the judge, is taken as somewhat symbolic of his function. In Europe the advocate, as well as the judge, is expected to robe for his appearance in court. The lawyer of good taste will not worry about his dress, because instinctively it will be that which is suitable to his station in life—a member of a dignified and responsible profession—and for an important and somewhat formal occasion.

· · ·

Is Advocacy a Lost Art?

Certainly not. So long as controversies between men have to be settled by judges, proficiency in the art of forensic persuasion will assure one of first rank in our high calling. In the judicial process, as practiced among English-speaking peoples, the judge and the advocate complement each other, for, as Thoreau said, "It takes two to speak the truth—one to speak and another to hear."

But if not a lost art, advocacy is an exacting one. When he rises to speak at the bar, the advocate stands intellectually naked and alone. Habits of thought and speech cannot be borrowed like garments for the event. What an advocate gives to a case is himself; he can bring to the bar only what is within him. A part written for him will never be convincing.

If you aspire to such a task, and I address particularly the younger men at the bar and in the schools, do not let your preparation wait upon a retainer. There is not time to become an advocate after the important case comes to you. Webster, when asked as to the time he spent in preparing one of his memorable arguments, is said to have replied that his whole life was given to its preparation. So it is with every notable forensic effort.

The most persuasive quality in the advocate is professional sincerity. By that I do not mean that he believes in his case as the Mohammedan does in his Koran. But he must believe that under our adversary system both sides of every controversy should be worthily presented with vigor— even with partisan zeal—so that all material for judgment will be before the Court and its judgment will suffer no distortion. He must believe with all the intensity of his being in law as the framework of society, in the independent judicial function as the means for applying the law, and in the nobility of his profession as an aid in the judicial process. He will feel equal disdain for a judge partisan in his favor and one partisan in his opposition. The opportunist, the lawyer for revenue only, the cynic, will never reach the higher goal.

The effective advocate will not let mastery of a specialty foreclose that catholicity of interest essential to the rounded life and the balanced judgment. He will draw inspiration not alone from the literature of the law, but from the classics, history, the essay, the drama, and poetry as well. It is one of the delights and intellectual rewards of the legal profession that it lays under tribute every science and every art. The advocate will read and reread the majestic efforts of leaders of his profession on important occasions, and linger over their manner of handling challenging subjects. He will stock the arsenal of his mind with tested dialectical weapons. He will master the short Saxon word that pierces the mind like a spear and the simple figure that lights the understanding. He will never drive the judge to his dictionary. He will rejoice in the strength of the mother tongue as found in the King James version of the Bible, and in the power of the terse and flashing phrase of a Kipling or a Churchill. And the advocate will have courage, courage to assert his conviction that the world is round, though all about him men of authority say it is flat. Most memorable professional achievements were in the face of opposition, abuse, even ridicule.

The advocate may be summoned often to other forums, but he will appear in the Supreme Court of the United States only when that tribunal has been satisfied that decision of his cause is important to the body of federal law. Emphasis on the public interest in a just and uniform legal system has submerged emphasis on special equities and individual interests which properly prevail in trial and intermediate courts.

Adequately and helpfully to present a case—as it is about to be transformed into a precedent to guide future courts, to settle the fate of unknown litigants, perhaps to become required reading for a rising generation of lawyers—will challenge and inspire the true advocate. Decisional law is a distinctive feature of our commonlaw system, a system which can exist only where men are free, lawyers are courageous and judges are independent. To participate as advocate in supplying the basis for decisional law-making calls for vision of a prophet, as well as a profound appreciation of the continuity between the law of today and that of the past. He will be sharing the task of reworking decisional law by which every generation seeks to preserve its essential character and at the same time to adapt it to contemporary needs. At such a moment the lawyer's case ceases to be an episode in the affairs of a client and becomes a stone in the edifice of the law.

As I view the procession of lawyers who pass before the Supreme Court, I often am reminded of an old parable. Once upon a time three stone masons were asked, one after the other, what they were doing. The first, without looking up, answered, "Earning my living." The second replied, "I am shaping this stone to pattern." The third lifted his eyes and said, "I am building a Cathedral." So it is with the men of the law at labor before the Court. The attitude and preparation of some show that they have no conception of their effort higher than to make a living. Others are dutiful but uninspired in trying to shape their little cases to a winning pattern. But it lifts up the heart of a judge when an advocate stands at the bar who knows that he is building a Cathedral.

[196] Address by Robert H. Jackson, Associate Justice, Supreme Court of the United States, delivered upon the Morrison Lecture Foundation before the State Bar of California at San Francisco, California, August 23, 1951.

❖❖❖❖❖❖❖❖❖

197 · Where the People Stand

There was a time in this country when only the tabloid newspapers in our big cities thrived on a steady diet of crime stories. But in the past year, the front pages of even our most respectable news organs have been transformed into a daily diary of crime, gambling, and scandal. A veritable hurricane of muckraking has cut a wide path through our national life. You never seem to know who or what will be implicated next.

The first reaction of most people is that this is shocking news. Perhaps bribes of the basketball players in New York were the most shocking of all. The exposures of the gambling and rackets underground of the Costellos and Lucianos had already been widely talked about. Even the connection between politics and the underworld, or politics and graft is not new in American life. But from the mink coats which hang on White House coat racks to the reported wild betting sprees of Senator McCarthy at race tracks, to the bigger-time, organized crime of the underworld syndicates, to the All-American players whose lives have been wrecked, we seem at first glance to be a nation overpopulated with corruption.

When you ask people about it in public opinion surveys, you find a good deal of indignation over these activities. People tend to shake their heads and bemoan the fact that people in high places or people who are so well-known should get themselves involved in scandals, such as these. What is more, people also tend to say, by a wide margin, that steps should be taken to wipe out the instruments of gambling. For instance, when the Minnesota Poll asked a cross section of people in that State if they were in favor of having slot machines in their state or would they want them kept out, some 73 per cent said they wanted them out. Only a very small 3 per cent of the public there said they would like to have them, and these people thought they would be all right if they were taxed and regulated by the State government.

Of course, people will tell you, too, that there are all kinds of gambling. In the recent Kefauver hearings across the country, we have been getting a below-the-surface look at the machinations of organized gambling in this country. The Senate Committee reported a few weeks ago that there existed, in fact, an underworld government, of which a New York syndicate and a Chicago syndicate divided up the areas of operation, and Lucky Luciano, the deported white slave czar, was the impartial arbiter between the two mobs. The Committee's hearings have turned up evidence to show that bookmaking, horse race betting, numbers, punchboards, odds-making on sports events, and elections, have all been carefully knit into an efficiently run business. And these so-called illegal businesses in gambling have, in many cases, been merged with actual legitimate business.

But organized <u>gambling</u> has been the target of the recent investigations. It isn't organized murder, such as in the case of Murder, Inc. It isn't a band of kidnappers or bank robbers. The big money in crime apparently lies in gambling. And it is here that the Kefauver Committee, and State Legislative Committees, and District Attorneys have hit pay dirt. It is estimated that betting on sports events alone comes to roughly 15 billion dollars annually. In baseball, each of the major league teams plays 154 games a year. Across the country, there are bookmakers who

take bets daily on each of these games. It is estimated that 6 billion dollars is bet on baseball
alone. Another major area for betting is horse
racing. A good deal of the betting at the tracks
is legal. A good deal through private bookmakers
is not. The total take on horse racing by the
bookies alone is estimated to be about another 6
billions a year.

Basketball, which has been rent asunder by the
recent fixes, apparently attracts one billion dollars
worth of betting in a given year, while football
bets total roughly the same amount. Hockey grosses
some 670 millions in betting each year. And, interestingly enough, boxing, which for many years has
been accused of being run by gamblers and mobsters,
and of having its share of fixes, attracts only a
relatively small 300 millions a year. As a matter of
fact, just taking the amount of betting estimated
to be spent in a given year on sports alone, taking
that as one big business, this enterprise does more
business than all but 6 industries in the United
States. Only the food, steel, oil, auto, chemical
and machine tool industries have a greater volume
of business.

But then, there's a good deal more gambling than
just on sports, that goes on and is apparently controlled by organized mobs in this country. For
instance, more people, according to a recent survey,
bought a number on a punchboard in 1950 than bet on
some sporting event. And one-third as many people
as bet on sports played the numbers last year. And
as many people played slot machines as bet on sports.
So it might be that _more_ people spent _more_ money
last year on punchboards, numbers, and slot machines
—all of which are a part of organized crime's
enterprises—than on sports events. If you add up
all these bets and gambling activities in terms of
dollars, it would not be an overstatement to say
that gamblers deal in over 30 billion dollars worth
of business a year, one of the biggest businesses
in the United States. It totals more than twice the
income the automotive companies take in from the
sale of cars. Needless to say, this industry doesn't
pay any corporate taxes, and many of the key individuals no doubt haven't paid in full on their
income taxes.

It would seem to be little wonder that the path
of gambling cuts such a wide swath through American
life. But what is perhaps most curious about the

recent investigations and disclosures is that there appears to be some confusion over emphasis. Is the purpose of the Kefauver Committee, for instance, to expose those illegal practices of the leaders of organized gambling, or is it to outlaw gambling? If it is to catch the leaders of gambling in illegal practices and send them off to jail, will this in itself end the practice of income tax dodges, sub-rosa slot machines, numbers, and other gambling activities? Well, as with any nationwide organization, apparently one of the things which holds the crime syndicate together is a national wire service which does nothing but transmit gambling information —odds on anything that is bet on, which horses are running, and so on. It has been proposed that this private wire service be outlawed. A law would be passed by Congress making it illegal for any gambling information to be sent across state lines. By over a 3 to 1 margin, the people of this nation say they are in favor of such a law, and only one-quarter of all the people who gamble themselves want <u>no</u> such ban.

Even then, however, while things would be made tougher for those who run organized gambling, it would still be difficult to keep new gamblers from cropping up to take the place of the ones who are sent off to prison. Or, if all gambling were outlawed, that would indeed be a difficult thing to enforce. The facts from a recent survey are well worth thinking about. It was found that some 57 per cent of the people in this country gamble during the course of the year in one thing or another. Close to 6 out of every 10 people admit to gambling in some form. As might be expected, men gamble more than women, but still some 5 out of every 10 women gamble, too. Now, some of the people who gamble never saw a bookmaker in their life, and probably never will. For instance, 37 per cent of the people have played raffles for churches or lodges, and 21 per cent more regularly play bingo, while 19 per cent play cards for money. Most of these bets are among friends, done for purely social purposes.

But let's take up that last one I mentioned— playing cards for money. During wartime in the Army, for example, many a GI filled his coffers full for several years from his regular games of poker or "21." Part of our folklore are card sharps who play as part of gangs, part of organized gambling. So the line between playing cards for money purely on a fun

basis, and playing in a straight gambling sense,
can become a thin one. But what is perhaps a better
illustration is the thinner line which exists between
bets on sports events. Two friends might well bet
each other a few dollars on the outcome of a baseball
game. But some who bet with friends also bet with
bookies on the ball games. Similarly on elections.
Some make friendly bets, while others place bets to
make money. And even on punchboards, which have
recently been reported as the largest source of
underworld revenue, we've seen some very worthy
causes which have used punchboards as a means of
raising money.

The big question in outlawing gambling is where
to draw the line; how many people can you ask to
change their habits of recreation? On the other hand,
the argument is made by some that if you legalize
gambling, won't it be open encouragement to irresponsible spending by many who stay away from
organized gambling because of its underworld and
sub-rosa status.

Also the argument is made that if you once make
gambling legal, then why not have all gambling
sponsored by the government? And—so the argument
goes—the government could take the money made from
its gambling revenues and pay for the expense of
running its operations. This, of course, has from
time to time been put forth by people as a substitute
for increased taxation. This idea is the proposition
of a national lottery. There are those who say, "If
we are such a nation of odds-makers and gamblers,
why then don't we have a national lottery and get
all the gambling spirit out of our bones?" As a
matter of fact, the public was asked about a national
lottery sometime ago, and the results are interesting, indeed. It was found that, while 12 per cent
were undecided or couldn't understand what it was,
and 32 per cent or roughly one-third were opposed
to the idea, a good majority of 55 per cent of the
people were in favor of such a lottery.

One trouble with a national lottery, however,
is that it has been tried many times before. Before
France had its present tax system, it had a national
lottery to raise money for the government. But
unfortunately, the lottery didn't work so well, since
the government officials who were running the lottery
used it to make themselves rich. There was no way
in which the French could make the men who ran their
national gambling operation honest.

Speaking of gambling in foreign countries, it
may be of interest to know that in England, surveys
on gambling have repeatedly turned up the fact that
just about the same percentage of people gamble as
they do here in America. They play the numbers, slot
machines, bet on horses, elections, and take punchboard numbers, just as we do here. But more of the
British bet on the Sweepstakes than we do.

If history has any meaning as far as gambling is
concerned, two things would appear to be certain:
it is probably impossible to abolish the instinct
of the human being to gamble on one thing or another,
and it is not feasible or wise to engage in national
lotteries. But these two suggestions lie at the
extremes of the gambling problem. One would outlaw
gambling entirely, the other would give it not only
legal status but would make it a prime government
function. The answer probably lies somewhere in
between. And that seems to be where we are today
in America, as we go through the biggest wave of
exposure we have witnessed in 30 years.

Of course, it is hard to tell whether gambling
is really on the increase here in America, or not.
Just because gambling has been exposed more, and our
headlines read like a precinct detective's casebook,
is no reason to suppose this sort of thing hasn't
been going on for a long time in the past. George
Gallup reports that a wartime survey he made showed
that only 45 per cent of the people interviewed
reported that they gambled, as opposed to the present
day 57 per cent. But that survey in 1944 didn't
include men in the armed forces, where it would be
supposed the ratio of gambling would be a bit higher
than for the population as a whole.

But even if close to half the people like to
gamble year in and year out, the size of organized
gambling and its criminal overtones cannot be
ignored. Senator Kefauver said recently that the
network of the underworld could actually imperil the
security of the nation in a time of emergency, and
remember organized gambling is probably the biggest
privately-run business in the country. The biggest
problem facing the Kefauver Committee, and perhaps
all of us as a nation, on the subject of gambling,
would appear to be how to distinguish and draw a
sharp line between relatively harmless and harmful
gambling. Are raffles, card playing, and bingo on
the safe side? Are the numbers game, slot machines,
and bookies on the dangerous side? Suppose you agree

they are, how you can keep the safer forms of gambling from drifting over to the more harmful side is
something this observer hasn't heard any answer to.

And, while there are some people who point to
the recent gambling scandals as a sure sign of the
complete moral decadence of America, there are others
who would say that gambling is an attribute as
firmly attached to human instinct as the desire to
eat or sleep. Undoubtedly one of the reasons why
there has been so much public interest recently in
the Kefauver Committee hearings lies in the fact
that so many people gamble themselves, in addition
to the fabulous tales we have been told about the
leaders of organized gambling in this country.

What we are going through as a nation in this
whole muckraking experience is not entirely clear.
Neither is it clear what we will do about it. We
say gambling is bad. But we continue to gamble. It
may be a subject on which there are real and honest
differences of opinion. But the 61 per cent who say
they've usually lost when they bet, don't go on to
say this has cured them of betting!

Good evening.

197 Elmo Roper, "Where the People Stand," March 25, 1951. Reproduced through
the courtesy of the Columbia Broadcasting System.

⟡⟡⟡⟡⟡⟡⟡

198 · The Drainage Level

Most of them thought John Wolff was going crazy. He was not aware
of it himself. Only he liked to repeat things he knew. And he also dictated to himself letters to his wife every week, though he hadn't money
to smuggle them out if he had been able to write them. He would ask her
to write what she was doing and then he would say what had happened
in the prison. The letters sounded pretty much alike even to himself. He
got tired of them. The day after the captain delivered the news of Bur-
goyne's surrender, he wrote Ally about it; but then he could think of
nothing to add. The Mr. Henry who had first welcomed him to the caverns
asked what the trouble was. "I'm writing my wife, Alice," explained John
Wolff, "but I can't think of anything new to tell her."

"Have you described this lovely home of ours?" said Mr. Henry.

"No, I haven't."

"Why don't you? Take a look around and see what there is to see."

Several men laughed, but John Wolff did not mind. It was an idea.

He began looking round and made up his letter, about the air shaft and the beds and the queer beach of sand and the water. "The water is queer," he said, "The water keeps dropping down off the walls all the while and the water don't never get higher nor lower." He realized that he was saying something nobody had noticed.

Suddenly John Wolff came out of his daze and he had a long fit of the shakes. But they were not the damp shakes that everybody had. He was shaking with excitement. He went and looked at the water.

He said, "Has anybody ever tried to wade out there?"

"It's too deep," one of the men said.

"Has anybody tried to swim?" asked John Wolff.

A roar of laughter went up. One of the men reached out and rattled the chains connecting his ankle and wrist fetters. "Try and swim with forty pounds," he suggested. John Wolff stood in their midst looking at their faces, gaunt and filthy with rock dust and charcoal smoke and unwashed beards. It came to him that he must look like that himself. His hand went to his beard. He had never had a beard before. He had always shaved.

Then his eyes grew cunning. He felt them growing so and closed the lids lest the other men should see it, and he went and lay down. They were still making jokes about him when the guard opened the door and shouted at them to "Heave up!" for their exercise.

From his bed, John Wolff watched them clambering toilsomely up the ladder, their chains clashing against the iron rungs, as they fought upward with one hand and carried the night buckets with the other. The smoke from the braziers drew into the guardroom and the guard stepped away from the door. John Wolff lay there till they had all gone up.

"Hey, you!" the guard yelled. "What's your name, Wolff!"

John Wolff didn't answer.

"Come up."

John Wolff remembered all the filth he had ever heard and sent it up to the guard. The guard laughed. "All right," he said. "Stay down. Stay down for a week." Wolff was a harmless man, not worth coming down for and lugging up and flogging. He slammed the trap shut.

John Wolff got up. He clanked slowly down to the beach, looking at the water. Then he started rummaging in the straw beds. Some of the prisoners had bought pieces of plank from the guard, to put under the straw. He hadn't any himself because they cost a shilling a foot. Moving with the slow, half-hopping motion the irons forced him to use, he took down planks and put them in the water. They floated soggily. He got more. He laid them on top of each other, side by side. Then he waded out and straddled them and tentatively pulled up his feet. The planks sank under him and he rummaged for more. He finally had enough to float him and he tied them together with strips torn from his blanket.

He straddled the raft and pushed it out with his feet. He paddled with his hands. The weight of the irons made his hands splash no matter how careful he was. But he had only a little way to go to get out of the brazier lights.

John Wolff had thought a long time about which shaft to choose. But as he could not make up his mind he chose the farthest. When he entered it, the noise of his splashing diminished. The light behind him was circumscribed by the low ceiling of the shaft and the flat level of the water. Looking back, it seemed to him that he had come a great distance. He could not see far ahead, because the shaft made a turn. He paddled slowly round that, and then in the darkness that instantly became complete he felt the front of his rafte strike the rock. The blow was very slight, but it almost knocked him forward off balance. He barely saved himself by lifting his hands and bracing himself against the rock wall. He realized that the drift was filled to the ceiling, and that there was no way out. He felt all round the water level to make sure and then tried to turn his raft.

There was not room to turn it in the darkness, and he had to back out. It was a laborious and painful process. His arms dragged and his legs had gone cold and numb, except for the ache the cold made in his ankle scars.

When he came back into view of the sand beach and the smouldering braziers and the mussed straw of the beds he had despoiled of planks, he was sobbing with exhaustion. He lay forward along the boards, eyes shut. From a vague sense of habit he started dictating a letter to Ally.

"The right drift is full of water so I can't get out that way. I shall have to try the other one. It is so hard to paddle."

Then it occurred to him that he could not wait another day. It would take almost as long to get fifty feet back to shore as to paddle into the next drift. In either case he would not have time to put the planks back under the straw. They ducked men who monkeyed with the beds of others. It took two weeks to get dry.

John decided to paddle into the next drift.

Again the splashing he made seemed to crash against the upward walls of the air shaft. But again the noise was shut off when he finally entered the second drift.

He had been working for an hour to cover his hundred feet or so of progress and the men should be coming down soon. He forced himself to keep at it until the last reflected light of the water was left behind. Then he came to a slight curve and continued round that, and then he stopped.

He had a sudden new sensation. The sweat was pouring out of his skin. It was the first time he had sweated for months. It made him feel weak, as if the whole energy of his body had been put to work at the process of creating sweat in him; but at the same time he felt an access of courage because he was able to sweat.

It gave his hands power to paddle on. Behind, and far away, shut off by the rock wall, he heard the muffled clanking as the men started coming down the ladder. He kept on.

It was dark now, and he was scraping the side of the drift. But he kept paddling. When he heard his name called behind him, the sound was dim and the echoes that entered the drift were mere whispers of his name,—*John Wolff, John Wolff,*—like voices for a person departing this world.

His arms lifted and fell and lifted. He had gone a long way. He was not completely conscious any more of what he was doing. He was quite unprepared when the raft struck a projection of the wall, dumping him sideways off the board into the water. His last flurry broke the wrappings of the raft and the boards came apart. He thought he would drown. Then he struck bottom. He stood up and his head came out of water. Against his wet face, in the dark, he felt an icy draft of air.

He started wading. The bottom was quite smooth, but the water deepened. It reached his chin. He knew that he was going in the right direction, because the air still drew against his forehead.

The boards were now out of his reach and it was too dark to see anything, anyway. John Wolff stood still in the water, thinking aloud: "Dear Ally, the water is up to my mouth. It is getting deeper. But there is surely air coming along this drift and I can't get back and I figure to go ahead. It is better to drown than to stand still in water. It is not very cold water, but it makes me shake some. Otherwise I am well and hoping you are the same . . ." He drew a deep breath and took a full stride forward.

The water fell away from his chin, from his throat. He felt the cold air against his wishbone. He drew another breath and took still another step and the water dropped halfway to his waist. He shouted.

It was thin sound and it was drowned by his sudden threshing in the water. All at once he was reaching down, holding tight the chains to his ankles and floundering knee-deep along a narrow stream. The air was cold all over him. He went on for half a dozen yards and shouted again. There was light on the righthand wall. Faint, but actual light. Daylight. He turned the corner to the left and saw the dazzle on the water which now ran downhill quite fast through a small tunnel that seemed to narrow to the dimension of a large culvert. He had to bend and get on his knees. He took another turn as he dragged himself in the water, and he saw ahead of him the gray of woods in October.

But between him and the woods was a wooden grille.

It shocked and amazed him to find that grille after so long and baffling a distance. It seemed to him a malicious manifestation of the godlessness in man. In its way it seemed to him infinitely more wicked than the trial which had sent him to prison in the first place.

He dragged himself up to it and put his hands against the lower bar and rested his head on his hands. The shakes were getting hold of him again. He closed his eyes, and let go of his body.

He felt the grille shaking as he shook and opened his eyes. It came to him that the wood was old and the joints the crossbars made with the frame were very rotten. He braced his feet against a stone and threw his weight against the grille.

The whole business gave way, tumbling out under him down the steep hillside. He fell with it, with a last clank of his irons, rolled over down the slope, and came to rest with his face upward, seeing the breast of the hill against the sky. He lay still, weeping.

A cold rain was falling steadily.

[198] Walter D. Edmonds, *Drums along the Mohawk* (Boston: Little, Brown & Co., 1936), pp. 281–286. Copyright, 1936, by Walter D. Edmonds.

❖⟫❖⟫❖◄❰◄❰◄❖

Bibliography

Addison, Joseph, *Selections from Addison's Papers, Contributed to the Spectator,* ed. Thomas Arnold. Oxford: At the Clarendon Press, 1882, 528 pp.

Adler, Mortimer J., *How to Read a Book.* New York: Simon & Schuster, 1940, 398 pp.

Aldington, Richard, ed., *The Viking Book of Poetry of the English-speaking World.* New York: The Viking Press, Inc., 1941, 1,272 pp.

Andersch, Elizabeth G., and Lorin C. Staats, *Speech for Everyday Use.* New York: Rinehart & Company, Inc., 1950, 218 pp.

Auslander, J. A., and Frank Ernest Hill, eds., *The Winged Horse Anthology.* New York: Doubleday & Co., Inc., 1929, 669 pp.

Austin, Margot, *Lutie.* New York: E. P. Dutton & Co., Inc., 1944, 34 pp.

Baird, A. Craig, and Franklin H. Knower, *General Speech.* New York: McGraw-Hill Book Co., Inc., 1949, 500 pp.

Bartlett, John, compiler, *Familiar Quotations,* ed. Christopher Morley and Louella D. Everett. Boston: Little, Brown & Co., 1941, 1,578 pp.

Bates, Ernest Sutherland, ed., *The Bible Designed to Be Read as Living Literature.* New York: Simon & Schuster, 1936, 1,271 pp.

Benchley, Robert, *Chips off the Old Benchley.* New York: Harper & Brothers, 1949, 360 pp.

————, *The Treasurer's Report.* New York: Harper & Brothers, 1930, 306 pp.

Benét, Stephen Vincent, *America.* New York: Rinehart & Company, Inc., 1944, 122 pp.

————, *The Stephen Vincent Benét Pocket Book,* ed. Robert Van Gelder. New York: Pocket Books, Inc., 1946, 414 pp.

Bennett, Arnold, *How to Live on Twenty-four Hours a Day.* New York: Doubleday & Co., Inc., 1910, 103 pp.

Bessey, Mabel A., and Isabelle P. Coffin, *Active Reading.* New York: Appleton-Century-Crofts, Inc., 1941, 351 pp.

Bisland, Elizabeth, ed., *Life and Letters of Lafcadio Hearn.* Boston: Houghton Mifflin Company, 1906, 2 vols.

Blackman, Clifton, and Dwight Hillis Plackard, *Blueprint for Public Relations.* New York: McGraw-Hill Book Co., Inc., 1947, 355 pp.

Boleslavsky, Richard, *Acting: The First Six Lessons.* New York: Theatre Arts Books, 1933, 122 pp.

The Book of Common Prayer. New York: The Church Pension Fund, 1945, 611 pp.

Boyd, James, *Drums.* New York: Charles Scribner's Sons, 1925, 490 pp.

Brooks, Charles S., *Like Summer's Cloud: A Book of Essays.* New York: Harcourt, Brace & Co., Inc., 1925, 262 pp.

Brooks, William F., *Radio News Writing.* New York: McGraw-Hill Book Co., Inc., 1948, 200 pp.

Broun, Heywood Campbell, *Collected Edition of Heywood Broun,* compiled by Heywood Hale Broun. New York: Harcourt, Brace & Co., Inc., 1941, 561 pp.

Brown, John Mason, *Accustomed As I Am.* New York: W. W. Norton & Co., 1942, 201 pp.

Burke, Edmund, *Select Works,* ed. E. J. Payne. Oxford: At the Clarendon Press, 1926, 3 vols.

———, *Speech on Conciliation with America,* ed. Sidney Carleton Newsom. New York: The Macmillan Co., 1913, 124 pp

Cairns, Huntington, Allen Tate, and Mark Van Doren, *Invitation to Learning.* New York: Random House, Inc., 1941, 431 pp.

Cather, Willa, *On Writing.* New York: Alfred A. Knopf, Inc., 1949, 126 pp.

Charnley, Mitchell V., *News by Radio.* New York: The Macmillan Co., 1948, 403 pp.

Clark, S. H., and Maud M. Babcock, *Interpretation of the Printed Page.* New York: Prentice-Hall, Inc., 1945, 402 pp.

Clemens, Samuel L., *How to Tell a Story.* New York: Harper & Brothers, 1897, 233 pp.

———, *The Innocents Abroad.* New York: Harper & Brothers, 1869, 2 vols.

———, *Life on the Mississippi.* New York: Harper & Brothers, 1917, 527 pp.

———, *Mark Twain's Autobiography.* New York: Harper & Brothers, 1924, 2 vols.

———, *Mark Twain's Speeches,* ed. Albert Bigelow Paine. New York: Harper & Brothers, 1923, 396 pp.

Colby, Frank Moore, *Imaginary Obligations.* New York: Dodd, Mead & Co., Inc., 1910, 335 pp.

Commager, Henry Steele, *Heritage of America.* Boston: Little, Brown & Co., 1939, 1,152 pp.

Cooper, Lane, *Two Views of Education; with other papers chiefly on the study of literature.* New Haven: Yale University Press, 1922, 321 pp.

Corson, Hiram, *The Aims of Literary Study.* New York: The Macmillan Co., 1895, 153 pp.

Coulter, John G., *Plant Life and Plant Uses.* New York: American Book Company, 1913, 464 pp.

Crocker, Lionel G., and Louis M. Eich, *Oral Reading.* New York: Prentice-Hall, Inc., 1947, 507 pp.

Cruikshank, R. J., *Charles Dickens and Early Victorian England.* New York: Chanticleer Press, Inc., 1949, 308 pp.

Cunningham, Cornelius Carman, *Literature as a Fine Art.* New York: The Ronald Press Company, 1941, 303 pp.

Daly, Joseph Francis, *The Life of Augustin Daly.* New York: The Macmillan Co., 1917, 672 pp.

Dasent, Sir George Webbe, *Popular Tales from the Norse.* Translation from the *Norske Folke-eventyr* of Asbjørnsen and Moe. New York: G. P. Putnam's Sons, 1908, 443 pp.

Day, Clarence, *This Simian World.* New York: Alfred A. Knopf, Inc., 1936, 98 pp.

Dickens, Charles, *Martin Chuzzlewit.* New York: Harper & Brothers, 2 vols.

Dickey, Dallas C., Robert T. Oliver, and Harold P. Zelko, *Essentials of Communicative Speech.* New York: The Dryden Press, Inc., 1949, 338 pp.

Dickinson, Emily, *Bolts of Melody,* ed. Mabel Loomis Todd and Millicent Todd Bingham. New York: Harper & Brothers, 1945, 352 pp.

———, *Poems by Emily Dickinson,* ed. Martha Dickinson Bianchi and Alfred Leete Hampson. Boston: Little, Brown & Co., 1947, 484 pp.

Donne, John, and William Blake, *The Complete Poetry and Selected Prose of John Donne and the Complete Poetry of William Blake.* New York: Modern Library, Inc., 1946, 1,045 pp.

Duerr, Edwin, *Radio and Television Acting.* New York: Rinehart & Company, Inc., 1950, 417 pp.

Eastman, Charles Alexander, and Elaine Goodale Eastman, *Wigwam Evenings.* Boston: Little, Brown & Co., 1909, 253 pp.

Eastman, Max, *Anthology for the Enjoyment of Poetry.* New York: Charles Scribner's Sons, 1947, 329 pp.

———, *Enjoyment of Laughter.* New York: Simon & Schuster, 1948, 367 pp.

Edmonds, Walter D., *Chad Hanna.* Boston: Little, Brown & Co., 1940, 548 pp.

———, *Drums along the Mohawk.* Boston: Little, Brown & Co., 1939, 592 pp.

Eginton, Daniel P., *Better Speech for You.* Permabooks. New York: Doubleday & Co., Inc., 1949, 235 pp.

Eliot, T. S., *Notes towards the Definition of Culture*. New York: Harcourt, Brace & Co., Inc., 1949, 128 pp.

Emerson, Ralph Waldo, *Essays*. Boston: Houghton Mifflin Company, 1903, 445 pp.

Fadiman, Clifton, *Reading I've Liked*. New York: Simon & Schuster, 1945, 906 pp.

Fairbanks, Grant, *Voice and Articulation Drillbook*. New York: Harper & Brothers, 1940, 234 pp.

Fielding, Henry, *Tom Jones*. New York: P. F. Collier & Son Corporation, 1903, 4 vols.

Flesch, Rudolph, *The Art of Plain Talk*. New York: Harper & Brothers, 1946, 210 pp.

Fowler, H. W., *A Dictionary of Modern English Usage*. Oxford: At the Clarendon Press, 1949, 742 pp.

————, and F. G. Fowler, *The King's English*. Oxford: At the Clarendon Press, 1925, 370 pp.

Franklin, Benjamin, *Autobiography*. Rinehart Edition. New York: Rinehart & Company, Inc., 1948, 176 pp.

————, *Poor Richard's Almanac*. Boston: Houghton Mifflin Company, 1886, 88 pp.

————, *Satires and Bagatelles*. Detroit: Fine Book Circle, 1937, 139 pp.

French, Joseph Lewis, ed., *The Best of American Humor*. New York: Garden City Books, 1941, 401 pp.

Frost, Robert, *The Pocket Book of Robert Frost's Poems,* ed. Louis Untermeyer. New York: Pocket Books, Inc., 1946, 262 pp.

Fry, Roger, *Vision and Design*. London: Chatto & Windus, 1929, 302 pp.

Gassner, John, *Producing the Play;* with *New Scene Technician's Handbook* by Philip Barber. New York: The Dryden Press, Inc., 1941, 744 pp.

Gibbon, Edward, *The History of the Decline and Fall of the Roman Empire*. New York: Heritage Press, 1946, 2 vols.

Gilbert, Sir William, *Iolanthe*. London: G. Bell & Sons, Ltd., 1910, 224 pp.

————, *The Yeomen of the Guard*. London: Macmillan & Co., Ltd., 1929, 102 pp.

Glasgow, George M., *Dynamic Public Speaking*. New York: Harper & Brothers, 1950, 315 pp.

Goldstein, Harry, *Reading and Listening Comprehension at Various Controlled Rates*. Contributions to Education, No. 821. New York: Teachers College, Columbia University, 1940, 69 pp.

Gould, Jay Reid, and Sterling P. Olmsted, *Exposition, Technical and Popular*. New York: Longmans, Green & Co., Inc., 1947, 126 pp.

Grahame, Kenneth, *The Golden Age*. New York: John Lane & Co., 1902, 241 pp.

Griswold, Glenn, and Denny Griswold, *Your Public Relations*. New York: Funk & Wagnalls Company, 1948, 634 pp.

Guides for Management from Current Opinion Trends. New York: Opinion Research Corporation, n.d., 58 pp.

Hamilton, Edith, *The Great Age of Greek Literature.* New York: W. W. Norton & Company, 1942, 347 pp.

Hawthorne, Nathaniel, *The Scarlet Letter.* Rinehart Edition. New York: Rinehart & Company, Inc., 1947, 251 pp.

Hebel, J. William, and Hoyt H. Hudson, eds., *Poetry of the English Renaissance: 1509–1660.* New York: Appleton-Century-Crofts, Inc., 1938, 1,068 pp.

Herendeen, Jane, *Speech Quality and Interpretation.* New York: Harper & Brothers, 1946, 382 pp.

Herzberg, Max J., and Leon Mones, *Humor of America.* New York: Appleton-Century-Crofts, Inc., 1945, 417 pp.

Hoag, Victor, *It's Fun to Teach.* New York: Morehouse-Gorham Co., Inc., 1949, 199 pp.

Hoffenstein, Samuel, *Poems in Praise of Practically Nothing.* New York: Liveright Publishing Corporation, 1928, 217 pp.

Hoffman, William G., *Public Speaking for Businessmen.* New York: McGraw-Hill Book Co., Inc., 1949, 412 pp.

Hollowell, Lillian, *A Book of Children's Literature.* New York: Rinehart & Company, Inc., 1950, 697 pp.

Holmes, Oliver Wendell, *The Autocrat of the Breakfast Table.* Everyman's Library. New York: E. P. Dutton & Co., Inc., 1906, 350 pp.

The Holy Bible. King James Version.

Hubbard, Kin, *Abe Martin: Hoss Sense and Nonsense.* Indianapolis: Bobbs-Merrill Company, Inc., 1926, 128 pp.

Huxley, Thomas Henry, *Autobiography and Selected Essays,* with introduction and notes by Ada L. F. Snell. Boston: Houghton Mifflin Company, 1909, 138 pp.

————, *Readings from Huxley,* ed. Clarissa Rinaker. New York: Harcourt, Brace & Co., Inc., 1920, 160 pp.

————, *Science and Education.* New York: Appleton-Century-Crofts, Inc., n.d., 451 pp.

Irving, Sir Henry, *The Drama.* Boston: Joseph Knight Company, 1892, 201 pp.

Irving, Washington, *The Sketch Book.* Chicago: Scott, Foresman & Company, 1906, 476 pp.

Keller, James, *You Can Change the World.* New York: Longmans, Green & Co., Inc., 1948, 387 pp.

Kelly, Amy, *Eleanor of Aquitaine and the Four Kings.* Cambridge, Mass.: Harvard University Press, 1950, 431 pp.

Kready, Laura Fry, *Study of Fairy Tales,* with an introduction by Henry Suzzalo. Boston: Houghton Mifflin Company, 1916, 313 pp.

Lagerlöf, Selma, *The Treasure.* New York: Doubleday & Co., Inc., 1925, 158 pp.

Lawrence, T. E., *Seven Pillars of Wisdom*. New York: Doubleday & Co., Inc., 1935, 672 pp.

Lewis, Clive Staples, *The Screwtape Letters*. New York: The Macmillan Co., 1944, 160 pp.

Linscott, R. N., ed., *Omnibus of American Humor*. New York: Popular Library, 1932, 192 pp.

Loomis, Roger Sherman, and Donald Lemen Clark, eds., *Modern English Readings*. New York: Rinehart & Company, Inc., 1950, 1,062 pp.

Lowell, Amy, *Men, Women and Ghosts*. Boston: Houghton Mifflin Company, 1916, 363 pp.

Lowrey, Sara, and Gertrude E. Johnson, *Interpretive Reading*. New York: Appleton-Century-Crofts, Inc., 1942, 607 pp.

McBirney, James H., and Kenneth G. Hance, *Discussion in Human Affairs*. New York: Harper & Brothers, 1950, 432 pp.

McLean, Margaret Prendergast, *Oral Interpretation of Forms of Literature*. New York: E. P. Dutton & Co., Inc., 1936, 380 pp.

Manser, Ruth B., and Leonard Finlan, *The Speaking Voice*. New York: Longmans, Green & Co., Inc., 1950, 404 pp.

Marquis, Don (Donald Robert Perry), *Chapters for the Orthodox*. New York: Doubleday & Co., Inc., 1934, 314 pp.

Masefield, John, *The Poems and Plays of John Masefield*. New York: The Macmillan Co., 1923, 3 vols.

Melville, Herman, *Moby Dick*. Rinehart Editions. New York: Rinehart & Company, Inc., 1948, 566 pp.

Mencken, H. L., *The American Language*. New York: Alfred A. Knopf, Inc., 1936, 769 pp.

Miller, Clyde R., *The Process of Persuasion*. New York: Crown Publishers, 1946, 234 pp.

Millett, Fred B., B. G. Whiting, and Alexander M. Witherspoon, eds., *College Survey of English Literature*. New York: Harcourt, Brace & Co., Inc., 1942, 2 vols.

Monroe, Alan H., *Principles and Types of Speech*. Chicago: Scott, Foresman & Company, 1949, 658 pp.

Morley, Christopher, *Pipefuls*. New York: Doubleday & Co., Inc., 1924, 274 pp.

Nelson, Severina E., and Charles H. Woolbert, *The Art of Interpretive Speech*. New York: Appleton-Century-Crofts, Inc., 1946, 588 pp.

Norris, Frank, *The Octopus*. New York: Doubleday & Co., Inc., 1930, 635 pp.

O'Neill, James M., ed., *Foundations of Speech*. New York: Prentice-Hall, Inc., 1946, 499 pp.

Parker, Dorothy, *After Such Pleasures*. New York: The Viking Press, Inc., 1933, 232 pp.

Parrish, Wayland Maxfield, *Reading Aloud*. New York: Thomas Nelson & Sons, 1941, 506 pp.

Pearson, Hesketh, *Dickens: His Character, Comedy, and Career.* New York: Harper & Brothers, 1949, 361 pp.

Peattie, Donald Culross, *An Almanac for Moderns.* New York: G. P. Putnam's Sons, 1935, 396 pp.

Perry, Bliss, *And Gladly Teach.* Boston: Houghton Mifflin Company, 1935, 315 pp.

————, *A Study of Poetry.* Boston: Houghton Mifflin Company, 1920, 396 pp.

————, *A Study of Prose Fiction.* Boston: Houghton Mifflin Company, 1902, 406 pp.

Phelps, William Lyon, *What I Like.* New York: Charles Scribner's Sons, 1933, 718 pp.

Quiller-Couch, Sir Arthur, *On the Art of Writing.* New York: G. P. Putnam's Sons, 1916, 302 pp.

Repplier, Agnes, *Eight Decades.* Boston: Houghton Mifflin Company, 1937, 304 pp.

Riggs, Lynn, *Roadside.* New York: Samuel French, Inc., 1930, 158 pp.

Robb, Mary Margaret, *Oral Interpretation of Literature in American Colleges and Universities.* New York: The H. W. Wilson Company, 1941, 242 pp.

Roberts, Kenneth, *For Authors Only, and Other Gloomy Essays.* New York: Doubleday & Co., Inc., 1935, 446 pp.

————, *Northwest Passage.* New York: Doubleday & Co., Inc., 1937, 709 pp.

————, *Oliver Wiswell.* New York: Doubleday & Co., Inc., 1940, 836 pp.

Roughead, William, *The Murderer's Companion.* New York: The Press of the Reader's Club, 1941, 365 pp.

Ruskin, John, *Sesame and Lilies,* ed. Sybil Wragge. London: J. M. Dent & Sons, Ltd., 1920, 190 pp.

Saidla, Leo E. A., *Essays for the Study of Structure and Style.* New York: The Macmillan Co., 1939, 717 pp.

St. John, Christopher, ed., *Ellen Terry and Bernard Shaw: A Correspondence.* New York: G. P. Putnam's Sons, 1931, 334 pp.

Sanders, Gerald DeWitt, and John Herbert Nelson, eds., *Chief Modern Poets of England and America.* New York: The Macmillan Co., 1936, 796 pp.

Sanford, John A., and Selma W. Schneider, *A College Book of Prose.* Boston: Ginn & Co., 1941, 566 pp.

Santayana, George, *Soliloquies in England and Later Soliloquies.* New York: Charles Scribner's Sons, 1923, 264 pp.

Saroyan, William, "The Beautiful People," in *Three Plays by William Saroyan.* New York: Harcourt, Brace & Co., Inc., 1941, 275 pp.

Sayers, Dorothy L., ed., *The Omnibus of Crime.* New York: Harcourt, Brace & Co., Inc., 1929, 1,177 pp.

Schubert, Leland, *A Guide for Oral Communication.* New York: Prentice-Hall, Inc., 1948, 286 pp.

Schwab, Gustav, *Gods and Heroes.* New York: Pantheon Books, 1946, 764 pp.

Seitz, Don C., *Artemus Ward.* New York: Harper & Brothers, 1919, 338 pp.

Shakespeare, William: See any standard edition of the plays and poems.

Shaw, George Bernard, *The Art of Rehearsal.* New York: Samuel French, Inc., 1928, 12 pp.

————, *Dramatic Opinions and Essays,* ed. James Huneker. New York: Brentano's, 1906, 2 vols.

————, *Sixteen Self Sketches.* New York: Dodd, Mead & Company, Inc., 1949, 207 pp.

Sidney, Sir Philip, *The Poems of Sir Philip Sidney,* ed. John Drinkwater. New York: E. P. Dutton & Co., Inc., 1910, 320 pp.

Sitwell, Edith, *The Canticle of the Rose.* New York: Vanguard Press, Inc., 1949, 290 pp.

Smith, C. Alphonso, *What Can Literature Do for Me?* New York: Doubleday & Co., Inc., 1913, 220 pp.

Smith, J. M., and Edgar J. Goodspeed, eds., *The Complete Bible.* Chicago: University of Chicago Press, 1948, 1,130 pp.

Smith, Logan Pearsall, *All Trivia.* New York: Harcourt, Brace & Co., Inc., 1934, 209 pp.

Soper, Paul L., *Basic Public Speaking.* New York: Oxford University Press, 1949, 394 pp.

Spender, Stephen, *Poems.* New York: Random House, Inc., 1934, 68 pp.

Stout, Rex, *And Be a Villain.* New York: The Viking Press, Inc., 1948, 216 pp.

Taylor, Deems, *The Well-tempered Listener.* New York: Simon & Schuster, 1940, 333 pp.

Teasdale, Sara, *The Collected Poems of Sara Teasdale.* New York: The Macmillan Co., 1940, 311 pp.

Thoreau, Henry David, *The Heart of Thoreau's Journals,* ed. Odell Shepard. Boston: Houghton Mifflin Company, 1927, 348 pp.

————, *A Week on the Concord and Merrimack Rivers.* Boston: Houghton Mifflin Company, 1893, 531 pp.

Thurber, James, *My Life and Hard Times.* New York: Harper & Brothers, 1933, 153 pp.

Toynbee, Arnold J., *A Study of History.* New York: Oxford University Press, 1947, 617 pp.

Tresidder, Argus, *Reading to Others.* Chicago: Scott, Foresman & Company, 1940, 529 pp.

The Union Prayerbook for Jewish Worship. Cincinnati: The Central Conference of American Rabbis, 1940, 395 pp.

Untermeyer, Louis, ed., *Modern American and British Poetry*. New York: Harcourt, Brace & Co., Inc., 1939, 1,218 pp.

Utterback, William E., *Group Thinking and Conference Leadership*. New York: Rinehart & Company, Inc., 1950, 248 pp.

Van Doren, Carl, ed., *Modern American Prose*. New York: Harcourt, Brace & Co., Inc., 1934, 939 pp.

Van Doren, Mark, *The Private Reader*. New York: Henry Holt & Co., Inc., 1942, 416 pp.

———, ed., *An Anthology of World Poetry*. New York: A. & C. Boni, 1928, 1,318 pp.

———, ed., *Masterpieces of American Poets*. New York: Garden City Books, 1932, 698 pp.

———, ed., *The New Invitation to Learning*. New York: The New Home Library, 1944, 436 pp.

Van Loon, Hendrick Willem, *The Story of Mankind*. New York: Liveright Publishing Corporation, 1921, 479 pp.

Waring, Fred, *Tone Syllables*. New York: Shawnee Press, Inc., 1944, 8 pp.

West, Rebecca, *Black Lamb and Grey Falcon*. New York: The Viking Press, Inc., 1943, 1,181 pp.

White, E. B., *Here Is New York*. New York: Harper & Brothers, 1949, 54 pp.

———, *One Man's Meat*. New York: Harper & Brothers, 1944, 350 pp.

———, *Quo Vadimus?* New York: Harper & Brothers, 1938, 219 pp.

White, Paul W., *News on the Air*. New York: Harcourt, Brace & Co., Inc., 1947, 420 pp.

Wilde, Oscar, *The Poems and Fairy Tales of Oscar Wilde*. New York: Modern Library, Inc., 1932, 214 pp.

Wilder, Thornton, *Our Town*. New York: Coward-McCann, Inc., 1938, 128 pp.

Wilson, George P., *A Guide to Better English*. New York: Appleton-Century-Crofts, Inc., 1942, 527 pp.

Wodehouse, P. G., *Thank You, Jeeves!* Boston: Little, Brown & Co., 1934, 307 pp.

Wolfe, Thomas, *The Face of a Nation*. New York: Charles Scribner's Sons, 1939, 322 pp.

———, *Short Stories*. Baltimore: Penguin Books, Inc., 1947, 150 pp.

———, *A Stone, a Leaf, a Door*. New York: Charles Scribner's Sons, 1945, 166 pp.

———, *Of Time and the River*. New York: Charles Scribner's Sons, 1935, 912 pp.

Wooley, Catherine, *Read Me Another Story*. New York: The Thomas Y. Crowell Co., 1949, 161 pp.

Woolf, Virginia (Stephen), *The Moment, and Other Essays*. New York: Harcourt, Brace & Co., Inc., 1948, 240 pp.

Woollcott, Alexander, *The Woollcott Reader*. New York: The Viking Press, Inc., 1935, 1,010 pp.

Wyatt, Sir Thomas, *The Poetry of Sir Thomas Wyatt,* ed. E. M. W. Tillyard. London: The Scholartis Press, 1929, 180 pp.

Wylie, Elinor, *Collected Poems*. New York: Alfred A. Knopf, Inc., 1933, 311 pp.

MAGAZINES

Anonymous, "The Happy Ham," *Time,* LIX, No. 13 (March 31, 1952).

———, "How to Read Aloud at Home," *Time,* LIX, No. 13 (March 31, 1952).

———, "Psympel," *Newsweek,* XXXII, No. 12 (September 29, 1948).

———, "The Talk of the Town," *New Yorker,* XXIV, No. 44 (December 25, 1948).

Brown, John Mason, "Seeing Things," *Saturday Review of Literature,* XXXIII, No. 4 (February 3, 1950).

Bullard, E. F., "The Technical Man's Role as Interpreter," *Journal of Petroleum Technology,* II, No. 7 (July, 1950).

Buurma, E. C., "Teleprompter Aids the Orator," *Radio Age,* XII, No. 2 (April, 1953).

Johnston, Alva, "Who Knows What Is Funny?" *Saturday Evening Post,* CCXI, No. 6 (August 6, 1948).

Kernodle, George R., "Basic Problems in Reading Shakespeare," *Quarterly Journal of Speech,* XXXV, No. 1 (February, 1949).

Laughton, Charles, "Storytelling," *Atlantic Monthly,* CLXXXV, No. 6 (June, 1950).

Nathan, George Jean, "First Nights and Passing Judgments," *Esquire,* X, No. 5 (November, 1938).

Prentiss, Henrietta, "The Master Key to Understanding," *Theatre Arts Monthly,* X, No. 9 (September, 1926).

Scriven, R. C., "Words for Nicholas at Nine," *Punch,* CCXXI, No. 5787 (September 26, 1951).

Stokes, Sewell, "A Lament for Lost Speech," *Theatre Arts Monthly,* XXIII (April, 1939).

NEWSPAPERS

Anonymous, "Editorial," New York *Times,* October 13, 1941. On adverbs.

Ford, Ed ("Senator"), "Being Funny Isn't Much Fun," *New York Times Magazine,* June 25, 1944.

Index

Index

IV